HORTICULTURE AND ENVIRONMENT

HORTICULTURE AND ENVIRONMENT

Darshana Nand

KALPAZ

ISBN: 978-81-7835-941-0

₹ 910

First Published 2013

Published by

Kalpaz Publications
C-30, Satyawati Nagar,
Delhi - 110052 Ph.: 9212142040
E-mail: kalpaz@hotmail.com
Laser Typesetting : Lucky Graphic, Delhi
Printed at : G. Print Process, Delhi

Cataloging in Publication Data—DK

Courtesy: D.K. Agencies (P) Ltd. <docinfo@dkagencies.com>

Darsìana Nanda, 1930-

Horticulture and environment / Darshana Nand.

p. cm.

Includes bibliographical references and index.

ISBN 9788178359410

1. Horticulture—India. 2. Horticulture—Environmental aspects—India. 3. Crops—Environmental aspects—India. I. Title.

DDC 635.0954 23

In loving memory of my beloved wife
Smt Usha Srivastava
(13th Nov. 1934 - 3rd May 2008)

Contents

Preface

Horticultural Science is a vast subject, consisting of scientific cultivation of fruits, vegetables and flowers. The author has been working on research and development of these for the last many decades. Simultaneously, the research papers and articles were got published from time to time in various journals, magazines and newspapers from time to time. Only some of the papers are joint in which names of all the authors have been clearly indicated. Some have been added by courtesy. Where names have not been mentioned, these have been authored by self. Environment/pollution cannot be placed aside. Some write-ups remained unpublished. The present book 'Horticulture and Environment' is, as a matter of fact, a compilation of the above. Further, besides encouraging horticulture, the author is still campaigning for neat and clear environment through personal requests and publishing in newspapers. It is understood that this book may be useful for general public, research and other students to make basis for further research on the subject. This book should prove useful for libraries also. In the last I cannot ignore to write that my eldest son Er. Ambrish Kumar, General Manager Ranbaxy laboratories Ltd. Gurgaon has struggled much in making this 02-02-2012 manuscript in a printable form.

Allahabad
10th January 2013

Darshana Nand

1

Introductory Informations for Orcharding

In every day diet, fruits are very important. These, alongwith green and other vegetables, have essential vitamins and minerals in themselves, which are required to keep the body healthy. Fruits may be taken after purchasing from market and also after self growing on a large scale in orchards and on a smaller scale in kitchen gardens. In kitchen gardens short lived and quick growing plants like banana, papaya, phalsa, guava, strawberry, rasp-berry, karonda, custard apple, Amrapali mango, pineapple and others may be grown. On a large scale orcharding, growing of fruits like Mango, Guava, Aonla, Litchee, Grapes, Jack fruit, Monkey Jack, Mahua, Tamarind, Bael, Kaitha, Carambola and Citrus fruits, etc. may be done. Before establishing an orchard, there are some main points which must be kept in mind. This is important because these are long term crops and a mistake done in the beginning cannot be rectified in future. For example, the distance of plantation between two plants of mango is 12 to 16 metres and if one has no knowledge of it, he may plant the mango orchard even at 3 metres apart. As such the result will be that these plants will grow very tall, dense and almost no or very less branching. There will be almost no fruiting. If there will be some fruiting that will be only on the top of the tree, where there is Sun light. Similarly, growers should have other important information also for a successful orcharding.

Selection of Site

Selection of site for establishing an orchard should preferably be done near a road or at such places from where marketing and transport of fruits are easy. If orchards of Dasehri are to be established, site should be selected somewhere in Malihabad or near about. For Langra mango some land in Varanasi, Farukhabad and Patna should be selected. For Guava plantation, orchards may be established near Sulem Sarai Area and Sayed Sarawan area of Allahabad (now in Distt. Kaushambhi), Kanpur and Lucknow also. For Litchee cultivation places like Dehradun in Uttarakhand and Muzaffarpur in Bihar (Now perhaps in Jharkhand) should be selected. For Aonla growing places like Pratapgarh, Varanasi, Faizabad, Tamil Nadu and arid areas in Rajasthan be selected.

It will be better if the orchards are near 'Haats' and markets, so that perishable fruits like Phalsa, Jamun, fully ripe papayas, raspberries and strawberries, carambolas, etc., may easily be disposed off, before these are destroyed.

Climate and Soil

Climate and soil are also very important for fruit growing. If the site selected for orcharding is of hill climate and on a great height from sea level, Apples, Pears, Apricots, Plums, Peaches, Almonds, Walnut, Chestnut and Cherries will suit. These plants shed their leaves in winters and are planted on hills in winters when these are in dormancy. In the climate of plains and valleys also evergreen trees like mango, Citrus, Guava, Litchee, Jamun, Jack fruit and Bael etc. should be grown. Plants like grapes, phalsa, mulberry, pear, fig also attain dormancy though these are also grown in plains but shed their leaves in winters. Plantation of orchards of these plants should be done in winters only after plants are pruned in December/January.

Most of the plants grow well in loam/sandy fertile loam soil. However, some of the fruit trees may grow also in unfertile and arid area soils and wastelands. Such fruits are Aonla, Ber, Mahua, Jamun, Wood apple (Kaitha), Bael, Monkey jack, Cluster figs (Goolar), Lasora, Karonda, Phalsas, Khejari (Prosopio cineraria). Grows vigorously in arid areas of Rajasthan near Bikaner and others. A very good fodder tree, pods are utilized for preparing curries and pickles - The tree is a very good wind break Kareal (Tenti) and other plants also.

Suitable Arrangements of Drainage

All the plants do require watering during or after plantation, but these do not tolerate water-logging. All the rain or irrigated water must be well drained off except some plants like ber and guava which carry on in low lying and some water-logged areas.

Wind Breaks

At the time of laying out an orchard, rather before laying out, wind break plants like mango seedlings, Desi tall bananas, Jait (Sesbania aegyphace) Khejari (Phosopis cineraria) should be planted on western and northern sides of the orchard to protect the orchards from heavy storms (to save branches from breaking and fruits from being shed), cold and hot wind.

Preparation of Soil and Layout

If the land selected was being cultivated earlier its all right. If the soil was not cultivated earlier layout of the orchard should after 2-3 ploughings and planking by square/hexagonal system and the place of actual plantation of the fruit plant may be located at proper distance and the point be pegged. Digging and filling of pits should be done in the months of April - May - June.

Plantation

Plantation is filled up pits should be done in the centre of the pits with earthen ball around the roots. After plantation, soil should be gently tightened all round the plant. Plantation should be done when the weather is cloudy or some light drops of rains are there. However, plantation in evening is always better. If there are no rains plants should be lightly irrigated.

Irrigation

Irrigation of plants and trees should be done from time to time specially to newly planted orchards. Each individual plant should be covered by thatches to save young plants from hot sun and hot wind in summers. These should also be protected likewise in winters from frost and cold wind.

Thalas should be prepared for each plant for irrigation and should be widened according to the spread of drip of the plant. Proper weeding and hoeing must be done from time to time to let the plants grow healthy.

Those plants which shed their leaves in winters like grapes, phalsa, fig, mulberry, pear, peaches and plums should never be irrigated in winters, till they sprout up in February-March.

Inter-cropping

In newly planted orchards or those which have inter spores must be covered with seasonal vegetable to have income so far as there is no income from the orchard.

Planting Distances

Plant mango seedlings, Khirin and Tamarind at 16 x 16 metres. Vegetatively propagated Laugra, Chausa and Fajli mangoes, jack fruit, monkey jack, carambola, mahua, chilbil, Panamla, Dillenia (Chalta) and Kadamb, at 12 x 12 m; Grafted a Dasehri mango 10.5 x 10.5 m; Grafted amprapali mango 2.5 x 2.5 m (8.25 x 8.25 feet); Aonla, Litchee, Ber, Kaitha, Bael, Jamun, Lasora, Spondias, Sweet Spondia (meeth amra), Mulberry, Loquat, Sapota, Coconut 7.5 x 7.5 m; Guava, Custard apple, fig 6 x 6 m; Lime and other citrus 4.5 x 4.5 m; Pomegranate 4 x 4 m; grapes 3 x 3 m; Banana, Papaya, Karonda, Phalse 1.8 x 1.8 m; Pineapple 0.75 x 0.75 m; Raspberry 0.75 x 0.75 m; Strawberry 0.45 x 0.2 m.

Some Other Important Points

Water sprouts - Remove all water sprouts conical and green shoots growing very vigorously, straight upwards on plants. This occurs mostly on citrus fruits.

Sprouts from Rootstocks

Any sprout seen on root stocks of grafted or budded plants should immediately be rubbed off.

2

Mango - The King of Fruits

Mango is a very important tasteful fruit of our country. It is the choicest fruit not only of India but of the whole world. An evergreen fruit tree of the family Anacardia-cea the mango is botanically known as Mangifera indica. It grows upto a height of 40-50 feet (12-15 metres) and almost equally densely spreading. As such it becomes very shady. Other fruits of mango family are hog plum (amra), cuddapah almond, (chironji), cashewnut (Kaaju), and Pistachio or green almond (pista).

In Sanskrit mango is named as 'aamr' and 'chut'. In Hindi, besides 'aam' it is also called 'amb', 'aamb', 'ambria' and also 'rasaal.' In Bangla the name of mango is 'aam,' while in Gujarati is 'aamri.' in Rajasthani 'amlia,' in Sindhi and Kashmiri 'amb,' Kumauni 'aamrn' Irani 'ambaah' and Arabi 'ambai.' In Karnataka mango is known as 'maava,' in Kerala 'kutam' or maavee' and in Portugal 'mang'. In Andhra Pradesh its name is 'naaamidi' and 'maavi'. The English name 'mango' has been derived from the Tamil name 'mange' or 'manke'. In Malaya and Java it is called 'mange,' or 'mangga,' while in China 'mang-kwo'.

Nutritional Importance

Besides a fruit by all, mango fruit is very nutritious as well. It is specially rich in vitamin-A, lack of which in daily meals gives rise to blindness. It is also highly medicinal. Every 100 gm, of ripe mango pulp makes available vitamin A 4800 i v. carbohydrate 11.8 gm, protein 0 6 gm, fat 0.1 gm and sugar 11-20 gm. The pulp also provides iron 0.3 mg, calcium 10 mg, phosphorus 20 mg, nicotine acid 0.3 mg and 50 calories of heat energy. Mango contains tanin also.

Vitamin-C is also an important vitamin, which is required in the highest quantity in diet among all the vitamins. Each 100 gm pulp of ripe mango contains 13 mg of Vitamin-C. However, differences in this respect have been found in various varieties. In langra mango this quality of vitamin-C increases to 131.75 mg, while in the pulps of dashehri, Alphonso, Neelam and Amrapali, its quantity is 37 mg, 33.5, 31.0 and 35.0 mg respectively Unripe mango is also rich in vitamin-C and iron. Tartaric acid and malic acid are also available in unripe mango in sufficient quantity. Smaller-sized unripe mangoes are richer in vitamin-C than bigger ones. Each 100 gm unripe mango pulp provides moisture 90 gm, protein O.7 gm, fat 0.1 gm, carbohydrate 8.8 gm and iron 4.5 mg.

Medicinal Value

Dried blossoms of mango when used give relief in the case of chronic dysentery and diarrhoea, oil is also extracted from mango blossoms. A few drops of this oil when dropped in nostrils, relieve one from headache. Use of bark of mango is said to relieve the troubles of gout and diphtheria (a kind of breathing trouble). The gum oozed out of mango tree branches and sap from fruit pedicels are useful for filling up the cracks created in heels of the foot. Resin is also extracted from its gum. An extract of bark of the tree when taken is said to give relief in the case of bleeding. Mango leaves are aromatic. These also have resin in them. Leaves may, therefore also be used in place of bark.

The tea of green mango leaves, as such, if taken, give strength to the booy. It is said that powder of mango seed kernel is in useful in vomitings, dysentery, heart-burning, indigestion and other. Now fibrous young mango seed kernel, powder proves better. Its application on the belly relieves the blocked urine. Sucking juicy mangoes and taking warm milk, thereafter removes sleeplessness.

Types of Mango

Generally mangoes are of two type:- (i) sucking mangoes and (ii) vegetatively propagated (kalmi) mangoes. However, these can be distributed in five groups.

Sucking Mango

Sucking mangoes are juicy ones. These are relished only by sucking and cannot be cut in slices. These are digested very easily. Sucking, mangoes (chusua aam) are generally seedling mangoes and are also called deshi mangoes. These fruits are plucked from trees when fully mature and ripened in straw or keeping in closed room. Its plants are prepared by sowing its seed stones and bear fruit after nine or ten years. Due to cross- pollination in flowers of seedling mangoes, fruits of every tree are of different qualities. Some are sour, some very sweet flavoured and very delicious and so on. Some sucking mangoes of certain trees are so good that these are liked by all. However, these varieties cannot be established unless these are propagated by vegetative means (grafting etc.).

Tapka Mango

Those fruits of sucking mangoes, which completely ripen on the tree and drop on the ground. They are known as 'tapka aam.' People like very much to relish such mangoes, provided the fruits of that particular seedling tree are tasteful. Tapka mangoes are more delicious than those of ordinary sucking mangoes, though these are also sucked.

Katua Mango

Those fruits which can be cut-into slices and then relished are called 'katua aam.' Actually these are the mangoes which are 'kalmi aam' and these are propagated by grafting. Such vegetatively propagated plants/trees bear fruits having true characters of fruits of their mother plant/tree. Dasheri, langra, chausa, Bombay, Alphonso, pairi, Benganpalli, Beneshain, Amrapalli and mallika are some of the examples of 'katua aam' (grafted mangoes) the so-called 'kalmi aam' possess the same characters of their mother tree from which scions (shoots) were used for grafting. In grafted mangoes good and bad points-both are truly available as in their mother-plants. These bear in 4-5 years.

Tukhmi Mango

The plants or trees propagated by sowing the seed stone of a particular variety is called 'tukhmi aam' of that variety. If seeds of dasheri are sown the fruits obtained from those trees are called tukhmi of dasheri' (dasheri kaa tukhmi). Similarly one may have tukhmi of langra, tukhmi of chausa, tukhmi of Bombay green or Bombay yellow and so on. People sow such seeds thinking that their trees will produce fruits of original characters of the variety, rather there are differences also.

Wild Mango

Those mango trees growing wild or growing themselves are wild mangoes. Fruits of such trees bear smaller fruits than deshi mangoes.

Tasteful Varieties

Mango is the only fruit which has more than one thousand varieties. However, qualities of a few of these are presented here with.

Dashehri

This is a mid season choice variety of mango which ripens in June. Fruits are longish oval, often beakless, medium to large-sized. On ripening the fruit is of attractive yellow colour. The pulp is yellow or attractive orange-yellow, coloured fine-textured, fibreless, sweet flavoured and very delicious. Its keeping quality is very good. It can be kept safely on room temperature for several days. It originated in village Dashehri of Lucknow.

Daily about 120 trucks loaded with about 1,000 packets of Dashehri mangoes on each are transported from fruit belts (mango belts) of Lucknow to Delhi, Mumbai, Gujarat, Jalandhar, Kanpur and Gorakhpur fruit mandies. Besides these, mangoes worth about Rs. 90 lakh are sold every day in Dubagga fruit mandi of Lucknow. On the other hands 20 trucks loaded with Dashehri mangoes and 10 trucks loaded with sucking mangoes are also purchased daily for preparing preserved products of mango by processing.

Banarsi Langra

The fruit of Banarsi Langra is also a mid season variety. The fruit is medium-sized oval or a bit rectangular of green or milky green colour on ripening. Pulp is soft orange coloured good flavoured, very sweet. It originated in Varanasi. Though its keeping quality is not very good, but it is also liked by many being a famous variety of Varanasi. These are exported to Sri Lanka, Nepal, Bangladesh and Pakistan. Their demand is also going on increasing in Gulf countries.

Alphonso

This is the best variety of mango. This variety is grown on a large scale in Ratnagiri district of Maharashtra and in Gujarat also. The fruit on ripening is very attractive of golden yellow colour, very smooth and shining the fruit is medium sized and obliquely oval in shape. Also it is a mid-season variety of pleasing sweet flavour, very sweet and tasteful with fibreless and fine-textured attractive golden yellow coloured flesh. Its keeping quality is very good. Its slices may be canned.

Alphonso mango is also known by various other names like 'aapoos', 'hafoos' 'alphonse' and 'badami' out of so many varieties, the maximum export to foreign countries from India is only of the varieties Alphonso and Dashehri. Alphonso being at number one due to its high durability.

Pairy

Pairy is next to best variety (Alphonso) of India. It is a variety of Maharashtra and south India. The fruit is small to medium sized oval with a developed broadbeak. The fruit is with a pleasant flavour sweet and very tasteful. Its leaves are long with enlarged thick apex.

Other Mid Season Varieties

Other mid season varieties of mango are Sůfeda Lucknow, Sufeda Malihabad, Rataul, Kapuri, Tikari, Khasulkhas, Husne-ara, Zardalu and some others. Fruit of Sufeda Lucknow are medium sized, with whitish light yellow coloured skin with prominent beak. Its pulp is very sweet with pleasant flavour. It can also be suckod.

On the other hand, fruits of sufeda Malihabad are small sized roundish oval and very tasteful. The variety Rataul is also good and tasteful and if of attractive golden yellow colour and roundish in shape. It originated in village Rataul of district Ghaziabad. The variety Kapuri of Gorakhpur, Tikari of Karinganj (Farrukhabad) are the same as Banarsi langra of Varanasi. Fruits of Khasul/khas and Husneara are of attractive golden yellow colour. The basal portions of the fruits (towards padicel) are of attractive vermillion colour fruits of the variety Zardalu are of Apricot yellow colour and good flavoured and tasteful.

Banganpalli

It is a famous variety of Andhra Pradesh, which originated in the village/ town of Banganpalli of A.P. The fruit is medium to large-sized attractive golden yellow-coloured, slightly flattish and obliquely oval in shape. It is also smooth and shining. The flesh is yellow, fibreless good flavoured tasteful, sweet with some sourishtinge. The tree flowers in winters in south India and therefore, it's fruits are available in plenty in the markets of northern India from the very beginning of March-April..

Other Early Ripening Varieties

Bombay green, Bombay yellow, Bride of Russia and Safdor Pasand are very delicious early varieties of mango, which ripen in May. On ripening the fruit of Bombay green remains green while those of Bombay yellow turn yellow in colour. These are medium sized roundish oval in shape. Skins of fruits of the varieties bride of Russia and Safdar pasand are golden yellow in colour. Their basal portions are beautiful vermillion coloured and very attractive. Gaurjeet is an important earliest ripening variety of Gorakhpur. Its fruits are of golden yellow colour, small to medium in size and roundish in shape. It starts ripening from the very beginning of May. Its pulp is of attractive golden yellow colour with sweet pleasant flavour and taste. Gaurjeet fruits may also be very well relished by sucking and enjoying the thick pulp.

Some Late Ripening Varieties

Among the late ripening varieties of mango, says which ripen in the month of July—August and onwards, 'Samar Bahisht chausa'— the so called "Khajri' is the chief one. Chusa ripens in July- August. Its fruits are large-sized longish and broad of golden yellow colour, smooth, shining and very attractive. The apical portion of the fruit is conical or cornered, slightly some more above of which lies the beak of the fruit in the form of a protuberated point only. Its skin is very thin. The pulp is light yellowish in colour fine-textured very sweet smelling and very delicious.

Fruits of Fajri are very large and remain green on ripening: Pulp being reddish yellow colour though sweet, is loose textured Fajri Zafrani remains yellow on ripening. Its fruits are more tasteful than Fajri. Its flesh is yellowish.

Neelam

Neelam is a very later ripening variety of south India. Its tree is comparatively small sized, specially when other mango trees are very huge-sized. Neelam is a regular bearing variety, whereas other varieties are alternate bearers. The fruit of Neelam is medium-sized approximately 8 cm long and 7.0 cm broad and 180 gm in weight. Its beak is prominently broad. It ripens from middle of August to the end of September. On ripening the fruit is greenish yellow in colour.

However, on wrapping in newspaper the whole-fruit becomes completely golden yellow in colour. Its pulp is yellow in colour, which is very attractive fibreless sweet, tasteful and fine textured with good flavour. Its fruits are also durable.

Varieties Named Under Various Bases

Several varieties of mango have been named on different bases such as:

(1) On the basis of Emperors, Kings and Persons Eg. Jahangir, Nisar Pasand, Rehmat Khaas, Himayuddin, Laila-Majnu, Amrapali, Mallika, Kavas Ji Patel, Gopalbhog, Raja Ram, Chandra Kiran, Krishnabhog, Taimurlang, Meer Jaafar, Alif Laila, Peter.

(2) On the basis of Name of Place Such as Dashehri, Safeda Lucknow, Safeda Malihabad, Husne-ara, Asaugia Deoband (Saharanpur), Rataul, Maldah (West Bengal), Bainganpalli (south India), Bangalore Bombay bottle, Murshidabadi, Brindabani, Malgova and Singapuri etc.

(3) On the basis of Weights and Measures Haathijhool, Pansera Fajri, Raja Ram (2 kg), and Laatkampur (1.75).

(4) On the basis off Time of Ripening Bhaduria or Bhadaila or Bhadauhan, Barahmasia, Dofasli and Sawania and others.

(5) On the basis of Flavour and Taste Lemon, Baal, Saunfia, llaichi, Gulabjamun, Kakarhia, Rasgulla, Mithua, Gulakhas, Gajaria, Batasia, Kachmuha, Karela, Kesar, Shakarkand, Kharbooza, Aamlet, Kesar, Kamchan, Kacthmeetha.

(6) On the basis of Shape and Colour Sharifa, Karela, Laddu, Bhoora, Totapari, gola, seepia, Bombay green, Bombay yellow, Swarnrekha, Zardalu, Fajri Zarani, Sundarja, Turai, Chitla, Sinduria, Neelam, Haathiphal, Kuharha, Chikna.

(7) On the basis of Designation, Caste and Others Jailor, Jamadar, Collector, Prince, Sukul, Panditawa, Buddhu ka kelwa, Raspumia Kotwalpasand, Taimuria, Himsagar, Fakirwala, Romani, Aminheera, Raanipasand, Dilpasand, Nazukbadan, Baneshan, Farmamdeen, Bathua, Vanraj, Dilkash, Dilfareb, Dilruba, Lambbhadra, Nawabpasand, Langra, Chausa, Alphonso, Ooor, Rajapuri, Mussarat, Sundarja, Sardar, Mahbooba, Singara, Stakirt, Motidana (10 gm) and Khaparia etc.

Hybrid Varieties of Mango

Two regular fruiting varieties of mango have now been evolved through hybridization by the Division of Horticulture and fruit technology, Indian

Agricultural Research Institute, New Delhi. These varieties are known as 'Mallika' and 'Amrapali'. These are very tasteful and sweet flavoured varieties pulp of which are very sweet fibreless and fine textured. Fruits are large in size. Though trees of these varieties are smaller, however trees of Amrapali are smaller than those of Mallika.

Amrapali is known as a dwarf variety of excellent quality, fruiting profusely every year. The tree grows to a height of 2 metres. Mallika has been developed by crossing the female part of flowers of Neelam with the male part of flowers of Dashehri variety (Dashehri Neelam).

On the other hand, Amrapali variety was evolved by crossing the female part of Dashehri with the male part of Neelam (Neelam Dashehri). Actually 'Amrapali' was a beautiful dancer of Vaishali, who was all of a sudden seen in a mango orchard (Amra-kunj). That is why that dancer girl was named as 'Amrapalis'. Only on that basis this newly evolved hybrid variety of mango was named 'Amrapali'. The fruit of Amrapali is oblong, more or less like Dashehri but smaller than Dashehri and larger than Neelam. Its flesh is very attractive deep orange coloured and very sweet flavoured and delicious. Availability of vitamin-A in the pulp of Amrapali is 2-1/2 to 3 times more than the quantity available in Dashehri and Neelam.

Between 1974 and 1982 Dr. P.K. Majumdar, Dr. D.K. Sharma and Dr. N.R Singh of Division of Horticulture and Fruit Technology of IARI New Delhi jointly studied the qualities of Amrapali, Dashehri and Neelam in various aspects. These findings were (1) Average weight of a fruit 143.0155-0 and 100-Ogm respectively (2) Pulp 74.8, 68.0 and 59.1% in the same order (3) Total soluble solids % 22.8, 24.0 and 18.0 (4) Total sugar % 17.2, 15.2 and 16.4 (5) Acidity % in the form of citric acid 0.12, 0.19 and 0.28. (60 Ascorbic acid (vit. C) mg/100 gm pulp—35.0, 37.0 and 31.0 (7) Total carotene pigment (in the form of B-carotene pigment/vitamin A microgram/100 gm—16,830, 7,452 and 5, 275 in the same order, i.e., in pulps of Amrapali, Dashehri, Neelam.

High Density Orcharding

High density orcharding is a technique of establishing on orchard with a view to reduce the distance of planting to have maximum number of plants per unit area in comparison with other varieties and simultaneously to have better yield regularly every year. For this less growth in trees is a must, i.e., this practice is possible in dwarf trees and not huge trees.

Since there is a problem of alternate bearing in mango, therefore, Amrapali variety was selected for high density orcharding by the horticultural scientists of Indian Agricultural Research Institute, New Delhi (mentioned earlier), so as to have satisfactory yield regularly from the very beginning of fruiting.

For high density orcharding of Amrapali mango, plantations were done at 2.5x2.5 metres apart (8.25x8.25 feet). As such 1,600 plants could be accommodated per hectare of orchard, against an average of 100 plants per hectare of huge-sized trees of other commercial varieties of mango like langra, chausa, fajri and several others. Yield of these varieties have been estimated as 8.67 tonnes from these 100 plants of one hectare orchard, which is far less than Amrapali. As regards the yield of Amrapali in high density orcharding mentioned above, the yield in the 4th year per hectare was 11.5 tonnes, while in the 7th year it raised to 22.2 tonnes.

The year-wise details are like this. In the year 1979, i.e., in the 4th year of plantation as mentioned above the yield per tree was 7.19 kg and per hectare it was 11,504 kg. In 1980 (5th year) the yield was 8.36 and 13,376 kg in the same order. Again in 1981 (6th year) it was 10.36 kg and 16,576 kg, while in the year 1982, i.e., in the 7th year of plantation, the yield per tree obtained was 13.93 kg and it was 22,288 kg per hectare. Fruits were picked between the 2nd and 3rd week of July and ripened afterwards. These plants were raised by veneer grafting on root stock of mango seedlings.

Plantation of Amrapali were done on various growers' fields and in Government gardens and nurseries of Bulandshahar, Ghaziabad, Meerut, Allahabad and others earlier, about more than two decades back by planting the root stocks and veneer grafting them in situ with the help of IARI (Horticulture and Fruit Technology Division), New Delhi staff and the author. Scion sticks of Amrapali were sent by Dr P.K. Majumdar the then Head of Horticulture and Fruit Technology Division through Mr K.B. Nigam horticulture scientist and a trained technical person to these places as and when required and demanded. The root stocks of mango were veneer grafted with the scion sticks of Amrapali brought by them then and there. Now Amrapali grafts are available for supply and plantation of orchards in various government gardens and nurseries of the state.

Utilization

As mentioned earlier ripe mangoes are relished and enjoyed by sticking them fresh into pieces or by sucking their juices depending upon the varieties and types of mangoes. However fresh ripe mangoes may also be had and enjoyed in the form of mango milk shake, mango chaat, salad, mango kulfi, ready to serve syrup (sharbat) mango ice-cream and others.

Again taste of mango can also be had and enjoyed in the off season by processing these in many ways. Jams, Jellies, squashes, syrups, juices, nectars, mango toffee, fruit bar, aam papar (amaavat), preserves (murabba), sweet 'chutneys' and others may be prepared and preserved for future use. The slices of 'katva' mangoes like dasheri, chausa and alphonso (so-called kalmi ones) varieties may also be canned or bottled in syrups after peeling for off-season use.

Likewise unripe mangoes are also important. These may be turned into hot and sweet pickles 'chutneys' and preserves green mango pulp or their slices may be dried for use in curries, cooked pulses and 'karhi' (liquid cooked preparation from gram flour) green mango pulp powder (aamchur) may also be prepared and packed for future use in food preparations fresh peeled slices of green mangoes are similarly used in pulses, curries etc. green mango peels exclusively are also utilized in preparimg hot pickeles.

Best use of unripe green mangoes in summer reason in the scorching sun and hot wind (loo) is to use its preparation- 'panaa' (aam-paani) to save from the ill-effects of 'loo'. For this green mangoes are either boiled in water or cooked in hot ash. The pulp is then thoroughly taken out and prepared as a drink with salt crushed mint leaves and others. A tumbler of mango panaa if taken before start of going out specially in noon and one tumbler after return is helpful in saving one from the attack of hot wind (loo). In case one becomes victim of 'loo' spreading the pulp of the cooked green mangoes mentioned above on soul of the foot and palm relieves him from the trouble.

Young growing small mangoes (amiya, tikora, tikola, karry) are also utilised in preparing pickles, chutney, salad, ready to serve sharbat. These are also used in curries and other food preparations.

The importance of mango stone cannot be overlooked. The mango seed kernel yields 8-10% edible oil. Its oil is also used in preparing soap. The powder of the seed kernel is mixed with wheat flour and utilised in preparing chapaties. Its kernel makes available carbohydrate 69.2%, fat 16.3%, protein 5.56% and starch 90%. After extracting oil from mango seed kernel, the left over are given to animals to eat and the peels of the mango stone are used as fuel. Dry mango leaves are utilised for covering mango stones spread in soil for raising seedling root stocks. These save plants from the attack of white ants due to presence of resin in leaves green mango leaves are used at religious occasions and social functions. Mango wood is burnt in 'Hawan' or 'yagya'. Wood is also used in preparing furnitures and packing boxes. Its bark is used in colouring leather. Its gum is used for pasting.

Historical Background

Mango is being grown in India from time immemorial. This is confirmed by its historical background also. When Alexander attacked India in 327 years B.C., he stayed only in a mango orchard. He knew about mango in the valley of Sindh and later on this fruit was taken to other countries also. In the 7th century, while touring India the Chinese pilgrims wrote much about mango in their diaries.

Fa Hian and Sung

I have described about such a mango orchard in their diaries, which was offered to Lord Buddha by a female disciple - Aamradharika for worship. Information regarding mango was received in China through the Chinese pilgrim Hyauansong after he came to India in 9th century. Only after his visit to India and return to China, mango growing became a practice in China also.

Other foreign pilgrims like Ibnehaukul in 9th century, Ibnebatuta in 13th century and Lyudo Visideyarthma in 15th century have also highly praised the qualities and other good points of mango. In the year 1331 mango travelled and reached Africa. Since then Africans started growing mangoes in Somali land on North-eastern side of Africa. The well known poet and saint Ameer Khusro has very beautifully praised mango and he accepted mango as the king of fruits. He liked mango fruit so much that he used to say that mango can be tastefully taken in any stage whether it is ripe or unripe, grown up or only in a growing stage.

Moghuls were very much fascinated by mangoes. They were rather mad behind mangoes. They felt proud of themselves in establishing mango orchards of various varieties at different places. The Moghul emperor Akbar loved mangoes so much that he got a mango orchard of different varieties established in Darbhanga (Bihar), having one lakh plants/trees. This famous historical mango orchard later on was known as 'Laakhi Bagh' of India. In the year 1510 Abul Fazal gave detailed references of Laakhi Bagh mangoes in his book Aaine Akbari.

Mango plants reached around the border areas of Persian gulf by the 16th century. Also in 1600 mango travelled to Philiphines and in 1665 to Mulucca. In 1690 mango plants were brought to England, where these were being grown in glass houses. However, the mango trees of knew gardens of England could actually come to fruiting stage only during the year 1818. Further, most probably in the year 1878 or even a bit earlier, the traders of Spain brought- mango plants from Philippines to Mexico, where so many big orchards of mango were planted.

It was presumed when Portugese came to India, the Portugese administrators of Goa created in themselves great love for mango. It is also said that from that very time they started preparing mango plants by grafting (Kalmi plants), when in India mango plants were being propagated by Inarching (Bhentkalam) since very early periods. However, when they went back from India, they took large number of mango grafts with them. This resulted in large scale mango orcharding in Western countries. In 18th century mango grafts were taken by them to Brazil and then to Western Islands.

In Hawaii mango got a place between 1800 and 1820. After this it reached Florida in the year 1861 or 1862, Azores in 1865, Queens land in 1870, California between the years 1880-85 and in the end of 18th century to Yemen. In the year 1905, mango orcharding also started in South Italy.

Egyptians had also planted some mango grafts successfully in their country after having these from Mumbai in the year 1825. In the year 1929, mango travelled from Egypt to Israel. In Israel mango got so much honour through wide publicity and expansion that this country is now being regarded one of the leading mango growing and mango producing countries.

In this way mango plantation and production besides India (including Pakistan), spread extensively throughout the whole world. This included the countries and areas of south eastern Asia, Maldives, Indonesia, Java, Philipphines, Hawaii Islands, Pacific Island, South China, Queensland, Egypt, Sudan, Madagascar, border area of tropical countries of Africa, Yemen, United Arab Republic, Persian gulf countries and Israel. These countries grow and produce mangoes on a large scale. In Florida, Mediterranean regions and California mango is grown only on limited scale. However, India continues to be the largest mango producing country of the whole world.

Production, Area and Distribution

Among the total production of mango in the whole world the contribution of India is 62.2 per cent of the total area covered under fruits in India mango orcharding contributes about 44% of that area. As such India grows mango in an area of 11.0 lakh hectare of land, producing thereby about 111.0 lakh tonnes of mango every year.

Uttar Pradesh is the leading state in mango production among all the states of India, where mango orchards cover an area of 4,84,000 ha. This area is about 44% of the total area covered under mango in our country. This produces 34, 41,000 tonnes of mango. This production is 31.0% of the whole production of mango (111.0 lakh tonnes) in the country.

In mango production next to Uttar Pradesh, the states of Bihar and Andhra Pradesh are second and third, where mango production is 13.5% and 13.48% of total production of mango in the country in the same order. After these three states other states in mango production in the same order are—West Bengal, Orissa, Kerala, Tamil Nadu, Maharashtra, Madhya Pradesh, Karnataka, Tripura, Punjab, Assam, Meghalaya, Lakshwadeep, Andaman, Jammu and Kashmir, Himanchal Pradesh, Sikkim and Rajasthan.

In Uttar Pradesh, Government (Horticulture Department) have declared 14 fruit belts to protect mango orchards. In Lucknow most of the areas of Malihabad and neighbouring places are covered with the delicious variety of International fame Dashehri originated in the village Dashehri of Malihabad from the mother tree of Dashehri variety, is still standing there. This tree is more than 200 years old. Mango orchards in an area of 14000 hectares are lying only in mango fruit belts of Malihabad, Maal and Kakori when fruiting is good these orchards yield about two lakh tonnes of mango fruits.

As stated earlier the mango variety 'Banarsi Langra' is the proud of Varanasi (U.P.). In Varanasi most of the mango plantations are of Banarsi langra. This variety originated from the mother tree found in the campus of State Bank of India Varanasi (Main branch), situated near Collectorate and bridge of the river Varuna, Varanasi. In Varanasi district the area under mango orchard is in 1,500 ha of land. Out of these 60% orchards are only of Banarsi Langra variety. Chief growing areas of this variety in Varanasi are Chiraee gaon, Cholapur, Sewapuri, Chaubepur, Pindra, Bara gaon, Harahua, Pilakhani (Rohania) and Kashi Vidyapeeth block development areas. These produce about 5 lakh tonnes of mango.

Religious and Cultural Importance

Mango is tightly related with Indian culture and religion. Pages of Sanskrit and other old religious 'granthas' of India are covered with the praises qualities and importance of mango fruit. Mango trees and fruits have also been very artistically pictured carved on Baudh monuments like those of Bharhut and Saanchi and also on other old historical and religious monuments. These have also been pictured on the walls of caves of Ajanta and Elora. Medicinal values importance and specialities of mango have been well described in Charaksanhita also. Importance and utility of mango have also been included in various folk songs, folklores, poems and religious stories of our country.

According to a 'Pauranik' story when Lord Bramha after evolving earth broadcasted in the soil after creating different kinds of seeds of various fruits flowers and grains the residents of earth under the leadership of Maharaja Manu prayed God for evolving such a sweet juicy fruit, which has sweetness of fruits, aroma of flowers and nutrition of food grains.They also prayed that this fruit should be within the reach of every poor and rich person. After hearing and accepting their request Lord Bramha poured a drop of water from his 'kamandal' on the ground. Just after this mango plant sprouted from the holy soil of India. This is how mango originated. Most probably only for this reason it is said that mango came on earth from Heaven and that is why mango is also called as 'Deva-phal.'

In India guests are made to stay honourably in mango orchards, where they take rest with great pleasure for saints and 'rishi'- 'Munies' Mango orchards are regarded not less than their 'Aashrams'.

Regarding the origin of mango, there are so many opinions. The Sanskrit old poet Rishi Valmiki has described the mango orchards of Ceylon in a very interesting and artistic manner. It is also said that mango was brought to India from Ceylon by Lord Hanuman, whereas it has also been opined that mango was already being grown in India since the period quite earlier than that. As such on the basis of these opinions and presumptions besides Mayanmar,

Thailand and Malaya, India was also regarded as the birth place of mango. However, in every case the original place of birth regarded for mango is India.

Mango is such an attractive fruit that there are other Pauranik stories also on mango. Once God himself was taking round in a mango orchard. There being so much impressed with mangoes, God drew a figure of a beautiful lady with the juice of mango fruits. After that God gave life to this figure as a result of this a beautiful dancer girl 'Urvashi' came into existence. Again, there was a competition of race between two sons of Lord Shankerji— Ganesh and Kartikeya to win one mango fruit which was with their mother Parvati for this they had to take three rounds of the whole Universe and after that who reaches back first, will get the mango. Kartikeya riding on peacock flew in the air and started taking solvind of the universe. On the other hand Ganeshji riding on mouse took three rounds of his mother and father regarding them to be the whole universe/world and was back quite early and won the mango.

As indicated earlier, green and dry leaves of mango and dry wood juices are utilised in performing 'Yagya' and 'hawan' and other religious occasions. By burning dry wood of mango with other 'hawan' material the environment further becomes clean due to the presence of resin in them 'Green mango leaves are used in kalash poojan', preparing 'bandanwar' and stretching them on doors, temples in various religious and other social functions and in festivals marriages etc.

During spring season the sweet voice of cuckoo in a singing style informs one regarding the arrival of mango season after a gap of one year. The inflorescences coming out on mango trees spread their sweet smell in the whole orchard of mango and also at places surrounding there. This sweet smell of mango inflorescences along with songs of cuckoos encourage the poets to write or sing their poems. On the holy occasions of the religious festival of Basant Panchami, it is customary to wear yellow (basanti) clothes by Indian males and females in Hindu families and see the inflorescence of mango. At this holy occasion Goddess Saraswati is worshipped and cultural programmes are organised in Her honour.

In the drama named as 'Abhigyan Shakuntalam' the poet Kalidas has described the mango orchards and mango inflorescences in spring season in a very interesting style.

Mango Festival

In mango season mango feasts are organised in the form of mango festivals or mango parties. This is done by prospective and progressive mango growers who invite their nears and dears to eat and enjoy veritable varieties of mango of different castes, shades, shapes and sizes. These also include mangoes of various kinds and groups, i.e., kalmi (katua) and sucking mangoes etc. The gentries of the area are also invited.

In Puducherry mango festival is celebrated every year on a very large scale at a function in a place "kairekal" situated there. There is also an interesting story behind the mango festival of Kairekal. A religious minded poetess of Kairekal had two mangoes. Her husband had shown his desire to her to eat these two mangoes after lunch. In the mean time a guest reached there, had his meals and after that demanded one mango to eat, who had it. On the other hand when her husband asked for the next mango after eating one, his wife was very much worried. The guest could not be refused for one mango and simultaneously it was also essential for her to serve the second mango to her husband.

She, therefore, started praying God to save her position. After some time there was a mango in the hands of that lady, who served that to her husband. Actually, God was examining her. Since then it is said that due to God's kindness the area of Kairekal is always full of mangoes in the season. This may only be said as 'Ishwariya chamatkar'.

Mango Shows and Parties

In mango season mango shows are organised by Horticulture Department at an all-India level and also on State level. In these shows, different varieties of mangoes are displayed by various mango growers and nursery men, which are open for public. This is done with a view to make the general public, mango growers and mango lovers aware of the importance and qualities of such mangoes. Technical know-how is also given there for successful mango orcharding. Such mango shows are also sometimes organised on division or district levels.

Various parties feasts and festivals of Nature's precious gift-mango, are organised every year at places like Delhi and Saharanpur by Tourism department. These are also organised on International level. 'Aaam Mahotsava 2002' is being organised in Delhi from 6th July, 2002. These festivals and functions consist of different types of mangoes. Besides progressive mango growers, mango feasts and festivals are also organised by big hotels also. To enjoy the mango parties best, it is good to have a full tumbler of cold milk after having tasteful slices of Dashehri, langra, chausa and other, such varieties of mango in full buckets. Feast parties of sucking mangoes give special enjoyment to crazy lovers of this natural gift. For this sucking mangoes are placed under water and people sit all around each bucket in several groups and start sucking them. Within few minutes all the mangoes of the bucket disappear. If these mangoes are again added to buckets, these also disappear soon and one will only find peels and stones aside. There are competitions also between these groups and the group which take maximum mangoes win the game. Mango is such a tasty fruit that one never seems satisfied with only few mangoes. He wants to go on taking or sucking as many mangoes as he could, though he has also to keep in mind that 'excess of everything is bad.' This is how people enjoy sucking mangoes.

How Mangoes should be Eaten

Mango fruits just plucked from the tree or taken out from the ripening store or from 'paal' possess much heat in their pulp whether these are juicy or slicing ones. As such before eating mangoes, the first and foremost work to be done is to dip them in cold water and continue for 5-6 hours. After this the mangoes should be washed twice or thrice by gently rubbing these with hands. This is also necessary because these days the mango traders use calcium carbide in stores for hastened ripening which is harmful for health. Only after such processing the mangoes reach a stage to be eaten safely. The best time to start eating mangoes is after 2-3 rains. Even then above practices must be adopted in every case. If mangoes are taken otherwise one may become victim of diarrhoea and other stomach troubles.

Before sucking juicy mangoes, the hood of the pedical should be removed and then a few drops of juice should be leaked out so that the actual juice to be sucked is free from resinous material (Chenp). Earlier than this each mango is softened by gently pressing it between the thumb and fingers of hands all round. Sucking mangoes are easily digested. If the varieties are to be taken after slicing, the hood of the fruit along with a little flesh should be removed with a sharp knife by placing its point vertically and moving all round. This practice makes the pulp free from resin as it lies in the fruit just under the pedical. Such varieties may be sliced with peels or sliced alter peeling and then relished. Some relish by having broad slices and eating the pulp with spoon, who enjoy much in this practice. Such 'katua' or slicing mangoes are also relished as sucking mangoes. For this the fruit of Dashehri, langra or any such variety is softened like sucking mango and tastefully sucked with thick juice. This is more digestible in comparison to slices. The thick juice sucked thus are very palatable. It has been opined that the mango pulp in the form of juice or slices if kept for some time and taken afterwards are less digestible as by coming in contact with air the pulp becomes heavier. However, being such a delicious fruit, there is always the possibilities of one to eat mangoes more than what is actually required. In such cases or always if possible jamun fruits should be taken after mangoes. Jamun is aid to digest the mangoes. Taking cumin water (jal-zeera or a little powder of dry ginger (south) and salt equally serve the purpose. After having mangoes in normal way taking a tumbler of cold milk as indicated earlier, or cold milk lassi is useful and this may be a supplement for meals. Mango pulp may also be taken after mixing with cold milk (as milk mango shake) but it should be borne in mind that in no case should the pulp be sour. Milk should also not be taken after eating sour man goes. Taking milk with mango is supposed to provide sufficient energy to body.

Climate and Soil

Tropical and sub-tropical climates are quite suitable for mango growing. It thrives well in plains from commercial point of view, though it can grow in region upto an altitude of 1500 metres above the sea level. However, for commercial growing regions above an altitude of 600 metres is not recommended. It flowers and fruits well in valleys of hills. Hot and cold winds and frost are unfavourable specially for young plants of mango. Cloudy weather, humid atmosphere and rains are harmful during flowering. Dry atmosphere encourages profuse flowering. Hailstorm, cyclone and rains during flowering and start of fruiting destroy the mango crop.

Well-drained deep loom porous soil suits well simultaneously, it should be rich in organic matter. Heavy, sandy and socky soils should be avoided.

Propagation

Mango is propagated by seeds and vegetative means. As such seedling plants and vegetatively propagated (kalmi) plants of mango grafting of mango (Enriching - Bhent Kalam) in India is being practised from very olden days. Though an easier and cheaper method of 'Veneer grafting' has been evolved, but in Malihabad still the method of 'inarching', which is in general called as 'frafting' is adopted for propagating a grafted or kalmi' mango plant. 'Grafting by approach' is also used for the term Incharging. This is an attached method of grafting, in which the scion stick (soot of desired variety) of mother-plant tree remains attached with the root stock till the union of stock and scion is complete. In a detached method of grafting, the scion stick is first detached from the mother-plant and then it is attached with the root stock, which after union given rise to a 'kalmi' plant of desired variety. However, in any method of grafting the availability of suitable and healthy root stocks is a must.

Raising Mango Root Stocks

For mango root stocks its seedling plants are good enough. For raising these freshly collected mango stones are spread in the prepared beds under old friting mango orchards. These are spread flat in soil in a way that each mango stone lies side by side but should not overlap any. This is done in June-July or even earlier. After spreading, the seeds are covered with thick layer of dry mango leaves which has been hinted earlier regarding the use of leaves. The leaves should always be kept moist under such conditions these germinate in a fortnight and the plantlet starts growing. The mango leaves keep moisture in themselves for a longer period, which also save the plants from attack of termites due to the presence of resin in leaves. Further due to leaves being lighter than soil, these allow the least resistance to germinating plants.

After the plantlets of mango (amola) cange their coopesish leaves into green ones (in a month or so after germination) and the mango stones are still attached to roots, these are released from soil. For this a broad bladed khurpa is inserted in soil in such a slanting manner that after pushing the blade forward 20-25 plants are released at a time with only 1-1/2 inch long tap roots and stone being attached to roots. These plantlets are without soil and can be shifted in baskets very easily in large number at a time for further growth in the nursery.

Inarching

For inarching or any type of grafting the root stock should be a mango seedling of one year age, healthy and disease- free. The plant should be 2-3ft. in height and its thickness should be like that which is between the thickness of ring and little finger. In May-June the scion sticks of mother plants (say of Dashehri bending near ground should be selected and for a particular scion the position of planting the root stock should be marked.

The root slock of one year as prepared earlier should be lifted from the nursery and planted on the marked position. When root stocks are established in soil, the steps for actual grafting should be taken during July-August-September for this 1/3 (one third) part of thickness of stock. The scion stick should be brown in colour and equal in thickness to that of the root stock should clearly and smoothly be peeled off up to a length of 4-5 cm at a height between 25 to 30 cm from the ground. Simultaneously the selected scion stick should also be peeled off likewise including bark and wood starting the peeling from 15-20 cm below the top. Both the peeled portions should then be brought together, joined wrapped with a mango leaf and tied tightly with a soft rope up to a little above and below the peeled portions. In eight weeks due to the growth of Cambium layers in cats of both scion and stock, these unite with each other and become one plant (graft-a clone). During this period the root stock, is nourished by the food material in soil and the scion is nourished by the mother-plant/tree. After their union and becoming one plant, the scion is nurtured by the food material of soil through its root stock. Since the scion till then remains connected with the mother plant, it continues feeding on the mother plant also. As such growth starts in scion portion. Cut and remove the top portion of the stock then from about 2 cm above the joint of the graft. After 10-15 days make a half (1/2) cm wide 'V' shaped notch on the scion 2 cm below the joint to 1/3 depth of thickness of the scion stick. After fifteen days remove again 1/3 portion of thickness from the notch of scion. Then fifteen days after severe the scion from the mother plant by giving a final cut to the notch. Thus a graft of desired variety is prepared, the scion of which grows on the roots of seedling plant root stock. This plant will bear true to type fruits. Two months after, the graft is lifted from there with earthen ball and planted in nursery beds for further growth. These grafts are supplied for planting and establishing new mango orchards. Before lifting from nursery the string or rope tied on the joint should be gently removed. During this period this should also be watched that there is no-growth on the stock (portion below the joint) the success in inarching is though, between 80 and 90% but the method becomes cumbersome and costly, because the rootstock has to be lifted and taken to mother to mother plant for attached grafting.

Veneer Grafting

This is a detached method of grafting, which is easier and cheaper than inarching. This is carried on from April to September. The success in this method is also 80-90% for veneer grafting first the scion stick of the desired variety of mother plant is prepared for actual grafting. The scion stick should be 3-6 months old. About 7-8 days before grafting the selected scion should be defoliated. As such the food material in the scion stick collect in auxiliary buds and in vegetative bud at the top of the shoot and therefore, these buds become plump. On the other hand the root stock for inarching are good enough for veneer grafting also for veneer grafting the root stock may remain planted in nursery or may be planted earlier at the final place where the orchard is proposed to be established and veneer may be done direct in situ.

Now the prepared scion sticks are cut and collected in thick moist cloth or moist moss grass from the mother plant, each being atleast 15 cm length. A stating longitudinal downward cut of 3-4 cm length is given on the stock at a height of 20 to 25 cm from the ground and then, a horizontal cut is given at the base of the cut so as to only remove the peeled bark and wood from the stock. A similar longitudinal cut is given on the lower portion of the scion and the bark and wood is removed so as to match the cut made on the stock. The scion is then placed on the stock in such a way that the cut and peeled portions of these face each other. The graft union is then tied with soft rope or a soft polythene strip. When the growth starts in scion after union, the top portion of the stock is cut and removed from 1-2 cm above the joint of root stock and scion rest of the operations are just like those of inarching. In this method scion sticks may be taken or sent from one place to the other easily for grafting.

Cleft Grafting

Claft grafting is more or less similar to that of veneer grafting. The scion sticks are prepared just like those of veneer grafting. The lower portion of the scion up to a length of 3-4 cm are peeled with bark and wood in a slanting manner on both the sides like a wedge. The root stock is then beheaded at a height of 20-25 cm from the ground. Then a sharp knife is passed from the top middle of the thickness of the beheaded stock downwards up to a length of 3-

4 cm. The wedge of the scion is then inserted in the crack of the stock from top downwards to matchy the joints of each other. These are lied and later on the graft through cleft or wedge grafting comes in existences.

Stone Grafting

Sprouted mango stones are utilised for stone grafting, while the semi-mature terminal shoots of 12-15 cm length which have acquired green colour from purple colour is used as scion grafting is done as cleft grafting. Success is obtained in this method to the extent of 75 to 80%. The grafts are first placed in a polythene house for 12-14 days in the nursery. The humidity maintained during this period should be more than 80% and this is during this period that stock and scion unite and the scion starts sprouting. After sprouting plants are transferred into hots and put under shade of trees or green house for some time before disposal. Though it is cheaper and easier and require less time, even then there are mortalities during final transplanting. Moreover, there are problems for poly houses and green houses for growers. This is mostly possible in institutions.

Budding

Budding in mango was tried earlier but could not show promise.

Soft Wood Grafting

Soft wood grafting is done like Cleft or wedge grafting on newly emerged flush of copperish coloured leaves and stem. The scion stick should also be of the same thickness and should be defoliated 7-8 days earlier than actual grafting so as to make the auxiliary and terminal buds active and plump. This method is good for in situ grafting in July and August.

Goottee

Plants by Goottee can also be raised by applying 10,000 pm Indol butyric acid or Napphthalene acetic acid hormone in lanolin paste soradix powder may also be applied for better rooting plants raised by goottee or aerial layering may be planted for establishing mango orchards or for using as root stock.

So Many Varieties in a Tree

One tree of mango can produce several varieties of mango fruits. This may be made possible by detached method of grafting technique. In the mango orchard of Haji Kalim Ullah Khan of Malihabad (Lucknow), there is a tree of certain variety of mango over which different branches have been grafted with 200 varieties work in this direction was started by him in the year 1987 and by 1995 twenty four varieties have already fruited. Now most probably some more branches were grafted and total varieties in that tree have based to 275. Another tree of mango of 77 years of the variety 'Al-Muqarrar' is also in Malihabad over which Haji Kalim Ullah Khan has grafted 315 varieties which include

Dashehri, Alphonso, Banganpalli, Neelam, Romani, Ameer pasand, heart shaped Asi-ul-Mtuqarrar, bright red Husn-e-ara, bitter gourd like Karela and others.

Top-working Mango Trees

Mango trees which are of undesirable varieties may be turned into profuse be using improved varieties. This is done by beheading main branches in February. New shoots then sprout from their tops. These are later on grafted with choice varieties.

Planting

Mango grafts are planted at a distance of 10.50 to 12.0 metres (35-40 feet) apart each way in rainy season from July-August to September and even up to October. If there are proper and sufficient arrangements for irrigation water, these may be planted in February-March also. As such by laying out and planting at 35 feet (10.50 metres) apart, the number of plants which will be accommodated per acre of land will be 35 and per hectare 87, while on planting at 40 feet (12 metres) apart the number of plants will be 27 and 67 in the same order.

Actually the trees of Dashehri variety are smaller in size than those of langra, chausa and fajri etc. Therefore, these may be successfully planted at 35 feet (10.50 metres) apart, while others mentioned above at 40 feet (12 metres) apart. The trees of Neelam are further smaller and as such these may be planted at 25x25 feet (7.50x7.50 metres) accommodating thereby 69 and 172 plants per acre and per hectare respectively.

Before planting, pits 2-3 feet (60-90 cm) wide and deep are dug in April and May after lay out and left in open hot sun for about a month. These are then filled up tightly with surface soil, 1/3 part of Farm yeard Manure (F.Y.M-cowdung manure) and 3-4 kg of bone meal per pit 15 cm. above the soil surface. On the upper portion of each filled upfit 50 gm of aldrex is sprinkled and mixed in soil to save plants from the attack of termites.

As mentioned earlier Amrapali mango, trees being dwarfer in size may be planted only at 8.25x8.25 feet (2.50x2.50 metres) apart. In this way per acre and per hectare accommodation of plants will be 640 and 1600 Nos in the same order. Seedling mangoes if planted as an orchard or along roads etc. the distance between two plants each way will be 50 feet or 15 metres. The accommodation of plants will, therefore be 17 and 42 nos in the same order. However, in any case if the layout is done by hexagonal system (equilateral triangular system) instead of simple square system, the accommodation in number of plants will increase by 15%. The site selected for mango or charding should be within the reach of proper sunlight and no water-logging should be there.

When there are 2-3 rains and the raised soil in each pit comes at the level of surface of soil, then plants should be planted in the Centre of the filled up pit in evening or at any time when it is cloudy. After plantation the soil should be tightened all round taking care that the earthen ball round the roots may not be broken. Further plantation should be done to a depth up to which the mark of soil is there on the stem of the plant.

Irrigation: If there are no hopes of rains after plantation, plants should be lightly irrigated soon after plantation. Later in winters irrigation should be done at an interval of 15 days and in summers at 7 days. When hot winds blow and the Sun is very hot the period between two irrigations may be reduced to 3-4 days, irrigation should be avoided during flowering.

Weeding, Hoeing, Inter-cropping: Weeding and hoeing should be done after 2-3 irrigations to keep the soil free from weeds and for proper aeration in soil. Inter-cropping of seasonal vegetables should be taken in the vacant spaces between plants. This will add to income of the grower. Again, hoeing and weeding of these will further help the main fruit of plants also in growth due to proper aeration in soil.

Manuring: For proper growth of mango plants manuring should also be done from time to time. If neem cake is dissolved in irrigation water, this will save the plants from attack of termites, besides irrigating the plants and adding nitrogen and other nutrients. In absence of neem cake, mahua or ground-nut cakes may also be used. These cakes are nitrogenous manures.

A mango plant of one year requires 10 kg of farm yard manure (FYM), 100 gm Nitrogen, 217 gm urea, 50 gm phosphoric acid, 312 gm single super phosphate and 100 gm potash. This dose should be increased every year up to 10 years. As such the requirement of manure and fertilizers for a tree of 10 years or above will be F.Y.M 100 kg N, 1000 gm 200 gm potassium sulphate, P 500 gm (2.17 kg urea) (312 gm single super phosphate) and K 1000 gm (200 kg potassium sulphate). Application of farm yard manure and other organic manures as essential to keep the soil texture porous. Half the quantity of total manure and fertilizers should be applied in June-July after harvest and rest of the half in the month of November-December at bud-break. Irrigate the plants soon after manuring. Manures should be applied from just below the drip of the tree towards trunk leaving 30-40 cm space from the trunk. These should be sprinkled all round and mixed in soil after digging and also by adding some surface soil to these.

Save plants from frost, loo, animals, strong wind: Mango plants and trees are very susceptible to frost, young plants should be thatched individually on north and west side and the top portion to save from frost and cold wind. This practice is adopted for saving the plants from hot Sun and loo as well. The top thatch in the case of frost should be removed in day time while in the case of loo and hot sun, it should be removed in night. In the case of grown up bearing trees, smuding should be done in night to create heat in the orchard. For this leaves should be collected at various places in the mango orchard and these are smoked in night. Again to save from frost the soil should be kept moist. Fencing with barbed wire and protective hedges like those of Ingadulsis and Karonda of the whole orchard should be done all round the orchard or deep furrows be prepared to save plants from animals. If possible individual plants may also be fenced. Besides saving specially young plants of orchard from animals, the fruiting trees should also be saved from strong wind and storms cyclones etc. For this wind breaks of trees or plants like Jamun, seedling mangoes, banana plants of cooking varieties and mulberry should be planted on Northern and Western sides of proposed orchards much earlier than these are established. These plants should be planted at a distance of 8-10 feet alternating so that a dense screen may be formed to fight with the storm and cyclones.

Remove sprouts from root stocks: Care should be taken to rub immediately the sprouts if any seen on the root stocks below the joints of the graft. This is important as such sprouts if not removed may create adverse effects on growth of plants (scion portion).

Remove blossoms from young plants: When grafted plants are planted in orchards, these start flouring even the next year. Allowing such blossoms to flourish in such a young stage is not advisable, as the plants may become weak. These should be de-blossomed soon after appearance. This practice should be continued atleast up to three years. Only from the fourth or fifth year the trees should be allowed to flower and fruit be allowed to flower and fruit.

Pruning and Training of Plants: The newly planted young growing plants in the mango orchard should be trained through pruning from time to time in such a way that the tree may form a strong framework. For this there should be a main stem (trunk) up to a height of 75-90 cm (2.5 to 3 feet) from the ground. This should be made stout and healthy. From the top of this main stem 4-5 branches should be allowed to grow all round in a balanced way, so that Sun light may reach in every part of the tree. This will help the tree to flower and fruit well.

A mango tree ordinarily grows to a symmetrical shape. However, in certain cases if the plant goes on growing in upward direction and does not throw out side shoots the top of the main stem should be cut on the above height. This will allow side shoots. Even if other portions of side branches are in shade, but the terminal ends receive proper Sun light, these will flower and fruit. As such one should be careful in removing and pruning side shoots. In general no annual pruning is done in a mango tree, except when shoots are growing too long or these are diseased ones cross each other or growing downwards etc. However, whatever pruning is done after the rainy season is over.

Fruit Drop: After mango blossoms come to fruiting stage, there are some natural fruit drops. However, to save further drops, besides irrigation, a solution of 4 ml Naphthalene Acetic Acid in 9 litres of water should be sprayed first at the end of March and second in the middle of April. Spraying only with water from time to time on the growing fruits will further save the fruits-drop and will also help in increasing the size of fruits.

Powdery Mildew: During cloudy weather and damp atmosphere, white powdery material deposit on leaves and mango blossoms and tender shoots. This hinders the photosynthetic functions of leaves and growth of blossoms and fruits for prevention/control dissolve 2 gm sulfex or 0.5 gm bavistin or one ml kerathane L.C. in a litre of water and spray thrice after 15 days interval first spray should be done at the time of emergence of blossoms in January. No spraying should be done during opening of flowers. This is caused by the fungus 'odium mangiferal'.

Phoma Blight: Brown spots are produced on old leaves of mango and in serious cases these drop off for control dissolve 3 gm copper oxychloride in a litre of water and spray on leaves. The fungus 'phoma glomerata' is the cause of this disease.

Die Back Disease: Mango branches start drying from apical to basal end. Under such cases these dry portions should be pruned off up to green portion and cut green ends should be painted with boardeous mixture (5-5-50). In serious cases defoliation also takes place. The disease die back is caused by a fungus 'Botryodiploidia theobromae.'

Anthroachose, Redsust, Sooty mould, Bacterial canker and some others also need timely attention for control of mango diseases.

Pests of Mango: Besides diseases, there are many pests which harm the mango crop.

Indioserus species or Mango hoppers: Mango hoppers are small green wedge shaped pests, which harm the mango crop throughout India. The adults and nymphs both hop from one place to the other on the mango tree, picture the leaves, tender shoots and inflorescence and suck up the sap from them. The pests make these portions weak. These hoppers also secrete sweet black material called honey dew on leaves and in serious cases the whole leaves become black, checking the photosynthetic activities of leaves. The leaves also drop off and the inflorescence dries up. This pest also gives rise to the disease sooty mould, caused by the fungus capnodiurn mangiferum, due to secretion of honey due. Mango hoppers are most active from February to April and then again from June to August.

To prevent and control the attack of mango hoppers (commonly known as bhunga or lassi keer or phudka), dissolve in a litre of water either 1 ml monocrotophos (Nuvacron 40 cc), or 1 ml methyl parathion 50 EC (folidol) or 1 ml Methyl-o-demeton 25 EC (Metasystox) or 0 5 ml phosphamidon 100 EC (Dimecron) or 0.5 ml phosphamidon 100 EC (Dimecron) or 3 gm Carbaryl dust (Sevin).

Spray one of these solutions just at the emergence or inflorescence in the beginning of January. Second spray should be done when the inflorescence reaches its full size, but before blooming, say at the end of January. Again a third spray should be done at the pea-stage, i.e., at the end of the March, when fruits attain the size of peas. A mango tree requires about 20 litres of solution at a time for full drenching. Pesticides should be changed in every spray as far as possible.

Mango Mealy bug (Droslcha mangiferae): These are small oval shaped insects, adults and nymphs of which crawl on the tree from the ground and suck up the sap from inflorescence, tender shoots and young fruits. This pest is covered with lime-like white powder and attack the crop collectively by assembling in masses at various parts. In severe cases the attacked parts may not be seen except white masses of these bugs. The flowers fruits, shoots dry up and drop off. As such the crop is destroyed. Mealy bugs are very active from December to May. The adult males are small and winged. The females are bigger wingless, who damage the crop. The best way to prevent the mango crop from the attack of mealy bug (ordinarily called Gujhia keet) is to make such arrangements that they may not reach the flowers and fruits of the tree in the month of April. May the females after being fertilised by the males crawl down the tree and take shelter in the cracks of soil under the mango tree. There they lay eggs in large number in white masses and remain lying there till November/December, when they hatchout minute pink to brown coloured nymphs, who start crawling up the tree. Later on these turn as if covered with white powder.

To prevent the mealy bugs from crawling up the tree polythene bands of 30 cm width (400 gauge) should be wrapped all round the trunk of the tree at a height of 60-70 cm from the ground in early November the upper and lower ends of the polythene bands should be tied after wrapping and then some portions of trunks should be sealed with wet clay.

The nymphs thus slip from the polythene sheets and fell on the ground, when they crawl on the tree. Similarly, instead of polythene banding; grease banding may be done in the same manner. A ready-made such band known as Ostico band is also available. When these are wrapped around the trunk, the nymphs when crawl on the tree get themselves pasted with grease and die.

However, if grease handing or other measures could not be taken and the bugs climbed on the tree spray solution of either one ml of methyl parathion or one ml of manocratophos or 4 gm of carbaryl dust dissolved or mixed with one litre of water.

Again 2% dust of methyl parathion should be dusted all round the trunk of the tree from just below the grease or polythene band up to the lowest portion near the soil. This dusting should be done by typing the just in a cloth and thumping that on trunk all round.

Further, some cultural practices may also be adopted to control the attack of this pest. When the female mealy bugs come down from tree in the soil and lay eggs in April-May the soil under the mango tree should be ploughed. The eggs and bugs lying in soil thus come on the surface of soil and as such by heat of the Sun and surface soil all these die.

This practice may be repeated once or twice. Even in the month of November, when young nymphs hatched out of eggs are in a position to crawl on the tree, the soil is ploughed these may die before climbing on the tree. For this about 200 gm of methyl portion dust will be required per tree. Dusting the same quantity around the trunk in soil also kills the nymphs.

Gall Midges: These are small insects First of all these insects attack the flowering buds. These lay eggs on flowering buds, tender inflorescence axis and newly set tender fruits. The eggs hatch out maggots, which enter the portions where they hatch out.

The maggots, thus, feed inside inflorescence, tender shoots and fruits, which later on shed on the ground after yellowing or drying. These are active from January to March. The mature larvae drop down in the soil for pupation and remain lying there till next January, when they dispense and start their actions. These are 'Erosomyta indica.' Besides attack on inflorescence at bud burst stage and on young fruits and tender shoots, these also attack young leaves. There are also two gale midges 'Dasineura amramanjarse' mature larvae red and 'Procystiphora mangiferae mature larvae orange which also infest and damage the crop likewise. These species pupate in buds which swell up and look larger and thicker than normal buds. The flowers infested with 'Dasineura amramanjarae' have red coloured petals.

However, to control from these midges Dimethoate 1.5 ml or Monocrotophos 1.0 ml of Fenetrothion 10 ml or Diazinow 10 ml may be mixed in a litre of water and be sprayed at bud burst stage of inflorescence, fruit formation stage (mustard seed stage) and then at peasize stage at the end of March. Ploughing the soil around the trunch of the tree and dusting with methye paratheon will kill the pupating or dispausing larvae in soil.

Scale Insects

Several species of these insect pests harm the crop. The nymphs and adult scale insects suck the sap of tender leaves shoots and other parts and reduce the vigour of the tree. In severe damage they also secrete honey dew resulting in the growth of fungus. Among various species, pulvinaria polygonata scale insect is the most damaging one. These are most active from February to October. To control the pest either of these pesticides should be sprayed. Quinalphos 25 E.C. 2 ml or monocrotophos 40 E.C. 1.25 ml or Methyl parathion 50 E.C. or Methyl-O-Demeton 25 E.C. 2 ml or Dimet hoate 30 E.C. 1.6 ml Dissolved in a litre of water. First sprays should be done at full emergence of inflorescence in February but before blooming. Second spraying should be done 15-20 days after first one when the fruits reach mustard-size stage. A third spray should also be done in October after adding nor gm wettable sulphur. In every spray the pesticide should be changed.

Mango shoot gall maker or shoot gall psylla (Apsylla cistellata). In March-April females of this pest lay eggs on back side of mid-ribs of leaves as well as in later axis of new leaves. Eggs hatch out nymphs during August-September and they crawl to nearby buds in leaf axils and suck the sap from their cells. As a result of this green conical galls are formed in September-October and fruit setting does not take place. For control the galls along with nymphs should be collected and burnt from November to February.

Also spray 2 ml of either Dimethoate 30 E.C. or Ouinalphos 25 E.C. or Mono crotophos 40 E.C. mixed with one litre of water. The first spray should be done between 15th to 25th August and then two sprays at an interval of 10-15 days. While spraying the lower portion of leaves should be fully drenched.

Flowering and fruiting: Although the grafted plants of mango start flowering the next year but commercial flowering and fruiting starts in the 4th or 5th year of plantation. A reference in this respect has been given in earlier chapters. Actually the bud break starts in the end of December or beginning of January. The blossoms come out, start developing and by February-March the mango tree is seen full of well developed mango blossoms, when flowers also start opening. These blossoms come out from terminal buds of last years (1 year-old) ripe shoots. Sometimes flowering and fruiting also take place in axils of leaves very common in the variety Barahmasi mango. At this very time new vegetative shoots also come out on mango trees, which conveys the message that these shoots will become of one year age (ripe) next year and will sharply fruit.

Vegetative growth in mango trees take place in the months of April-May, July-August and October-November. However, even under such conditions blossoms come out in shoots not reaching the age of 8-10 months, if not complete one year. A mango blossom (bour) is full of in numerable flowers. These blossoms have two types of flowers, 90 per cent of which possess male flowers. Rest 10 per cent flowers are almost perfect ones. These bear both male and female organs and actually these are the flowers which may develop into fruits.

However, out of these 10 per cent bisexual (perfect) flowers of mango, 50 per cent flowers remain unpollinated and 45 per cent flowers drop off due to physiological disorders. Again, out of these 1.0 per cent perfect flowers, only 1/10th of these reach final maturity. As such a successful and satisfactory mango crop can be said only if a blossom of mango has at least 10 per cent bisexual flowers. In this way maximum three ripe fruits can be had from one blossom (bour) of mango for this it is also said in another way that only 0.2 to 0.3 per cent flowers of a blossom form fruits.

Within two weeks of opening of flowers in the blossom, small green fruits (Tikora, amiya, tikole) start appearing. By the end of March these attain the size of peas. As indicated earlier, as soon as fruits of mango appear on the tree, these should be regularly irrigated at an interval of 15 days. This will help the fruits to increase in size and will also save from fruit drop.

In commercial varieties of mango like Dashehri, Langra and Samar-bihisht—Chausa, self pollination is not possible. Therefore, these require pollen grains of other varieties for pollination. Dashehri flowers suit for pollination with pollen grains of the variety 'Bombay green,' whereas for Langra, Chausa (Khajri) and Rataul, the pollen of Dashehri and for Himsagar pollen of Langra mango suit well. As such while establishing mango orchard plan should be made in a way that pollinating agent varieties are there somewhere near about or few rows of these are included in the orchard so that trees may be pollinated through insects.

Alternate Bearing: In general mango bears in alternate year or sometimes after two years. As such there is a serious problem of alternate and irregular bearing in mango orcharding. When the whole trees of the mango orchard are loaded with mangoes, that period is known as 'on year.' During on year there is no vegetative growth on trees and as such no mature shoots are available next year to flower and fruit. Therefore, the trees do not fruit next year and that is called 'off year.' In off year vegetative growths take place profusely, which after attaining an age of about one year come to fruiting and that period again becomes 'on year'. Alternate bearing in most of the varieties are hereditary and in some cases it occurs as the soil is highly exhausted during the heavy fruiting 'on year.' To some extent such problems may be achieved by heavy manuring.

To overcome alternate bearing, if immediately after flowering half portion or 1/4 portion of flowers are removed from the tree, new vegetative shoots will come out, which will mature to bear in the next 'off-year'. 'In this way one may not be mangoless. Similarly, trees of half portion of the orchard maybe deblossomed in the 'on year,' which will bear in the next 'off year.' In this way the crop may be regulated to have some mangoes every year.

Again some varieties are regular bearers by heredity. To overcome alternate bearing these varieties may be included in the mango orchard. Such varieties are Neelam, Romani, Himsagar, Banglora and Dashehri to some extent. Besides these hybrid vareties, Amrapali and Mallika are regular bearers. Orchards of these varieties may successfully be planted to get regular crops of quality mangoes.

Diseases of Mango: Many serious diseases destroy the mango crop chief of these are Mangomal formation, black tip, internal necrosis and others.

Mangomal Formation: In this disease mango blossoms form in bunches from their normal shape and do not fruit. Though the number of flowers in malformed bunches are more than normal, but the bisexual flowers are lesser in such blossoms. However, the fruiting in malformed inflosescences does not take place at all. Some scientists opine that this virus disease is caused by some small mites, while others say that this is due to physological disorders. So far no conclusion has been arrived at. Since it is an infectious disease, these should be cut from the tree, collected at a place and burnt to ashes. If these are not cut and removed, firstly these infect other inflorescences and secondly these unnecessarily use the food material from the tree.

To save the mango trees from the attack of malformation disease, a solution of 200 ppm (parts per million) acetic acid hormone should be sprayed and drenched on the whole tree. For this 200 mg NAA should first be dissolved in a little alcohol. Then this should be made into a litre after adding a little water to it.

After spraying when the flowering buds at the terminal ends start cracking in the end of December or the first week of January, these should be nipped off before these become 1-2 cm long. After spraying and nipping terminal buds from top shoots 4 to 5 healthy inflorescences come out from axillary buds and horizontally spread up all round. By that time the temperature also rises up. which becomes unfavourable for the spread of this infectious disease. Rise in temperature encourages more production of bisexual flowers in the blossom. Again the pollinating insects become active. After 2-2-1/2 months of nipping, these blossoms take their full shape and size. As such these blossoms remain free from malformation and also there is an increase of 3-4 times yield than normal, due to production of 4-5 blossoms in a shoot instead of one blossom. Even if the spraying of NAA could not be done in October and only outer terminal buds are pinched off the tree will yield much more higher crop.

Black Tip Disease: Black tip is a disease, which attacks growing mango fruits in the month of April through the gases present in smokes coming out of brick-kilns. When brick-kilns are operated, the smoke of coal reaches the mango orchard with the flow of air. Actually the gases ethylene, sulphur dioxide and carbon-monoxide harm the crop. Out of these sulphur dioxide gas is supposed to be most harmful and then ethylene gas. When these gases reach the hanging growing mango fruits on trees of the orchard, these are first absorbed through the tips (beak end), which create a brownish soft spot. Gradually, these spots move upwards. Later on these become black and dry up. In serious cases even some portions of stones are also visible at the apical ends of fruits. Once the fruits get affected with black tip disease, the whole crop destroys and there are no curative measures. Therefore, one preventive measures can be taken.

For preventing the spread of this disease prepare a solution of 0.5 to 1.0 kg of borax with 100 litres of water (0.5 to 1.0 per cent) with 1/2 kg washing soap. Instead of borax, the same quantity of washing soda (sodium carbonate) may be used. After preparing the solution the first spray should be done in mango orchards in the last week of March when the fruits have reached the pea-stage. Second spraying should be done 15 days after the first one and again the third spraying be done fifteen days after the second spray.

Besides these, if the mango orchards are established within 5-8 kms of brick kiln, the chimney of the kiln should be at least 15 metres (50 ft) above the ground. Again, the orchard should be layed out in the direction from north to south of brick kiln, as those planted in the east-west direction of the kilns, the smoke of the kiln flows with the wind and reach the fruits of the orchard. New orchards, therefore, should be planted in north-south direction of the brick kiln. Again, no brick-kilns should be allowed to be constructed within 8 km of the mango orchard, or if established should not be allowed to function during the mango season or it should be got closed down further, all the mango groves of various areas should be got declared by government as fruit (mango belts) so that the crops may not be harmed in many way under certain laws. Mango orchards of Malihabadi, Mal and Kakori have already been declared fruit belts.

Internal Necrosis of Mango: In this disease spongy brownish spots are produced at the tips of hanging green fruits on the tree. This disease occurs due to deficiency of boron. Gradually this brownishrot moves towards basal end and the fruit drops on the ground before ripening. As a preventive measure 0.8 to 1.0 per cent solution of borax in water should be sprayed at pea stage (last week of March) and then further two sprays should be done each at an interval of 15 days. Besides this 150 gm borax powder should be applied per tree as manure in January-February and then another dose in September-October.

Mango is the King of fruits. It is so delicious that it is liked by all. Ripe and raw mangoes all are very well utilized in one or the other form. In earlier articles mango varieties, its propagation and its various cultivation techniques and other important aspects have been dealt with (NIP Alld. 4th, 11th, 25-July 2002; 1st, 8th, 22nd, 29th August 2002; 5th, 12th, 19th, 26th Sept. 2002.) Diseases and pests of mango were also discussed. Few more pests, ripening, harvesting, yield and export possibilities have been dealt with in this article.

Stem Borer (Batocera Rufomaculata)

This is a beetle which lays eggs in cracks of trunk or strong branches of the mango tree. Grubs of the beetle bore the stem and make tunnels. They feed inside tunnels and the tree or branches become weak and in severe damage dry up. For control put in the tunnel through a syringe petrol or a solution of either ml. Dichlorovos 7 E.C. or 1.5 ml Endosulfan mixed in a litre of water and plug the tunnel with wet clay.

Bark Eating (Caterpillar Indarbella Quadrinotata)

Caterpillars of this moth eat away bark of branches and also feed on their wood by entering the branches, after preparing small holes, leaving brownish excreta and pieces of eaten wood and bark like saw dust outside the hole spread in webs already spun by them. The branches and trees thus become weak. To control the menace, first the excreta in webs should be removed, then a thick wire should be pressed in the hole to kill the caterpillar, if inside. After this, a piece of cotton soaked in petrol or diazinon should be inserted in the hole and plugged with mud. Dichlorovos and endosulfan as for stem borer may also be used in place of petrol.

Picking, Ripening, Marketing and Export

From flowering to maturity of fruits, it takes 4-5 months. However, from fruit - set to fruit maturity, it takes lesser time. In Dashehri and Langra varieties maturity of fruits reach about three months after fruits set. Picking of fruits from the tree should only be done when these are fully mature. Picking fruits in immature stage and repening these artificially by other means like calcium carbide make these insipid in taste and create shrinkage. These are also harmful. When fruits lose their immature green colour and start acquiring whitish and yellowish tinge but still hard, the fruits may be regarded as mature. Besides this, a mature fruit will produce a dull sound after thumping with a finger, if few half ripe fruits drop on the ground from the tree, this is also a sign of mango fruit maturity. At such stages fruits may be picked up. All the fruits of a tree do not mature at a time. This is because flowers of some branches of a tree bloom earlier and some later on. Even then all the branches come to bloom and fruit set within a month of starting blooming and setting. That is why all the fruits of a tree should not be harvested at a time, otherwise mature / ripe fruits will mix up with immature /unripe fruits and it will be very difficult for the grower / contractor in marketing these fruits. For export or transporting from one place to the other, fruits must be harvested at such a stage when these are quite hard. This is an important point to keep in mind, so that fruits may not be spoiled in transit. However, according to the time of ripening mango fruits of almost all the varieties are harvested from the months of May to July - August. Again for domestic use ripening sort fruits may safely be picked from the mango tree.

Harvesting of fruits should never be done by giving jerk to branches or by beating the twigs and fruits with sticks or logs, as by adopting these practices fruits may be bruised or cracked by the sticks and also by dropping on the ground. Harvesting should be done by climbing on the tree or on a stool ladder by means of a curved sickle tied at the top of a log fitted with a net-led bag to receive the fruits. Harvesting should be done in morning hours, after which these should be collected in shade for further operations. For sending outside, the fruits should be graded immediately and suitably packed. A mango harvester has also been evolved for harvesting.

For sending/ disposal of fruits in the local market or for domestic use, harvested hard fruits should be collected in airy stores and covered with paddy straw, dry banana or mango leaves or newspaper sheets or shavings for ripening at room temperature. Calcium carbide should never be used for ripening fruits, as these are very unhealthful. For transporting mango fruits from one place to the other trains, trucks, steamers, boats and aeroplanes are in use, according to needs and facilities available. From export point of view, now arrangements are being made for packing machines. Arrangements are also being made for air-conditioned vehicles for transporting mango packs up to aerodromes.

Yield : A vegetatively propagated (Kalmi) mango tree of 3 - 4 years may yield 20 - 25 fruits, while a tree of 5-6 years may yields 50 to 75 fruits. Trees reaching the age of 10 years may produce 300 to 500 fruits and from those trees which are 10 to 15 years old 1,000 fruits may be expected per tree. A tree from 15 to 20 years may yield 1,500 fruits, while that above 20 years up to 40 years may produce up to 3,000 numbers of fruits. The yield goes on decreasing after 40 years age. Seedling mango trees are hardier than vegetatively propagated trees. The life of seedling trees are also more than those of 'kalmi' mangoes.

An yield of fruits upto 10,000 in number has been recorded from a 70 year old seedling (beejoo) mango tree. This yield can only be expected in an on year and this too under favourable conditions and when all the scientific methods for its orcharding have been strictly and timely followed. However, in other conditions 200 fruits from a tree or 1 to 3 fruits per panicle or per bunch may be supposed as satisfactory, though a panicle (bunch of flowers) bears more than, 10,000 flowers. In apanicle, most of the flowers are male, which go on dropping by and by.

3

Tips for Identifying Mango Varieties

Classification of some Important Mango Varieties on the Basis of Folding, Twisting, Waviness, Crinkling and Reflection of Leaves

Introduction

The varieties of mango, in India alone, are numerous. According to Mukherjee (1948), there are about 1,000 horticultural varieties of mango in India. Horticultural varieties are restricted to vegetatively propagated plants only.

Varieties are often distributed under wrong names by some nurserymen which causes considerable chaos and confusion. Thus, the fruit grower is very easily cheated at the time of purchasing young nursery plants. Likewise, a purchaser of an established orchard in an unbearing state may be cheated if he is not skilled in identifying the trees of different varieties. Thus a plantation of an inferior variety or a mixture of varieties becomes a curse to the grower which continues throughout his life, particularly in the case of mango, whose economic life is long.

Therefore to escape this difficulty and for the sake of enhancing and increasing our fruit, production and securing a standardised quality of produce, a properly evolved system of classification must be found whereby such mixtures can be eliminated in the nursery or field before the plants have established, themselves permanently.

Undoubtedly, the classification of varieties on the basis of leaf characters is the most outstanding and the most promising means of classification and its importance can never be overemphasised.

Thus, like apple, peach and other varieties of fruits, mango varieties can also be identified in the nursery as well as in the orchard, if the following method is adopted.

So an attempt has been made to classify seventeen varieties of mango on the basis of folding, twisting, waviness, crinkling, and reflection of leaves, which might prove helpful in the proper identification of varieties.

Review of Literature

The taxonomical importance of leaf characters has been shown by various workers in varieties of different fruits they have worked on. But in mango classification only a few workers like Kinman (1918), Popenoe (1927, 1941), Naik (1947), Mukherjee (1948), and Naik and Gangolly (1950) have thrown light on leaf characters of different varieties.

Kinman (1918) classified fourteen imported and five Puerto Rican varieties of mango. Naik and Gangolly (1950) classified 325 varieties of South Indian mangoes.

Almost all of the above workers have given due consideration to folding, twisting, waviness, crinkling and reflexion of leaves at the time of mango classification.

Materials and Methods

The work of classification was conducted during the years 1950-52 with seventeen varieties of mango. The trees of these varieties are growing in a good healthy condition in the Botanical Garden of the Government Agricultural College, Kanpur. All of them are horticultural varieties which are flourishing well and giving a satisfactory yield.

Selection of Varieties : The following varieties of mango were selected for study : Baramasi, Bombay Bottle, Bombay Green, Chaupatia, Dasehri, Fajri, Gola Khurja, Gopalbhog, Langra, Langra Khurja, Maldah, Mewa Saharanpur, Pairi, Samarbihishtchausa, Sufeda Malihabad, Sufeda Lucknow, and Variegata Khurja. All the varieties except a few are leading commercial varieties of India.

Selection of Shoots and Leaves : First of all normal healthy shoots were selected at random on the exposed parts of typical trees of each variety, which were in normal growth and health and had attained bearing age. On such shoots fully grown leaves, which had acquired their mature green colour, were selected from the mid portion of the shoot for studies as suggested by Sefic and Blake (1937), in peaches, Tydeman (1936) in apples and Naik and Gangolly (1950) in mangoes. Selection of shoots and leaves was limited to the current season's growth which had completed its growth period for the season, as suggested by Sefic and Blake (1937) in peaches and Naik and Gangolly (1950) in mangoes.

Observations, Results and Discussion: The characters like folding, twisting crinkling, waviness and reflexion of leave were studied for classification.

One of the most important advantages in such characters is that the observer can identify the trees of a variety at a glance.

Naik and Gangolly (1950) have grouped the folding of the lamina of mango leave under two heads :- (i) Strongly folded and (ii) Slightly folded. But in this experimen it was thought suitable to divide it into three groups :- (i) Strongly folded—when the lamina is folded up to the extent that the margins almost meet together (ii) Slightly folded—when margins of lamina are folded upwards to make a wide 'U' or 'V', (iii) Folded—which consists of a degree of folding in between the first and second groups.

Twisting of the leaf blade is a characteristic feature in some varieties of mango while only the spiral curve or twist of the apex is in others. In some varieties the wavy margin of the leaf blade is a character and in others crinkling of the leaf blade or curving of the leaf backwards on the midrib has also been found to be a suitable basis for classification.

Either of these characters may, insteacd of occuring individually in a variety, also be manifested in conjunction with other characters, e.g., folded leaves with wavy margins and folded and twisted leaf blades.

The observations on the selected leaves of each variety were recorded by making regular visits to the orchard for the sake of confirmation and the results obtained in these investigations in all the seventeen varieties of mango are as follows :

Baramasi : Twisting or a spiral curve of the apex of the leaf blade of this variety along with waviness of the margin can make not only a scientist but also a layman confident of the variety. Sometimes the twisting of the apex extends up to a portion of the lamina.

At the time of vegetative growth in the month of September, or October, the young vegetative shoots have been found terminating in panicles and the leaves which appeared earlier on these shoots also bore flowers and fruits in their axils.

Trees of this variety can be identified at any time of the year.

Bombay Green : Leaves of Bombay Green are 'folded' in nature with wavy margins. By these characters varieties can be identified at the first glance over the tree by an observer even from a distance.

Chaupatia : The leaf blade in this variety is 'strongly folded' which is of a great diagnostic value.

Dasehri : The characteristic feature in Dasehri is the flat nature of the leaf blade along with very slight folding and waviness in the margin.

Fajri : Reflexion of the apices of the leaves is the characteristic feature of this variety.

Gopalbhog : Leaf blades of Gopalbhog are twisted and folded in nature and are very dark green.

Maldah : Maldah leaves are 'slightly folded' and without waviness in margins.

Pairi : Of all the varieties of mango studied in this investigation, Pairi and Gopalbhog have been found to be such that they can be identified very easily and can be differentiated from each other as well as from other varieties at a glance over the trees. The most characteristic feature in Pairi is the 'twisting' nature of the leaf blade along with its folding, larger size, and very distinctive accumuinate tip (sharp pointed with a long drawn tip). The length of the leaf blade of Pairi is about the double of that of Gopalbhog. Its colour is light green.

Samar-Bihisht-Chausa : Leaves of this variety are 'reflexed and crinkled'. Sometimes they are a bit twisted.

Variegata Khurja : The most characteristic feature in this variety that strikes the observer on the first vision of the tree is, the 'waviness' of the leaf margin to a very great extent along with its flat nature.

Trees of Bombay Bottle, Gola Khurja, Langra, Langra Khurja, Mewa Saharanpur, Sufeda Lucknow and Sufeda Malihabad possess almost 'flat' leaves without any extent of waviness or folding.

By the above results it is clear that the leaves of varieties Baramasi, Bombay Green, Fajri, Chaupatia, Gopalbhog, Maldah, Pairi, Variegata Khurja, Samar-bihisht-chausa and Dasehri possess altogether different characters and hence they can be identified and differentiated between each other easily and with almost no complication.

Those varieties having almost flat leaves, e.g., Langra, Sufeda Lucknow etc. may also be separated from any of the above ten varieties. These varieties require more extensive study because it is not essential that the same character be employed for identifying all varieties. A particular character may be of a great value for one variety but not of the least for another. So by an extensive study, varieties may be classified on other bases also.

Summary and Conclusion

Seventeen varieties of mango, standing in the Botanical Garden of the

Government Agricultural College, Kanpur, have been classified on the basis of the folding, twisting, crinking, waviness and of the leaf blades. These characters have been found to be of a great diagnostic value in the trees of this orchard.

Acknowledgements

The author is highly thankful to Sri S. N. Singh, Assistant Botanist, National Botanical Gardens, Lucknow and Ex-Assistant Professor of Horticulture, Dr. V. P. S. Chhonker and Sri P. N. Bajpai, Assistant Professors of Horticulture, Government Agricultural College, Kanpur, for their keen interest and guidance throughout the progress of this investigation.

1. Kinman, C. F. (1918). The mango in Puerto Rico—*Puerto Rico Agr. Exp. Stn. Bull.* 24,1-30.
2. Mukherjee, S.K. The varieties of mango and their classi-fication. *Bull. Bot. Soc. Bengal,* 2(2),' 101-33, Oct. 1948
3. Naik, K. C. (1947). South Indian fruits and their culture.
4. Naik, K. C. and Gangolly, S. R. (1950). A monograph on classification of South Indian Mangoes.
5. Popenoe, W. (1941). Manual of tropical, and subtropical fruits.
6. Popnoe, W. (1941). The Mango—A study in systematic pomology. *Tropical Agriculture*, 18 : 23-25
7. Sefic, H. J. and Blake M. A. (1937). The classification of varieties of peaches by means of leaf characters. *Proc. Amer. Soc. Hort. Sc.* 35, 246-50.
8. Tydeman, H. E. (1936). Variation in the 'Paradise' apple root stock. *Journ. Pom. Hort. Sc.* 14, 1925-1926.

Bombay green

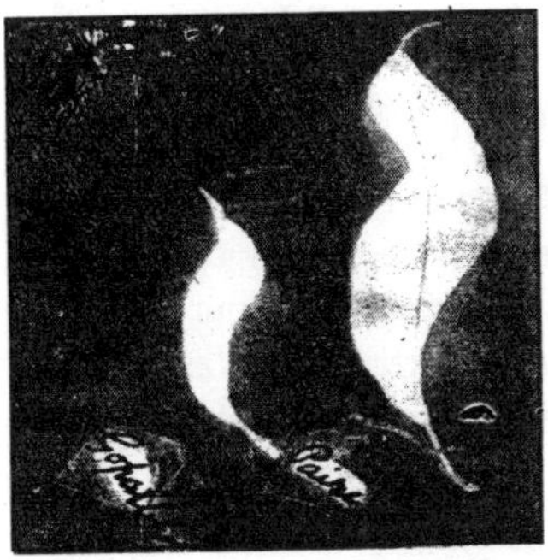

Maldah

Colour of Young Growing Leaves as a Means of Identifying Mango Varieties

Introduction and Historical Review

Colour of young growing leaves is of a great diagnostic importance for different varieties of mango, the choicest fruit of India. It is a constant character which is not prone to variation even under the diverse conditions of mango culture.

One of the most important advantages in colour studies of young growing leaves is that if there is any difficulty in taxonomy of different varieties of mango trees in the orchard or young plants in the nursery by means of mature leaves or other vegetative characters, this character may very well be employed for their indentification or confirmation at the time of vegetative growth in different flushes.

The importance of foliage in taxonomical studies of fruit trees has been clearly shown by Alderman and Shoemaker (1925), Winter (1925), and Thomson (1932). Upshall (1924, 1925) employed the abundance and scarcity of yellow pigment in leaves of apple for varietal classification.

Mukherjee (1948) classified 72 varieties of mango ccuring mostly in Bihar and Bengal. Colouration of emerging leaves in different varieties was also kept in view at the time of classification.

Shaw (1914) postulated that leaf colour was not helpful in identifying different varieties due to scarcity and abundance of greenness depending on the vigour of the tree. This statement, however according to Naik and Gangolly (1950) applies to only mature leaves. Distinctive colour of mango has been found to be of a great taxonomical importance, if descriptions are made at three different stages of development by means of some standard colour dictionary. They classified 325 varieties of south Indian mangoes on different bases, colour of young leaves being one of them.

An attempt, therefore, has been made to describe colour of young growing leaves of seventeen varieties of mango which may help in their identification.

Thus, the fruit grower may not be so easily cheated or jeopardised at the time of purchasing young nursery plants or orchards of established trees in an unbearing stage by being provided with wrong varieties.

Materials and Methods

The colour studies of young growing leaves of mango varieties were started in the year 1951. Trees of all the seventeen varieties are growing in a good healthy condition in the Botanical Garden of the Govt. Agricultural College, Nawabgunj, Kanpur. They are all horticultural varieties.

Selection of Varieties

The varieties selected for study were Baramasi; Bombay bottle, Bombay Green, Chaupatia Dasehri, Fajri, Gola Khurja, Gopalbhog, Langra, Langra Khurja, Maldah, Mewa Saharanpur, Pairi, Samar-bihisht-chausa, Sufeda Lucknow, Sufeda Malihabad, and Variegata Khurja. All of these varieties except a few are the leading commercial varieties of India.

After selection of varieties, ten healthy vegetative buds which were well swollen and were to sprout up soon were selected on the outer perimeter of the trees of each variety. Buds were tagged and dates of their sprouting were recorded. From the day the leaves sprouted from the bud, daily a portion of young leaf was picked up after sunrise and the colour matched by employing the methods given by Maerz and Paul (1930). Up to the time the leaves were in a folded condition after sprouting from the bud, the same colours (colour of dorsal surface of leaves) were noted. After their unfolding, colours of ventral surface of the leaves were recorded by visiting the orchard regularly. This practice of visiting the orchard regularly and observing the colour was continued for about fifteen days for a variety till the leaves attained their green colour. In this way colour of young growing leaves of different varieties of mango made two to three distinct changes. Only those distinct colours were recorded in the results. Observations were taken in the month of September and October, 1951 when the trees were in vegetative flush. Later on in the month of March 1952 when the major flush started, results of all the seventeen varieties of mango were confirmed.

In the matter of colour descriptions of leaves, standard colour dictionaries by Maerz and Paul (1930) and Ridgeway (1912) were brought into use.

Experimental Findings

The time taken in unfolding of young leaves sprouted from vegetative buds of mango, was two to three days. There was almost no change in colour of folded leaves.

Colour of folded leaves and distinct change in colour of ventral surface of unfolded leaves of different varieties of mango under study were found as in the table:-

Table 1

Sl.No.	*Name of Variety*	*Colour of folded leaf*	*Colour of young their unfolding till full (upper-surface)*	*Leaves after growth*
1.	Baramasi	Courge Green (21, L, 3)*	Romantic Green Olive Green Citrine Rhubarb Old moss	(14, L, 3) * (15, L, 4) * (14, L, 6) * (14, L, 2) *
2.	Bombay bottle	Old moss (14, L, 2)*	Metallic Green Chamois Bistre Green	(15, L, 6) * (11,9, 5) * (13, L, 5)*
3.	Bombay Green	Light Brownish Olive (XXX, 19", K)	Saccardo's Olive Medal Bronze Cameo Brown Sayal Brown	(XVl,19,m,) (IV, 19, m) (XXVIII, 7"K) (XXIX, 15",i)
4.	Chaupatia	Rainette Green (XXXI,27", i)	Saccordo's Olive Dark Olive Yellowish Olive	(XVI, 19', m) XI; 21", m) (XXX, 23",K)
5.	Dasehri	Courge Green (XVII, 25, i)	Oil Green Yellowish Olive Dull Citrine Yell-owish Oil Green	(V, 27, K) (XXX, 23",K) (XVI, 21', K) (V, 25, K)
6.	Fajri	Courge Green (21, L, 3)*	Chrysolite Green Colonial buff Oil Yellow	(19, k, 3)* (10, G, 2)* (12, L, I)*
7.	Gola Khurja	Drab (XLV1, 17")	Buffy Olive Brownish Drab Deep Chrysolite Green	(XXX, 21", k) (XLV, 9",') (XXXI, 27",1)
8.	Gopalbhog	Chrysolite Green. (19, K, 3)*	Palm leaf Olive Sheen Airedale	(14, L, 1),* (13, k, 3,)* (14, F, 6) *
9.	Langra	Deep Chrysolite	Rainette Green Light Yellowish Olive	(XXXI 27") (XXX, 23",f)

		Green. (XXXI, 27,"-)	Wood Brown Yellowish Olive	(XL, 17", i) (XXX, 23", k)
10.	Langra Khurja	Chrysolite Green. (19, k, 3)*	Russet Green Oasis Old moss Old Gold	(20, k, I)* (20, L, 2)* (14, L, 2)* (14, k, 5)*
11.	Maldah	Rainette Green (XXX, 27", i)	Jade Green Buffy Citrine Fawn Colour	(XXI, 27", K) (XVI, 19', K) (XL, 19', K)
12.	Mewa Saharanpur	Courge Green (21, L, 3,)*	Citron Green Rose Ash Devon Cigarette Anti-que Brown	(19, K, 2)* (6, J, N)* (14, K, 11)*
13.	Pairi	Benzo Brown (XLVI, 13" ",i)	Mignonette Green Ecru Olive Citrine	(XXXI, 25", i) (XXX, 21", i) (IV, 21, K)
14.	Samar-bihisht-chausa	Courge Green (21 L, 3)*	Certosa Russet Green Bittre Green Chartreuse Green	(20, L, 3)* (20, K, I)* (13, L, 5)* (II, L, I)*
15.	Sufeda Lucknow	Deep Chrysolite-Green (XXXI, 27",-)	Rainette Green Light yellowish Olive Deep Chrysolite Green	(XXXI, 27" i) (XXX, 23", i) (XXXI, 27", i)
16.	Sufeda Malihabad	Light Cress Green (XXXI, 29", i)	Kronberg's Green Deep Olive Saccardo's umber	(XXX1, 25, K) (XL, 21"', K) (XX1X, 17", K)
17.	Variegata Khurja	Deep Chrysolite Green (XXXI, 27",-)	Mignonette Green Citrine Olive Citrine	(XXX1, 25", i) (IV, 19, K) (XVI, 21", m)

Discussion

The above table reveals the fact that the colour of young growing leaves is of a great taxonomical importance by which different varieties of mango may be very easily identified. This is because every variety differs from the other in colour at one or the other stage of leaf growth. Hence it seems possible that classifying or describing the varieties of mango on basis of colour of young growing leaves only, may surmount the botherations of mango classification on other bases. In some varieties such peculiar colours were seen which were not found in other varieties in any of the developmental stages of young leaves e.g. Fawn colour in Maldah, Saccardo's Umber in Sufeda Malihabad, Certosa in Samar-bihisht-chausa, Cameo Brown in Bombay Green, Yellowish-Oil Green in Dasehri, Wood Brown in Langara and Cigarette Antique Brown in Mewa Saharanpur.

These varieties may be very easily identified. In the same way other varieties may also be identified by studying distinct changes taking place in the colour of young leaves.

Summary and Conclusions

Seventeen varieties of mango standing in the Botanical Garden of the Govt. Agricultural College, Kanpur, have been described by means of colour of young growing leaves.

From the results obtained in these investigations it is concluded that colour of young growing leaves is very useful means for identifying different varieties of mango.

Acknowledgements

I wish to express my deep sense of gratitude and indebtedness to Sri S. N. Singh, Asstt. Botanist, National Botanical Gardens, Uttar Pradesh, Lucknow and Ex-Asstt. Professor of Horticulture, Dr. V. P. S. Chhonkar and Sri P.N. Bajpai, Asst. Professors of Horticulture, Govt. Agricultural College, Kanpur for the guidance and thoughtful criticisms throughout the course of these investigations.

Size and Shape of The Terminal Vegetative Bud Useful in Classification of Mango Varieties

Introduction and Review of Literature

Mango, the king of fruits, is the leading commercial fruit and the most fancied among the people of India. Recognised as one the choicest fruit of the tropics it has been raised from time immemorial in India, attaining an importance unexcelled in any part of the world.

There are numerous varieties of mango in India. Varietal mixtures are often distributed by nurserymen which, while purchasing young nursery plants, may create a great confusion to the fruit grower, if he is not skilled in identifying the varieties. Similarly the purchaser of an established orchard in an unbearing state may also be jeopardised if he is not skilled in distinguishing between the trees of different varieties. Thus a grower, who plants an unsuitable variety by erroneous identification, is put to a great loss and all his efforts in making the plant attain the bearing stage is squandered.

Therefore, to solve this problem some proper means of classification and description of varieties must be evolved by which different varieties of plants or trees may be easily indentfied. Thus such mixtures of varieties can easily be separated in the nursery or field before the plants have permanently established.

Therefore, it is evident that by classifying the varieties on the basis of vegetative characters the aforesaid problem can be easily surmounted.

Different workers like Burns and Prayag (1915, 1920), Kinman (1918), Mukherjee (1948), Naik and Gangolly (1950), Nand (1955), Pope (1929), Popenoe (1923), Rolphs (1915), Venkataratnam (1951), Watt (1891), Wester (1920), Woodhouse (1909), and Woodrow (1904) have classified and described different varieties of mango from different regions of India as well as from other countries.

Most of the above workers, except a few, have attached importance to fruit characters only. Out of them Kinman, Mukherjee, Naik and Gangolly, and Popenoe have given weight also to leaf characters for varietal classification.

Nand (1955) has described some important varieties of mango by means of colour of young growing leaves and found it a useful means for their identification.

However, no work appears to have been reported on classification of mango varieties by means of characters of terminal vegetative buds, which may help much in identifying young plants and trees of different varieties in an unbearing state.

The present study was, therefore, taken up to classify some important varieties of mango by studying the characters of the terminal vegetative buds.

The greatest advantage in using the terminal vegetative buds for classification of mango is that the trees or plants can easily be recognized in any of the major or minor vegetative flushes.

Materials and Methods

The varieties selected for study were Baramasi, Dasehri, Bombay Bottle, Bombay Green, Chaupatia, Fajri, Gola Khurja, Maldah, Mewa Saharanpur, Pairi, Samar-bihisht-chausa, Sufeda Lucknow and Variegate Khurja. All the trees are growing well in the Botanical Garden of the Government Agricultural College, Kanpur. They are securing similar manurial and irrigational treatments.

When the major vegetative flush synchronised in March 1952, twenty five healthy and fully grown terminal vegetative buds were selected for study from the exposed parts of typical trees of each variety.

After selection of bud, the greatest diameter and length of all the twenty five buds of a variety were measured in m. ms. by means of a screw gauge, after which they were averaged. By means of these data, the percentage ratio between the average greatest diameter and average length of a bud of each variety was also calculated.

The shape of the bud was also described by employing the terms : (i) Conical and sharp pointed, (ii) Short and thick, (iii) Small and plump and (iv) Large and thin. Other terms like 'Large and thick' and 'Slender and thin' were also employed where necessary.

The work in this experiment was carried outon the line of the work done by Condit (1941) in classifying fig varieties. For describing the shape of the bud, help was taken from the diagrams of terminal vegetative buds of fig varieties given by him (Condit 1941).

Observations, Results and Discussion

The average maximum diameter, average length, and percentage ratio between the average maximum diameter and average length of the terminal vegetative bud of each variety were recorded in m. ms by the aforesaid methods.

Likewise, the shape of the terminal vegetative bud of each variety was also described by using the terms mentioned previously.

Data, which were collected, are given in the following table :

Sl. No	*Name of Variety*	*Average maximum diameter of the terminal vegetative bud in m. ms.*	*Average length of the terminal vegetative bud m. ms.*	*Percentage ratio between the average maximum diameter and average length of the terminal vegetative bud*	*Shape of the terminal vegetative bud*
1	2	3	4	5	6
1.	Baramasi	4.93	12.26	40.21	Like the spur of a temperate
2.	Bombay Bottle	5.20	14.55	35.73	Conical and sharp pointed
3.	Bombay Green	8.02	13.45	59.59	Short and thick
4.	Chaupatia	7.72	15.84	48.73	Large and thick
5.	Dasehri	8.53	17.50	48.74	Conical and sharp pointed
6.	Fajri	7.43	13.70	54.24	Do
7.	Gola Khurja	4.85	10.90	44.49	Short and thick

8.	Gopal-bhog	6.40	8.36	76.55	Short and thick
9.	Langra	5.63	15.40	36.54	Slender and thin
10.	Langra Khurja	5.50	10.82	50.83	Conical and sharp pointed
11.	Maldah	8.70	14.15	61.40	Large and thick
12.	Mewa Saharan-pur	6.01	15.02	39.94	Curved like a hook
13.	Pairi	8.30	12.10	68.58	Short and thick.
14.	Samar-bihisht-chausa	7.85	13.80	56.88	Large and thick
15.	Sufeda Lucknow	5.70	11.20	50.89	Conical and sharp pointed
16.	Variegata Khurja	6.75	13.40	50.37	Conical and sharp pointed

By the above table it is evident that there is a marked difference between the diameter and length of the terminal vegetative buds of different varieties of mango.

The average maximum diameter of the terminal vegetative bud of mango varies from 4.93 mms (Baramasi-minimum) to 8.53 mms (Dasehri-maximum), while the average length of the bud varies from 8.36 mms (Gopalbhog) to 17.50 mms (Dasehri-maximum). Both of the length and diameter have been found to be the maximum in Dasehri among all the varieties under study.

Besides the size, the percentage ratio between the average greatest diameter and the average length of the terminal vegetative bud has been found to be of a great taxonomical importance in some of the varieties of mango which is clear from the above table e.g. Bombay-Bottle 35.73% (minimum), Dasehri 48.75%, Sufeda Lucknow 50.89, Langra 36.5%, Pairi, 68.58% and Gopal-bhog 76.55% (maximum).

Almost none of the characters outweigh in importance the shape of the terminal vegetative bud which is a very diagnostic feature in mango varieties. Though the shape has been grouped under four main heads as previously mentioned, nevertheless, varieties falling under the same head may also be separated from each other by studying the individual peculiarities. Maldah, Samar-bihisht-chausa and Chaupatia all possess large and thick type of terminal vegetative buds. But the bud of Chaupatia is very blunt pointed while that of Maldah is sharp pointed but somewhat triangular in shape. The bud of Dashehri is conical and sharp pointed but its tip is a bit curved which is of a great diagnostic importance. The variety Mewa Saharanpur has got its terminal vegetative bud curved like a hook which is of a great help in identifying this variety.

The vegetative buds of Langra have been found 'Slender and thin' and very characteristic in nature. Of all the varieties of mango studied, the terminal vegetative bud of Baramasi was found to be the most characteristic which had a shape of its own kind and looked like the spur of a temperate fruit. The terminal vegetative buds of Bombay Bottle, Fajri, Langra Khurja, Sufeda Lucknow, and Variegata Khurja are conical and sharp pointed.

The varieties Bombay Green, Gola Khurja and Gopalbhog possess 'Short and thick' terminal vegetative buds.

The above results were also confirmed in July-August 1952 and February-March when the trees were in vegetative flush.

All the above characters have been found to be constant in all the verieties of mango under study which are very helpful in identifying different varieties.

Summary and Conclusion

Sixteen important varieties of mango growing in the Botanical Garden of the Govt. Agricultural College, Kanpur have been classified by means of shape and size of the terminal vegetative buds.

It is concluded that the shape and size of the terminal vegetative bud employed in classifying and describing different varieties of mango for the sake of correct identification. Out of them shape of the terminal vegetative bud of mango varieties furnishes one of the simplest diagnostic characters for use by practical growers any nurseryment.

Acknowledgements

Grateful thanks are due to Sri S.N. Singh Ex-Assistant Professor of Horticulture, and Senior-Scientific Officer, National Botanical Garden Lucknow, Dr. V. P. S. Chhonker and Sri P. N. Bajpai, Assistant Professors of Horticulture, Govt. Agricultural College, Kanpur for their continued interest and helpful suggestions.

Fresh and Preserved Specimen of Leaf Helpful in Classifying Mango Varieties

Emphasis on diagnostic characters of vegetative parts of mango varieties have been given by Kinman (3), Popenoe (10, 11), Mukherjee (4) and Naik and Gangolly (5). As a result of detailed studies made on various aspects of leaf characters of mango varieties (6), findings on the basis of (i) colour of young leaves (ii) shape and size of terminal vegetative buds and (iii) folding, twisting, waviness, crinkling and reflexion of leaves were reported earlier (7, 8, 9). However, results on measurements and various other characteristics in fresh and preserved specimens of leaves were not reported. These are, therefore, presented in this paper.

Materials

Seventeen varieties of uniform mango trees (Baramasi, Bombay Bottle, Bombay Green, Chaupatia, Dashehri, Fajri, Gola Khurja, Gopalbhog, Langra, Langra Khurja, Maldah, Mewa Saharanpur, Pairi, Samar-Bahisht-Chausa, Sufeda Malihabad, Sufeda Lucknow and Variegata Khurja), were selected in the Horticultural Gardens of Government Agricultural College, Kanpur. Normal shoots of the current season, which had completed their growth for the season, were marked at random on exposed parts of these trees. Fully mature leaves situated on mid-portions of such shoots were utilized for these studies.

Methods and Results

Methods adopted and results obtained on various aspects are presented below:

Fresh Leaf

Pose of Leaf : Angles of one hundred leaves formed with the shoots were measured on the tree of each variety with a protractor, averaged and grouped (5) as (i) Erect or Upheld (when the angle formed by the leaf with the shoot was less than 45°), (ii) Drooping or Downheld (when the angle was almost 90° or above) and (iii) Spreading or Outheld (a position between 'Erect' and ('Spreading'). Data collected in this direction are presented in Table 1 (Col3). It is obvious that all the varieties could be grouped under the head 'Spreading' or out helds. However some of the varieties like Gola Khurja, Pairi, Sufeda Lucknow, and Sufeda Malihabad differ from Baramasi, Dashehri, Maldah, and Variegata Khurja.

Table 1. Showing pose weight, thickness and area of leaf; thickness of pulvinus width ratio between length of pulvinus and (W), length (L), W/L ratio of leaf-blade ; length of pulvinus, length of mid-vein and midvein in leaf of different varieties of mango

Sl. No.	Name of variety	Angle (pose) leaf with the shoot	weight of fresh leaf (gm.)	Thicknes of lamina (fresh leaf) mm.	Area (fresh leaf) Sq.cm.	Thick-ness of pulvinus leaf) mm.	Greatest width (W) of lamina (pressed) cm	Length (L) of lamina (pressed) cm	Percentage W/L rati (pressed)	Length of pulvi-nus (press-ed) cm	Length of peti-vein (pressed) cm	Length of mid (press-ed) cm	Percent-age Ratio between length of petiole & midvein (pressed) cm.
1.	Baramasi	58.22°	1.63	0.23	41.28	2.71	4.10	16.00	25.50	0.90	1.80	16.00	11.25
2.	Bombay bottle	61.11°	2.73	0.31	85.91	4.85	5.84	18.89	30.91	0.86	2.92	18.89	15-45
3.	Bombay green	64.30°	2.52	0.25	75.46	3.41	5.61	19.64	28.56	0.81	2-75	19.64	14.00
4.	Chaupatia	69.30°	1.64	0.30	39.21	2.97	4.22	15.88	26.51	0.64	3.12	15.88	19.64
5.	Dashehari	52.33°	2.12	0.21	74.49	3.74	4.63	18.92	24.50	0.99	2.95	18.92	15-59
6.	Fajri	64.80°	3.23	0.27	112.74	5.44	6.59	22.40	29.44	1.09	2.94	22.40	13.12
7.	Gola Khurja	70.22°	2.36	0.27	81.59	3.92	5.27	21.26	24.79	0.99	3.62	21.26	17.02
8.	Gopal bhog	53.22°	1.60	0.41	40.11	4.30	3.80	16.87	22.53	0.99	2.60	16.87	15.41
9.	Langra	62.08°	2.56	0.25	91.97	3.69	6.06	21.21	29.05	1.11	2.71	21.21	12.71
10.	Langra Khurja	63.44°	3.16	0.25	90.75	4.69	5.69	22.78	24.99	1.16	3.32	22.78	14-57
11.	Maldah	55.81°	2.81	0.31	95.97	5.44	6.20	19.99	31.03	1.14	3.17	19.99	15.85
12.	Mewa Saharanpur	69.35°	2.87	0.28	94.13	4.06	6.23	21.18	29.44	1.24	3.50	21.18	16.52
13.	Pairi	70.77°	3.43	0.26	111.64	5.67	6.04	26.54	22.78	1.22	3.92	26.54	14.77
14.	Samar-Bahisht -Chausa	67.80°	4.14	0.28	120.00	5 .00	7.20	23.28	30.93	1.43	3.42	23.28	14.69

Sl. No.	Name of variety	Angle (pose) leaf with the shoot	weight of fresh leaf (gm.)	Thick- of lamina (fresh leaf) mm.	Area (fresh leaf) Sq.cm.	Thick- ness of pulvin leaf) mm.	Greatest width (W) oflamina (pressed) cm	Length (L) of lamina (pressed) cm	Percentage W/L rati (pressed)	Length of pulvi- (press- ed) cm	Length of peti- vein (pressed) cm	Length of mid (press- ed)cm	Percent- age Ratio between length of petiole & midvein (pressed) cm.
15.	Sufeda Lucknow	70.11°	2.14	0.24	71.69	3.55	4.97	19.16	25.96	0.90	3.73	19.16	14.24
16.	Sufeda Malihabad	73.02°	2.05	0.27	72.82	4.23	4.62	20.47	22.59	0.99	3.11	20.47	15.19
17.	Variegata Khurja	52.37°	2.06	0.28	65.01	3.47	4.97	18.44	26.95	0.64	2.88	18.44	15.61

Weight of Leaf: After taking observations on pose of leaf, twenty five fresh leaves of each variety were collected in a cellophane bag one hour after the sun-rise. These were weighed on a physical balance to find out the weight of a fresh leaf.

In most of the varieties, the average weight of a leaf was about 2.0 gm., which could be differentiated with Samar-Bahisht-Chausa, Gopalbhog, Chaupatia, Baramasi, Pairi, Fajri, and Langra Khurja (Table-1 Col. 4).

Thickness of Lamina : Thickness of lamina was then measured in the middle portion of the leaf-blade near the edge on both sides of the mid-rib with the help of a screw gauge (five leaves at a time). Lamina of Gopalbhog was found maximum in thickness, while the minimum was in Dashehri (0. 21 mm). In other varieties it ranged between 0.21 and 0.31 mm. (Table 1 Col. 5).

Area of Leaf Blade : This was determined by applying Darrow's matching method (1) with a slight modification. Results obtained show that leaf of Samar-Bahisht-Chausa could be differentiated easily with that of Gopalbhog, Chaupatia and Baramasi (Table 1 Col. 6) .

Thickness of Pulvinus: Maximum diameter of pulvinus of a fresh leaf was measured with a screw gauge. Data collected have been presented in Table 1 (Col. 7). It may be seen that the thickness of pulvinus is of diagnostic importance in varieties Pairi (5.67 mm maximum) and Baramasi (2.71 mm minimum). The variety Chaupatia could also be separated easily from Fajri, Maldah, Pairi, Samar-Bahisht-Ehausa, Bombay Bottle and Gopalbhog as the difference between the thickness of pulvinii of these varieties and that of Chaupatia are remarkable. Likewise, Bombay Green, Dashehri, Langra, Sufeda Malihabad and Variegata Khurja could also be separated from Fajri, Maldah, airi and Samar-Bahisht-Chausa.

Preserved (Pressed) Leaf

After collecting above data on fresh leaf all the leaves were pressed to dry for studies in herbarium.

Greatest Width (W) and Length (L) of Lamina and W/L Ratio

Greatest width and length of lamina of all the twenty-five pressed leaves of a variety were measured to the nearest 100th. cm. Thus the percentage W/L ratio was calculated and as such on the basis of W/L ratio, leaves were classified into the heads: (i) very narrow (below 20 per cent), (ii) narrow (20-24 per cent), (iii) medium (25-29 per cent) and (iv) broad (above 30 per cent), as suggested by Seffick and Blake in peaches (12).

Observations recorded are presented in Table 1 (Col. 8, 9, 10). It is obvious that the width of lamina was maximum in Samar-Bahisht-Chausa (7.20 cm) and minimum in Gopalbhog (3.80 cm). Width in other varieties, however, varied from 4.1 to 6.59 cm.

The length of lamina in Pairi was maximum (26.54 cm), while it was minimum in Chaupatia (15.88 cm.).

W/L ratio of Dashehri, Gola Khurja, Gopalbhog, Pairi, and Sufeda Malihabad was 'Narrow', while it was 'medium' in Baramasi, Bombay Green, Chaupatia, Fajri, Langra Khurja, Mewa Saharanpur, Sufeda Lucknow and Variegata Khurja and 'Broad' in Bombay Bottle, Maldah and Samar-Bahisht-Chausa.

Length of (i) Pulvinus (ii) Peticle (iii) Mid-vein and (iv) Ratio between Peticle and Mid-vein of The Leaf:

The pressed leaves of each variety were utilized for this purpose : Data collected in this direction have been shown in Table 1 Col. 11, 12, 13, 14.

The length of pulvinus was minimum (0.64 cm.) in Chaupatia and Variegata Khurja and maximum in Samar-Bahisht-Chausa (1.43 cm.). In other varieties, it ranged between 0.81 and 1.43 cm.

The length of petiole in Baramasi was 1.8 cm. (minimum), while it was 3.92 cm. (maximum) in Pairi. In other varieties it varied between 1.8 and 3.92 cm.

The ratio between the length of petiole and midvein has shown encouraging results in Baramasi (11.25 per cent-minimum), Gola Khurja (17.02 per cent) and Chaupatia (19.64 per cent-maximum).

Shape or Outline of the Leaf : Shape of leaf was classified under the following two heads (12):

(i) *Oval-lanceolate* : Leaf having its maximum width in the centre was grouped under this head. To observe accuracy, grouping under this head was limited to the leaf having its broadest point within 1 cm. from the mid-point towards the base.

(ii) *Ovate-lanceolate* : Leaf having its broadest point near the leaf base was grouped under this head. This was limited to the leaf which had its broadest point beyond 1 cm. from the mid-point towards the base of the leaf blade. Shape of leaf was found as a distinct varietal character in mango. The varieties Baramasi, Bombay Bottle, Challpatia, Dashehri, Gola Khurja, Gopal bhog, Langra Khurja, Maldah, Sufeda

Lucknow and Sufeda Malihabad were 'Oval-lanceolate' and the remaining were 'Ovate-lanceolate' (Table 2, Col. 3).

Magnitude of apex and base of lamina: The magnitude (angle) of leaf apex was measured with a protractor at a point 2.54 cm. from the leaf tip, while that of the base at a point 1.77 cm. from the juncture of the lamina and petiole (12). As such on the basis of angles formed by the apex and base of lamina, mango varieties were classified as under :

Apex— (i) acuminate (less than 25°), (ii) sharply acute (25°-29°), (iii) acute (30°-34°), (iv) broadly acute (35°-39°) and (v) broad (40 and above).

On the basis of apex of leaf, all the varieties fell under the group "Broad". The narrowest angle formed by the leaf apex was in Gopalbhog (45.0°), while the broadest was in Samar-Bahisht-Chausa (68.76°). In Pairi, Sufeda Malihabad, Chaupatia and Dashehri, apex angles were almost similar to the narrowest angle and as such these, alongwith Gopalbhog, could easily be differentiated with the leaves of Samar-Bahisht-Chausa and also with those of Bombay Bottle, and Maldah, whose apex angles were more or less equal to that of Samar-Bahisht-Chausa (Table 2, Col. 4).

Base- (i) narrow acute (less than 60°), (ii) acute (60°-74°), (iii) broadly acute (75°-84°) and (iv) obtuse (85° and above).

On the basis of magnitude (angle) of base of lamina, the varieties Baramasi, Chaupatia, Dashehri, Gopalbhog and Sufeda Malihabad were grouped as 'narrow acute', while Bombay Bottle, Bombay Green, Gola Khurja, Langra Khurja, Mewa Saharanpur, Pairi, Sufeda Lucknow and Variegata Khurja were 'acute'. The remaining varieties i.e. Fajri, Maldah and Samar-Bahisht-Chausa were broadly acute. None of the varieties were 'obtuse' (Table 2, Col. 5).

Shape of Apex and Base of Lamina

Apex : Shape of the leaf apex was divided under three heads (5):

(i) *Acuminate* : When the leaf tip is sharp pointed with a long drawn tip.

(ii) *Acute* : When the leaf tip ends in a blunt point.

(iii) *Sub-acuminate* : When the leaf tip is in between 'acuminate' and 'acute'. Apices of leaves of Pairi, Sufeda Lucknow, Langra, Langra Khurja and Fajri were found 'acuminate' (Fig. I : 1, 2, 3). These could easily be differentiated with Bombay Bottle and Bombay Green, which possessed 'acute' apices (Fig. I: 4, 5). Leaves of the remaining varieties i.e. Baramasi, Chaupatia, Dashehri, Gola Khurja, Gopalbhog, Maldah,

Sl. No.	*Name of variety*	*Shape of leaf (based on distance from mid-point to the broadest point of lamina on the mid -rib in cm.)*	*Angle (magnitude) of leaf apex*	*Angle (magnitude) of base of lamina*	*Shape of leaf apex*	*Shape of base of lamina*	*Nature of cross vein of a leaf*	*Number of pairs of cross-veins in a leaf*
1	2	3	4	5	6	7	8	9
1.	Baramasi	OV.L. (0.65)	51.00° (BR)	56.90° NA	SAM	NP.	A	20
2.	Bombay bottle	OV.L (0.96)	66.18° (BR)	69.28° A	A	NP	A	31
3.	Bombay green	OT.L (1.42)	59.28° (BR)	66.24° A	A	NP	BR	25
4.	Chaupatia	OV.L (0.54)	50 .94° (BR)	52.52° NA	SAM	NP	A	29
5.	Dashehri	OV.L (i.o4)	50.12° (BR)	56.34° NA	SAM	X	VA	25
6.	Fajri	OT.L (2.40)	61.16° (BR)	77.46° BRA	AM	R	A	26
7.	Gola Khurja	OV.L (1.00)	57.08° (BR)	60.04° A	SAM	NP	A	25
8.	Gopalbhog	OV.L (0.80)	45.00° (BR)	45.44° NA	SAM	X	VA	24

1	2	3	4	5	6	7	8	9
9.	Langra	OT.L (2.07)	61.20° (BR)	73.80PA	AM	X. 1	A	24
10.	Langra Khurja	OV.L (0.85)	58.38° (BR)	69.84° A	AM	R	A	25
11.	Maldah	OV.L (0.56)	67.43° (BR)	81.37° BRA	SAM	X. I	VA	27
12.	Mewa Saharanpur	OT.L (I.50)	64.92° (BR)	73.64° A	SAM	X. 1	A	20
13.	Pairi	OT.L (3.40)	46.76° (BR)	72.00° A	AM		BR	37
14.	Sarnar-Bahist Chausa	OT.L (1.90)	68.76° (BR)	82.78° BRA	SAM	R	BR	25
15.	Sufeda Lucknow	OV.L (0.90)	53.34° (BR)	60.48° A	AM	NP	A	24
16.	Sufeda Malihabad	OV.L (1.10)	48.11° (BR)	57.77° NA	SAM	X	A	30
17.	Variegata Khurja	OT.L (1.40)	54.30° (BR)	60.64° A	SAM	NP	A	28

OV.L = Oval-lanceolate : OT.L = Ovate-lanceolate : BR = Broad NA = Narrow acute : A = Acute

BRA = Broadly acute : SAM = Sub-acuminate : AM = Acuminate : X = Clearly tapering in straight line

X.r = Tapering in straight line with a little curve : R = Roundish : NP = No peculiarity:

VA = Very acute.

Mewa Saharanpur, Samar-Bahisht-Chausa, Sufeda Malihabad and Variegate Khurja had 'sub-acuminate' apices (Fig.1 : 6) . In addition, the apex of Pairi leaf was found very peculiar, as characterised by a long drawn tip (Fig. 1:1).

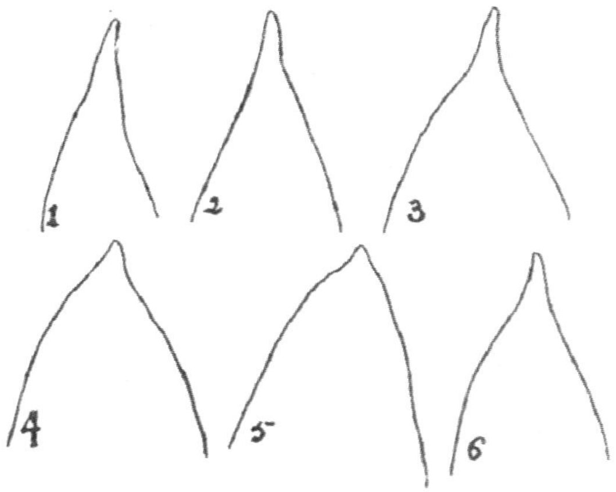

Fig.1

Base **:** Base of leaf-blade was grouped under the head 'narrow', 'apering' and 'broad'. Bases of Lamina of Dashehri, Gopalbhog and Sufeda Malihabad were found very diagnostic, as their margins were clearly tapering in straight lines (Fig. II : 1, 2, 3). Bases of leaf-blades of Maldah, Mewa Saharanpur and Langra, though had their margins almost in straight lines, were found with a slight curve (Fig. II : 4). Leaf-blades of Fajri, Samar-Bahisht-Challsa and Langra Khurja were having roundish bases (Fig. II : 5, 6) . Bases of leaf-blades in Pairi were of two shapes, (i) Narrow for about 3 cm, followed by broadening with a little curve (Fig. II : 7) and (ii) Broad and roundish. Rest of the seven varieties had no characteristic features.

Nature and Number of Pairs of Cross-vein : Nature of cross-veins was judged on the basis of angles formed by these veins with the mid-rib limited to the first three or four veins from the base of leaf-blade towards the apex. These were classified as 'very acute' (45° or below), 'broad' (70° or above) and 'acute' (between 45° and 70°).

Leaves of Dashehri, Gopalbhog and Maldah were found having very acute' veins. The veins of Gopalbhog, however, were comparatively slightly broader than those of Dashehri and Maldah. Cross-veins of leaves of Bombay

Green, Pairi and Samar-Bahisht-Chausa were 'broad'. Leaves of the remaining eleven varieties had 'acute' veins, though the veins of Langra and Mewa Saharanpur were narrower than others (Table II Col. 8).

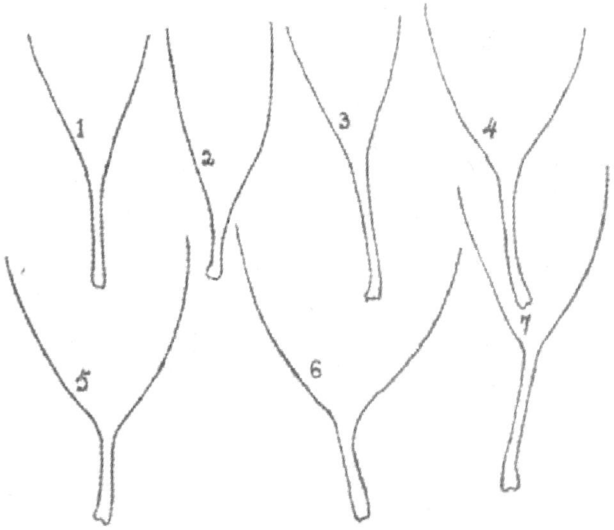

Fig. 2

Number of pairs of cross-veins in a leaf was counted with a view to find out if this could be made a basis for signifying different varieties.

The results in most of the varieties were found insignificant except in Pairi (37-maximum) and Baramasi alongwith Mewa Saharanpur (20-minimum). In other varieties the number of pairs of cross-veins varied from 24 to 30 (Table II Col. 9).

Discussion

Classification of mango varieties on the basis of leaf-characters is a difficult job. However, Hayes (2) opined that work in this direction will be a valuable contribution to the complex problem of mango. In the present investigations, emphasis has mainly been given to studies on herbarium specimens and measurements of leaf-characters. Contrary to this, Naik and Gangolly (5) pointed out that herbarium specimens are not useful for a study of minute and very striking characters, which are clearly manifested in the field and get obliterated in the preserved specimens. The author though, fully agrees with this view, is of the opinion that studies on herbarium specimens and measurement of leaf-characters in mango are extremely useful where such characters are not helpful in the field.

Nand (9) reported that leaves of both Gopalbhog, Pairi are 'folded and twisted' on the tree. Thus these can easily be distinguished in the preserved specimens to remove confusion on the tree, as in Pairi and Gopalbhog the width of lamina was 6.04 cm. and 3.80 cm respectively, while the length was 26.54 cm and 16.87 cm in the same order. Again, base angle of the leaf-blade in Pairi was recorded as 72.0°, while that of Gopalbhog as 45.44°.

Further, leaves of Sufeda Malihabad and Langra look almost similar on the tree due to their leaves being flat in nature (Nand, 9). Results obtained in respect of these varieties in the present investigations show great promise, as the W/L ratio of Sufeda Malihabad and Langra are 22.59 and 29.05 per cent respectively. Further, the apex angle of leaf in Sufeda Malihabad is 48.11° and that of Langra is 61.20°. Again, the base of the lamina of Sufeda Malihabad forms an angle of 57.77° against 73.80° in Langra.

Inspite of the above encouraging results, the present investigations also revealed that sometimes consideration of a single aspect was not purposeful. In Gopalbhog, apex and base angles of leaf blade (lamina) are almost equal (45.0° and 45.44° respectively). On the other hand, apex angles of Gopalbhog (45.00°) and Pairi (46.76°) are approximately similar. Thus by considering only apex angle of these two varieties, it may not be possible to eliminate their plants from each other. However, this could be made possible by considering both apex and base angles together, because in Gopalbhog the base angle is 45.44° and in Pairi it is 72.0°. Similarly, the apex angles of Pairi (46.76°) and Sufeda Malihabad (48.11°) are approximately equal but there is a great difference between their base angles (72.0° and 57.77° respectively). These two varieties, therefore, could easily be separated from each other. Further, apex angle of Gola Khurja (57.08°) and base angle of Sufeda Malihabad (57.77°) and Dashehri (56.34°) were almost equal. Leaves of Gola Khurja, therefore, could easily be differentiated from both Sufeda Malihabad and Dashehri.

The angle formed by the base of lamina of Fajri is 77.46°, while that of Chausa is 82.78°. The nature of cross-veins of Fajri leaves are 'acute', while 'broad' veins are formed in Samar-Bahisht-Chausa. Thus, these two varieties can be separated on the basis of angle formed by the base lamina and nature of cross-veins in leaf.

Summary

Seventeen important mango varieties of Horticultural Gardens.

Government Agricultural College, Kanpur were classified on the basis of nineteen leaf-characters during 1950-52. All the bases of classification except few were found useful for identifying and ascertaining mango varieties.

Acknowledgement

Grateful thanks are due to Sri S. N. Singh and Drs. V. S. Chhonker and P. N. Bajpai for valuable suggestions from time to time during the course of these studies.

References

1. Alderman, W. H. and Shoemaker, J. H. (1945). Use of leaf characters in Proc. identification of plum varieties Proc. Amer. Soc. Hort. Sc. Vol. 22, p. 48.
2. Maerz, A & Paul, M. P. A dictionary of colour Mc. Graw Hill Book Co.
3. Mukerjee, S.K. (1948). The varieties of Mango and their classification Bul. Bot. Soc, Bengal 2 (2) :101-33. Oct. 1948.
4. Naik, K. C, and Gangolly, S. R. (1950). A monograph on classification and nomenclature of South Indian Mangoes.
5. Ridgeway, R. (1912). Colour Standard and Colour Nomenclature, Washington.
6. Shaw J. K. (1914). The study of apple trees characters and its bearing on variety substitution. Proc. Amer. Soc. Hort. C. Vol. II, pp. 112-120.
7. Thomson, C. R. (1932). Identification of red currant varieties. Annual report of the Agr.-Hort. Research Stn., Long Ashton, 1931-32, pp. 23-39.
8. Upshall, W. A. (1924). Identification of varieties of fruit trees from leaf characters and other growth characters. Scientific Agriculture, 4 (1924), No. 6, pp. 184-89.
9. Upshall, W. A. (1925). Govt. Inspection of nurseries to eliminate variety mixture.
10. Winter, J. D. (1925). Use of plant characteristics in identification of red raspberry varieties, Proc. Amer. Soc. Hort. Sc. Vol. 22 pp. 261-64.
11. Burns, W. and Prayag, S. H. (1915). Mango classification. Agr. Journ. India, 10, 374.
12. Burns, W. and Prayag, S. H. (1920). The book of mango. Bombay Dept. Agr. Bull 103.
13. Condit, I. J. (1948). Fig. characteristics useful in identification of the varieties Hilgardia, 14 (1), 1-68, May, 1941.
14. Kinman, C. F. (1918). The mango in Puerto Rico. Puerto Rico. Agr. Exp. Stn. Bull. 24, 1-30.
15. Mukherjee, S. K. (1948). The varieties of mango and their classification. Bull Bot. Society Bengal, 2 (2), 101-330, Oct. 1948.

16. Naik, K.C. and Ganguly, S.R. (1950). A monograph on classisfication of South Indian Mangoes.
17. Nand, Darshana. (1955). Colour of young growing leaves as a means of identifying mango varieties. Agr. College Journ. Kanpur. Jan. 1955, 15-19.
18. Pope, W.T. (1938). Mango culture in Hawaii. Hawaii Agri. Exp. Stn. Bull. 58.
19. Popenoe, W. (1923). Manual of tropical and subtropical fruits.
20. Rolphs, P. H. (1923). Mangoes in Florida University of Florida.
21. Venkataratnam, L. (1951). Mangoes in Hyderabad. Ind. Journ. Hort. 8(4) Dec. 1951.
22. Watt, G. (1891). The Mango classification.
23. Wester, P. J. (1920). A description list of mango varieties in India. Agr. Review, 18 (4).
24. Wester, P. J. (1920). The mango-Philipine Bureau Agr. Bull. 18.
25. Wood-house A. C. (1909). Mango in Bhagalpur, Quarterly Journ. Dept. Agr. Bingal 2, 108.
26. Woodrow, G. M. (1904). The mango : Its culture and varieties.
27. Darrow, G. W. (1932). Plant Physiology by Miller.
28. Hayes, W. B. (1950). Personal communication.
29. Kinman, C. F. (1918). The mango in Puerto Rico-Puerto Rico Agri. Exp.Stn. Bull. 24.
30. Mukharjee, S.K. (1948). The varieties of mango and their classification. Bull. Bot. Soc. Bengal, 2 (2), 101-33.
31. Naik, K. C. and Ganguly, S. R. (1950). A monograph on classification and nomenclature of South Indian mangoes. Govt. Press, Madras.
32. Nand, Darshana. (1952). Classification of some important mango varieties on basis of leaf character. M. Sc. (Ag.) Hort. Thesis, Agra University. (Govt. Agr. Col., Kanpur) pp. 1-92 (1955). Colour of young growing leaves as a means of identifying mango varieties.
33. Kanpur Agr. Col. Journ. 14 (1) : 15-19. (1957). Size and shape of terminal vegetative bud useful in classification of mango varieties. Kanpur Agr. Cel. Jorn. 16 (1 & 2). 152-57. (1958). Classification of some important mango varieties on the basis of folding, twisting, waviness, crinkling and reflexion of leaves. Gardening, 1 (5): 25-33.

34 Popenoe, W. (1923). Mannual of tropical and subtropical fruits. Macmillan Co. New York. (1941). The Mango. A study in systematic pomology. Trop. Agriculture. 18:23-25.

35 Sefick, H. K. and Blake. M A. (1937). The classification of varieties of peaches by means of leaf characters. Proc. Amcr. Soc. Hort. Sc. 55: 246-50.

4

Secrets of Mango Grafting Practices

Securing quality grafts in a desired number continuously for years is an important point in mango nursery practices from commercial point of view. Observations made on this line by the author in Malihabad in the last week of August 1961 compaired with those made earlier elsewhere, along with his own views, have been summarised, discussed and concluded in the following paper.

Raising of Root Stocks

Mango stones are collected in the months of May and June and spread in nursery beds either in open field or under shade of mango trees. While spreading, care should be taken that seeds do not overlap each other. Shade protects young delicate seedlings from direct sun. Hays (1957) has reported that seeds when spread in beds are covered with sand or garden soil or may be left uncovered and kept moist. In Malihabad seeds are covered with thick layers of dry mango leaves. If rains fail beds are irrigated to keep the leaves and seeds moist. Leaves retain moisture in them for longer which stimulate germination. Leaves also provide the least resistence to germinating seeds and prevent them from the attack of white ants.

Seeds germinate in about a month's time. When seedlings attain the height of 9"-12" and delicate coppery leaves start turning green, they are transplanted in nursery beds for their future use as root stocks. For transplanting young seedlings following practices are adopted:

1. The general practice in vogue is that seedlings are lifted from soil with their tap roots and cotyledons intact after which they are set out in nursery beds at 10"-12" apart.
2. Bajpai (1955) has reported that in Malihabed young seedlings are pulled up from the soil with a little force to let the tap roots break, taking care that cotyledo's remain attached with seedlings. They are transplanted in rows 1" apart and 9" from plant to plant.
3. The author observed in Malihabad that young seedlings are uprooted individually with their cotyledons. Their tap roots are then cut to a

length of 1"-1/2" by vertical use of Khurpies. Seedlings are then set out in nursery beds at 5"-6" apart.

4. Another method observed by the author in Malihabad was that broad bladed Khurpies are used horizontally with a little slant in the soil so as to cut the tap roots of seedlings to a length of 1"-1 1/2" and release several seedlings at a time from the soil with their cotyledons attached with them. Seedlings are then planted in nursery beds at 5"-6" apart.

By adopting first method root stocks or grafts are to be lifted from soil essentially with larger size of earthen balls. This also encourages higher percentage of mortality during lifting due to growth of long tap roots deep into the soil.

Method No. 2 allows easier lifting of plants with smaller size of balls, as a portion of tap root is broken in pulling out young seedlings. Chances of mortality in this method are lesser.

The third method is a modification of method No. 2 in which plants are pulled up with a view to break a portion of tap root. It is just possible that in some cases a desired portion of root is broken while in other cases only a very little portion or more than required portion is broken. By practising the third method tap roots are cut to a desired length. This allows smaller size of earthen balls with plants during lifting. Chances of mortality in this case are very little.

Method No. 4 is a further modification of second and third methods. This method is a quicker one as several seedlings are released from soil at a time and the problem of individual uprooting or lifting of young seedlings is removed. Secondly it makes possible to lift root stocks and grafts with smaller size of earthen balls. Thirdly chances of mortality are little. The only disadvantage in this method is that great care is to be taken at the time of using khurpies in the soil as a little negligence may destroy a larger number of young seedlings. This method, however, seems to be the best of all.

After young seedlings are transplanted in well prepared nursery beds, proper manuring, watering, weeding and hoeing should be done in them from time to time to get healthy root stocks for their use in the next year.

Principles Underlying Severing of Tap Roots of Young Seedlings and Attachment of Cotyledons with Them

Transplanting of plants is one of the most important practices of nursery management. At the time of transplanting of young seedlings, if tap roots, which grow deep into the soil are intact, they create difficulty in future transplantings of root stocks and grafts, as they require larger size of earthen balls with them at the time of digging from soil.

When tap roots are cut or broken, seedlings produce adventitious roots which allow easy lifting with smaller size of earthen balls, which further facilitates their handling from one place to another.

Attachment of cotyledons with young seedlings at the time of first transplanting is essential specially when tap roots are cut. When roots are severed, plants get shock and remaining portions of roots are not able to absorb food material immediately direct from soil as adventitious roots are also not so much developed till then. Till these roots are well developed, young seedlings are nourished from the food material stored in the attached cotyledons. Even when tap roots are not severed, cotyledons are kept attached with the saplings and those saplings from which cotyledons get detached are rejected for transplanting. This might be due to the reason that tap roots developed till then might not be able to nourish the seedlings independently from soil and therefore presence of cotyledons in such cases also becomes essential.

Plantation of Mother Plants and Securing Healthy Scions from Them

The author observed in Malihabad that nurserymen are not particular in planting mother plants at any regular distance. Mostly they plant at 5'-10' apart and in some cases even upto 20' apart. The distance from 5-10' seems to be sufficient. After planting each mother plant is sufficiently manured to give out healthy scions. Inarching should be started when mother plants are 3-6 years old. Some nurserymen at Malihabad are of the view that mother plants should not be used for grafting before five years as such grafts do not produce true to type fruits, but there does not seem to be any scientific reason behind this view. This practice might be applicable only in such cases where varieties are doubtful and are required to be confirmed which can be done in fifth or sixth year by studying the varietal characters of fruits when first crop is taken. This problem can however be overcome by studying varietal characters of different vegetative parts such as leaves, vegetative buds and shoots, etc. as done by various workers like Mukherjee (1948), Naik and Gangolly (1950), Nand (1955, 1957 and 1958) and others.

To obtain grafts on a large scale regularly every year, scions from mother plants in the nursery should be utilized in rotation after dividing the plot of mother plants into portions. For example, in a newly laid out nursery if mother plants are planted in the year 1962, the whole land may be divided into four plots as under:

1	2	3	4

Scions of mother plants of plot No. 1 may be started with for grafting in the year 1965 (3 years age) and mother plants be left for vegetative growth in the next year, i. e., 1966 to be used again for scions in 1967. This practice may be followed in every alternate year for about 8-10 years.

Similarly grafting with scions of mother plants of plot No. 2 may be started in 1966 (4 years age), plot no. 3 in 1967 (5 years age) and plot no. 4 in 1968 (6 years age) and for future the same practice be followed in every alternate year as for plot no. 1. Thus desired number of grafts may be had regularly every year from different plots except for a few years in the beginning as it is clear from diagram No. 1 given below :

Diagram I showing number of plots of mother plants to be utilized for grafting every year (when planted in 1962).

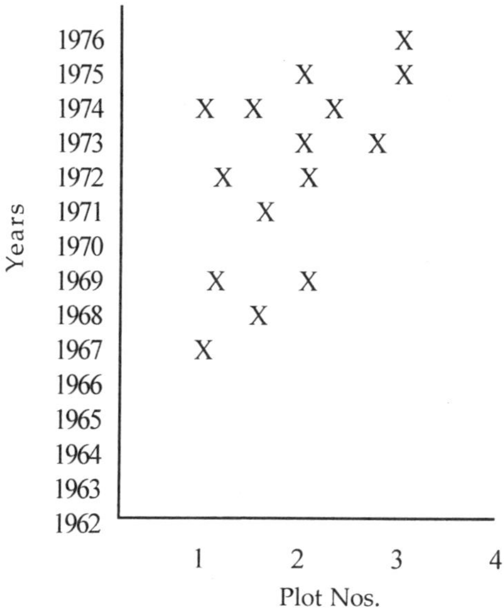

The above diagram (No. 1) shows that grafts from two plots can very well be taken every year continuously for eight years (up to 1974) except for the first two years in the beginning of 1965 and 1966. It is also clear from the above diagram that in 1975 only one plot is left for grafting, as plants of plot No. I due to their being old are removed after taking grafts in 1973. To maintain the continuity of availablity of scions from two plots each year, new plants may be planted in plot No. 1 in 1972 in between the spaces of old mother plants, where they will grow for a year, after which old mother plants will be removed after taking grafts in 1973 thus providing open space for growth of new plants. Grafting with new mother plants will be started in 1975. If this rotation is practiced in each plot, one may be able to get grafts from two plots every year continuously for long, but in such cases the plots must be filled up with fresh fertile soil due to continuous removal of rich soil with earthen balls of plants. To get rid of this trouble the whole land may be changed after 10 or 15 years and a fresh nursery be laid out. While laying out the nursery for planting mother plants care should be taken that plan should be made in such a way that all the mother plants may not have to be used at a time, otherwise a time will come when there will be no mother plant for grafting. Care for producing root stocks according to the availability of scions, should be taken so that scions may not be wasted for want of root stocks.

Sometimes mango grafts are planted at 20' apart each way. After they give out healthy scions, plants are utilized for grafting purposes by (i) felling of alternate trees in each alternate row both ways and (ii) by felling of all the trees in each alternate row (adjacent to the previous row) both ways. The remaining plants are thus left at 40' apart each way which are allowed to grow into a mango orchard. As a matter of fact this method is employed for utilizing the remaining spaces between the plants of a newly planted orchard by planting mother plants for grafting purposes. Grafts by this method can be taken only for a few years because mother plants will have to be removed in the fifth or sixth year to take first successful crop from the orchard trees. If mother plants are not removed at this stage, they grow huge in size and affect the yield. Felling of such mother plants also become very difficult. No rotation can be followed in this method and a time comes when there are no mother plants left for grafting purposes. The above method is also clear from diagram II given below:

Diagram II

Showing utilization of plants for grafting and establishment into orchards, at 40' apart.

● X ● X ● X ● X ●
X X X X X X X X X
● X ● X ● X ● X ●
X X X X X X X X X
● X ● X ● X ● X ●
X X X X X X X X X
● X ● X ● X ● X ●
X X X X X X X X X
● X ● X ● X ● X ●

● These plants will be left for establishment of orchard.

X These plants are meant for felling for taking grafts.

Lifting of Root Stocks, their Placing and Planting Near Mother Plants

Seedling root stocks when 1 —1 1/2 years old are dug up from soil in the months of June to August and planted near scions of mother plants by either of the following four systems :—

1. Flat System

Felling of mother plants from three to six years of age is done in early rains and their branches spread up flat to the level of the ground after bending them with the help of rope, wire and pegs. Weak, unhealthy and other shoots hindering in grafting operations or several shoots growing from a point should be removed from mother plants to let the remaining shoots grow healthy for their use as scions. Fellng of trees for grafting purposes after six years is not advisable as a lot of labour, time and material is wasted in felling such old trees.

When scions of spread up branches are ready for grafting, the soil under mother plants is well smoothened after proper weeding and hoeing. After this two or three types of symbols each symbol signifying a certain thickness are marked on the ground near scions exactly at the place where stocks of the same thickness are actually to be planted so as to let the scion and stock come in contact with each other easily and conviniently at the proper position. For example if scions of 0.8, 1.00, and 1.5 cms. thicknesses, are available, they may be signified with the symbols, +, + + , and respectively.

When such symbols are marked on the ground, seedling stocks of different thicknesses (out of those already dumped) are placed at different marks accordingly. When a sufficient number of seedling root stocks are placed near desired scions, they are planted in the soil. This work of finding out exact spot near desired scion for planting root stock of equal thickness is rather more important than actual grafting in Malihabad. This practice allows healthy and superior quality of graft, and must be encouraged.

The practice elsewhere in vogue is that after dressing up the soil seedling foot stocks are planted at places near mother plants with the least consideration of thickness, maturity and contact of scion with stock. Grafts thus obtained are of inferior quality.

At some places one root stock at a time is taken to the mother plant and planted near a selected scion but this method is combursome and time taking.

2. Mound System

In bearing trees where branches are spreading and drooping near ground, root stocks are planted near scions on mounds of soil prepared under them as high as required so as to enable them to come in close contact with each other. In this system grafts and fruits are taken at a time from the same tree. This system can only be applied on a small scale.

3. Machan System

When trees are tall, branches high and varieties remarkable and rare, root stocks planted in pots or jooties are placed near selected scions on machans prepared under trees for grafting operations.

4. Mixed System

In flat system if some branches of mother plants could not be spread up completely flat on the ground, small mounds of soil should be prepared under such branches and stocks planted over them so as to reach the desired scions.

Actual Grafting

After about fifteen or twenty days of planting, the stock is inarched with the scion by the ordinary technique after removing about 1/3 portion of wood of their thicknesses to a length of 1 1/2"-2" at a height of 9"-1" from the ground level. Generally after giving cuts in scion and stock they are tied together with a string for union. The practice in Malihabad is that cut portions of scion and stock are first tied with a piece of string after which wrapped with a green mango leaf and then again tied with another string. The union in this way is complete within four to six weeks, whereas it takes about eight weeks by the ordinary method. This practice of tying should be encouraged among the nurserymen as wrapping with leaf prevents the graft union from the direct touch of rain water and sun which facilitates early and complete union.

Inarching should be started in the month of July, so that all the grafts prepared during rains may be transplanted to nursery beds latest by the end of October. As a matter of fact the period of June to October is the busiest in all the nurseries as grafting operations and supplies of plants are to be done in full swing at the same time. It was observed by the author that root stocks were being planted near scions in nurseries of Malihabad and most of the nurserymen were not able to start actual grafting till then. Grafts in which union between scion and stock are not complete by October are left under mother plants and tranplanted in beds in February and March. Inarching is also done in February and Match and the grafts prepared during this period should be transplanted into beds in next rains. When union is complete between scion and stock, strings should gently be cut and removed from grafts. Till grafts (attached or detached with mother plants) remain planted near mother plants or in nursery beds, proper weeding, hoeing and watering should be done in them from time to time to make the graft union complete and strong.

Grafting operations are almost stopped during rains causing there by a great loss to nurseries. To get rid of this loss, large sized umbrellas having wooden stands in their centres should be brought into use. These stands are fixed vertically in the ground and under their shade grafting operations remain continued even if it is raining. These umbrellas also prevent grafters or budders from intense heat of sun during grafting or budding operations.

Acknowledgements

My grateful thanks are due to Sri Ram Surat Singh, Director of Agriculture, U. P., Lucknow who lead me to make these observations. I am also thankful to Sri T. S. Chauhan and Dr. A. Prasad, Dy. Directors of Horticulture, Lucknow and Allahabad and Sri S. K. Shukla, Superintendent, Govt. Gardens, Allahabad for their encouragement in making these observations and writing of this paper.

References

1. Bajpai, P. N. (1955). Mango Nursery Practices in Malihabad Kanpur, Agr. Coll. Jurn. 14-(2) 5-6, 1955.
2. Hayes, W. B. (1957). Fruit Growing in India, 1957.
3. Mukherjee, S. K. (1948). The varieties of Mango and their classification. Bull. Bot. Soe. Bengal 2 (2), 101-33, Oct. 1948.
4. Nand, Darshana (1955). Colour of young growing leaves as a means of identifying Mango Varieties. Kanpur Agr. Coll. Journ. Jan. 1955, 15-19.
5. Nand, Darshana (1957). Size and shape of terminal Vegetative bud useful in classification of Mango Varieties. Kanpur Agr. Coll. Journ. 152-56, February 1957.
6. Nand, Darshana (1958). Classification of some important mango varieties on the basis of folding, twisting, waviness, crinkling and reflexion of leaves. Gardening, 35-38, June 1958.
7. Naik, K. C. and Gangolly, S. R. (1950). A monograph on classification and nomenclature of south Indian mangoes.

5

Delicious Guava Varieties of Allahabad Origin

Guava (Psidium guajava) is actually a fruit of Central America. It is very tasteful and nutritious and belongs to the family Myrtacea. Its leaves are aromatic. In Hindi it is called as 'amrood' or 'safiri'. In Sanskrit it is named as 'drirhbeej', 'bahubeej' and 'perik'. In Bengal it is named as 'Piara' and 'Goachiphal'. In Maharashtra it is called as 'Peru' and 'Jaam' whereas in Gujarat it is called as 'Jamrookh' and 'Jaamphal'. Chief guava growing areas in the world are California, Florida, Brazil, Mexico, Hawai Island, Peru, Southern China, Sri Lanka, Myanmar, Quba, Pakistan and India. In France and Algeria guavas are found growing wild.

In India guava was introduced in 17th century. Since then, its expansion took place with such a fast speed that guavas are now being produced commercially in Uttar Pradesh, Bihar, West Bengal, Madhya Pradesh, Gujarat, Andhra Pradesh, Maharashtra and other areas also. Now guava has become so popular in India that people take this as an Indian fruit. It is being counted as one of the chief fruits of India, where guava covers an area of about 1.02 lakh hectares as guava orchards, producing thereby approximately 10.15 lakh tonnes of guavas every year.

However, Allahabad has adopted this sumtuous delicious guavas in such a fine manner that Allahabadi guavas have now become famous in the whole world. This credit goes to the village Aboobakarpur (Bhabhakkarpur) in Chail tehsil of Allahabad near Sulem Sarai (about 6 km from Allahabad now included in Kaushambi district). Aboobakarpur is the main place where alongwith its adjoining villages and areas, original historical Allahabadi guava orchards are existing. Since decades from there the area of guava plantation spread in the interior parts of Development Blocks of Chail. Mooratganj and other areas. As a result of this, several good varieties were selected from the above historic guava orchards.

Allahabad Safeda : The world-wide name and fame of Allahabadi guavas started with the variety Allahabad Safeda, which was evolved and developed through selection in these historic guava orchards of Aboobakarpur. This variety is a 'FIND' for Allahabad. The fruit of Allahabad Safeda variety of guava is medium sized roundish and about 170 gm in weight. The skin of the fruit is thin beautiful whitish creamy in colour smooth and shining with small reddish dots here and there.The basal portion of the fruit is roundish and its stalk is fixed perpendicularly in a shallow sinus. The apical or stigmatic portion of the fruit is flattish round with a narrow persistent calyx, sepals converging towards each other.

The pulp is charming white, sweet, crisp, soft, melting and of an excellent taste with a pleasant flavour. The storage quality of the fruit is medium. The total soluble solids (TSS) in juice of the pulp is 12.6% and the acidity (citric acid) is 0.24%. The pulp also makes available 187.94 mg vitamin-C per 100 gm pulp, 6.096% reducing sugar (glucose, i.e., grape sugar and fructose, i.e., fruit sugar), 1.780% nonreducing sugar (Sugar from sugar-cane i.e. sucrose), 0.370% tannin, 0.647% starch, 0.304% pectic substances and 3.132% crude fibre.

Its trees are more or less spreading with broader leaves and slightly folded margins. Allahabad Safeda variety of guava is loved and liked by all in our country as well as in foreign countries.

Apple-coloured Guava : The next gift of Allahabad guavas is the variety 'Apple - Coloured'. In common language this variety is named as 'Sebi, Sebia or Surkha Amrood'. The fruit of this variety is bright red from outside and whitish inside. It is very attractive and looks like an apple. People, by mistake, think these fruits as apples, when placed in lots and seen from some distance. This variety is also becoming a choice variety among others and is getting name and fame. The fruit is roundish, medium-sized and about 112 gm in weight. The skin of the fruit is slightly unsmooth and filled with reddish dense dots throughout, making thereby the fruit red in colour. The basal portion (stalk end) of the fruit is flattish and the apical portion (stigmatic end) roundish. The fruit stalk is perpendicularly fixed in a deep sinus. The persistent caly area is wide but almost closed. The pulp is creamy white, soft, melting and crisp, tasteful, sweet with a pleasant flavour. The durability of the fruit at room temperature is better than that of Allahabad Safeda. The T.S.S. of the pulp is 11.8% and acidity (as citric acid) 0.548%. The pulp also contains reducing sugar 2.987%, Non-reducing sugar 1.805%, tannin 0.202%, starch 0.592%, Pectic substance 0.834% and crude fibre 5.372%). As regards vitamin-C, one hundred gram of pulp makes available 139.751 mg of vitamin-C. The growth of the tree is slightly upright.

Chittidar: The third variety of guava selected in the above area of Allahabad is Chittidar. This is more or less similar in qualities as those of Allahabad Safeda. The skin is thin creamy white with very small red dots scattered throughout its body. The fruit is medium sized and roundish or slightly oval. The basal portion of the fruit is obtuse and slanting. The apical portion is roundish or slightly flattish. The pulp is yellowish white, comparatively more sweet with flavour. Durability of the fruit at room temperature is better than other varieties. The tree of Chittidar guava grows in an upright way.

Red-fleshed Guava : Red-Fleshed Guava is also a selection from the historic guava orchards of village Aboobakarpur area (Sulemsarai) of Allahabad district (now in Kaushambi). The speciality of this variety is that outer portion of this is whitish and the inner portion of the flesh is red. The fruit is medium to large-sized and about 170 gm in weight. It is oval round in shape, smooth and shining. Actually the skin is thick and pinkish creamy in colour, with few very small pinkish dots. The apex of the fruit is obtuse or flattish, while the basal portion is roundish. The fruit stalk is thin which is inserted in a shallow sinus at the basal end in a slanting way.

The flesh of the fruit is actually attractive pink in colour soft, melting, slightly sourish sweet, very tasteful with a pleasing flavour. Its seeds are small, smooth with reddish tinge. The fruit on the whole is of medium quality and of less durability. The TSS of the juice is 12.37% and the acidity in the form of citric acid is 0.40%. The pulp also makes available reducing sugar (glucose, i.e. grape sugar and fructose, i.e., fruit sugar) 4.0% non-reducing sugar (sucrose, i.e. sugar from sugar-cane) 4.93%, tannin 0.134%, starch 0.60%, pectic substance 1.624% and crude fibre 4.58%. The pulp of red-fleshed guava also makes available 62.50 mg of vitamin-C per 100 gm of pulp. The tree grows in an upright manner but different branches grow to an un-uniform height. Leaves are large narrow, longish margins slightly wavy and apex pointed. Slices of red-fleshed guava are very decorative on the dining table.

To preserve the historic guava orchards and to keep the name and fame of Allahabad guavas alive guava orchards of 53 villages of Chail development block, 3 of Mooratganj development block and three of Nagar Maha Palika Allahabad (Sulem Sarai, Aboobakarpur) were got declared as fruit-belt by the Uttar Predesh Shasan, Lucknow through the Department of Horticulture U.P. Lucknow in the year 1987. This declaration forces one to preserve these orchards and see that these are not cut. Cutting these orchards will be unlawful and may be taken as a crime. The administration is also supposed to look after these affairs. The declaration of the above fruits belt consisting of 59 villages in all was done through krishi (4) Anubhag Govt. Order No. 6516/12-4-211-87 dt. Lucknow 22nd December, 1987. This has been published in Uttar Pradesh Govt. Gazette Asaadhaaran Vidhaoee Parishishta Bhaag-4, Khand (Kha) (pariniyat aadesh), Lucknow Thursday, 24th December, 1987. This fruit belt covers 2000 hectares of land under guava orchards.

About 50% orcharding of guava (of the whole country) is done in Uttar Pradesh. Guavas are being grown commercially besides Allahabad in Lucknow,

Faizabad, Varanasi, Pratapgarh, Mirzapur, Fatehpur, Farrukhabad, Etawa, Aligarh, Meerut and other parts of Uttar Predesh. Chaka and Karha areas of Allahabad district, Shamshabad and Kaimganj areas of Farrukhabad district, Basrehar of Etawa and areas from Nawabganj to Bithoor along river Ganga in Kanpur district are growing very good guavas on a large scale. The above fruit belt area of Allahabad (Allahabad and Kaushambi now) covers 2000 hectares of land under guava orchards having many varieties. These yield 40,000 tonnes of guavas every year. A wonderful variety of guava was seen in the above fruit belt by the author in December 1987 as a chance seedling and was selected for growing and multiplying. The speciality of this variety is that the outer and inner (pulp) portions both are red. Actually its tree was found in Sulem Sarai area in village Umarpur Neenwan Bhagtana (Aboobakarpur) in the orchard of Sri Jagannath Prasad Kushwaha. The fruit is apple-coloured outside and red fleshed inside and, therefore, this Allahabad's fifth natural gift was named on the line of Allahabad Safeda as 'Allahabad Surkha'.

The plants of the variety 'Allahabad Surkha' were multiplied in Khusroobagh. Allahabad by patch budding and 25 such plants were got planted there author in an area of 0.1 hectare (1/4 acre) of land as mother plant/ orchard on 30th July, 1988. Plants of this variety are being propagated there from these mother plants and are being supplied to the growers on demand. Main charateristics of this variety are described as under.

Allahabad Surkha : As stated earlier Allahabad Surkha variety is also a gift of Allahabad and has been evolved by selection. The fruit of this variety is roundish of medium to large size (8x8 cm) and about 200 gm in weight unsmooth. Most of the outer portion is apple coloured and shining. Those parts which are not reddish are pinkish creamy in colour as of red-fleshed variety. The basal portion of the fruit is flattish. Fruit stalk is thin about 3.0 cm long and inserted in a shallow sinus in a slanting manner. The apical portion of the fruit is roundish and the calyx is closed.

The pulp is dark pinkish in colour, tasteful, soft, very sweet, having pleasant flavour fruits remains in good condition for four days at room temperature. One fruit counted 342 seeds, weight 4.426 gm. Seeds are very hard. TSS of juice of the pulp is 13.75% and acidity 0.40%. Total sugar in the pulp is 10.2%. One hundred gm of pulp makes 150 gm of vitamin-C available.

The tree grows upright vigorously. It is dome-shaped and compact. Leaves are large, dark green, long and elliptical. Veins and midrib of leaves towards upper portion are sunken, while those at the basal end are protuberated. Leaves of upper portion of a shoot are slightly folded and those at the lower portion flat. The variety is a heavy bearer. Besides these guava varieties of Allahabad origin, there are many other good guava varieties.

Other Guava Varieties -2

In earlier issues of this series, the last guava variety indicated there in was 'Allahabad Surkha', which was selected in Fruit (Guava) belt area of Allahabad in December 1987 in village Aboobakarpur. Just after this variety was found, it was called 'Red-Flashed-Apple-Colour Guava', but afterwards as already mentioned, on the line of variety 'Allahabad Safeda' it was named as 'Allahabad Surkha' (Indian Horticulture, July -September 1991 issue ICAR New Delhi) to further keep the name and fame of Allahabad alive. The block of this variety (plants got planted by the author on 30 July 1988) in Khusroobagh, Allahabad has been name-plated as 'Allahabad Surkha, Year of plantation is also written 1988-89.

However, there are also so many other varieties of guava, which do need mention. Guava fruit, in general being nutritious and tasteful is a rich source of vitamin-C. It contains five times more of vitamin-C than in the juice of Santra and 40 to 50 times more of vitamin-C than that available in apple. Again, among all common fruits, the richness of vitamin-C in guava is considered as next to that of Aonla. It possesses in itself 299 mg of vitamin-C per l00gm of pulp. The maximum amount of vitamin-C is available near the skin lesser than that in the outer pulp and minimum in the inner pulp in the ratio of 12:5:1. The guava fruit also possesses moisture 76.1%, total solids 23.9%, carbohydrate 14.5%, protein 1.5%, fat 0.2%, calcium 0.01%, phosphorus 0.04% and fibre 6.9%. One hundred gm of guava pulp also makes available vitamin B-1 (Thiamine) 30 mg, vitamin B-2 (Riboflavin) 30 mg. Nicotinic acid (Niacin) 0.2 mg and Iron 1.0 mg. Iron is available in and around seeds of the guava fruit. Therefore, one must take guavas with seeds and without peeling. Besides vitamin-C, guava contains thrice more of Iron, 2 1/2 more each of Calcium and Nicotinic acid, twice more of Phosphrous and 1 1/2 times more each of Thiamine and Riboflavin in comparison to those in Apple pulp. The calorific value of guava is 66 calories per 100 gm of pulp.

Guava fruits may also be utilized by canning or bottling its slices for off seasons use. These may also be transformed and preserved in the form of jams, jellies, drinks, cheese, toffees, pickles, salad and others. It is highly medicinal specially for cleaning the bowels. As regards other varieties, some of these are mentioned herewith.

Seedless Guava. The fruits of seedless guava variety have no seeds and therefore these have a special taste and flavour. It is sweet and very pleasant and of a good quality. The fruit is medium-sized (5.8 x 4.7 cm) pear-shaped longish round and about 72 gm in weight. Skin thin and light yellowish in colour with ununiform surface and pinkish large dots distributed sparsely. The fruit on the whole looks as if it has been divided in four parts. The basal portion of the fruit is flat and sunken, making thereby a shallow sinus, in which the fruit-stalk is inserted perpendicularly. The apical portion of the fruit is flat and the calyx covering the stigmatic point is wide but closed by the sepals.

The flesh of the fruit is white soft or slightly hard with pleasant flavour as mentioned above. The whole fruit is filled up with pulp except a little vacant space in the middle inside. Though there is an improvement in the quality of the fruit of seedless guava, but simultaneously its keeping quality at room temperature is very alarming. It can hardly be durable for two days and as such should be disposed off as early as possible. The tree grows upwards with dense branches and leaves. Leaves are large, stiff elliptical. This variety is a little shy - bearer. The trees of this variety or the plants/trees propagated on root stocks of this variety show signs of resistance to the deadly disease guava wilt.

Sardar Guava. A delicious variety of guava-L-49 (Lucknow-49) was selected and developed from a seedling Allahabad Safeda variety grove in Ganeshkind fruit, Research Station, Poona (Maharashtra) by late Dr. Sardar G.S. Cheema, an eminent Horticulturist of India. In Maharashtra and southern parts of India this variety was already being grown commercially. In Uttar Pradesh it was introduced later on and now this is also being grown on a large scale. This is specially because this variety is also more or less resistant to guava-wilt disease.

The fruit is medium to large sized (7.2x7.4 cm) roundish to ovate, about 200 gm in weight, skin of the fruit is thin greenish yellow slightly unsmooth with few medium sized dots scattered over the whole body from stalk end to stigmatic end, i.e. in the length of the fruit there are few some raised ridge - like appearance. The stalk of the fruit is perpendicularly fixed in a shallow sinius of the roundish base, while at the stigmatic end, the apical portion of the fruit is flattish with broad open calyx.

The flesh is creamy white, soft and crisp with slightly sweet and pleasing flavoured taste. About 215 seeds are contained by the fruit which are 1.9 gm in weight. The keeping quality of the fruit at room temperature is quite good. The pulp of the fruit contains total soluble solids (TSS) 13.57%, pH 4.0%, citric acid 0.55%, vitamin-C (ascorbic acid) 202.5 mg per 100 gm pulp, reducing sugar (grape sugar and fruit sugar) 3.93%, non-reducing sugar (sugar from sugar cane) 5.0%, tannin 0.168%, starch 0.660%, pectic substances 1.261% and crude fibre 0.676%.

The tree grows vigorously with dense branches and leaves. It grows upright-spreading. The growth of the tree is upto a height of 4-5 metres and spreads to a width of 8-9 metres. Due to spreading branches the side branches bend towards ground. Leaves are thick, leathery light green in colour, smooth elliptical, margins folded inwards. Base of leaf is round and apex is obtuse. Veins of front surface of leaves are sunken, while those at back are protuberated. New shoots of the tree are brownish green, ridged and layered. A heavy yielding variety. Later on L-49 variety of guava was renamed as 'Sardar Guava'. This was done in honour of late Sardar Dr. G. S. Cheema.

Pink Fleshed Guava. In the fruit belt of Allahabad another variety of guava was found in the guava orchard of Sri M. U. Ahmad (Majju Miyan) of Sayed Sarawan. The fruit from outside is smooth creamy white just like Allahabad Safeda and there is no symptom of any pinkish tinge on the skin as in the case of red-fleshed variety. Even then the flesh of this variety is light pinkish inside. The skin of this fruit is thick (about 0.2 cm in thickness). The fruit is roundish, medium to large sized (7 x 7.5 cm) and 250 gm in weight. It contains 384 seeds. The base of the fruit is roundish. The stalk is thick (0.4 cm) and 0.8 cm long and inserted in a deep sinus the apex of the fruit is flattish with a broad open persistent calyx.

The flesh of the fruit is crisp, sweet with a very pleasant flavour and is tasteful. It is very durable and can be safely stored at room temperature for 4-5 days.

The tree is medium to large-sized. The leaf is light green in colour, longish oval or ovate in shape, which measures 10.5 x 5.0 cm in size. The apex and base both form acute angles. Sometimes the apex of the leaf seems pointed and the leaf stalk is 0.8 cm in length. The mid-rib and leaf stalk of front side are groved, while those on the back side are ridged. The veins coming out from the mid-rib are nineteen in number on both sides towards margin. A heavy yielder.

Mirzapuri. 'Mirzapuri' variety of guava was selected and developed from a seedling of Allahabad Safeda variety in Mirzapur of Uttar Pradesh. The fruit is roundish and 3.5 x 3.8 cm in size. The skin is smooth on which some small dots are scattered all over. The basal portion of the fruit is slightly conical and the fruit stalk is perpendicularly inserted in the medium-sized sinus. The apical portion of the fruit is roundish. The pulp is soft and acidic sweet with a slight flavour. Keeping quality of the fruit is good. The tree is 3-4 metres high. Branches densely spreading. The leaf is longish oval 1 x 5 cm in size. Apex and base of leaf both are obtuse but the apex is pointed. Leaf slightly folded inwards fruiting medium.

Ahmad Ishkwala. This variety is also a selection from Allahabad Safeda seedling. The fruit is medium to large-sized (9.95x8.9 cm), roundish to oval and 170 gm in weight. The skin is greenish yellow and thick. The outer portion of the fruit further is rough, groved and protuberated all through. The base is roundish and the fruit stalk is small, which is fixed perpendicularly in a sinus of medium depth. The apex of the fruit is also roundish and the persistent calyx is broad but the sepals are fully closed and covering the stigmatic point. The flesh of the fruit is white or creamy white of medium thickness, but the pulp just below the skin is creamy in colour. It is soft, sweet and tasteful with pleasant flavour. Its TSS is 11.0%. The pulp contains total sugar 7.50%, reducing sugar 4.15% and acidity 0.24%. One hundred gm of pulp contains 198.50 mg of vitamin-C. Seeds comparatively large-sized, 195 in number and 2.0 gm in weight. The fruit may safely be stored at room temperature for 4-5 days.

The tree of the variety Ahmad Ishkwala is about 5-6 metres high, which grows vigrously. The leaf is thin, large in size (16.0x6.9 cm), longish with entire margin, the leaf - stalk being of 9.0 mm in length. The apex and base of the leaf both form acute angles. The front portion of the leaf is dark green and back portion green.

Kothrud. Kothrud is a good variety. The fruit is medium-sized (6.5 x 5.4 cm), longish like a pear and 112 gm in weight. Outer portion of the fruit is light yellow in colour, smooth, glossy and uniform. The skin is thin, apex of the fruit is roundish and the base is slightly tapering with a shallow sinus, having a small thin stalk fixed therein.

The sub-epidermal layer of the pulp of the fruit is yellowish and the inner pulp pinkish, granular medium sweet with a pleasing flavour. TSS of the pulp (juice) is 11.07%, pH 4.5%, acidity 0.48%, reducing sugar 4.17%, nonreducing sugar 2.03%, pectic material 1.45 and vitamin-C 80.0 mg per 100 gm of pulp. Durability of the fruit is very poor. It can safely be kept hardly for two days only. Seeds are hard, small, smooth, pinkish or light orange in colour, 222 in number per fruit which are 1.13 gm in weight. These seeds exist loosely in the pulp.

The tree is small in size, which grows with a medium vigour up to a height of 2.5 to 3.5 metres. Branches of the tree are spreading all round but making the canopy of the tree ununiform. Leaf is longish of medium size (13.9 x 5.1 cm). Apex of leaf is acute, while the base is obtuse. The front part of the leaf is green, while the back portion is light green and the margin is wavy. The outer bark of the trunk and branches is light brown and the inner bark greenish white in colour. The variety Kothrud is a heavy yielder. One tree yields about 700 fruits.

Surkh Chitti Neputani. This variety also appear to be selected and developed from Allahabad Safeda seedling. It is an excellent variety and in some respects it appears better than Allahabad Safeda. The fruit of Surkh Chitti Neputani is medium to large-sized (8.45 x 7.30 cm) and 193.5 gm in weight. It is roundish or oval in shape. The skin is thin, smooth, uniform, light yellow in colour and filled with attractive red-coloured dots. The basal end of the fruit is tapering with a deep sinus, fixing therein a small fruit-stalk in a perpendicular position. The apical end of the fruit is roundish with the open medium-sized persistent calyx.

The layer of pulp just below the skin is greenish and other parts of the pulp are creamy white, soft, sweet and have pleasant flavour. The pulp responses to 12.50% TSS, 8.65% total sugar, 3.75% reducing sugar, 0.48% acidity and 182.50 mg vitamin-C per 100 gm of pulp. Seeds are loosely settled in the pulp. Seeds are comparatively large-sized and 193 in number, which weigh 2.6 gm. The upper layer of the seed is soft keeping quality of the fruit is encouraging. The fruits maintain their good quality for 5-6 days at room temperature.

The tree grows very vigorously to a medium height of 4-5 metres with densely spreading branches giving the canopy a roundish shape. Leaves are thin, elliptical and of medium size (12.3 x 5.2 cm). The apex of the leaf is acute and the base obtuse. The leaf margin is entire and front and back portions of leaf - both are green. The leaf stalk is small (5.0 mm), fruiting heavy. An average tree yields about 660 fruits, which weight 125 kg.

Chakaiya Rahman Nagar. This appears to be a selection from Allahabad Safeda variety. The fruit of Chakaiya Rahman Nagar is very attractive of roundish flat shape. The quality of the fruit is excellent. The fruit is medium to large in size (6.6 x 7.6 cm) and 200 gm in weight. The skin is thin greenish yellow, slightly rough. The basal portion of the fruit is roundish with a deep sinus having a medium sized stalk therein. The apical portion of the fruit is also roundish with medium broad open calyx.

The pulp is creamy white, soft of sweet taste and pleasing flavour. The layer of pulp just below the peel is greenish. The TSS of the pulp juice is 12.50%. The pulp also contains total sugar 8.70%, reducing sugar (glucose) 3.30%, acidity 0.48% and vitamin-C (ascorbic acid) 175.10 mg per 100 gm pulp. The durability of the fruit is 4-5 days at room temperature. Seeds are small, smooth and light brownish in colour. The outer layer of the seed is soft. Seed loosely exist in the pulp. These are 210 in number which are 1.68 gm in weight.

The tree grows vigorously straight upwards upto a height of 5-6 metres. The branches and leaves grow densely, forming thereby a uniform canopy of the tree. Leaves are large-sized (14.3 x 6.4 cm) thin and oval in shape with entire margin. Leaf stalk is medium-sized (9 mm in length). The leaf apex is acute angled, while its base is obtuse angled. The front and back portion of the leaf are green and light green in the same order. This variety is a medium yielder. A tree of the variety Chakaiya Rahman Nagar yields about 385 fruits, which are approximately 78 kg in weight.

Gutaniwala. The fruit of the guava variety Gutaniwala is almost oval in shape and of medium size (8.98x8.38 cm), which weigh 164 gm. This variety is also said to be a selection from Allahabad Safeda. The base of the fruit is tapering roundish with a shallow sinus having inserted in itself a small fruit stalk. The apical part of the fruit is roundish with medium broad persistent calyx, the sepals of which close and fully cover the stigmatic point.

The skin of the fruit is greenish light yellow in colour thin and rough. The pulp just below the skin is greenish white. Other portions of pulp are creamy white in colour juicy, sweet, crisp, delicious with pleasant flavour and 11.8% TSS. The flesh also contains total sugar 7.62% reducing sugar 4.90%, acidity 0.50% and 189.0 mg of vitamin-C per 100 gm of pulp. Seeds comparatively larger, hard brownish smooth and loosely filled in the pulp. These are 170 nos in a fruit which weight 1.7 gm. The durability of the fruit is 3-4 days at room temperature.

The tree is medium sized which grows upright. Leaf large sized (14.3 x 6.5 cm), thin and pointed with entire margin. The leaf stalk is about 9.0 mm in length. The apex and base of leaf - both make acute angles. The front and back- both portion of the leaf are green in colour. The tree fruits very well and yields 740 fruits, which weight approximately 122 kg.

Bassateen Edfina. This variety of guava was developed on the basis of experiment conducted at the Horticultural Research State Sabahia (Alexandria), Egypt. The trees of Bassateen Edfina fruit very well. In Sabahia fruits of this variety are available from middle of September to the end of November, while in Edfina these are available upto the first week of December. The fruit is medium-sized (6.0x5.5 cm) with a narrow base and broad roundish apex and looks attractive. The pulp is sweet, tasty and soft with a pleasing flavour. It contains less and soft seeds. The fruit is further rich in vitamin-C with its TSS as 11%. On the whole the fruit of this variety is of a good quality.

Koheer Safeda. This is a hybrid obtained at Fruit Research Station Sangareddy, Andhra Pradesh by crossing the variety Koheer (female) with Allahabad Safeda (male). The fruit is large - sized and of a good quality. It is also rich in vitamin-C. This variety (Koheer x Allahabad Safeda) is also a heavy yielder.

Tasty Nutritious Guavas

Some more delicious varieties of guavas are detailed herewith :

Waber Supreme. The fruit of the variety Waber supreme is small to medium in size (5.6 x 4.8 cm.) and about 70 gm. in weight. The shape of the fruit on the whole is oval round. The base of the fruit is roundish with a narrow deep sinus inserting therein a medium sized stalk in a slanting direction. The apical portion of the fruit is roundish having its persistent calyx open and of medium breadth. The skin of the fruit is thin, smooth and whitish green. The pulp just below the skin is greenish. The main pulp is creamy white in colour, soft, sweet and with pleasing flavour. The TSS of its juice is 12.0%. The pulp contains Total sugar 8.10%, Reducing sugar (grape sugar or glucose) 4.50%, acidity 0.32% and 169.50 mg of vitamin-C per 100 gm of pulp. The seeds 285 in number, weighing 2.0 gm in a fruit are loosely filled in the pulp. These are small, light almond coloured, smooth and hard.

The tree grows upright vigorously and reaches a height of 6 - 7 metres. The branches and leaves of the tree are dense, but form an ununiform canopy. Leaves are large (14.5 x 5.0 cm), thin, elliptical, pointed with entire margin. The apex and base of the leaf are acute with a leaf stalk of 0.8 cm length. The front part of the lamina is green and the back portion light green in colour. The variety Waber supreme is a high yielder. One tree yields 920 fruits, which weigh 65 kg.

Bangalore. The fruit is medium-sized (6.9 x 6.4 cm.) and 110 gm in weight. It is oval - round in shape. The base of the fruit is roundish with a deep sinus having a medium-sized stalk fixed therein. The apex is also roundish with an open calyx of medium width. The skin is thin greenish yellow and smooth. Pulp just under the skin is yellowish and other portions of the pulp are creamy, thick, soft, sweet with a pleasing flavour and 11.50% TSS. The pulp further possesses in itself. Total sugar 7.25%, Reducing sugar 3.10% and 182 mg. Vitamin - C per 100 gm. of pulp. Seeds small, light almond coloured, smooth hard, 240 in number in a fruit, which are about 1.7 gm. in weight. The fruits, which are about 1.7 gm. in weight. The fruits remain durable for 3-4 days at room temperature. The tree grows vigorously to a medium height of 4-5 metres. The branches and leaves grow in a dense form. The branches spread all round in a symmetrical way, giving the tree a roundish canopy. Leaves are thin and large-sized (14.48 x 6.88 cm.), oval in shape, pointed with entire margin. The apex and base of the leaf - both form acute angles having its stalk, 9.0 mm in length. The upper surface of lamina of the leaf is dark green and the lower (back) surface light green in colour. The variety Banglore is medium to heavy bearer. About 530 guavas weighing 58.5 kg. may be had from a tree of this variety.

Surkh Goodi : The fruit of this variety is medium-sized (7.25 x 6.0 cm.) roundish and 125 gm in weight. The skin is thin, greenish yellow, smooth and uniform.

The base and apex both are roundish. The basal position of the fruit has a shallow sinus inserting in itself a medium-sized fruit stalk. The apex of the fruit bears an open calyx of medium width. The flesh of the fruit is light red, soft and of sweet flavour taste, but the portion just below the skin is greenish. TSS of the juice is 11.0 %. The pulp makes available total sugar 7.41%, Reducing sugar 4.0%, acidity 0.29% and vitamin - C 179 mg. per 100 gm. pulp. Seeds large, smooth of light almond colour and hard in number which are 2.2 gm in weight.

The tree grows straight upwards vigorously and reaches a height of 5 - 6 metres. The growth of branches and leaves are not dense, but the growth and shape of canopy is formed symmetrical. The leaf is thin, medium sized (12.7 x 5.6 cm.) longish with a short stalk (7.0 mm). The base of the lamina is roundish and the apex is obtuse which is dark green in colour on front surface and light green on back surface. The fruit is durable for 3- 4 days at room temperature. The tree of the variety Surkh Goodi fruits very well. One tree yields 630 fruits which are about 78 kg. in weight.

Anaaka Palle. This variety is a heavy bearer. The fruit medium or small in size (4.1 x 4.3 cm.) roundish or oval and about 38 gm. in weight. The basal part of the fruit a slightly tapering with a shallow sinus, inserting in itself a thin stalk. The apical portion of the fruit is flattish. The outer portion of the fruit is pinkish yellow, slightly rough and protuberated here and there with small red sots scattered densely throughout over there. The skin is thin. The flesh is pinkish in colour, granular with sweet tasteful and pleasant flavour. Whitish yellow small spots also exist on the flesh. The fleswh just below the peel is yellowish. When the fruit is not fully ripe or when it is less ripe, the outer portion is greenish yellow in colour. Seeds are light brownish in colour, small, smooth and 144 nos. in a fruit weighing 0.8 gm.

The tree attains a height of 3 - 4 metres and grows vigorously with dense branches and leaves. The branches spread uniformly all round giving a roundish shape to the canopy. The bark of the tree is brownish in colour and its under portion is greenish white. Leaves are medium sized (12.8 x 4.5 cm.), thin, oval and pointed. The front surface of the lamina is green and the back portion light green in colour, with its apical portion acute and the basal one roundish. The margin of leaf (lamina) is entire and smooth. The leaves on smearing produce turpentine smell.

The fruits remain durable for five days at room temperature. A tree of the variety Anakapalle yields as many as 1,000 guavas.

Hafzi. This is a roundish and smooth fruit variety. The flesh is reddish soft sweet flavoured but comparatively lesser in sweetness.

Selection 8. This variety of guava was selected at Indian Institute of Horticultural Research, Hessargatta Lake, Bangalore from a tree left for open pollination. The fruit is large sized and keeps very well for several days at room temperature. T.S.S. of the fruit juice is 12.5% and the yield per tree is 240.5 kg.

Safed Jaam. A hybrid developed by crossing the variety 'Allahabad safeda' (femal) with koheer (male) at Fruit Research Station, Sangareddy, (Andhra Pradesh). On the whole the fruits were found bigger in size and of good quality. The seeds in the fruit are soft and lesser in number. The yield of the variety 'Safed Jaam' is also good.

Hybrid-1. A variety developed by crossing with 'Allahabad Safeda' at Indian Institute of Horticultural Research Bangalore. In this hybrid, a three year old plant yielded 192 kg guava fruits. The TSS of the pulp was 12.5%.

Striped. The striped variety of guava has been developed in Rewan of Madhya Pradesh. In common language it is named as 'Dhaaridaar'. The fruits, besides other characteristics, have stripes over them and look attractive.

Surkh Chitti Abuwalla. This variety of guava appears to be a selection from the variety Allahabad Safeda. The fruit is roundish of medium-size (7.0 x 6.4 cm) and 100 gm in weight. The base of the fruit is roundish with a deep sinus inserting therein a medium sized fruit stalk. The apical portion of the fruit is roundish with a medium-sized open clayx. The skin is thin greenish yellow, smooth and uniform with some red-coloured dots scattered all round the fruit. The flesh just below the skin is whitish yellow. Remaining part of the flesh of the fruit is white, soft, very sweet with a pleasant taste and flavour, having 13.0% TSS. The pulp of the variety 'Surkh Chitti Abuwalla' also makes available reducing sugar 4.31%, total sugar 8.36%, acidity 0.30% and vitamin-C 152 mg per 100 gm pulp. Seeds which are small, smooth, hard and of light orange colour are loosely distributed in the flesh. These are 220 in number and 1.35 gm in weight.

The tree grows very vigorously and attains a height of 4-5 metres. Its branches are also spreading but these do not form a uniform canopy. The leaf is medium-sized (11.45 x 5.20 cm) longish pointed with a small (6.0 mm long) leaf stalk. The lamina of the leaf is green on the front side and light green on the back side with wavy margin. The apex of the leaf is acute, while the base forms an obtuse angle. Fruits of this variety are durable for 3-4 days at room temperature. Fruiting heavy. One tree yields about 830 fruits, which are 83 kg in weight.

Behat Coconut. It is a selection from the village / town Behat of district Saharanpur (Uttar Pradesh). The fruit of this variety is large-sized, longish round and greenish yellow in colour. The skin is slightly rough. The pulp is white, sourish sweet with a pleasant taste and lavour. The tree has spreading branches, which are densely distributed all round the tree. Behat Coconut variety of guava is also a heavy yielder.

S.E.S. 6550. It is a good variety. The fruit is medium-sized (6.8 x 5.8 cm) and 148 gm in weight. The basal portion of fruit is roundish with a deep sinus inserting therein a medium sized fruit stalk. The apical part of the fruit is also roundish with a broad open calyx. The fruit peel is greenish yellow, thin and smooth. The pulp just below the skin is greenish. The main pulp portion is thick, soft, very sweet with a fine pleasant tasteful flavour. The TSS of the fruit juice is 13.0%. The pulp contains total sugar 8.9%, reducing sugar 5.72%, acidity 0.24% and vitamin-C 151 mg per 100 gm of pulp. Seeds are small, smooth, hard, light almond coloured and 256 in number weighing 1.35 gm.

The tree grows vogorously in an upright direction and the branches are spreading also. The branches, shoots and leaves of the tree remain dense and these give a roundish symmetrical shape to the canopy of the tree. The leaf is large-sized (16.3x6.4 cm) oval with a 0.7 mm leaf stalk. The upper surface of the leaf is green and the lower surface of the leaf is also green. Fruiting of the tree is good. About 565 fruits weighing 78.5 kg may be yielded from a tree.

Nashpati. The fruit of this variety is large-sized long like the shape of a pear. Its size is 8.4 x 6.4 cm and weight about 520 seeds. The fruiting is also less to medium.

Karela. The fruit of the guava variety 'Karela' is large sized long with rough surface, furrowed and ridged in the length. The shape is like a pear or is irregular. It is 8.2 cm in length and 7.5 cm in thickness and 238 gm in weight. The peel of the fruit is thick, green or greenish yellow with small dots here and there. The basal portion of the fruit is tapering and the apical portion forms obtuse angle. The flesh of the fruit is white, granular, sweet, melting with pleasing taste and flavour. Fruiting is less. One fruit contains 330 seeds. Keeping quality of the fruit at room temperature is medium.

Sindh. The fruit of this variety is roundish or oval. The pulp is white or with some reddish yellowish white tinge and soft.

Dharwar. Its fruit is longish oval. Not good in quality.

Nashik. The fruit is of the shape of a bottle. The apical portion is roundish, while the basal portion is narrow like the neck of a bottle. The skin is yellow and rough. Not a good variety.

Dholka. The fruit of the variety Dholka is big-sized. The tree grows vigorously.

Lucknow. The fruit is roundish and the tree is bushy. The pulp is acidic in taste.

In Allahabad district, besides earlier mentioned famous varieties, some local good varieties of guava like KAKARAHA, DANDUA, LALKA and CHAPTA (CHKAIYA) are also grown in village Aboobakarpur and adjoining areas of Sulem Sarai in the fruit (guava) belt area. These are also popular. The variety 'Chapta' is a medium sized flattish fruit and comparatively more sweet.

Guava Varieties of other States. Uttar Pradesh guava varieties are also grown in other states of India. However, other varieties are also grown in those states which are more popular there. Most of these have been collected at fruit Research Station Basti (U.P.) and found promising. These are :

Andhra Pradesh. The popular guava varieties in Andhra Pradesh are 'Red Fleshed', 'Banarsi', 'Smooth Green', 'L-49', 'Allahabad Safeda', 'Chittidar', 'Sefeda' and 'Hafzi'. Besides these, two more varieties - 'Nagpur Seedless' and "Saharanpur Seedless' are also popular there.

Tamil Nadu. 'Nagpur Seedless', 'Hafzi', 'Chittidar', 'Banglore', 'Anaakapalle', 'Banarsi' and 'Smooth Green' are popular in Tamil Nadu.

Maharashtra. The varieties grown in Maharashtra are 'L-49', 'L-24', 'L-46, 'Kothrud', 'Sindh', 'Dharwar',. 'Nashik', 'Dholka', Seedless' and 'Behat Coconut'.

Kerala. The guava varieties 'Behat Coconut' and 'Hafzi' are popular in Keral. These varieties are grown in Dharwar and Nashik also.

West Bengal. All varieties of Uttar Pradesh alongwith a chief local variety 'Barueepur' are grown in West Bengal and these are very popular there.

Bihar. 'Allahabad Sefeda', 'Seedless', Red-fleshed', Chittidar' and a local variety of Bihar 'HAREEJHA' are most popular in Bihar.

Assam. In Assam the guava varieties which are very popular besides those of Uttar Pradesh are 'Madhuri Aam', 'Safri or Piara', 'Soh Priyam' and 'Aam Safri'.

Other Guavas Varieties - Harvesting - 4

According to a news from Lucknow bureau an orchardist - Sri Ram Bilas Maurya of village Bulakihaar, Malihabad (Lucknow) has developed a new variety of guava named as 'Malihabadi Barahmasi Amrood'. Its fruits have pleasant flavour with a fine taste. A large number of plants of this variety are planted in villages Bulakihaar and Mujaasa. Their trees yield fruits having 600-900 gm weight per fruit. Some are even of a kg in weight (United Bharat, Allahabad 21st Dec. 2004). It is felt that the State Government/Department of Horticulture, U.P. should form a committee of horticultural experienced experts. This committee should visit the site at proper time and go in details about the existence of the variety and qualities of fruits and make a wide publicity accordingly among the growers, as and when needed. These should also be multiplied in government gardens. A variety 'Lalit' has also been developed at Central Sub-tropical Horticulutre Institute Lucknow.

Diseases - Many diseases and pests harm the guava crop. However, the most deadly among these is the guava-wilt. No concrete solution could be found out so far, though efforts are being made by various institutions and organisations. BIOVED Research and Communication Centre Allahabad has also taken up this work. Central Sub-tropical Horticultural Institute, Rehmankhera Lucknow has started rejuvenation of trees to get rid of this deadly hazard. The scientists of this Institute have cut guava-wilt affected trees at a height of 1 1/

2 metre in Kaushambi and Allahabad districts and claim that guava-wilt will be over and the trees will become healthy (United Bharat Allahabad, 20th May 2004, and United Bharat 31st May 2004 page 4). Anyway, if this practice comes successful, it will be a great achievement for the state as well as the country. The varieties 'Sardar Guava' and 'Seedless' show resistance towards guava-wilt (Amrood ki Baghwani, 1988, 105 Zero Road, Allahabad).

Besides, so many sweet and delicious varieties of guava, there are some sour varities also, which have their own importance. These may specially be utilized in making ready to serve drinks, syrups, squashes, jams, jellies, preserves, chutney and pickles. These sour variety may not be taken fresh, but may very well be utilized as salad.

Patil. This sour variety of guava is rich in vitamin-C, acidity and pectin. The flesh is pink in colour.

Supreme. The 'Supreme' sour variety of guava has a white coloured pulp. This is rich in acidity, vitamin-C and pectin.

Florida Seedling. This is a pink-fleshed sour variety of guava, which is rich in vitamin-C, pectin and acid.

White Fleshed Sour. This sour guava variety is white fleshed and is rich in acidity, pectin and vitamin-C.

Spear Acid. The flesh of this sour variety of guava (spear acid) is pink in colour. This is rich in acidity, vitamin-C and pectin.

Arica Florida. The flesh of this sour variety of guava is reddish and rich in vitamin-C and other contents like other varieties.

Webber X Supreme

The variety was had through crossing the variety 'Webber' by 'Supreme' and is pink-fleshed and sour. This is rich in pectin, vitamin-C and acidity.

Portugal, Seed Rolfs, Seedless triploid 'Ruby', 'Supreme x Ruby', 'Barafkhana', 'Bhadri Sebia', 'Chakiya Mahmood Nagar', Hybrid Supreme' and 'Ishaqwala' are also some other common guava varieties for eating fresh.

The genus Psidium, besides the species guajava (Psidium guava - the common guava) has several other species also, used in various purposes. Psidium cattleianum, P. cattleianum var lucidum, P. guineense, P. pumilum (China guava), P. cujavillis, P. chinensis (red fleshed), P. chinensis (white fleshed), P. corecium, P. mole, P. caudatum, P. pedicilatum, P. resticatum and P. polycarpum are chief of these.

Psidium guineense is known as guinea guava or Brazillian guava. Its fruits though resemble the common guava, are not of good quality. The branchlets and shoots are round unlike those of common guava, which are 4-angled and cross-sections of which are square in shape.

Psidium cattleianum also known as strawberry guava or cattley guava is the most important species after the common guava. It grows in the form of a shrub or bush having small green glossy thick ornamental leaves. The fruits are also small (approx. 3.0 cm thick) and purplish. The fruits are generally used in Jelly making or eaten fresh. The whole plant is very ornamental. Other species are used as root stocks for budding or grafting or for certain other purpose. Among several trials done in Basti P. catlleianum has been found to be most outstanding. The variety Allahabad Safeda was better in growth and yield on this stock. However, fruits of better quality were recorded on the root stock of P. pumilum. Seeds were much reduced on root stock of 'Seedless guava'. All these root stocks along with those of 'P. cujavillis' and 'Florida seedling' were found wilt-resistant except 'Allahabad Safeda', which shows susceptibility towards guava-wilt disease. Trials conducted at Allahabad resulted in excellent quality 'Allahabad Safeda' fruits on P. pumilum root stock, which was also wilt resistant.

To have a pleasing taste and flavour of marvelous guavas while eating, it is important that fruits should be harvested at suitable time at proper stage. The harvested fruits should also be properly handled afterwards. From flowering to ripening the guava fruits take about five months. When fruits set, these are dark green hard and very small. These go on developing in growth and size. The main crop of guava is obtained during winters, which goes on up to March. On ripening the skin of the fruit attains a yellowish tinge. It also attains softness. However, harvesting should be done at such a stage that the fruits have attained yellowish tinge but these are still hard and not soft. This stage of fruits will help in transporting from one place to the other. This will be the proper stage of picking for export purposes. Also fully ripe fruits if picked up should immediately be disposed off in local mandi for eating fresh or turning them in various guava products as damage starts in fruits just after four days.

Picking should be done by standing on stool ladder or by climbing on the tree where possible. Picking may also be done through logs in netted bags fixed at the top of the log. Though the tree starts yielding fruits from the third year, satisfactory production may be had in 5-6 years age of the tree. One such tree may yield 1000 to 2000 fruits, weighing 200 to 250 kg (2 - 2 ½ quintals). As such about 400 quintals of guavas may be had from an orchard of one hectare land. If the fruits are to be stored for 3-4 days according to variety, these should be stored at a cool and airy place. If stored in cold storage it should be stored at 11.11°C (52°F) for a week, but after taking out from cold storage, fruit should be disposed off soon.

For packing guava fruits for sending outside, first of all sorting and grading of fruits should be done. All bruised, cut, rotten, and diseased fruits should be taken out from the lot of fruits and then the remaining one should be graded into small, medium and large size, so that prices of these may be easily had accordingly. The fruits after grading should be packed in pine-wood boxes or baskets. Paper shavings should first be placed inside at bottom of packing boxes. Each fruits should then be wrapped in paper and then placed in the packing box. The upper surface of the layer of fruits should also be covered with paper shavings. The packing boxes should contain at the most 10-20 kg fruits according to the packing box. The wooden boxes are closed by wooden pieces and therefore these may easily be handled if these are piled up one over the other. However, there are problems in safety of fruits, if packed in baskets. In such cases the upper portion of the basket is sewn from side after covering with chatti and then hardening sides, bottom and top portions of basket with wooden sheets by placing and fixing these in such a way that the baskets may be lifted and placed here and there without any damage to fruit. As such fruits inside the basket remain safe. After packing the fruits the packages are transported to the required places for sale.

Maturity Standard in Guava

Guava (Psidium guajava L.) fruits are highly perishable. After harvest, fruits remain durable hardly for 3- 4 days at room temperature. On maturity, the guava fruits just start yellowing, but still hard. This is the proper stage for harvesting. At this stage, fruits are fit for transport and export. If such fruits are left on tree, these start softening, which further continue yellowing and ripening. Fully ripe fruits if picked, should immediately be disposed off in local market for fresh consumption. Such guava fruits may also be preserved as tasty jellies, jams, cheese and toffees. Picking of fruits should be done either by climbing on tree or stool-ladder. Picking may also be done by means of harvesters. However, under all circumstances, there should be no injury or bruising in fruits. These also should not drop on ground. Very soft guavas should be eaten soon according to requirements. Such fruits should not be stored. If these are left for 7 - 8 days at room temperature, there are greater chances of their being poisonous.

"Poster paper presented for Public Awareness in First Indian Horticulture Congress during 6th to 9th November 2004, in IARI Campus, New Delhi."

6

Aonla

Aonla-A Nutritious Horticultural Produce

Aonla is an Indian sumtuous fruit. It has so many such medicinal qualities that it may more or less be called a medicine. In English it is called Indian Gooseberry, Emblic, My robalan or Malacca, Tree but it is familiar among the public by its common Hindi name 'AONLA'. It is also known as Amla, Aunra and Aurha. In Sanskrit aonla is named as Aamlaka, Dhaatriphal, Pancharasa, Amritphal, Shreephal, Aamlaki, Vayastha and Trishyaphala. In Bengal, aonla is known as Aamlaki, Aamro, Amla, Aamla and Ambolta. Its Marathi name is Aanwali, Aanwalkaathi, Aanwala, Aawali, Kaathi, Aanwal, Oval kaori, Aawale and Aawali. Its Gujarati name is Aanwala, Aamla, Aamli and Aamlanu Jhaarh. In Arabi, aonla is called as Aamalaj while its Persian name is Aamlah, Aamlaya. Aamlajaye and Anwala. Being of the family Euphorbiaceae, it is botanically known as Emblica officinalis, Gearth. Its earlier botanical name is Phyllanthus emblica, L.

The most important good quality of this horticultural produce, i.e. Aonla fruit is that it is extremely rich in vitamin-C. This is only vitamin-C, which is required in much more amount in everyday's human diet as compared to requirements of all other vitamins. It is richest in vitamin-C among all the commonly grown and used fruits. One hundred gm. of aonla pulp makes available 600 - 750 mg. of vitamin-C, though two fruits. Barbedos cherry and seabuckthorn are richer than aonla, but actually these are not in common use. By regular use of aonla fruit, one may get rid of diseases developed from vitamin-C deficiency. Availability of vitamin-C in aonla has been reported even upto the extent of 1000 mg. per 100 gm. of aonla pulp (UNI Lucknow, 24th February 2000, N.I.P. Alld. 25th February 2000).

Again, an amount of vitamin-C as high as 1800 mg. and further even 2000-3500 mg. per 100 gm. pulp have been reported in some wild growing aonla fruits ('Innovative approaches in aonla processing' CISH, LKO; 'Khaadya prasanskaran udyog vikas men aonla prajaatiyon kee upyogita' N.D.U. Agri. and Tech. Faizabad - Brochure issued on 'Aonla evam prasanskrit utpaadon kaa viparan/ niryaat vishayak sangoshthi, 27th January 2005, Hotel, Kaanha Shyam, Allahabad, Govt. of U.P.). Fresh aonla juice possesses 20 times more of vitamin-C than in that of fresh orange. Generally 200 mg. of synthetic vitamin-C, which is used by people, is equal to only 8.7 mg. of naturally available vitamin-C complex in aonla fruit (INFA, New Delhi, 22nd January 1997. Northern India Patrika, Allahabad, 23 January 1997, 04).

Aonla fruit is so nutritious that one may remain disease free if it is consumed daily. Even an ordinary every day aonla consumer may feel vigour and immunity to fight with many types of diseases. The practice of consumption of Aonla fruit daily may bring one's youthfulness back. In ancient period Rishi Chyavan, whose Ashram was said to be situated somewhere near the border of Pratapgarh and Sultanpur districts. (U.P.), had regained his vigour and youth (Kaya - Kalp) by regular use of aonla fruit and its medicinal produce Chyavanprash'. This was Rishi Chyavan, who prepared this useful medicine (Chyavanprash). Late Pt. Madan Mohan Malviya had also utilized aonla fruits in his old age, who later on had regained his vigour (Kaya Kalp). Even in the preparation of the useful medicine. 'Triphala' for the three fruits of (1) Aonla, (2) Yellow myrobalan or Chebulic myrobalan i.e. 'Harara' (Terminalia chebula Retz-family Combretaceae) and (3) Belleric myrobalan or Bastard myrobalan i.e. 'Bahera' of 'Vibhitaka' (Terminalia bellirica Roxb. Syn. Myrobolanus bellirica Gaertn. - family Combretaceae), the main roll is of AONLA. Besides these two medicines several other medicines and cosmetics are prepared from aonla. Raw, fruit of aonla is laxative, diuretic and antiscorbutic. In dried form it is medicinally used in diarrhoea and dysentary. Phyllembin is found in Aonla pulp to the extent of 6.3%. It has been found to have mild depressant action on central nervous system. Aonla fruits have been reported to have antibiotic activity against a wide variety of microorganisms. It is also considered as a good liver tonic (Dictionary of Economic Plants in India, ICAR, New Delhi 1983).

Besides vitamin-C, an aonla fruit makes available moisture 81.2%, protein 0.5%, Carbohydrate 14.1%, Calcium 0.05%, phosphorus 0.02%, Fat 0.1% and Fibre 3.4%. Again, 100 gm aonla fruit pulp possesses 1.2 mg. Iron, 59 I.U. (International Unit) Vitamin-A, 30 mg. Vitamin B-1 (Thiamine), 0.2 mg. Nicotinic acid (Niacin) trace of Vitamin-E and 59 calories of heat (calorific value). Fruits also-contain Galic acid 5.0%, Tannin 28% in pulp and 21% in fruit peels. Aonla seeds also yield 16% oil. Naturally available Agalic acid and Galic acid in the pulp are antioxidants. Dried aonlas are equally good. Dry aonla fruits possess in themselves Moisture 1.83%. Unripe dried aonla pulp posesses 35% tannic acid. In ripe aonla dried pulp the availability of tannic acid is reduced. It has Ether extract 11.3% which includes also Galic acid. Further, dry aonla pulp makes available Alcohol extract as 36.10% including sugar and tannic acid. In addition to these, dry aonla pulpcontains gum 13.74%, Albumin 13.08%, mineral salts 4.12% and total solids 17.80. Aonla leaves also possess tannic acid to the extent of 18.0%. Inspite of various constituents in an Aonla fruit it is dominated by the acidity and astringency present in its juice. Fruits like tamarind, unripe mango and karonda etc. which are sour and acidic, increase acidity in the body after these are consumed. Even then Aonla being sour fruit, instead of increasing, it controls the acidity. Similarly, the acidic fruit wood apple (limonia acidissima or Feronia Iimonia - Kaitha) encourages constipation but Aonla acts against constipation. The durability of sourness (acid affect) alongwith astringen. (tannin affect) are mainly due to the presence of Polyphenols or Leuco Anthocy-nins in Aonla fruit. That is why vitamin-C and other nutritious elements in aonla do not spoil and remain preserved even after boiling or drying the fruit, while in ordinary course vitamin-C is spoiled by heating. The possibilities of spoilage of vitamin-C are also removed by dipping the aonla fruit in boiling water for 2-3 minutes and then dipping in a concentrated salt solution. Again, besides availability of Polyphenols and Leuco Anthocynins, the importance of vitamin-C in aonla fruit is further increased also due to the presence of Bioflava-noids in the fruit.

Aonla- A Nutritious Horticultural Produce

Aonla being so much valuable, has been considered as a very pious tree, which is also worshiped in India. It has now become a very important fruit of the whole world. Its tree is of medium size with ash coloured trunk and branches. The aonla tree sheds its leaves for some time in January-February and resprouts in the first week of March. Leaves are simple but appear like leaflets arranged on the midrib of a compound leaf. Actually that is not midrib but a branchlet coming out of a branch, which bears whitish flowers, small leaves and then fruits in due course of time. The fruit on an average is approximately roundish to flattish, greenish to whitish, about 4.5 cm. in length, breadth and thickness and about 50 gm in weight. The aonla fruit is longitudinally divided into six or sometimes 7-8 segments, through thin whitish, smooth or furrowed stripes. The fruit further holds in itself tightly a hard, sharp-ridged stone. On drying the ripe fruit, first the pulp of the fruit dries up and cracks away into its segments, releasing the stone away or sometimes partially holding it.

The stone later on dries up, cracks, bursts and releases away 6-8 dark brownish coloured seeds which are about 9.0 mm in length and 4.5 mm. in breadth. Aonla tree's wood, bark, leaves, flowers, fruits, seeds, roots - all parts are either of medicinal and industrial importance or of domestic and other importance.

About the evolution of Aonla tree, there are many Pauranic stories. According to one story in ancient times, when the whole universe was perished, Brammha Ji had whole-heartedly devoted himself in deep meditation of God.

During that very period Brammha Ji was so much impressed in affection of God that a drop of affectionate tears dropped on the ground from his eyes. This drop immediately turned into and appeared, there as a huge tree. All the deitees and Devotees were wonder struck after seeing this tree. In the mean time, a message was announced from God like this. 'This is an aonla tree and is the best of all trees and is very much loving to God.' Another such story is also there. Lakchmi Ji and Paarvati Ji were going on pilgrimage. In the way Paarvati Ji expressed her views to Lakchmi Ji that, she wanted to worship God with some self- imagined new liquid. Lakchmi Ji also expressed her views to Paarvati Ji that she wanted to worship Trilochan Mahadeo by some new liquid. After this shining clear tears dropped on the ground separately from the eyes of both the deities. From this very liquid, an Aonla tree appeared on the ground in the month of Magh (some time in January - February) on Ekaadashi of Shukla Pakch. Then by seeing the Aonla tree all saints and deities were full of joy. From that very time, the Aonla tree was included among pious trees/plants like Bael (Aegle marmelos) and Tulsi (Occimun sp.) and is worshiped. Now Hindu ladies and gents pay their respects to the tree with flowers and garlands every year on Ekadashi of Shukla Pakcha in the month of Magh. With this belief and respect Hindu families have their meals as prasaad under the Aonla tree on Chaturdashi of Shukla Pakcha in the month of Kartik every year and wish for their good luck.

Expansion of Varieties and Area

From the last several decades only BANARSI AONLA was known to people, as this was the only Aonla grown in aonla orchards of Banaras (Varanasi) from ancient times. That is why this has been named as Banarsi aonla. It is a very famous variety and the best for reparing preserves (morabba). Its fruits are translucent, fibreless, white shining, very beautiful, smooth and round like small ball. The size of fruit is 4.6 x 4.7 cm, which is 70 gm. in weight. The acidity in the fruit as 2.34%, T.S.S. 13.0% and the amount of vitamin-C in the pulp is 625.21 mg. per 100 gm. pulp. Shelf-life of fruit is 10 days but a shy bearer. The tree of Banarsi aonla grows high and the branches are spreading. Some aonla orchards were also planted earlier in Pratapgarh fort Uttar Pradesh in an area of about 1.2 hectare land according to available information. Most probably plants of this orchard were also brought from Varanasi and these might be some selections or so. However, these plants were grown there as a special variety. Since these grew in the fort of Raaja Sahab of Pratapgarh, this variety was named as 'FORT', 'QILA'or 'RAJBAGH'. The branches of its trees are drooping and, therefore, this was also called as 'HAATHIJHOOL'. This variety has also been named as, 'FRANCIS'. The fruit of the variety Qila is large-sized, round, yellowish green, translucent with small light whitish dots all over the body and some, blackish tinge on the basal side. Its size and weight are 4.44 x 5.14 cm and about 66 gm. respectively. Fruiting and keeping quality good. Its fruits are also suitable for making preserves. A resident of village Gonde (6 km away from Pratapgarh on Allahabad - Faizabad Road - towards Faizabad). Sri Jagatpal Singh brought two aonla plants from Pratapgarh fort and planted in his village sometime in the year 1932 and then made developments in this direction up to the year 1936.

Gradually, the area in this village was increased to six hactares by the above orchardist. The varieties included in his aonla orchard by then were 'Qila', 'Red tinged' and 'Chakiya'.

After Sri Jagatpal Singh, his son Sri Ram Shiroman Singh was looking after these aonla orchards which were fruiting very well. He expanded his aonla orchards to the area of 20 hectares of land during 1955 to 1960, whom the author had an occasion to meet and have a round of his orchard with him. Now aonla orchards of Gonde village are looked after by his son Sri Tej Bahadur Singh with whom also the author had a chance to discuss about aonla orchards. These orchards are being looked after by his brother Sri Ramesh Bahadur Singh also. The variety - CHAKAIYA is also a gift of Pratapgarh. It is also named as 'GOOLARAHIYA; as it is more or less of the shape of a 'cluster fig.' goolar (Ficus glomerata syn. F. Goolierea) fruit. The fruit of CHAKAIYA' is green shining smooth, flattish, translucent, more or less fibreless good for 'morabba' making. The apical portion of the fruit is slightly roundish and the basal porton is flat. It is 4.3 x 4.95 cm. in size and 36.43 gm. in weight. This variety fruits in bunches and is a heavy bearer. The tree grows upwards. Two more varieties 'Madhupur Conical' and 'Madhupur Turbid dark green' were found out by the author in village Madhupur in the orchard of Th. Adya Prasad Singh during the years 1956 to 1958.

The fruit of 'Madhupur Conical' variety of aonla is conical at the apex and roundish at base (like the shape of a 'lattu'). It is whitish light green in colour, 5.08 x 4.69 cm in size and 58.30 gm in weight, smooth, shining, translucent with less fibre. Keeping quality good. Good for preparing preserves.

Its shelf life is fifteen days (some outstanding varieties of Aonla: 'Bhadri Abhinandan Granth Special Issue of Gardening', U.P. Fruit Development Board, Lucknow, 1969, pp.11-15). The fruits of Turbid Dark Green' is dark green opaque and 3.04 x 3.55 cm. in size and 43.72 gm in weight. The apical part is roundish and basal portion is roundish flattish. with less fiblire in the fruit.

The tree growns-high with spreading branches. It is a shy bearer. Fruits make tasteful preserves.

Aonla A Nutritious Horticultural Produce

Further Varieties and Expansion in Area —While aonla growing was progressing in Pratapgarh fort and in villages Gonda and Madhupur, these drew the attention of a very pretical and progressive orchardist of village Pathatia-(Post Gaura, district Pratapgarh) - Sri Mahabal Singh. He made up his mind to collect improved varieties of aonla and plant them as orchards in his village. He collected varieties 'Banarsi', 'Qila' and 'Chakaiya' in the year 1950 and planted an aonla orchard of 1.2 hectares, which was later extended to an area of 2.0 hectares. In the mean time Sri Mahabal Singh alongwith his grand son Sri Yashwant Singh who studied and worked hard propagated plants also. As such in his limited land he established his Aonla orchards of 4.4 hectares (11 acres) in all. Sri Mahabal Singh later expressed his views to the author to establish an aonla nursery, so that neighbouring people may also be benefitted by establishing their aonla orchards. It was a good idea and an aonla nursery was established in village Pathatia as 'Yashwant Nursery' which was got registered through the Department of Horticulture by the U.P. Fruit Development Board, Lucknow. As a result of their studies Sri Mahabal Singh also developed two improved aonla varieties - 'KANCHAN' and 'KRISHNA'. As narrated Sri Mahabal Singh to author, a grower Sri Ashok of village Ramapur near the village Pathatia) planted in his orchard a propagated (Kalmi) plant of the variety 'Qila' brought from the village Gonde. During growth and cultural operations the scion portion of the graft got broken and separated from the joint of stock and scion. This resulted into vigorous growth of the stock (seedling) portion which afterwards became a tree and started fruiting. When Sri Mahabal Singh, visited there, he liked the capacity of fruiting of the tree and the quality of its fruits very much. Therefore, he brought bud sticks from that tree and prepared many budded plants in his nursery. Then in the year 1970, he established Aonla orchard from these plants and when trees came to fruiting, this variety was named after the late daughter of his grandson Yashwant Singh as 'KANCHAN'.

The fruit of 'KANCHAN' is medium - sized, longish round, 3.3 x 3.2 cm in size, 20 gm in weight and light dirty green in colour with a translucent body. The six segments of the fruit are longitudinally divided by six clear white stripes. The sinus of the apex is very narrow but shallow and that of the base is slightly narrow and shallow. Durability of the fruit is good. Fruiting good, a regular bearer. Also good for making preserves. The tree grows high but branches are spreading. Narendra Deo University of Agriculture and Technology, Faizabad has taken up this variety in their collections and have named it as 'NARENDRA AONLA-4'. As regards the origin of the variety 'KRISHNA', to which N. D. University of Agriculture and Technology, Faizabad gave the name of 'NARENDRA AONLA-5', Sri Mahabal Singh further explained to the author that an orchardist Sri Narsingh Bahadur Singh of village Koyam, which as just by the side of his village Pathatia had an inarched (Bhent Kalam) plant of the variety a 'Chaikya' from his nursery in 1970 and planted in his orchard. In due course of time sprouts from the scion as well as stock got developed and branches of both started fruiting. The scion was 'Chakaiya', which was grafted on the seedling stock of 'Banarsi' Aonla. On fruiting, it was found that the fruits borne on branches off stock portion appeared to be good and were of large size. The fruiting was also heavy, while fruits borne on scion portion were smaller. In the mean time the branches from the root stock (Banarsi seedling) grew so vigorously that these dominated over growth of scion portion. Ultimately the scion portion dried up and the tree developed and flourished only from the branches of stock portion.

Mahabal Singh brought bud sticks from this tree and multiplied plants by budding and also planted orchard. On fruiting he named this variety as 'KRISHNA' after the name of his late daughter-in-law. The fruit of the variety; 'KRISHNA (NARENDRA AONLA-5) is medium to iange (4.6 x 4.7 cm) in size and 50 gm in weight. The shape of the fruits is flattish round and white with greenish yellow; tinge in colour. It is smooth shining and translucent. On full ripening the fruit attains reddish tinge near 6-8 longitudinal white stripes. The apical portion of the fruit is a bit conical or slopy and basal portion roundish. The upper portion of every segment of the fruit is slightly protuberated. The sinus of the apex of the fruit is very narrow of medium depth, while the basal sinus is of medium depth, medium width and round. Keeping quality very good. The fruit is nearly fibreless and excellent for preparing preserves. The are large sized and branches spreading. Fruiting heavy and a regular bearer.

NAREND R AONL A-7: This variety is locally named in Pratapgarh as 'NADIYA-KE-PAAR'. This is said to be selected from a seedling plant of the variety Fancis (Qila) by N.D. University of Agriculture and Technology, Faizabad. The fruit is medium to large in size and 40 to 50 gm in weight. Its shape is longish round. The body of the fruit is light yellowish; smooth and approximately with no fibre, free from necrosis disease. The branches of the tree grow upwards. Fruiting regular and very heavy. NARENDRA AONLA-10' has selected in Balwant Rajput college, Agra and was named as 'BALWANT AONLA' and is supposed to be used place of 'Banarsi' aonla. N. D. University has collected this variety and named as 'NARENDRA AONLA-10'. Besides above, 'Red tinged', 'Oval', 'Deshi', 'Narendra-6' (selection from Chakaiya) and Deshi varieties of aonla are also there. Small varieties also grow in forests, which may be improved with good varieties by top working. Again many varieties have been named by local nurserymen mostly of Pratapgarh, like 'Nai Jamuna, Amrit Bahar Chakaiya'. Rajendra Bahar Chakaiya', 'Alok Bahar', 'Saurabh Banarsi', 'Mangal Bahar Chakaiya', 'Shyam Bahar', 'Awadh Bahar' and others. Gujarat-1 variety of aonla has been developed in Gujarat. Experiments on Post Harvest Technology on aonla have been carried on in Horticulture Department of B.A. College of Agriculture Gujarat Agriculture

University, Anand Kheda and Anand districts of Gujarat have been mentioned as excellent pockets for aonla cultivation (National workshop on Post Harvest Management of Horticultural Produce Feb. 7-8, 2002, National Productivity Council Chandigarh, p. 201). Another variety 'GANGA BANARSI' has also been developed from village 'Gonde' of Pratapgarh (U.P.). Its fruits are large sized, milky in colour and bear in branches. These are more or less fibreless and are saved from fruit - drop.

Bears Heavily

Some analysis on various aspects of some aonla varieties was earlier done at Fruit Research Station, Basti. In 'Banarsi' aonla fruit its T.S.S. was 13.0%, Acidity 2.34%, Total Sugar 8.0%, Reducing Sugar 1.045%, Non-reducing Sugar 6.607%. Ratio between seed and pulp 1:21, presence of vitamin-C per 100 gm pulp 625.21 mg. These contents were available in the variety 'Fancis' as 11.5%, 2.52%, 7.0%, 4.085%, 3.05%, 1:22 and 583.00 mg in the same order. Similarly Chakaiya possessed 9.0%, 2.17%, 9.6%, 1.995%, 7.225%, 1:17 and 645.00 mg. 'Bansi Red tinged aonla made available 15.0% T.S.S., 2.32% acidity, 8.2 % total sugar, 1.382% reducing sugar, 6.77%, non-reducing sugar, 1:17 ratio between seed and pulp and 665 mg vitamin-C, while 'Deshi' aonla had 15.2%, 2.58%, 7.1%, 1.035%, 5.761%, 1.15. Ratio and 450 mg vitamin-C in the same order (Aonla aur uski Baghwa, Himanchal Pustak Bhandar, Gandhinagar, Delhi, 2002, 1152). Analysis of varieties has been done also at Narendra Deo University of Agriculture and Technology, Faizabad (UP.) on percentage of pulp, seed and fibre in variety 'Banarsi' as 34.10, 4 .5; 1.4; 'Krishna'(ND-5) 93.30, 5.3, 1.4; Chhakaiya 93.80, 4.2, 2.0; 'Kanchan (ND-4) 91.30, 7.2, 1.5 and ND-6 possesses 94.80, 4.4, 0.8; while Narendra Aonla-7 has pulp 93.30%, seed 3.5% and Fibre 1.2%. As regards presence of fibre in Chakaiya to its maximum as 2.0%, it is rather confusing as Chakaiya is approximately a fibreless variety from the very beginning of its appearance in Pratapgarh. It also fruits heavily and is good for making preserves. In another analysis there, the Banarsi variety made available. Total Soluble Solids 13.30%, Acidity 2.0%, Pectin 2.5%. Total Mineral Salt 0.8%, Phenolic Matter 3.1%, Vitamin-A 10.31.U. (International Unit) and Vitamin-C 826.4 mg per 100 gm pulp. In the same order 'Krishna' had 14.30, 2.4, 2.3, 0.40, 2.0%, 16.71 I.U. and 783.8 mg Vitamin-C. On the other hand likewise 'Chakaiya' possessed 10.00, 2.4, 3.40, 0.54,12.7%, 65.3 I.U. and 789.5 mg. Kanchan made available 11.30,1.6, 2.40, 0.60, 3.0, 24.5 IU and 711.4 mg vitamin-C per 100 gm pulp, whereas ND-6 had 11.80. 1.8, 2.7, 0.60, 2.8%, 61.2 I.U, and 788.1 mg. Narendra Aonla 7 possessed 10.80% T.S.S., 2.1% acidity. 2.4% pectin, total minerals 0.56 phenolic matter 2.8% and vitamin-A 50.00 I.U. and Vitamin C 767.2; mg per 100 gm pulp (Khaadya Prasanskaran Udyog Vikas men Aonla Prajaatiyon Kee Upyogita, Udyan Vigyan Vibhag, N D University of Agriculture and Technology, Faizabad - Brochure issued on 'Aonla evam prasanskrit utpaadon kaa viparan/niryat' Vishayak Sangoshthi, 27 January 2005, Hotel Kaanha Shyam, Allahabad Govt. UP.). Aonla is now being grown in Myanmar, Sri Lanka, China, Siam, East Indies etc. In India, it is grown in Rajasthan, Bihar, Madhya Pradesh, Himachal Pradesh, Jammu and Kashmir, Maharashtra, Punjab, Bengal. Haryana, Karnataka, Tamil Nadu, Andhra Pradesh, Gujarat, Uttaranchal and Uttar Pradesh. Aonia plants are also found naturally growing scattered or in groups. An hill-slopes, or in valleys of hills of Kumaon, Garhwal, Shivalik, Jhansi and Vindhyachal. However the maximum area is in Uttar Pradesh. In the year 1956-58, the area under aonla in Uttar Pradesh was 48 hectare (120 acres). Out of these the area in Pratapgarh was estimated as 18 hectare (45 acres) as surveyed by the author.

Aonla- A Nutritious Horticultural Produce - III

Further Extention in Area

In Uttar Pradesh aonlas are now grown in Pratapgarh, Varanasi, Allahabad, Faizabad, Sultanpur, Gonda, Basti, Gorakhpur, Lucknow, Kanpur, Agra, Saharanpur, Banda, Hamirpur, Jalon, Fatehpur, Etawa, Aligarh, Bareilly, Rae Bareilly, Mathura and other districts also. By and by the area under Aonla went on increasing in Pratapgarh, Uttar Pradesh and India. During 1956-58 the area covered in Pratapgarh was about 40% of the whole area in U.P. Generally the area under aonla in Uttar Pradesh was estimated on the basis of that covered in Pratapgarh. In recent few years knowing its utility and utilization of wastelands by planting thereon its orchards and earning handsome profit in plantation of its orchards, the area under aonla spread with a very fast speed. Now it has been estimated that out of the total production of aonla in the country, 85% production is only from Pratapgarh. Chief pockets of which are in village Gonda. In the year 2000, the area under aonla was estimated to be above 430 hectare in U.P. and in the whole country as 11,750 hectare ('Aonla aur uski Baghwani', Himanchal Pustak Bhandar, Gandhinagar, Delhi, 2002, 1-152).

Currently C.I.S.H. Lucknow has reported a very rapid surprising increase in its area, which raised to 60,000 hectares in India with a production of 2.25 lakh tonnes of fruits, while in Uttar Pradesh the covered area has been reported as 15,750 ha, producing thereby 63000 tonnes of aonla. According to another report there, the area covered in the country is 49,620 ha with the production of 1,50,500 tonnes of aonla fruits. On the other hand the Department of Horticulture Uttar Pradesh, Lucknow has estimated total area under aonla as 19,000 ha for Uttar Pradesh, with a production of 1,90,000 tonnes of fruits, the productivity being 7.9 tonnes per ha (Organic Aonla - a potential industrial commodity; Aonla kee aadhunik udyan vikaas kchetra men aonla utpaadan kee vartaman sthiti Brochure issued on 'Aonla evam prasanskrit utpaadon ka viparan/niryat' Vishayak Sangoshthi, 27th January 2005, Hotel Kaanha Shyam,

Allahabad, Govt. U.P). Srikant S. Mehta Salem (Tamil Nadu) has estimated the area under aonla in Andhra Pradesh, Karnataka, Tamil Nadu, Haryana, Punjab and Himachal Pradesh between 25,000 to 50,000 ha. On the other hand Tamil Nadu Govt. has announced an ambitious wasteland development programme, under which 20 lakh ha (50 lakh acres) of wastelands will be converted into productive lands within a period of 5 years. Aonla has been identified, as an important crop to play a dominent role in this programme (A case study on development of Aonla in Tamil Nadu - "Approaches for sustainable development of Horticulture" pp. 160-162". Personal communication 12th February 2005). As such the chances for development of this India's gift are very bright.

Soil and Climate

Aonla can stand very well in diverse soil and climatic conditions. Its plants are very hardy and can tolerate various adverse hardy situations. Aonla grows in alkaline, acidic, saline, degraded soils, also in banjar and even in usar having their pH as 9.5. It can also grow well in other types of soils and lands like some stony, dry soil, ravines, unfertile soil and other wastelands. It also grows in loam, sandy loam, clayey, heavy and light soils. In Chhattishgarh', about 7.5 lakh hectares of such lands are available in which aonla can do very well. Soils of these lands' consist of 50-60% stones, 30% fine sand and 5% each of clayey and river soils. These soil are called red laterite maata soil and has been found quite suitable for aonla growing, as found out in Gandhi Agricultural University, Raipur, Chhattisgarh. However, for a planned Aonla orcharding, well-drained some fertile loam or sandy loam soil is best suited. 'Actually aonla is a fruit of sub-tropical climate. However the climate for aonla varies from hot tropical plains to humid mid elevation hills and their slopes as referred, earlier. It is also grown in arid and sub-arid areas and coastal warm areas. Frost and extreme heat cold and hot wind make no harm to aonla trees and crop. It grows well up to an elevation of 1,200 metres. Aonla tree can bear the minimum temperature of freezing point and a maximum of 46^{0}C. It is an ever green tree but for a short period it sheds its leaves, leaving only branches like a deciduous tree. Shedding of leaves start, from the month of February and the tree becomes completely leaves-free by the end of March. During this process with the rise of temperature, sprouting also starts in the tree from the end of February and then flowers also appear.

PROPAGATION

Propagation of aonla plants are done by sexual (seeds) or asexual (vegetative) means. Plants grown by seeds do not bear true to type fruits, while trees prepared by vegetative means like grafting, budding, cutting or goottee etc. of a particular variety from a particular tree bear fruits just like their mother-trees bear.

Raising Seedlings

For establishing a nursery of seedling or vegetatively propagated plants, raising of seedlings is very important. These seedlings are utilized as root stock for grafting or budding and planting elsewhere. Ripe fruit of aonla (better if of Deshi varieties) are spread on neat and clean floor in the month of January. When these dry up and seed-stones crack, seeds are collected.

These seeds are dropped in a bucket full of water. Those seeds which float on surface of water are removed and those settled in bottom are taken out and dried in shade. These healthy seeds are then treated with Zinc-Manganese carbamate one kg of seed and 3 gm of ZMC. On the other hand, seed beds of the size 3.1 metre should be prepared in well manured and pulverizerd soil. For this 2-3 diggings of the soil should be done to a depth of 15-20 cm. Soil of each such bed should be mixed with 40 kg of cow dung manure and leaf-mould. When the seed bed is finally prepared, it should be raised, to 15 cm above soil surface, so that water may not stagnate in the bed. The soil of seed bed should also be treated to save young growing plants from damping off. For treating the soil a mixture should be prepared by dissolving 3 gm Zinc Manganese Carbamate in one litre of water and sprayed on the soil. Now seeds may be sown in rows prepared at the distance of 15 cm from each other in the breadth of the seed bed 4-5 cm deep in soil. Before sowing one must be sure that there is sufficient moisture in soil for germination. After sowing the soil should be smoothened and lightly pressed. Sowing of seed may be done in February to April. Seeds germinate within 10 to 15 days of sowing. After germination another spraying of ZMC should be done. To save plants from hot sun small light thatches should be prepared above the seed bed. From time to time these should be watered with a watering can having a rose, as and when needed. When aonla seedlings are 8-10 cm high, these should be transplanted in already properly prepared beds at the distance of 30-20 cm. For budding or utilizing grafting. The plants may also be transplanted in polythene bags filled with soil and manure. Seeds may also be sown in polythene bags and then budded or grafted at the proper time.

Aonla - A Nutritious Horticultural Produce- 5

Budding

For budding, one year old seedling of aonla is utilized as root stock. On the other hand, the bud with bark is taken out from the scion stick of the mother plant of a desired variety, e.g. Krishna, Kanchan, Narendra-7 or so, and is budded at a height of 15-20 cm from soil level on the stock plant. Ultimately the cambium layers of scion (bud) and stock (seedling) unite. After union, the bud of scion sprouts and grows on the food material supplied by roots of the root stock. When the growth of scion starts, the stock portion is gently cut and removed at 2 cm above the joint of scion and stock. As such this becomes a 'Kalmi' plant. The stock feeds the scion through its roots from soil and leaves of scion portion manufacture Carbohydrate with the help of their chlorophyll and feed roots of the stock. This cycle makes the tree grow on. The 'Kalmi' tree bears fruits exactly of the same character, which the mother plant was bearing. The best time of budding is that when the sap in scion and stock flows rapidly. At this stage the bark separates from the wood very easily.

There are many types of budding, e.g. 'shield budding', 'patch budding', 'ring budding', 'I budding' and others. The time between March - April to August-September was found suitable for budding. For 'patch budding, a rectangular patch of bark having a plump dormant bud (eye) is removed from the selected scion stick of the mother plant. To have the patch, two vertical cuts of the size 2-3 cm are given in the bark of scion stick at a distance of 1/2 cm. The selected bud should be in the middle. After that two horizontal cuts should be given both on the upper and lower side connecting the longitudinal cuts. All these cuts should be made with the help of a budding knife. The patch is then loosened and taken out from the scion stick. Such buds should be collected in sufficient number and kept in a wet cloth. Similar patches should be removed from the root stock at a distance of 15 to 20 cm above the soil level. One of the collected bud patches should then be fixed on the vacant space made at the root stock. This should be tied with a string of banana fibre, thin plastic, sun hemp or raffia grass. Tying should be started from lower end towards upper end leaving the plump bud (eye) uncovered. Union between stock and scion takes place within two weeks of budding. Later on sprouting of bud starts and goes on growing. The stock portion is then removed from the joint of stock and scion as indicated earlier. One must be cautious in all types of budding and grafting that strings by which these have been tied must be removed after union and start of growth. If this is not done in time the strings go on cutting the bark and sinking inside, which makes adverse affect on growth of the plant.

I budding was tried at Pratapgarh. For this only a longitudinal cut of 4-5 cm length is given on the aonla root stock in the second Week of September. A bud of the shape of shield is then taken out from the selected bud stick of the mother plant. For this a slanting cut is given in the wood from 1.5 cm below the selected bud and the knife is passed upwards with wood above the bud. Then a horizontal slanting cut is given from the upper end piece from the scion stick. This piece should be about 2.5 cm long. The selected plump bud should be in the middle of both length and breath of shield. The bark of this piece is loosened and the wood removed. This is then inserted, in I cut, so that the plump bud remains in the middle of length of the longitudinal I-shaped cut. This budding is also tied as usual, with banana or sun hemp fibre. Union takes place within two weeks but the bud remains dormant. This bud sprouts between the end of February and end of March and grows so vigorously that, the plant can be lifted for plantation in the next rainy season, as observed by the author (Science and Culture, 28, 486, 1962).

'T-budding' is another name of shield budding. It is called T-budding because after longitudinal cut in the root stock, a horizontal cut is given connecting the upper cut to about half the girth of the stock. The cut thus makes the shape of a T. It Is called 'Shield-budding' as the piece of bark taken out from, the scion stick of the mother plant is of the shape of a shield. In 'T' or 'Shield budding' the cut of the stock is loosened and the bark having the plump bud is inserted therein and tied as usual. Sometimes, the horizontal cut is given on lower side giving the shape of an inverted T. This is named as 'Inverted T-budding'. Similar operations are done in this system also regarding budding, tying etc. 'Modified ring budding' is also a system of vegetative propagation of aonla. In this method a plump healthy bud is selected on the scion stick of the mother plant.

After selecting the bud, a longitudinal cut is given on the back side of the plump bud about 3 cm in length in such a way that the plump bud of the scion may lie in the middle of the length. After this, two horizontal cuts are given all round connecting the upper and lower portion of the cut. This is then loosened and taken out from the scion stick. Similar cuts are given on the root stock, bark removed and the vacant space is replaced by the bud already taken out with bark from the scion stick by modified ring system.

BUDDING IN SITU

To save the plants of aonla from drying during lifting or transplanting, seedlings may be planted direct in situt i.e. where the orchard is to be planted. For this, lay out, digging of pits, filling of pits at proper distance and all operations for planting an orchard should be done earlier. Instead of planting a clone (plants raised by vegetative means), seedling of aonla should be planted in filled up pits and those which dry up may be replaced with new ones. When all seedlings are established, budding may be done on these. Seeds may also be sown there and budding may be done at the proper stage. By such plantations in situ one may establish a strong orchard. The roots of all such plants will be stronger. By planting sowing and budding in situ there will be saving of one year, which would have spent, in keeping the budded plants in nursery for one year.

Grafting

Attached method of grafting, i.e. Inarching is also applied in propagating aonla, mango, guava and others. In Inarching root-stock is lifted from nursery to the mother-plant. A suitable branch/scion of the mother-plant is bent to reach the root-stock. Then 1/3 portion of wood and bark of both scion and stock are peeled off to a length of 4-5 cm. Peeled portions of these are placed together and tied with strings. These take about two months to unite. This a cumber-some and costly method. Earlier this was the most common and successful method used for preparing a graft, but now it has been replaced by budding, veneer grafting and others. Grafting is done in rainy season.

GOOTTEE

Aonla plants may also be prepared by goottee with the application of seradix (powder hormone) at the peeled off portion of the bark near the bud, which give out roots after covering with moss grass or goottee soil. However, in the case of aonla, budding will be suitable for plant propagation.

Aonla- A Nutritious Horticultural Produce - 6

Preparation of Land

For establishing an aonla orchard it is very important to layout the orchard at proper distance at the right time, dig or plough the land and mix manure preferably organic manures in soil and perform other essential operations before actual plantation. Aonla plantations are done during rainy season and preparations are done during summers. The land selected for aonla growing should first be plou ghed atleast twice. Each ploughing should be followed by planking to break big soil pieces and smoothen the surface soil. After the soil of the land becomes smooth, lay out should be done at 09 metres apart each way, i.e. at a distance of 9 x 9 metres (30 x 30 feet). As such the points of plantations should be marked, where small pegs should be fixed. The number of pegs required per hectare will be 120 (48 per acre) and same will be the number of plants for plantation at each point.

The number of plants accommodated per hectare 120 and per acre 48 will be possible in square system of plantation which is mostly applied. In square system the distance from plant to plant and row to row will remain equal. It will remain same from both sides in a horizontal or vertical row. Four plants, opposite each other in two rows will make a square. In square system of plantation cultural operations are possible from two sides. However, by hexagonal system of plantation 15% more plants will be accommodated in comparison to that of square system. In Hexagonal system first the distances from plant to plant are marked on the base line. From each mark two arches are made forward for the next row. The point where two arches meet is the point of plantation for the next row. On the same pattern further rows are laid out. As such two plants on the base line and one point in the net row in between these two points make an equilateral triangle and six such triangles make a Hexagon and plants are planted on each corner or point. This system is called Hexagonal or Equilateral triangular system. Cultural operation like weeding, holling and irrigation etc. are possible from three ways in this system. After pegs are fixed, pits of the size of 90 x 90 x 90 cm. should be dug up around each peg. All such dug up pit's and soils taken out from pits should be made to remain open to hot sun for about a month so that soils may well be fried up in the burning heat of sun and all the pests, insects and weeds etc. may be vanished.

Filling Pits and Planting

Now each pit is filled up tightly with surface soil and 40 kg. Farm yard Manure (FYM). Cow dung manure or compost and pressed well. Filling should be done 15 cm. Above the soil surface, Further, about 156 gram super phosphate (2.5 gm. Phosphoric acid) may be mixed on upper surface of the filled up pits. Besides this, 50 gm Aldrex may also be mixed in soil on the upper surface. This will save plants from the attack of white ants. After completing filling work of pits, the pegs should be refixed in the centre of pits for demarcating the position. Planting of aonla should be done after atleast two rains during June - July, so that the heat of the soil inside the filled up pits may cool down and the raised portion of soil may come down at the level of soil surface.

Budded or grafted plants should be lifted from nursery with earthen balls and planted in centre of the filled up pit after removing the peg. Planting should be done after making a small pit of the size of the earthen ball holding all round roots of the plant. Plant should be planted so deep in soil that soil marks on basal portion of the plant remain parallel to soil surface. Then soil all round the earthen ball should cautiously be tightened with the wooden handle of a 'Khurpee'. Plants raised or transplanted in polythene bags should also be planted like wise after removing polythene. Similarly, aonla seedlings may also be planted for budding in situ. Aonla seeds may also be sown direct in filled up pits for raising seedlings and budding in situ. Efforts should be made to take up the plantation work in afternoon/evening or when the weather, is cloudy or having very light showers of rains.

Irrigation, Hoeing, Weeding, Manuring

Just after plantation, plants of aonla must be irrigated. Again when needed young plants should be irrigated after 7-8 days. Generally in rainy season no irrigation is required unless there is a long gap between two rains. Weeding and hoeling should also be done from time to time for proper aeration and growth of young plants. Weeding is also necessary to save the plants from infestation of pests and diseases. In young plants irrigation may be given through channels in athalaas made all round the young plants.

Manuring

Though aonla can grow in unfertile soil and may carry on with less of fertilizers and manures, yet for a commercial cultivation, all possible scientific methods for every operation should be applied. One year old aonla plant requires 10 kg. F YM 200 gm. Urea (about 100 gm. N), 312.5 gm. super phosphate single (50 gm P) and 150 gm Potassium sulphate (75 gm. K). These quantities should be increased every year up to 10 year. As such for a ten year old plant requirements of FYM will be 100 kg. urea 2000 gm (N 1,000 gm), Super phosphate single 3.125 gm (P 500 gm) and Potassium Sulphate 1,500 gm (K 750 gm). Plants above 10 year also will be fed by the quantities required for 10 year old plants.

When to Apply

Whole quantity of Farm Yard Manure and Super Phosphate along-with half quantity N and K should be applied in February for vegetative growth.

At this time tree sheds all of its leaves on the ground. After manuring these should be mixed in soil. Along with these the leaves on the ground will also be mixed in soil, which will further, make the soil fertile. Again the remaining half quantity of N and K should be applied before start of rains or just at the start of rains during June-July for development of fruits.

Where to Apply

Manures, fertilisers and water should be applied under the drip of the tree, so that feeding roots spread all round may utilize them. For 3 - 4 years 30 cm. wide and 20 cm deep furrow should be prepared all round under the drip: of tree in which manures should be mixed and then irrigation, should immediately be done. As the branches spread all round, the size of the furrow should be increased. On full growth of the tree the width of the furrow should be increased to one metre.

Aonla - A Nutritious Horticultural Produce- 7

Intercropping, Mulching, Irrigation in Established Orchards

Aonla trees reach fruiting stage, at the age of 9 - 10 years. During this period to have some return against the expenditure on maintenance of orchards, seasonal vegetables should be grown in vacant spaces. In rainy season and summers lobia, lady's finger, cluster beans (guar) and cucurbits maybe grown. Crops of cauliflower, turnip, cabbage, carrot, green peas, tomato, brinjal and others may be taken in winters. Besides these vegetables, crops of spices like fennel, garlic coriander, fenugreek, onion and others may also be taken. Besides these, fruits which require less space and fruit early may also be taken as intercrop. For this fruits like papaya, banana, strawberry, raspberry, pineapple and phalsa will do.

In established aonla orchards, irrigation should be done at 10 -15 days in summers, while in winters it may be done at 15 - 20 days interval in October - November and December for development of fruits. This irrigation will be better also for saving fruits from dropping. It has been mentioned earlier that like manuring irrigation should also be done under the drip of the tree. Irrigating the trees in basins made around the trunks of trees, therefore, are ineffective.

To save the number of usual irrigation, drip irrigation, irrigation by sprinklers and pitcher system are useful. However, mulching is another method of saving irrigation water. For this thick layers of wheat or paddy straw, sugar came trash, banana and sugarcane dry leaves, dry leaves of trees and leaves powder are good organic mulcbes. These save evaporation and keep the water soaked in themselves. Later on these mulches serve the purpose of organic manure and provide humus when these are mixed up in soil. Mulching by spreading sheets of black polythene on soil surface also show positive results. Black polythene sheets firstly save evaporation of water from soil, secondly encourages plant growth due to soil heat produced in soil below the sheets and thirdly subdue the weeds growth. At N.D. University of Agriculture and Tech. Umarganj Faizabad, spreading of black polythene in aonla orchards cultivar N.D. Aonla - 7 proved best with regards to growth of trunk and spread of canopy of the tree (J. Appl. Horti. 2 (1): 37-38, Jan. -June 2000) If the soil is usar sesbania cannabina syn. S. aculeata var. cannabina (Dhaincha) may be grown. Its plants should be turned in soil in rainy season. This will improve the soil fertility by fixing in soil, nitrogen from atmosphere and further improve the soil texture by adding organic matter in soil after ploughing the plants in field before flowering as green manure.

Further ploughing the orchard is also esseuntial. Few days after irrigation only light scrapping of soil surface by means of a hand be or so, will further be helpful in saving irrigation water, as hoed up soil layers will save water from evaporation. Ploughing the aonla orchards during September - October will mix up the grown weeds in soil, which will rot to form organic manure in soil. Another ploughing mentioned earlier, should also be done in Feburary or beginning of March, so that the leaves shed on the ground may mix up in soil and further provide humus to soil and improve its texture. When intercropping of vegetables is taken in an aonla orchard, an adition of 250 quintals of well rotten farm yard manure will further be required to have a good of vegetables, which will add as preliminary income to the grower.

Flowering and Fruiting

Aonla tree starts sheding its leaves from the month of February, sometimes even from the month of January. Leaves are fully shed by the end of March. The Author had also made some studies in this regard in Allahabad on aonla cultivar 'chakaiya'. During shedding, besides leaves, branchlets also shed afterwards and leave scars of shedding on branches. The dormant buds along the leaf scars start swelling. During this period sprouting of new growth also appear. In chakiya it was observed that first of all new tender branchlets appear on last year shoots which come but from the swelling buds left just by the side of scars. These branchlets are loaded with small roundish and flowering whitish buds. With the growth of branchlets the size of buds also go on increasing. By this time feathery bunches of green leaves also appear on tip portion of the branchlets. On further growth of the branchlets flowering buds and leaves start appearing separately on branchlets.

Flower buds with branchlets besides, appearing on new growth, also appear direct on last years branches (Aonla Aur USKA BAGHBANI, Himanchal Pustak Bhandar Gandhinagar, Delhi - 1, 2002, 1-152). This practice goes on.

Opening of flowers start by the end of March or first week of April. This continues for about three weeks, i.e. for near about 3rd week of April. Aonla flower is unisexual, Male flowers appear on every branchlet densely, but female flowers appear only on few branchlet to and these too on basal portion of the branchlet singly, but sometimes appear in a bunch of 2-3 flowers in number. The flowers which appear on aonla tree in all have only 0.06% female flowers. The ratio between Male and Female flowers is 1773-5 : 1 (Ind: J. Hort 14 (2) : 99-102, 1957). However, In different studies these ratios were found 197:1 and 307.9:1 (Same author). Male flowers start opening at 4 p.m. but most of them start between 6 and 7 p.m. Anthers start bursting either immediately or after 10 to 15 minutes of flower opening. Female flowers open in 72 hours after crossing various stages. The stigma of female flower is in a position to accept pollen only on the third day of flower opening. This receptively of stigma lying on the style continues for six days.

Pollen grains of flower are very light and pollination in female carries on by wind. After opening of flowers the stigma of the female flower rests on top of the style for 20 days and then drops off. The style on the other hand rests on the flower for 4 months. Even, at this stage there is no indication of formation of fruit and the overy appears to be lying in dormant stage. The style of the flower is covered by peel-like black layer. After 4 - 4 months of opening of flowers the ovary starts developing in July and August. These black layers crack and appear separating from the style and after five days these are fully removed. After this by the middle of August small roundish green fruitlets appear on branchlets of the tree. Gradually these go on developing. The fruits of Banarsi aonla fully mature and ripe by the end of December. In other varieties the development of fruits go on up to November.

Fruiting in aonla is very limited to the extent of even 12-18%. This is because the number of male flowers is comparatively too much in comparison to female flowers, as already indicated in ratio. The pollution and fertilization capacity in Aonla is good but the question of reaching pollen up to stigma is also limited as the pollen are very light and fly here and there with the wind. As such hand pollination gives better results.

Unfruitfulness

Aonla being such a nutritious medicinal fruit of great utility an God's gift of India is also facing many problems. Out of these unfruitfulness is the main problem. All varieties may not be self fruitful and therefore they require pollen of other varieties. It means their pollen are not self fertile. So one of the causes of unfruitfulness in Aonla is.

Self Sterility

This problem is generally faced in Banarsi aonlas. Their pollen are not self fertile and therefore, the trees bear less. Besides wind pollination takes place by insects also. Solution for this problem is solved if 5% trees of self fertile varieties are planted in a self infertile variety of aonla orchard like 'BANARSI AONLA'. In this way pollen grains of self fertile aonla varieties reach the stigma of self - infertile varieties very easily by wing insects. Therefore, the chances of fertilization and fruitfulness in Banarsi aonla variety become bright. Krishna, Kanchan, Narend.- 7, Francis or Fort, Chakaiya and Deshi are self-fertile varieties of aonla. If orchards of these varieties are planted there is no need of planting 5% of other varieties.

Aonla - A Nutritious Horticultural Produce - 8

Further Unfruitfulness and Remedies

In the earlier article it was suggested to plant 5% aonla plants of self-fertile varieties in a self-sterile aonla orchard, to make it fruitful.

Another solution for such orchards may be to TOP-WORK a branch of a self-sterile tree with the scion of self fertile variety. As such pollen grains of self-fertile top worked portion will reach self-sterile flowers of the tree easily, fertilize them and make the tree fruitful.

Again orchards of only self-fertile varieties like Chakaiya, Krishna, Kanchan, Narendra -7, Rajbagh and Deshi may be planted to get rid of unfruitfulness in aonla.

Selection of Wrong Scion is one of the main reasons of unfruitfulness in aonla. As stated earlier male and female flowers - both are borne on a branchlet. On some branchlets only male flowers or maximum number of male flowers are crowded. Some branchlets have maximum female flowers, while selecting bud sticks for budding, if buds are taken from those branches, the branchlets of which had only male flowers, the budded plant when developed to a tree, will remain unfruitful. If the branch or shoot has some female flowers on its branchlets and most of the branchlets had male flowers, the trees developed from such buddings may bear few fruits. When the buds are selected from those shoots which had maximum female flowers in their branchlets, the plants budded from these shoots, when developed into trees, will be fully fruitful. As such for budding or grafting only those shoots should be selected, which had maximum number of female flowers.

For selecting shoots of maximum number of female flowers, the grower / orchardist / nurseryman will have to be cautious at the time of flowering and fruiting. The desired selected bud stick as stated, should be tagged for identifying and at the time of budding or grafting only those shoots should be utilized. Tags should be kepts properly preserved on the tree and should not be destroyed, till the operation of budding or grafting are over.

Avoid Spraying during Pollination

During pollination of flowers specially when done by pollinating insects, spraying should be avoided, otherwise the insects may die or become inactive. Specially where cross pollination is needed, spraying will hinder in pollination and fertilization, with the result that the tree may not be fruitful.

Application of Manure and Water

To make the tree fruitful, besides other reasons and remedial measure, it is also necessary that manuring and irrigation should be done in time and in proper doze. Irrigation must be done soon after manuring.

Fruit Drop

After fertilization, the ovary of the female flower remains dormant for about 4 months as referred earlier. This is only in the middle of August that small green roundish fruits appear developing. During this long period of 4 months after fertilization and appearance of small fruits, there is an increase of growth inhibiting hormone in flowers fruity due to no fruit development. This hormone forces the fruits to drop. As such to control fruit drop, spraying of 100 to 200 p.p.m. Gibberelic acid (Solution of 100 -200 mg. G.A. and one litre water) should be done on fertilized flowers/fruits in the end of July. This operation will minimise the fruit drop as well as help in development of fruits.

Besides these drops 70% flowers drop during three weeks of flowering due to lack of pollination and genetic reasons. Another drop of flowers and fruits take place during June and September for lack of pollination and fertilization. Third drop takes place at different stages from the third week of August to October due to physiological disturbances.

Rejuvenation of Inferior Trees

There are many aonla trees/groves of inferior quality at various places. To change these into good varieties, rejuvenation of such trees may be done by Top working. For this cut the trunk of unwanted trees at a height of 120 to 150 cm. from the ground in the middle of February. Paint the cut portion with coaltar. After some time the trunk will start sprouting. Only 4 -5 healthy shoots growing all round should be maintained for further growth and rest be removed. These growing shoots will become strong within 3-4 months. Then at the proper time, budding may be done on these shoots by applying the methods of Patch budding, shield budding or others. The sprouts from these budding will grow and fruit, which will bear fruits of desired variety. Thus any such tree of aonla orchard, fruits of which are unwanted, may be changed into high yielding desired varieties by top working.

Diseases and Pests

Some diseases and pests also limit the aonla production. Care should be taken to keep plants and trees healthy. For this one should have a round of his orchard and trees from time to time.

Fruit hot— In fruit rot dark brown spots are produced in the fruit. Later on rotting of fruits are started. Ultimately fruits drop on the ground. The disease is caused by the fungus Pestolocia cuchenta. Spray of Foltak or Captafal 80% wetable powder 0-2% (2 gm. fungicide in a litre of water) should be sprayed from middle of September to middle or end of November.

Three such sprays may be done at an interval of one month. Besides these, 0.3% (3 gm. fungicide and one litre water). Copper oxychloride 50% wetable powder may also be sprayed. As far as possible the spraying fungicides should be changed in different sprayings.

Internal Necrosis- This disease is caused by boron deficiency, the pulp of the fruit becomes blackish inside the fruit. From outside the attack of disease is not detectable, but in Francis (Raj bagh) a shadow of blackish tinge appears on one side of the basal portion of the fruit.

A trial on this aspect was done in the orchard of Sri Mahabal Singh (Yashwant Nursery) in village Pathatia Pratapgarh on varieties Francis, Banarsi and Chakaiya and the incidence of disease was found as 68.8%, 1.8% and 0% in the same order. To meet the deficiency of boron, use 125 gm of Borax per tree like manure. Besides this spraay thrice 0.6% Borax solution in water on the tree (6 gm. borax and one litre water). First spray should be done in the end of April after fertilization of female flower. Second and third sprays may be done in July and September in the same order.

Rust— It is a fungus disease caused by the fungus Revenellia emblicae. When rust disease starts first light brownish protuberated spots appear on leaves. It appears that leaves have been affected by actual rust ('Zang'). In serious conditions leaves drop off from the tree. Such protuberated light brownish spots also appear on fruits and in very serious cases, these appear in patches. Thus fruits become disfigured and loose there value in market. In young plants growth is also affected when the disease spreads. To prevent the disease solution of 0.2% Zineb 75% wetable powder (Diathana Z-78-2 gm. fungicide in a litre of water) should be sprayed 3 - 4 times during August to September at an interval of 15 days. Besides 0.3% solution of this any copper fungicide like copper sulphate may also be sprayed. It will be better to change fungicides in various sprays.

Blue Mould - In blue mould disease, brown coloured spots appear on fruits as if that spot has soaked in itself water. Later on the brown colour changes into blue colour and later on rotting starts in fruits. The disease is caused by the bacteria Penicilium islandicum. P. oxalicum and Aspergillus nigre are also the sources of spread of the disease.

Aonla - A Nutritious Horticultural Produce - 9

Other Pests

There are some other pests and enemies of aonla crop.

Aphids

Small watery insects fly and gather in groups on growing tender leaves and shoots of aonla. During this period the aphids suck up juice of leaves and shoots. In serious cases these young shoots dry up. To control the attack of aphids Carberyl 10% dust or Fenitrothion 5% dust or Malathion 5% dust may be dusted. About 20 to 25 kg. of dust will be required for a hectare.

Besides dusting, spraying of one of these insecticides will also do. Monochrotophos 0.04% (0.4 ml. insecticide and one litre water), Dimethoate 30 EC 0.1% solution, 0.025% (1.25 ml insecticide with a litre of water), Malathion 50 EC 0.25% (2.5 ml. insecticide and one litre water) and others also.

Scale Insects

In tender growing shoots and fruits cotton like white material appear during March to May-June. Under the protection of these cotton-like appearances small brown coloured flattish insects rest and suck up the sap of shoots and fruits. For this 0.03% solution of Phosphamidon or Dimethoate or Methyl-0-dimton or Parathion or Diazinon may be sprayed on appearance of such symptoms. Again instead of these, 0.25% Malathion 50 EC may also be sprayed.

Bark Eating Caterpillar

The caterpillar of this pest eats away bark of shoots and branches and leaves behind material like saw dust, spread in webs. Later on it bores the woody portion, enters and remain inside and eat away the woody soft portion inside. The shoot in the long run dries up and in serious cases the tree also dries up. This caterpillar is known as Inderbel tetraonic. When such symptoms are seen first of all webs should be cleaned off, followed by inserting a thin wire in the hole to kill the caterpillar. Thereafter, some cotton wool lightly soaked in petrol or formaline should be inserted deep in the hole with the help of the wire and then plugged with wet clay. This operation should be done in September - October and February - March. Spraying in hole solution of 0.05% Nuvachron (Monochrotophos) or Dichlorovos (Nuvan) also does well. For this 0.5 ml. insecticide may be dissolved in a litre of water. Plugging the hole with Aluminum phosphide also serves the same purpose.

Shoot Gall Maker

This black coloured pest is active from July to September, which bores top of the shoot and remain sitting inside. The affected top portion changes into a hollow gall. This results in stopping the growth of the shoot above the gall. The gall should be cut and burnt as the pest remains inside the gall. The shoot gall maker pest is known as Betousa stylophora.

White Ants

For control of white ants 25 gm. of Carbofuron may be applied per tree in soil. Neem cake will also be useful.

Birds

Parrots, crows and other birds behave as enemies of aonla fruits. When fruits grow on trees, these birds specially parrot's cut the fruits, eat and damage the crop. For this watchmen should beat drums to make the birds fly away. Bird scares placed in the orchard make gun like noise and, therefore, birds do not come in the orchard or if they are there, they fly away. The grower should be cautious from thieves also specially when fruits are hanging on trees during development and maturity.

Picking, Yield and Disposal

When aonla fruits change their green colour and attain yellowish tinge, these may taken as ripe and may be picked up cautiously. Never pick the fruits with logs and donot the fruits drop on ground otherwise there will be bruising and injury in fruits which will encourage fungus growth. Picking may be done by climbing on the tree or by standing on stool ladder. Fruits after picking, may be collected in bags hanging on back of the harvester. Generally the stage of harvesting reaches in January. When fruits are ripe stones of these change from green to yellowish or brownish. By harvesting in January, fruits and their products like preserves, toffees and others will remain stable. Though for earning income growers start harvesting from October - November but under such cases these should be consumed soon, as these may not remain stable.

After harvesting proper grading should be done. Those fruits which are injured, bruised or cut or cracked or appear to be diseased should be taken out of the lot. These are then packed in baskets by spreading newspapers and transported for consumption. If fresh fruits are not easily disposed off these should be transformed in preserves, candies, toffees and other products.

Uttar Pradesh Govt. has now declared 56 aonla growing villages of Sadar, Mangraura and Sandwachandika blocks of Pratapgarh district as Aonla fruit Belt in the year 1993, so that these orchards may remain protected (Aonla aur uski Baghbani Himanchal Pustak Bhandar, Gandhinagar Delhi - 31). On the other hand Department of Horticulture

Uttar Pradesh has indicated that U.P. Govt. has declared 28 villages of Mangrora block and 41 villages of Sadar block as Aonla Fruit growing Belt in 1993 (Brochure on 'Aonla Evam Prasanskrit Utpaadon ka Viparan/Niryat vishayak Sangoshthi -Karyashala, Kanha Shyam, Hotel Allahabad 27th February 2005, UP. Govt.).

However, knowing various utilities of Aonla; its cultivation is going on increasing day by day rapidly. Now aonlas are also being exported to countries like America, Australia, Turky, Germany, China, Italy, Pakistan, Belgium, Sri Lanka, Saudi Arabia, Hongkong, Bahrene, Indonesia and others. Aonla growers of Pratapgarh should keep themselves in touch with National. Aonla Mission Pratapgarh, who should be responsible for proper disposal of India's Horticultural Produce, Aonla. Growers should not feel any difficulty in marketing, transport and export of their produce. Storage facilities of aonla fruits should also be made. Any grafted or budded plant the so called 'Kalmi' plant start flowering next year, but such blossoms should be plucked off if this is seen in aonla also. In Aonla the commercial crop may be had in 9th or 10th year. After acquiring this age, an aonla tree yields about 200 quintals of aonla fruits. As such one hectare of aonla orchard (120 trees) will yield 240 quintals of aonla fruits from 120 trees per year. In South India two crops are taken per year from aonla trees and therefore, their production per year may naturally be higher. So, please growers, go on growing aonlas and utilizing all waste and user lands. This will be very remunerative.

Some Outstanding Varieties of Aonla (Phyllanthus emblica, L)

Aonla (Phyllanhus emblica, L., Syn. Emblica officinalis) is the richest natural source of vitamin 'C' among all the fruits commonly grown in India. Banarsi Aonla of Vanarasi district, UP is famous all over the country for its excellent quality. This variety of Aonla has, however, been observed to be shy bearing. The reasons for this behaviour appear to be still uninvestigated. With a view to spot out some promising varieties of prolific bearing habit, survey of Pratapgarh district in U. P. was made during the years 1956-58 which has fairly a large acreage under Aonla (Appro. 45.0 acres). Fruit characters along with some vegetative characters of varieties of Aonla thus investigated, have been described in this paper. These varieties may be established by the names given below for further multiplication.

1. Fort or 'Qila' or Rajbagh

This variety is famous in district Pratapgarh. Rajbagh vraiety of Aonla is grown in Pratapgarh fort and from there it has been multiplied in other parts of the district. This variety is also more or less like 'Banarsi' with a little difference.

Form of the fruit—round; colour-light yellowish green with slightly blackish tinge; body— translucent with some whitish small dots; average weight of a fruit—65.58 gms. (1.12 chataks); size—4.44 cm. (1.75"—length x 5.14 cm. (2.05"—breadth); segments and streaks— fruit divided into six segments by white, groved, longitudinal streaks (streaks towards basal portion thicker than those towards apical portion); apical end of each segment—a bit protuberated; apex—round; base—round; apical sinus—slight or narrow deep; basal sinus— shallow, broad and round; keeping quality—good; quality with respect to moral be making— good; fibres—nominal; fruiting habit—prolific.

Branches of the tree are spreading in nature; branchlets—44.19 cm. (17.4') in length; leaves—1.65 cm. (0.65") x 0.39 cm. (0.155') in size.

2. Madhupur Conical or Lattu Shape

This variety was located in the orchard of Th. Adya Prasad Singh in village Madhupur of district Pratapgarh. The fruit resembles the shape of a 'lattu', an Indian term used for a wooden toy. Unlike other varieties of Aonla length of the fruit of this variety is more than the breadth which; along with the shape, strikes the observer first.

Form of the fruit—Conical; colour—whitish light green; body—translucent with some whitish dots; average weight of a fruit—58.30 gms. (1 chatak); size—5.08 cm. (2.0"—length) x 4.69 cm. (1.85"—breadth); segments and streaks—fruit divided into six segments by thick, white, deeply groved, longitudinal streaks from apical to the basal end; apex—conical; base—flat; apical sinus—clear, deep and narrow; basal sinus—broad and deep; keeping quality— good; quality with respect to Morabba making—good; fibres—nominal; fruiting habit—Prolific.

3. Chakaiya or Goolarahia

This is a common variety grown in Pratapgarh district. The name 'Chakaiya' or Goolarhia' has been derived from the Indian term 'Chakai' (a flat wooden toy) and 'Goolar' botanically known as Ficus glomerata. The fruit resembles the shape of a 'Goolar' fruit.

Form of the fruit—flat; colour—greenish; body—smooth, shining and translucent; average weight of a fruit—36.43 gms. (0.62 chatak); size—4.31 cm. (1.70"— length) x 4.95 cm. (1.95" —breadth); segments and streaks) fruit divided into six segments by thin, white, smooth, (ungrooved) longitudinal streaks from apical to the basal end; apex—roundish fiat; base—flat; apical sinus—slight; basal sinus—broad, deep and uniformally round; keeping quality—very good; quality with respect to Morabba making—excellent (which boiling the fruit for Morabba making, care should be taken that it is not boiled for a long period as its segmants may be separated); fibres—almost absent; fruiting habit—Prolific (bears in bunches).

Branches of most of the trees of this variety have been found growing upwards; branchlets 38.35 cm. (15.1") in length; leaves—1.52 cm. (0.6"—length) x 0.38 cm. (015" breadth).

4. Madhupur Dull Dark Green Colour

This variety was also located in the orchard of Th. Adya Prasad Singh in Madhupur.

Form of the fruit—round; colour—dull dark green; body—smooth to rough, opaque; average weight of a fruit—43.72 gms. (0.75 chatak); size—3.04 cm. (1.2"—length) x 3.55 cm. (1.4"—breadth); segments and streaks—fruit divided into six segments by whitish, longitudinal streaks; apex—round; base—round to flat; keeping quality—good; quality with respect to Morabba making—good, except that its colour is not attractive; fibres—nominal; fruiting habit —medium.

5. Red Tinged

The fruit of this variety is smaller than other varieties. The fruit has redish ting over the body which makes it very attractive.

Form of the fruit—round; colour—whitish light green with a part of its basal portion red tinged, body—translucent; average weight of a fruit—29.15 gms. chatak); size—3.8" cm. (1.5" —length) x 3.81 cm. (1.5"—breadth); segments and streaks—fruit divided into six segment by thick, white, longitudinal, smooth (ungoved) streaks; apex-round; base-round; apical sinus —small and narrow; basal sinus—broad and round; keeping quality—good; quality with respect to Morabba making—good except that due to smaller size there is some inconvenience in puncturing the fruits; fibres—nominal; fruiting habit—medium.

6. Other Varieties or Types

Besides the varieties mentioned above two types of Aonla fruits (i) 'triangular'and (ii) 'square' in shape have also been observed. They are light green in colour with yellowish tinge. The size and quality of fruits are quite good. The square one is divided clearly into four lobes by four white, longitudinal, groved streaks meeting at right angles at the basal and apical ends—thus giving a square shape to the fruit. Each lobe is further divided into two segments by a white longitudinal ungrooved streak. The whole fruit thus becomes eight-segmented unlike other varieties. The fruit of the triangular type is divided into three clear lobes by three white longitudinal, deeply grooved streaks—thus giving the fruit a triangular shape. Each lobe is further divided into two segments by a white ungrooved longitudinal streak.

The fruit thus becomes segmented. It is still to be confirmed whether they are separate varieties or only a few such fruits are found on trees of Banarasi or other Aonla varieties. In a few cases fruits having seven segments, which is also uncommon, were seen.

7. Scope and Limitations of Aonla Cultivation

Aonla is now being propagated by various methods of budding at different places during favourable periods (Singh, 1952; Nand, 1962; Teotia and Asthana, 1960). Its multiplication therefore, to other places may be done each. Cultivation of Aonla is a very profitable business. The plant is hardy and does not require much care. No watching is required during the fruiting season except from a few wild birds. For thieves also it is not easy to steal. Aonla fruits may be kept in a good condition for 10-15 days. It is hardly perishable and can stand rough handling during transport. The fruit is of a great medicinal value. It is very nutritious as well. It can very well be made into preserves, jellies, pickles and powders, etc. Attack of diseases and pests is also uncommon in the crop of Aonla.

8. Marketing and Location of Orchards

A brief account of marketing system and location of Aonla orchards, as surveyed, has been given in this paper with the idea that interested persons may take advantage of this information in multiplication and cultivation of these varieties.

Marketing : In district Pratapgarh Aonlas have been found growing in blocks of acres in the form of orchards. Cultivation of this fruit is now going on increasing day by day in this district, where it has become a good source of income. Generally, the whole orchard in given to contractors and the income thus obtained by the orchardist comes to Rs. 30 to Rs. 40 per tree.

Location of Orchards

S. No.	*Name of place*	*Approx. Acreage*	*Name of veriety*	*Name and address of orchardist.*
1.	Village Gonda Jagatganj	15.00	Fort, Chakaia Redtinged	Sh. Ram Shiroman Singh v.p.o. Jagatganj.
2.	Pratapgarh Fort	3.00	Fort	Raja Ajit Prasad Singh Pratapganj City.
3.	Pathatia	3.00	Banarsi Chakaiya	Th. Mahabal Singh, V. Patheatia Kalan, P.O. Gaura.
4.	Rajapur estate	5.00	Banarsi	Raja Pratap Bahadur

	(near Sangipur)		Chakaiya Fort	Singh, Rajapur Estate.
5.	Bhadri	5.00	Banarsi	Rai Bajrang Bahadur Singh, Raja Sahab of Bhadri. P.O. Bhadri.
6.	Tardih	0.50	Fort, Chakaiya Banarsi	Th. Baijnath Singh, V. Tardih, P.O. Garwara.
7.	Kharagpur	A few trees	Banarsi	Th. Bajarang Bahadur Singh, V. Khargpur P.O. Shahab Ganj.
8.	Narharpur	2.00	Banarsi	Sri Udairaj Singh, S/ O Sri Ram Pal Singh Vill. Narharpur. P.O. Konhdaur.
9.	Gutauli	1.00	Banarsi	Th. R.P. Singh Gutauli.
10.	Tala	1.00	Banarsi Fort Chakaia	Dr. R.P. Singh Tala.
11.	Purbara	4.00	Banarsi Chakaiya Fort	Sri Harihar Prasad. Purbara.
12.	Garhi Samdabad and Uchegaon.	1. 00	Banarsi	Khan Bahadur, Ali Hasan Khan. Garhi Samdabad.
13.	Katra Medniganj	1.00	Banarsi	Th. Harbax Singh, Katra Medniganj.
14.	Awwar	1.00	Chakaiya	Sri Raj Bahadur Singh Village and P.O. Awwar.
15.	Jethwara	A few trees	Banarsi	Raja Lal Pratap Bahadur Singh Vill. and P.O. Jethwara.
16.	Bhages	A few trees	Chakaiya Banarsi	Sri Lok Nath Singh Bhagesara
17.	Madhupur	A few trees	Madhupur conical, Dull dark green, Red tinged.	Th. Adya Prasad Singh Vill and P.O. Madhupur (Madhupur Conical requires attention with regards to its multiplication).

The contractors despatch these fruits to fruit preservation factories and other agencies to Amritsar and Calcutta. They start despatching in early October and continue up to the end of January and in some cases even up to the month of February. Packing for despatch is done after grading the fruits and placing them in baskets by spreading newspaper sheets in them.

Besides above orchards, good varieties of 'Banarsi'and 'Chakaiya' Aonla trees have also been observed existing in the orchards of Sarva Sri Munishwar Datt Upadhyaya, Ram Naresh Shukla, Shyam Shankar Misra, and Ram Prasad Vakil, who are specially interested in cultivation of Aonla and other fruits.

Acknowledgements

Grateful thanks are due to Dr. A. Prasad (now Director Horticultural Research Institute, Saharanpur), Sri S.K. Shukla, Superintendent Govt. Gardens, Allahabad and Th. Sheo Sewak Singh (retired Distt. Agr. Officer) for their encouragement during these investigations.

Budding in Aonla

(*Phyllanthus emblica*)

Singh[1] achieved 70% success in budding of Aonla in Saharanpur in the month of June. At the Government Farm Nursery, Pratapgarh, U.P., no remarkable results were obtained in June budding, which might be due to very hot weather conditions prevailing at that time. The author, on the other hand, obtained about 75% success there during the years 1956-58 by the process mentioned below.

A vertical cut l ½"-2" in length is given through the bark on a l- 1 ½ years old aonla seedling stock at a height of 6"-9" from the ground level in the second fortnight of September. The bark is then loosened from the wood, with the help of bone blade or back of the budding knife. A bud is then cut from a selected scion wood by passing the blade of the knife under it and thereby removing a 1"-1 ½" long shield shaped patch of bark. The small amount of wood attached with the bark should be removed. The bud is then inserted immediately under the bark of the stock through the vertical cut, which is then wrapped with banana fibre or raffia grass to hold it firmly in position. The bud after being united with the stock (within 2-3 weeks after budding) remains completely in dormant condition up to the end of January. From the second week of February, the buds start showing signs of sprouting and most of them actually sprout between the last week of February and the last week of March. The buds after sprouting grow so vigorously that they attain the height of 4'-5' by the next rains. These plants are supplied to the orchardists in the same season for establishment of new orchards of aonla.

References

1. Singh, L.B. (1952) : A new technique for Propagating Aonla Sci. and Cul. Vol. 17, pp. 345-46.
2. Nand, Darshana (1962) : Budding in Aonla (Phyllanthus emblica, L.Sci. and Cul. Vol. 28 (10), p. 486.
3. Teaotia, S.S. and Asthana, M.P. (1960): Propagation of Aonla by budding. Gardening. (1960) Vol. 2 (8) Sept. 1960, pp. 19-20.
4. L.B. Singh : Annual Report of the Plain Fruit Research Scheme, Uttar Pradesh, July 1953 to June 30, 1954.

7

Grow Papaya for Health

Among the early fruiting and less space covering nutritious fruit plants, papaya is one of the most important fruits grown in India and abroad. Papaya is a sweet and tasty fruit. Its plant starts fruiting within a year. Besides commercial cultivation, papaya may easily be grown in kitchen gardens for the benefit of family members. The papaya fruit possesses in itself water 90.75%, Total solids 10.4% and Acidity 1.15%. As regards availability of vitamin - A, its richness in papaya fruit is considered only just after mango fruit. A 100 gram of papaya pulp makes available 2020 I.U. (International Unit) of Vitamin - A. Again, its 100 gm. pulp contains Vitamin B - 1 (Thiamine) 0.04 mg, Vit. B - 2 (Riboflavin) 0.48 mg, Vit - C 45 - 50 mg, calcium 180 mg, Iron 2.1 mg, Phosphorus 11.1 mg, Protein 0.8 gm, fat 0.1 gm. and calorific value 43 calories.

The milky juice or latex of green immature papaya fruit contains a very large amount of a digestive enzyme named as PAPAIN. It is able to digest protein in our foods. Papain is of a great importance from industrial point of view, as it is used in preparing many digestive food and medicines. Latex is extracted from such green fruits as mentioned above which is further turned into papain. Papain is also present in leaves and stems of papaya. Papain is useful in making body, skin tender and in removing the spots of the skin. It is successfully used in manufacture of chocolate, chewing gum and many medicines as indicated earlier. Papain is also utilized as meat tenderiser Meat easily becomes soft soon, when cooked with papaya latex due to presence of papain. For this the pieces of flesh are wrapped in papaya leaves and placed for cooking. Papain is also useful in tanning industry, it saves wool and leather from shrinkage and also keeps them soft. It is also used in manufacturing body creams and many cosmetics.

Papaya is specially useful for polio patients. Papaya fruit is of a great importance in curing diseases of liver and spleen. Enlargements and also in stomach troubles. Papaya is used as a dessert fruit. Eating ripe papaya fruits clears the bowels and removes constipation. It is also comfortable in piles and gas troubles. It also increases hunger. Carbine, occurring in green parts and in seeds of papaya, has been reported to have been used as heart stimulant and as diuretic. It is also considered as amoebicide specially for amoebic dysentery (Dictionary of Eco. Plants ICAR., N.D).

There is a nutritious ingredient in papaya roots also, which makes the nerves of the body strong. Papaya latex when used on ring worms and scabies, these diseases are cured soon. Papaya leaves are used as poultice and this cures elephantis is also.

Ripe papaya fruits besides being eaten fresh. It also used in salad. The pulp is utilised also in preparing toffees, jams, jellies and refreshing drinks. Unripe fruits are utilized in preparing curries, pickles, preserves, petha, laccha, 'bari' and for taking fresh slices with salt and in 'salad'. Chutnies and 'Raayataas' are also prepared from green papayas. Green papaya slices are specially advised by doctors to be taken by the patients of jaundice.

Papaya is a native of South America and is grown in almost tropical and subtropical areas of the world. It was introduced in India by the Portuguese in 16th century. Since then, it spread through Pacific Islands, where papaya is a very common fruit now.

Papaya growing regions in the world are Hawaii, West Indies, Malaysia, California, Peru, Texas, Florida, South Africa, Kenya, Taiwan, Australia, India, Ceylon, Myanmar and others.

In India the orcharding of papaya is done in Tamil Nadu, Mysore, Maharashtra, Assam, Gujarat, Madhya Pradesh, Uttar Pradesh and Uttarakhand Vallies. Out of these at some places papayas are grown on a large scale. In Uttar Pradesh in Sarsaul town and development blocks of Kanpur Nagar and in Qayamganj of district Farrukhabad, besides others, papayas are grown commercially on a large scale. It observed by the author earlier.

Grow Papaya for Health

Climate: Papaya does well both in subtropical as well as tropical climate. However, warm and humid climate is the best, with the limitation that very humid atmosphere will be harmful. Heavy rains are also injurious, as there are many chances of spread of virus among the plants. Water logging is extremely harmful, which cause stem rot and damage the crop. Fast wind and storms directly exposed on papaya plants break the stem as it is weak and hollow. The plants may also be uprooted. Very cold atmosphere, cold wind and frost adversely affect the papaya crop. Similarly hot wind (loo) and scorching sun damage the crop. Places where the minimum temperature in winters does not go below 5°C and in summers where the range of maximum temperature is between 38° to 44°C are more suitable for papaya growing. However, in a warm climate, if the atmosphere remains dry instead of being humid, the fruits on ripening become more sweet. Anyway, the warm atmosphere is a must for papaya orcharding.

Soil : Well drained loam, deep loam, sandy loam, friable soil and rich in humus (with organic matter) are best for papaya growing. Rich alluvial soils of the banks and deltas of big rivers are also good enough. It does well also in black soils of Decan and laterite soils of Western Ghats. Aeration in soil is necessary. Only sandy, clayey, heavy, compact, marshy, stony and low-lying soils are unsuitable. Water logging in no way is tolerable. Even water should not continue touching the main stem or trunk.

Propagation: Papaya is propagated by seeds, as no vegetative methods of propagation could be possible, except to some extent by inserting healed cuttings in soil from branches sometimes coming out of the main stem or the trunk of the papaya plant/ tree. Seeds are sown in nursery bed in February - March or April to August. For this fresh seeds should be selected for sowing. The length of the seed bed should be 3 metres and one metre as its breadth. Also it should be prepared 15 cm. high from the ground level. For preparing the seed bed, first of all soil of the bed should be dug up and mixed up with well rotten fine compost. E.Y.M. or other organic matter, and the soil be smoothened for sowing.

Before sowing in beds, papaya seeds should be treated with Agrosan G.N.@ 1 part fungicide and 300 parts seed. Before treatment, slimmy covers should be removed from seeds to save the seedlings from damping off; treat the soil of the bed with 250 ml. formaline dissolved in 2.5 litre water per 20 square metre land. After treating the soil of the bed, it should be covered with polythene sheets for 48 hours. Treated seeds should be sown in treated soil only and that too only after a gap of fifteen days of soil treatment.

After soil and seed treatment, for actual sowing of seeds, prepare in the width of each bed 1 cm. deep rows at a distance of 10 -12 cm. Then drop the seeds in these rows at 2-3 cm. apart and cover the depth of row with finely sieved well-rotten Farm Yard Manure (FYM) or Compost. Then spread uniformly 5-6 mm thick layer of above sieved manure over the beds and press well.

For planting a hectare of land with papaya seedling a quantity of 200 to 250 gram of seeds will be required. Just after sowing seeds in nursery beds, irrigate in summers both times with watering can having a rose. Care should be taken that there is no over watering. Only water should absorb in the soil of the bed and should not flow below the raised bed.

Before germination of seeds and also after germination, arrangements, for temporary sheds should be made to protect the growing seedlings from hot sun and rains. However, morning sun is also essential for these young seedlings. Besides seed sowing in beds, these may be sown in wooden boxes, polythene bags, pots, trays etc. in case less number of seedlings are required. These should be filled with a mixture of one part soil, one part course sand and one part compost. Plants raised in beds, wooden boxes or polythene bags when attain height of 3 - 10 cm. these may be transferred in fresh polythene bags. In about two months the seedlings attain the height of about 15 to 25 cm., and this is the proper stage for transplanting the seedlings at the final place. Instead of transplanting the seedlings from beds direct to final place of planting, transplanting in polythene bags earlier is better. This practice saves plants from mortality. In every case seeds should be sown two months earlier than actual plantation at the final place.

For a large scale plantation transplanting every plant at the young stage in polythene bags may not be possible for final plantation. Under such circumstances seeds may be sown direct in polythene bags as indicated earlier, which may easily be shifted to final place of planting. Young 8-10 cm high plants may also be transplanted in newly prepared beds at a distance of 25- 30 cm. each way. These beds should also be well dug up and mixed with half to half soil and FYM or compost and sand as well. By transplanting in such beds, when the plants reach height of 25 - 30 cm for final plantation, these will have to be lifted from beds with earthen balls, which will be covered in joottee of kaans (Saeeharum) or unchafted paddy straw (Payaal) and tied and then taken to the place where papaya orchard is to be established.

As mentioned earlier though vegetative propagation by healed cuttings in papaya is possible, but to a very limited extent and on commercial basis it is not possible. This is because branching in papaya is not common. Even if some branches appear, only one cutting may be had from one branch as base (heal) of the branch from where it is removed from the main stern is a must. Therefore, on commercial scale papaya propagation is done only by seed.

Family Details and Sex Identification

Papaya belongs to the family Caricacea and is Botanically known as Carica papaya. Its English name is 'papaya' and 'papaw' as well. In Hindi or common language it is called 'papita' and 'Arand Kharbooza'. Its plant grows rapidly on a long straight stem, its stem or trunk grows up to a height of 3-4 metres unbranched, which is soft, tender and hollow. It is an evergreen plant. Actually its plant/tree is not like other trees but it is herbaceous, though sometimes, it is called a papaya tree. Being a herbaceous plant, it has large broad leaves (lamina) like the leaves of a castor plant, resting on long thick but hollow thick leaf - stalk. The plant looks like an umbrella. The basal portion of the leaf stalk (pulvinus) is swollen. Flowers and fruits are borne in leaf axil. Papaya is a dioceous plant. As such male and female flowers are borne separately on different plants. Flowers are creamy in colour.

Sex identification in papaya is a problem, which is directly related with fruiting. Since it is a unisexual plant, the male plant does not bear fruits. Fruits are borne only on female plants. Male flowers supply pollen grains through wind to female flowers for fertilization. Identification of male and female plants are not possible before flowering. Only it can be estimated in growing plants in the nursery. Out of plants planted at a time in the nursery, those which grow comparatively faster may come out as male plants.

As regards male plants, cream coloured small male flowers having tubular bases and coming out from axils of leaves are seen hanging in bunches on string-like stalks. These male flowers are 2.5 cm. long and the string - like stalks on which these flowers hang may be upto even about one metre long. Female flowers creamy in colour, thick and about 2.5 cm. in length are directly born on main stem in axils of leaves. These flowers have five thi*ck* petals, covering all around the creamy ovary with the stigma at its top. The ovary is just like the shape of a small papaya fruit and therefore female flowers may also be easily identified. This fruit-shaped ovary after fertilization develops into fruit.

The pulp of the fruit is thick. Green truits have whitish pulp and ripe fruits have yellowish-orange coloured pulp. The fruit is hollow. Its seeds remain attached on walls of the fruit inside. Unripe fruits have soft white unsmooth seeds and the skin of the fruit is green. In ripe fruits the skin is yellowish and seeds are black and covered with slimmy material, oval or roundish - oval in shape like seeds of black pepper female flowers bear three in number at a place. The middle one is larger in size— comparison to those two borne on each side. Sometimes only one female flower is also borne at a place.

Some plants of papaya are bisexual flowers are 3-4 cm. long and just like those of female flowers, except that these are comparatively a little thinner and are borne on thick and a bit longer stalk. These flowers are tubular at the basal end. Gradually these widen towards upper portion. Petals of bisexual flowers are creamy, thick and curled. The petals keep stamens and long ovary covered within inside. Bisexual papaya flowers yield oblong and longish fruits having less hollow portion inside and filled up with seeds. Sometimes ovary of bisexual plants are like those of female plants, but the androecium (male part) is irregularly arranged and appear as if pasted on the ovary. This is why fruits obtained from these flowers are disfigured and also having deep longitudinal stripes.

Besides these, there are many other phenomena regarding sex differentiation in papaya. Some-times, it may be seen in hanging male flower bunches, also few small green fruits hanging with them. This is because some-times few bisexual flowers also exist with male flower bunches. Sometimes it also happens that male plants when become old start bearing hermaphrodite flowers. Sometimes female and bisexual flowers - both appear on a single plant. This results in appearance of fruits of different shapes on a single plant. Sometimes some male parts of hermaphrodite flowers convert into female parts, resulting in deshaped fruits. There is no method of changing sex, but this may occur naturally all of a sudden. Fruits obtained from irregular sex or change of sex are abnormal in shape. When there is sex problem in papaya, for its remedy three plants may be planted at a place with the expectation that at least one female plant must come out. There should be a difference of 15 cm. between the two plants. After flowering, one healthy female plant should be retained and rest be remaked.

In a papaya orchard male plants are also essential and only female plants won't do. Since pollten grains from male flowers are required to famale flowers to fertilize and develop fruits, presence of some male plants near the papaya orchard is a must. Pollen grains of papaya reach female flowers from up to a distance of 4-5 kilometres through wind. However, as a safety measure 10% male plants should also be maintained in a papaya orchard for fruiting. Now some such new varieties of papaya have been evolved, most- plants of which are either female or bisexual. These varieties solve the exiting sex problem (though identification of sex in early stage still remains an unsolved problem).

Grow Papaya for Health

Varieties

As papaya plants are propagated only by seeds, maintenance of original characters of the parent plant is not possible in fruits of plants raised by seeds. This is due to the open pollination, pollen of which are received from different plants and varieties over the female flowers. It may only be possible when growing of other varieties are stopped in neighbouring fields to check their pollen grains reach female parts of flowers of growing plants. However, as indicated earlier, now many such varieties have developed in the country, plants of which bear a certain percentage or even 100% of bisexual flowers, on the plant, some of which are briefed in other paragraphs.

Honey Dew (Madhu Bindu)

The plant of Honey Dew variety is of medium size. The fruits start bearing from basal portion of stem of the plant. The fruit of this variety is long - roundish, weights 2.0 kg and attains yellow colour on ripening. The pulp is yellow coloured, sweet and tasteful and has less number of seeds inside.

Coorg Honey Dew

Coorg Honey Dew variety is a selection from among seedling plants of the variety 'Honey Dew' growing in orchards of Fruit Research Station, Chaithalli, Coorg. This selection was of hermaphrodite flowers and was named as 'Coorg Honey Dew'. Later on this bisexual variety Coorg Honey Dew got much popularity among the growers. The flowers of this variety possess both female and male parts. These fertilize and bear fruit by self pollination and do not require pollen from outside. As such the characters of this variety remain preserved also in future generations. Coorg Honey Dew is an important true to type variety of papaya suitable for commercial plantation as well as on home scale. The fruit of Coorg Honey Dew is medium to large sized and oval to long in shape. Its skin is smooth and turns yellow on ripening. The apex of the fruit has an under-developed nipple, with some raised and deep stripes towards the apical portion.

The pulp of the ripe fruit is orange coloured, juicy, tasteful, soft and compact. The hollow portion of the fruit is slightly more with lesser seeds. Since every flower of a plant has both male and female parts, only one plant may be planted at a place if Coorg Honey Dew orchard is being planted.

Washington

Washington is an improved Papaya variety of Maharashtra. Original characters of its previous generations were got preserved in this variety after segregating its plantation from other varieties. Thus the possibilities of obtaining true characters of the variety become better. The nodes of the stem and leaf stalks of this variety are purple coloured. In an experiment conducted at Poona earlier 60% plants were found female, 20% hermaphrodite and 20% male. The fruit of Washington is oblong with a purplish ring at the basal portion around the fruit stalk. It weighs from 1.5 to 2.0 gm. The skin of the fruit is green in an unripe stage and turns yellow on ripening. The pulp of the fruit is orange, sweet, tasteful and fine-textured with a pleasant flavour. Seeds are less in number and flowers are yellow.

Raanchi

Fruits in the variety Raanchi start bearing from lower portion of the stem (trunk) of the plant. In this variety the characters and qualities of the parent get preserved for many generations. The fruit is oval of medium size. On ripening the peel of the fruit becomes yellow in colour. The pulp of the fruit is thick, dark yellow in colour, sweet very tasty.

CO-1 (Coembatore-1) :- The variety Co-1 of papaya was developed in Tamil Nadu Agricultural University and Research Institute, Coimbatore. The plant is dwarf and starts bearing from a height of 60 cm from the ground. In this variety 60% plants are female and test are male. For this plants of Raanchi variety were segregated from other varieties up to six generations. Only after this true original qualities could be had in this variety. The fruit of CO-1 variety of Papaya is roundish in shape smooth skin, medium in size and about 500 gm in weight. The pulp of the fruit is golden yellow in colour, fine textured compact, juicy, sweet, tasteful and with a pleasing flavour. Keeping quality of the fruit is also good.

CO^2 (Coimbatore-2) :- The plant is of medium size. Flowers in a plant are hermaphrodite. The fruit is oval in shape with stripes over there. The fruit starts bearing at the trunk from the height of 100 to 120 cm from the ground level. The pulp of the fruit of CO^{-2} is pinkish and juicy. This variety is good for manufacture of papain.

Grow Papaya for Health-5

More Varieties Selection-7

The fruit of this variety is oblong or longish, of medium size and yellow in colour. Its nipple at apical portion has deep and protuberated stripes. The pulp is reddish in colour, compact and slightly juicy. This variety is also suitable for extracting papain.

Peradeniya

The fruit of this variety is small to medium-sized and roundish oval shaped. The flesh is orange in colour, firm, juicy and sweet. Its keeping quality is good. Good for extraction of papain.

Philippines

The fruit is medium-sized oval to oblong in shape. Its peel is yellowish green. The nipple at the apex of the fruit is clearly ridged and grooved. The pulp is orange coloured, soft, not compact and juicy. Keeping quality not satisfactory. However, it is good for the purposes of manufacturing papain. Indian Agricultural Research Institue, New Delhi - Regional Centre PUSA, Bihar has developed five such varieties of papaya, which more or less solve the present sex problem in papaya orcharding. For this efforts were made continuously for 16 years from 1966 to 1982. During this period so many varieties were collected from India and abroad and breeding, crossbreeding and selection work were done and continued. As a result of this only the variety Raanchi was found suitable at the above Regional Research Station. Therefore, by utilizing 'Raanchi' variety breeding and cross breeding work along with selection were carried on - on a large scale, which made possible to develop and establish five true varieties of papaya, which are 'Pusa Delicious' (Pusa 1-15) 'Pusa Majesty (Pusa 22-3), 'Pusa Giant' (Pusa 1-45), and 'Pusa Nanha' (Krishi Darshan -monthly magazine, New Delhi, May 1983, pp. 19-24).

Pusa Delicious

'Plants of this variety have no male flowers, but either female or hermaphrodite flowers. As such there is no need of pollengrains from outside for fertilization and plants fruit very well from their own pollen'. There is no difference between fruits obtained from female flowers and hermaphrodite flowers. The plant starts fruiting when it reaches a height of 80 cm. This stage comes at 8 - 9 months of planting. After fruiting, the plant attains the maximum height of 200 cm. The fruit is medium to large sized and roundish long in shape. It is 18 cm. long, 8 cm. wide and 1 to 2 kg. in weight. On ripening the colour of the fruit becomes dark yellow. The flesh is attractive dark orange in colour, 4 cm. thick, very sweet tasteful and with avery pleasant flavour. Sugar in the pulp of the variety 'Delicious' (of papaya) is quite rich, i.e. from 8 - 13%. After fruiting the number of fruits yielding in a plant is from 20 to 80 and these weight

35 to 40 kg. Ripe fruits are harvestable within a year of plantation. Though the life of a papaya plant is very short, but three crops may easily be had from this variety within three years. For plantation of a Delicious variety of papaya, only one plant should be planted at a place.

Pusa Majesty

All the plants of the variety Pusa Majesty of papaya are either female or bisexual. The plant starts bearing at a height of 50 cm. Once the plant starts fruiting it attains the maximum height of 175 cm.

The fruit is 1 to 2.5 kg. in weight, 17 cm. long and 9 cm. wide and of a special shape. The pulp of the fruit is yellow compact and very sweet, which is 3.5 cm. in thickness. It possesses 9 to 10 % sugar in itself. On ripening the fruits remain preserved for several days and do not rot. Therefore, this variety-has been found quite suitable for transporting to a long distance or exporting. This variety is also free from the attack of viral diseases. One plant yields 20 to 45 fruits which weigh 35 to 40 kg. Next year bisexual plants yield much more than the previous year to the extent 2 to 2 ½ times more. The plant fruits well for three years. A good variety for commercial purposes.

Pusa Giant

The plant of this variety is comparatively huge sized with strong and thick trunk and is resistant to strong wind and storm. Its plant starts fruiting at a height of 85 cm. and after fruiting for a year it attains the height of 220 cm. In this variety male and female flowers are found on separate plants. The fruit is large sized, with a length of 18 cm. and width of 10 cm. The shape is roundish long and its apical portion is conical. One fruit of Pusa Giant variety of Papaya weighs about 1.5 to 3.5 kg. The pulp is 5 cm. thick and contains 7.0 to 8.5% sugar. One plant produces 15 to 25 fruits which are up to 30 gm. in weight. Fruits of this variety are very useful for preparing curry, pickles and petha. Since male and female flowers are borne on separate plants, as a safety measure three plants may be planted at one place.

Grow Papaya For Health-6

Other Varieties

Pusa Dwarf -The plant of this variety is dwarf and starts bearing at a height of only 40 cm within eight months. After fruiting for a year this gains hardly the height of 130 cm. The height of the plant does not increase much even after 2-3 crops and therefore the growers feel convenient in plucking fruits. Its fruit is medium (12x8 cm.) in size, oval in shape, and 0.5 to 1.5 kg. in, weight. Its pulp is reddish with yellowish tinge and 3.5 cm. in weight. The pulp possesses in itself 8 - 9% of sugar. About 30-40 fruits may be had from a Pusa Dwarf plant which weight from 30 to 35 kg. This variety of papaya has been planted on a very large scale in Narendra Deo University of Agriculture and

Technology, Faizabad. As such this variety has gained much popularity in that area. Since male and female flowers are borne separately on different plants it will be proper to plant three plants at a place in this variety also.

Pusa Nannha - Pusa Nannha is a very dwaft variety of papaya. It starts fruiting only at a height of 30 cm. from the basal portion of the plant. Even after fruiting for 3 -4 years its maximum height reaches hardly one metre. The thickness of the stem of the plant is less. The yield per plant is also comparatively less in this variety, but due to lesser growth in the plant, these may be planted at a lesser distance, say 125 cm. apart each way. As such 6400 plants may be accommodated per hectare against 2500 to 3050 plants per hectare in normal case. The number of fruits borne per plant is less and therefore the yield per plant is also comparatively less (11 kg.) However, the accommodation of number of plants per hectare being more, the yield per hectare is also more than other varieties. The fruit of Pusa Nannha papaya is round in shape approximately 12x12 cm. in size. The pulp is sweet, yellow and 3 cm. thick. Pusa Nannha may be planted also in kitchen gardens as well as in pots. The orchard of this variety is safe from storms and being so dwaft there is no question of breaking stems of its plants.

Besides, above varieties Ceylon, Singapore and Barwani are other good varieties of papaya. Hayes (Fruit Growing in India, 1970, Kitabistan Alld.) has mentioned a local variety of papaya as 'Gujarat' besides 'Singapore', 'Ceylon' and 'Hawai'. 'Solo' has also been indicated there as a famous variety in Hawai Indian Institute of Horticultaral Research Hessarghatta Lake Post, Bangalore, has developed 'SURYA' 'Sunrise Solo X Pink Flesh); a good variety of papaya A visit by the author on 14th Novermber, 2002 during International conference on Vegetables held at Bangalore from November 11 - 14. 2002). 'Surya' is a hermaphrodite variety of papaya. Its fruits is more or less oval in shape with conical apex. The pulp is thick reddish pink, attractive and, very sweet. Two other new varieties were also developed there, which are IIHR - 39 and IIHR-57, (Also seen by the author in TV Samachar from Delhi in Ballia on 25th May 1993). Varieties like 'Saantakruz Giant Barwani Red, and Singapore pink have also been referred (Vigyan Pragati, November 1993 page 42). Another variety 'PANT' - It has also been developed from university of Agriculture and Technology, Pantnagar (Now in Uttaranchal).

A National workshop on 'Post-Harvest Management of Horticultural produce' was organised by National Productivity Council Chandigarh from February 7-8-2002 at of an Again Chandigarh. During this workshop a paper was submitted on Post Harvest Management of fruits and vegetables for export by Dr. O P. Singhal Principal Scientist IARI, New Delhi in connection with packing of many fruits for export including papaya. An regards papaya two varieties —TAIWAN -

783 and BOLOTYPES have been preferred therein. These are oval in shape, 250 - 500 gm in weight, yellow and orange - red in color with sweet juicy and thin pulp.

Seedless Papaya -Sometimes papaya fruits are seen with seeds at all and these fruits i.e. entirely seedless. Seedless fruits of papaya develop from purely female flowers, when by chance these do not fertilize by pollen of male plants. Though seedless papayas are a little smaller than fertilized fruits, yet these are sweet and tasteful, but due to lack of suitable technique of asexual (vegetative) propagation, seedless variety of papaya could not be established. However, seedless fruits of Honey Dew variety of papaya could be had by spraying 200 pm Gibberellic acid (200 mg G.A. and 1 litre water) on female flowers at Tamil Nadu Agriculture University, Coimbatore (Papaya in India, Farm Information unit, Agricultural Extension Directorate, New Delhi, 1974). These were though not entirely seedless, but one fruits contained 10-87 seeds against 50 to 800 seed in a normal fruit.

Producing Varieties by Sibmating - Continuous inbred by growing plants from seeds within a particular type of plant to get the original characters of fruits is called 'SIBMATING'.This is producing brother and sister plants from the same parents. For this seeds from the fruits of typical papaya plant, which present parental qualities like leaf, stem, fruit, leaf stalk etc. In the plant are selected and sown. Seedlings raised from these seeds are then transplanted in the field. When these plants flower, progenies conforming to the qualities and characters which formed the basis for original selection are tagged among the female as well as male plants. A day or two before opening of flowers male and female flower buds are covered with butter paper bags to avoid reaching of pollengrains from their papaya plants. From outside through wind. After opening of flowers, pollen grains from the bagged male flower collected in sterilized cotton wool and smeared on the stigma of the bagged female flower between 7 to 10 A.M. and covered with a fresh butter paper bag.

Within a week's time fruits set and then the whole bag is removed. When these sibmated fruits mature and become ripe, seeds from these fruits are collected. These are sown to get a second generation of plants. The methods adopted for selection, sibmating, will be the same. This practice is continued for several generations till all the inbred plants of papaya orchard bear fruits of uniform original characters. The varieties Co-I, Selection 7, Pusa Delicious, Pusa Majesty, Pusa Dwarf etc. are the results of sibmating, which were originally derived from 'Raanchi' papaya.

To protect the papaya varieties from degeneration, this may not be possible for every grower to adopt the technique of inbreeding or sibmaing. As, such they will have to purchase true seeds of a variety every time from universities of Agriculture and Technology, Kanpur, Faizabad, Pant Nagar,

A.A.I. (Deemed University), IARI New Delhi-12, IARI. Regional Research Station Pusa, Bihar, Indian Institute of Horticultural Research Hessarghatta Lake Post Bangalore. Uttar Pradesh Subtropical Fruit Research Station, Rehmankhera Lucknow, Horticultural Experiment and Traïning Centre Basti and Saharanpur and Department of Horticulture Uttar Pradesh, Lucknow.

However, to save from all above troubles for commercial growing of pepaya some large -sized papaya fruits may be had from market and seeds from these may be extracted and seedling be raised. These may be planted for having a papaya orchard. Of course one may not have uniform in size and quality but tasteful papayas will be there.

Layout of Orchard and Preparation of Soil

First of all 2 - 3 ploughings of the land should be done by a soil turning plough for planting a papaya orchard. During ploughing 400 quintals of well rotten Farm Yard Manure (Cow dung manure) should also be spread and mixed with the soil in the whole field. The soil should then be smoothened by planking after removing weeds and other foreign material from the soil. After the soil is smoothened, lay out is done at 1.8 metres (6 feet) apart each way and the place of plantation is marked. Pits of the size 50 x 50 x 50 cm. should then be dug up on every mark in April - May. After the soil of the pits and dug up soils are well dried up in the hot sun for at least a month these are filled up. For this, each pit is filled up with soil of upper surface mixed with 20kg of well rotten F.Y.M or compost and one kg. neem cake or bone meal or 500 gm. super phosphate single (80 gm. P). These pits are well pressed and filled up 15 cm. above the ground level. After one or two rains the raised portions come down to the level of the soil. If there is no rains the whole field may be watered. If the land was under cultivation of other crops and the ploughing was done up to 25 cm depth, there is no need of digging pits on the marks after lay out.

Plantation

After the filled up pits are ready for plantation, plants are planted in the center of the filled up puts. If the plant is in a polythene bag, polythene should be gently removed, so that soil around the plant, which was in the bag, may not be disturbed. If it is in 'jootee' that should be removed, then planted. In every case the soil around the roots of the plant should never be disturbed. Before plantation, a hole should be dug up in the centre of the filled up pits slightly larger in size than that of the earthen ball around the roots of the plant, so as to accommodate the earthen ball in the hole. The plant should be planted only up to the depth at which this was in nursery or in polythene bag. This could be judged from mark of soil on stem of the young plant. After plantation, soil all around the plant should be well-pressed and lightly irrigated if there are no rains.

Care should also be taken at the time of plantation that the plant may remain straight. The most suitable height is from 15 - 25 cm and about a month in age. It is also advisable to see if some root portions are visible outside the earthen ball, these should let remain in the same direction in tha soil. If there is any tap root it should be placed straight in the soil and if some fibrcus roots are seen these may be placed spreading all round. In no case roots should be folded. As referred earlier if no pits have been dug up and filled in an already cultivated soil it is supposed that ploughing, mixing manure, planking and layout have been done papay-: plantation. Under such circumstances, 10 kg. of FYM should be mixed in soil at each marked place of plantation and then 500 gm super phospnate or one *kg* of neem care or bone meal should he spread in a diameter of 50 cm all round each place of plantation.

If there is no certainty of male and female plants do plant three plants in a pit, thinking that out of these one plant must come out as female plant. The distance between these three plants should be 15 cm from each other. The healthlest fomale plant should be retained in a pit and rest be removed. If any pit or laid out mark remains temalesss, replantation of a female plant may be done there by having from other pits. However, 10% male plants should also be retained here and there in a papaya orchard.

However, if hermaphrodite varieties are being planted only one plant should be planted at a place. Examples of such varieties as already mentioned in earlier paris of thsi article are pusa Delicious (Cent per cent plants hermaphrodite or female), Pusa Majesty (all plants female or hemaphrodite), Surya (Bisexual), Coorg Honey Dew (Hermaphrodite), Washington (80% hermaphrodite and female), Coimbatore -2 (Hermaphrodite), Coimbatore - 1 (60% plants bisexual and rest male)

Time of Plantation

Papaya being an evergreen plant is fit for plantation during rainy season, i.e. from June-July to September - October. However, being prone to viral diseases, which spread rapidly during rains, it is considered best time when the rains are almost over or nearing to an end. As such second fortnight of September may prove more useful with regards to time of papaya plantation if there are good facilities of irrigation, papaya may also be planted during February-March, though the grower will have to be very cautious from hot wind and burning hot sun onwards. For this shades may be prepared and wind-breaks may be planted.

Wind Break

To save the plants from heavy storms cold and hot wind in winters and summers (in the same order), quick growing plants like Sesbania aegyptiaca (Jait) should be planted specially on Western and Northern side of the orchard.

For this seeds of these may be sown in situ (at the final place) during rains before actual plantation of papaya plants. Seeds germinate within a week and grow rapidly and form a dense wall-like structure. After germination, when plants grow up to a height of 20 - 25 cm. these may be thinned out to a distance of 90 - 100 cm from each other. This is a leguminous plant with deep tap roots in soil and therefore, when once established during rains, these require no care.

Intercropping

So far there is ample space between two plants of papaya each way in a papaya plantation, vegetable crops may be taken as intercrop specially, when no papaya fruits are available. During this period vegetable crops of cauliflower, cabbage, radish, garlic, onion, spinach, coriander, fenugreek etc. may become sources of early income. Onion, garlic, fenugreek, coriander leaves and dill (soya) may be harvested in green condition for fresh use and early income. Thus the occupied space becomes vacant for other intercrops.

Next year when plants reach a considerable sufficient height (depending on variety) seeds of beans (better it 'Rajani' variety) may be sown in July and the plants may be allowed to climb on naked parts of papaya stem (trunk). After flowering and fruiting one may have fresh beans throughout the winters.

When the land becomes more shady, crop of spinach may be taken throughout the yes. However, care has to be taken that the papaya crop is not affected in any case and area may not become very dense. In this way for the same piece of land crops of papay a and green vegetables may easily be taken. Again papaya plant itsalf may be taken as intercrop or as interfillars orchards of guava, mango and others.

The life of a papaya plant is hardly for 2 - 3 years and after that taking papaya crop from such plants will not be profitable. Therefore, to utilizes the same land for further papaya plantation, fresh papaya plants may be planted in between two plants each way, before the last crop that time the fresh plants will grow enough to bear papaya flowers and fruits in the mean time the old plants for which last crop or papaya was taken should be cut down from the base and removed. After cutting, digging and ploughing of land should be done so the fresh plantation may grow and flourish well. This papaya plantation will again continue for 2-3 years. Its first crop will be ready for harvest comparatively earlier.

Irrigation

Papaya is a shallow rooted plant and therefore watering from time to time is necessary. However, water logging around the plant in no case is desirable. Leaving the soil dry for a long period and suddenly irrigating plants may create an adverse affect on the crop. In summers irrigation may be done at every 5-7 days interval and in winters at an interval of 15 days. Irrigation should be done tnrough irrigation channels prepared between every two alternate row, which are connected with 'thaalaas' of every plant through sub-channels.

As a matter of fact small round raised rings (thaalaas) are prepared on the outer side around each plant after plantation and some raised soil should be there around the stem of each plant in slopy manner and pressed well to make it a compact slope of soil. This is done so that irrigation water may not touch the papaya stem directly, otherwise there will be stem root/foot rot and as such the stem will rot and got down from the base.

Size of thaalas are increased from time to time according to the spread of leaves. The raised ring of each thaala should be just below the drip of the plant, i.e. below the spread, rather a little away from there. Accordingly, the compact raised portion of soil should also be increased in size according to requirements. In the long run the slope around the stem may be about 15 cm. high and 30 cm. wide at the lower portion.

Hoeing and Weeding

For proper aeration in soil, hoeing the soil is a must. This will allow the roots to have air and light for better growth. Simultaneously weeding is also important as weeds consume food material of the crop and also harbour insects and pests. As such after every two irrigation, when the soil becomes trriable, hoeing and wedding should regularly be done specially when the plants are in growing stage. When one crop is over after a year, light ploughing or digging of soil as mentioned earlier should be done for the next crop and all operation are carried on as usual for the next crop.

Manuring

One crop of papaya requires 200 gm. Nitrogen (N), 80 gm. Phosphate (P) and 250 gm of Potash (K). Phosphate is provided at the time of plantation at the marked place after lay out or in the filled up pit. Rest of the manure's or fertilizers are divided into two parts. One part is provided in September - October and the remaining other part in February - March. The whole actual dose of fertilizers for a year according to N,F,K thus becomes 445 gm urea or 1 kg. of Ammonium Sulphate for Nitrogen (N), 500 gm. Single Super Phosphate lor Phosphate (P), and 500 gm. Potassium Sulphate or 416 gm. Potassium Chloride (MCP) for Potash (K) plus 20 gm. of farm yard Manure.

The fertilizers and manure are added all round the plant from the time of the compact slopy raised soil around the stem up to the spread of the plant on the outer side as irrigation was done. Those are sprinkled and mixed in soil by digging it to a depth of 8 - 16 cm or so. Care has to be taken that during digging after manuring roots may not get disturbed. After manuring watering may be done according to necessity. From timely manuring and Irrigation growth of plants go on properly, plants remain healthy and fruits ripen well. The above quantity of manure is in addition to these applied at the time of prepartaion of land and filling of pits or those applied at the time of plantation. These quantities are applying in fruiting plants of papaya. When male plants could clearly be detected there is no need of applying manure in these palnts. These plants pollinate the female flowers for fertilization and fruiting.

Flowering, Fruting and Thinning

After final plantation of papaya orchard, flowering and fruiting take place in six months. The fruits finally develop and mature within the next six months and the crop is harvested within a year. During development of green fruits many of them are densely populated. The bigger fruits sometimes press the smaller-sized fruits which become deshaped and flat. These also remain under developed. Such fruits, whether green or ripe, are less valued in the market. As such small fruits growing between large fruits or those pressed by larger or other fruits, should be thinned out time to time by catching the same hand and giving a twist. Such fruits may also be removed by cutting the fruit stalk through a sharp knife, taking care that other fruits are not injured.

After these fruits are thinned, remaining fruits will develop to their foul size, which will bring better price in the market. Those fruits which have been thinned may be utilized in preparing curries, chutney, pickles, preserves, petha and all other products mentioned earlier for utilizing green fruits.

Papaya plant if beheaded from the top, gives out many shoots in sides and callus formotion takes place at the cut end. To have fruits from these shoots only four shoots may be retained in a plant. In this way higher yield may be had. Either shoots if sprouted should be removed and should not be retained on plants. However, such extra shoots may be remcved with their heels (basal wide portion) intact, so that these may be utilized for vegetative propagation.

Plucking Fruits

From flowering and fruiting it takes six months to mature fruits and then it ripens. After fruits are fully matured, yellowish tinge may be visible between the stripes or at the apical (central) arid of the fruit. This is the symbol of ripening and plucking of fruits from the plants. At this stage if the skin of the papaya fruit is scratehed, it will ooze out white liquid. Liquid material (thinner than latex). Such fruits are then gently plucked by giving a light twist to the fruit and placed in basket by handing over to another person or by keeping the fruits in a bag hanging on the plucker's shoulder.

Plucking of fruits should be done by standing on stool or on a ladder. Handling of fruits between plucking and ripening is very important. That should be no injury or scratch on the fruit. During picking, fruits should not drop in soil. After pieking fruits should be placed in basket by first spreading news paper sheets in the basket. Fruits which ripen on the plant are more sweet and tasty. Under such circumstances if one is not cautious, crows eat and destroy ripening fruits on the plant. Sometimes, when papaya plant becomes very high many fruits remain cut of sight, which go on ripening and eaten by crows. As such for plucking such papaya fruits very high lackier should be used. However, any piece of bamboo or long stick should never be used for plucking, because the chance of injury and in infection in fruits become greater.

Ripening

After mature and yellow is tinged fruits are picked up, these are collected in a room wrapped in news papers or even covered with news papers. The room should then, be closed and too fruits with ripen within a week. According to requirement fruits may also be placed and covered in basket or wooden boxes. On ripening papaya fruits attain attractive golden yellow or reddish yellow colour. In no case calcium carbionate should be usad for ripening, as these make the fruits absorb poisonous gases. In Uttar Pradesh ripe fruits of papaya are available from January - February to May-June or even onwards.

Grow Papaya for Health-9

Marketing and Storage

From marketing point of view, papaya production should be done near cities and markets, for early and easy disposal. For transporting fruits from a long distance to the market, it is essential that truits should be packed when those are hard enough. Every fruit should be wrapped in news paper sheet and placed in baskets or wooden boxes. An average basket or wooden box can hardly accommodate 5-6 papaya fruits.

During packing, this point should also be under consideration that one fruit should not touch with the other fruit or should not touch directly walls or bottoms of packing boxes or baskets. In between fruits and fruits and walls and bottoms of boxes and baskets, wheat or paddy straw or paper shavings should be filled in. As such there will be no injury during movement in trucks or other vehicles and simultaneously fruits will also ripen in transit. It is also essential that one fruit should not be placed over the other fruit. Therefore packing should be done with only one layer of fruits. However, if fruits are smaller than average size, this may be done in two layers, with all precautions mentioned earlier.

If the fruits are fully ripe or nearing full ripening, these may be taken to mandies, or markets for sale. Such fruits cannot be sent to a long distance as fruits will destroy in the way. Fully ripe fruits can be kept at room temperature for 2-3 days at the most. However, these may be stored for 3 - 4 weeks at a temperature of 40 - 50^0 ft.

Yield

Yield of papaya fruits depends on female and hermaphrodite plants in the papaya orchard. Yield also depends on age of plants. The yield of fruits is good for the first three years and after that yield goes on decreasing by and by. It has already been indicated earlier that the economic life of a papaya plant is hardly for three years. Besides these, yield of fruits also depends on variety, soil, climate, cultural operations adopted etc.

One fruit of papaya weighs from 500 gm. to 2.5 kg and sometimes even up to 3 kg. Ordinarily one plant yields at least 25 - 30 healthy fruits which weigh about 30 kg. When better fruiting takes place one plant may yield even 60 -70 fruits. As such from 3025 plants per hectare one may have 900 quintals of fruits.

Preparation of Seeds

For collecling and preparing papaya seeds, large sized papaya fruits, which are fully ripe, sweet and tasteful are selected. These are longitudinally cut into two pieces with a sharp knife and seeds taken out in a wide and deep utensil. Add a little water and rub lightly the seeds with water. Keeping these between both palms. This practice will enable the seeds to be free from slimmy matter covering the seeds. Then decant water from the utensil along with slimmy matter floating in water. This practice may be repeated several times, till all the seeds are completely free from slimmy matter.

After seeds are free from slimmy material, these are spread in shade on old news-paper sheets, cloth sheets or in trays. When fully dry, these are collected and stored in black coloured air tight bottles for future use. These seeds may remain viable for more than a year. These should be placed in a cold dry place. Fresh seeds are best for germination. These germinate soon. Before storing seeds may be treated with some fungicides- like 1% Organo - mercurial dust (Agrosan GN, Ceresan dry, Hoxan etc.).

As already indicated earlier, no comimereial method of vegetative propagation has been found out as yet and is no such possibility in future also. This is also well known that plants raised from vegetative (asexual) propagation e.g. grafting, budding, cutting, layering etc. produce true to type fruits i.e. if the graft is of a Dasehri mango variety, the grown up tree from the graft will produce Dasehri fruit's exactly of the same character, irrespective of open/cross pollination of any variety.

If the stone (seed) of this grafted mango tree is sown, the tree will not produce fruits of the same character due to cross and open pollination (sexual propagation). Similar is the case with papaya, where only sexual propagation (propagation by seed) is possible. As such due to cross pollination or open and uncontrolled pollination, the fruits obtained, may be of different shape and sized good or bad in quality and others. Seed - sown plants of papaya may come out as unisexual also, most of which may be male plants. As such due to irregular and uncontrolled pollination of other varieties it becomes difficult, rather impossible to maintain the character of a particular variety in the next generation. Even if any how some good characters could be obtained by chance in the next generation, these will further be reduced or completely over in future generations.

As such once true seeds of a particular desired variety are sown, the fruits of first generation will be true to type, but during this period if the plants are left over as such for open cross pollination, fruits in the second generation will be different ones, unless controlled pollination is practiced. Therefore, to preserve the qualities of a particular variety in future generations, the only solution is that the seeds may be produced under controlled measures of pollination. If flowers of a particular variety of a female plant are pollinated by the pollen grains of the same variety and pollen of other varieties are beyond reach of the above desired variety, seeds obtained from such fruits will be true seeds. In this way to fruits prepare true seeds of a particular variety, above practice will have to be repeated regularly every year. Whenever a grower wants to establish a papaya orchard of a particular variety, having original qualities and character of the variety only true seeds will be required for sowing. For preparing true papaya seeds under contolled pollination, first of all such plants of a particular variety are selected, which possess original characters of the variety in their plants, leaves, flowers and fruits. New papaya orchard should be established by sowing seeds obtained from fruits of above selected ptants.

When flowerings take place in plants of the newly established papaya orchard. Such female and male plants should be tagged, which are having original qualities of the desired particular variety in them. Before tagging all the points should be well confirmed. Again, cover the male and female flowers of the tagged plants in tissue paper bags two days before opening of flowers, in such a way that no pollen can reach female flowers from outside and also that no pollen of male flowers could move outside the bag. When flowers open, pollen collected from the aged male flowers should gently be rubbed on the stigma of the bagged female flowers controlled pollination is done between 7 A.M. and 10 AM. To maintain purity, all to issue bags covering the male or female flowers, replaced with new ones. Fruits bear within a week after pollination After bearing of fruits, tissue paper bet all the flowers should removed and lot the try it develop freely. This submating or moreever breeding between plants and sister plants the same parant A referees of sibmating has go earlier also Seeds from fruits of above we be pure and of the variety the he seeds will so produce fruiis of lite same particulr variety when characters, out lot pure seeds same bagging and between time have to repeated.

GROW PAPAYA FOR HEALTH-10

Diseases Pests Enemies

Papaya plant faces many diseases and some of them are very serious.

Footrot

Footrot is a very fatal disease of papaya, which develops from a soil dwelling fungus, specially in rainy season. When the soil is wet, water logged and the water touches the basal portion of stem (trunk) of the plant at the ground level, the fungus becomes very active and the disease spreads very rapidly.

When the disease starts, the portion of stem of the plant, which comes in contact with water becomes soft and spongy. Gradualty this portion goes on soaking water. This results in injury and cracking of skin of stem and rotting of tissues. Oozing of foul smelling liquid also starts. Rotting later on spreads upwards in trunk and downwards in roots. Ultimately the plant falls down from the base on the ground. Such plants should be removed from roots and burnt.

Spread of disease of footrot can be prevented by keeping proper arrangements of drainage and avoiding water-logging when the atmosphere remains dry the disease is automatically checked. As indicated earlier irrigation water or rain water should never touch the stem of the plant directly. For this a high and wide slopy platform of soil should be made around the stem. In early stages disease can be checked also by proper hoeing, weeding and aeration of soil, besides proper drainage as stated above.

However, immediately after the start of disease is detected, the injured portion of the trunk is peeled off up to the green and healthy portion. Then the peeled portion should be painted with Blitox ointment, which is prepared by mixing 450 gm Blitox (Copper oxichloride 50% W.P.) and 225 gm. lime in 6.75 litre water. In addition to this Blitox - 50 should also be dusted all round the trunk of the plant in the ground including the trunk at the ground level.

Instead of above dusting, a solution of 6.3% Blitox or Captain in water (300 gm. fungicide in 100 litre water) should be sprayed at ground surface to make the soil fully drenched with the solution. Besides this, the soil may also be accordingly sprayed with 5.5:50 Bordeaux mixture.

Anthracnose

The disease of Anthoacnose in papaya is caused by a fungus, which develops on green under developed fruits and trunk of the plant when the southerly sun's rays directly scorch, these parts in winters. When the sun affects green fruits the affected position first becomes yellow. By and by the portion becomes soft. Later on this spot turns brown and spreads up to halt portion of the fruit, forming there on black coloured concentric rings. Pink coloured protuberated pustules are also observed over there. In the mean time the portion of trunk which is exposed to also burns away, becomes brown and sinks inside. By the summer sea- ant breaks down.

Only grown up plants of advanced age, which have become tail and have shed most of their leaves, are attracted by Anthracnose. Young growing and fruiting plants which have get leaves spreading all round the plant, are not affected as green fruits and stem get shade of leaves and are saved of sun's rays. However, if the grown up plants are covered with thick brown pieces of paper at the correct stage i.e. stage of possibility of occurrence of disease, it may be checked. Also the disease may be checked, if in the early stage green fruits and stem are sprayed with one part of Zineb or Zinc manganese crabamate mixed with 40 parts of water. After spraying fruits and stem may be covered with brown paper.

Damping Off

Damping off is a fungal disease, which causes young tender germinating or growing plants in the nursery to fall from base after rotting. The fungus develops in moist and damp soil over watering and water logging should be avoided, as referred earlier. Seed and soil treatment should also be done before sowing seeds. As regards seed treatment, 300 parts of seed should be treated with one part of 1 % organo = mercurial dust (Agrosan G.N.). For soil treatment mix 250 ml. formaline in 2.5 litre of water. This mixture is sufficient for treatment of 20 sq metre soil. After this treatment, the soil should be covered with a polythene sheet for 48 hours and sowing of seeds should only be done 15 days after soil treatment.

Mosaic

Mosaic is a viral disease, which is very dangerous. Though it is not a seed borne disease, it spreads rapidly in moist and dry conditions both, it spreads through aphids which suck juice of leaves and move from one leaf to the other and all plants are affected. The top leaves become yellowish and get crinkled. Leaves become small in size. The growth of plant and fruits also are adversely affected. Small roundish spots are also formed on fruits. These infect other plants also. The whole plantation is thus damaged. If the spread of disease is detected in the very beginning spray of 0.03% Methyl - 0 dimeton (0.3 gm. / ml. insecticide / 1 litre water). However, in very serious condition it is not advisable to let the plant continue. It should be uprooted and burnt.

Pests

No insect pests have been observed damaging the papaya crop. Only some serious diseases and some enemies damage the crop.

Enemies

When papayas ripe and become yellow on the trees, crow eat away the pulp by making holes in the fruit through their beaks. Other birds, squirrels and monkeys also damage the papaya crop. One should be cautious from thieves also. For safety 'Chatti' should be wrapped around the fruit at the time of ripening to keep the fruits out of sight of the birds, monkeys etc.

GROW PAPAYA FOR HEALTH-11

Manufacture of Papain

As indicated earlier regarding papain, growers should also be aware of extraction of latex and preparation of papain. Actually papain is the dry form of latex or milky juice of green immature papaya fruits, which is a digestive enzyme and is very important from industrial point of view. Manufacture of papain in Ceylon is already going on for a very long period. After manufacture, papain is exported from Ceylon to America and Europe. For extraction of latex with a view to manufacture papain, the papaya fruit should be green, raw, immature, hard and about three months old. The fruit should also be large-sized.

For actual tapping of latex about 3 mm deep, longitudinal incisions should be made on the fruits still hanging on the plant. Each incision should be 12-13 mm apart from each other. Care has to be taken that not more than four incisions should be made in a fruit at a time every day. To cover the whole surface around a fruit, in all five tappings at an interval of 4-5 days will suffice.

For tapping and collecting latex only non-metallic knife and utensils should be used. Metals react with latex, which get discoloured after reaction. For making incisions, knives or knives like instruments are prepared from bamboo pieces, which are very successfully used. Ivory blades are also utilized for making incisions. For collecting latex, glass, earthen or porcelain containers may be used. Aluminum containers have been found suitable metal, which does not react like other metals.

For collecting milky juice or latex from papaya fruits, morning time was found best, as the flow of latex in morning is abundant. Also morning time is good, for there is sufficient time for the whole day for drying of latex in sun. The fruits abound in latex, specially when the plant is young. When warm weather follows rains, it helps production of latex in large quantities.

After making incisions the latex should be allowed to tap for 2 - 4 hours in the container. The whole latex are then transferred and scraped on glass or porclain sheets and spread there on and dried in sun. If the latex does not dry completely the same day, it may safely be fully dried the next day without any damage. However, if tapping and collection are done early in the morning, it thoroughly dries up to midday. For latex collection large-sized aluminum trays are fixed on trunks of papaya plants in Tamil Nadu Agricultural University, Coimbatore. Latex flows in the trays which is dried later on.

Drying of latex should always be done when the whether is completely dry. Sun-drying may be hastened if the coagulated latex is pressed through a calendar. By adopting this practice papain will come out in small thread-like thin pieces which will dry soon. When fully dry the papain becomes crisp and can be turned into powder easily and placed in air tight bottles. The colour of sun-dried papain powder is white or cream coloured. In Europe and America such papain powders are further refined and turned in more better quality powders.

Drying of Latex Through Other Sources

Drying of latex, besides Sun is also done by other sources. In papaya orchards, which remain damp, humid and rainy for most of the period of the year, drying of lalex in sun is not possible. As such at such places some machinery or other heating arrangements are made, so that drying of latex may be done through artificial means. In West Indies and Ceylon a home-made drier is prepared.

For this a brick chamber is prepared about 2 metres in length, one metre in width and a metre in height. The top of this brick constructed chamber remains open. An opening is left during construction at the end to allow fuel for burning and producing heat. An iron sheet is then placed and adjusted 30 cm below the top and over this sheet 2.5 cm to 5 cm. thick layer of sand is spread to regulate the requirement of heat produced from the fire beneath. The coagulated latex is then spread upon a brown linen stretched on a frame fitting at the top of constructed brick drier. As regards use of fuel in drier such fuels, which produce smoke should not be used, as smokes spoil the drying latex or papain. As such coconut shells and charcoal should be used as fuel, as these do not produce smokes. Drying should be done by regulating the temperature below 38°C.

Yield of Latex or Papain

The yield of latex or papain from a papaya plant depends on many cultural operations and varieties etc. In Ceylon one plant yielded from 55 to115 gm dried latex in the first year. Next year this quantity is raised to 1 ½ times to that of the first year. It is economical to manufacture papain for only two years from a plant. In the third year the producer gets a diminishing return. An yield of 196 kg of dried latex per hectare of papaya plantation in Ceylon was considered good in the first year bearing. Later on the increase and decrease were similar to those indicated above for the yield per plant.

In Ceylon the best variety on an average produced 320 gm. of papain per plant and the best plant yielded over 460 gm. of papain. On the other hand, the "yield of papain in Tanganyika per plant varies from about 85 gm to 245 gm and 90 kg to 195 kg per hectare of plantation. Such experiments were carried out at H.B.T.I. (Harcourt Butler Technological Institute), Kanpur (UP India) with the same variety and the yield of papain per plant varied from 112 gm. to 450 gm. The yield of papain per plant from 'Gujarat' variety of papaya in Poona was recorded as 112 gm while the variety 'Singapore' produced double to that. A papaya plant in Coimbatore produces 200 - 300 gm. of papain. Its yield (goes even up to 450 gm. However, per hectare plantation of papaya yielded 250 to 375 kg of papain.

It may be noted that in those areas where chances are better for disposal as fresh ripe fruits for dessert purposes bringing high prices, growers should avoid papain production. However, where the grower has not to spend much on manuring, irrigation and other cultural operations and the crop is grown in rainfed areas, papain production may profitably be taken up. In Ceylon best results in papain production are obtained from rain-fed papaya plantations, which are done in well-drained loamy soil rich in humus and having plenty of organic matter. Selection-7 variety of papaya selected at Coimbatorc. Yields about 400 gm of papain per plant.

Disposal of Lanced Fruits

Fruits hanging on papaya plants which have been lenced for tapping latex for papain, continue growth on the plant, mature and ripe. However, the shape is a deformed, though these are more sweet in comparison to normal ripe fruits. These fruits will have to be disposed off in the market, though due to scratches on them and their unappealing appearance those may bring lower prices. On the whole papaya is a healthful profitable crop.

8

Carambola

Flowering and Bearing Behaviour of Carambola *(Averrhoa Carambola Linn.)*

Introduction

The carambola *(Averrhoa carambola* Linn.), is one of the important minor fruits of the tropics. It is extensively grown in India, Pakistan and China. Two varieties the 'Sour'and the 'Sweet' depending in their taste are commonly met with. The fruit is made into curries, tarts, stews, puddings, jams and pickles. The carambola crush is a refreshing drink. The fruit contains Vitamins A, B, C and useful minerals.

Before starting any systematic programme of improvement in a fruit crop the knowledge of its floral biology is most essential. However, no information on this aspect is available in carambola. The present studies were therefore conducted in this direction.

Materials and Methods

These studies were carried out during 1963-65, on well established carambola trees of the varieties 'Sour' and 'Sweet', growing at the Horticultural Research Institute, Saharanpur.

Observations on flowering and fruiting were made by visiting the trees throughout the period under study. Average size and weight of a fruit, was determined on the basis of ten mature fruits picked at random from all sides of the trees.

Twenty-five well developed panicles, each of 'Sour' and 'Sweet' varieties, were tagged at random on the trees. Flowers which opened in each panicle were removed every day, counted and recorded. The dates of opening of the first and last flower in panicles were also noted.

During various flowering flushes, dormant flowering buds swell up and appear as small, flattish protuberances. These burst into pinkish, feathery panicles (bud-burst stage). Ten such panicles, each of 'Sour' and Sweet', were selected at random on the trees and tagged. The length and maximum spread of these panicles were measured after every seventh day till the start of bloom.

The whole phase of floral bud development was divided into nine distinct stages from appearance of tiny bud to full bloom. In all fifty buds were kept under observation.

Anthesis

Fifteen panicles, each in 'Sour' and 'Sweet', were selected at random on the trees and tagged. The number of flowers, which were open every day, were finally recorded at intervals of two hours from 6 A.M. to 4 P.M. regularly for ten days. Flowers in which the petals were well expanded and the functional anthers were clearly visible were taken to be open. The open flowers were removed after every observation to avoid double counting.

Results

1. *Flowering and bearing habit :* Blossoms of carambola appear on naked shoots or on small branches from axillary or lateral buds in short panicles of cymes. These were also seen in axils of leaves ('sour' and 'sweet'). Besides, the 'sweet' was found flowering at the apical ends of growing shoot and looked like terminal panicles. Flowering and fruiting took place also on large and thick branches and even on trunks. Besides simple panicles, appearance of cluster panicles (double or triple) was not an uncommon feature in both varieties. The carambola flowered and fruited well both on exposed as well as unexposed portions of trees. Fruits were borne in clusters.

2. *Flowering and fruiting season :* Flowering in carambola took place in three flushes. The first flush appeared during April-May and the trees bloomed from the end of April to the second week of June. The peak bloom was seen from the end of April to the second week of May. Fruits ripened from July to September.

The second flush appeared in July-August. Flowers bloomed through out the month of August and continued up to the first week of September. The peak bloom, however, was observed in the third and fourth weeks of August. Fruits ripened during November and December.

The third flush appeared in September-October. Flowers bloomed from second week of September to the second week of November. The bloom was at its peak from last week of September to the first week of October. Ripe fruits from this flush were obtained during January-February.

The maximum yield was obtained from November to February i.e., from the second and third flushes. There was practically no difference between the varieties 'Sour' and 'Sweet' with regard to the above observations. In November only some of the flowers bloomed and these too dropped off. The remaining flowers dropped off just in the bud stage. It was noticed that a small sized (3-4 mm. in length) pinkish caterpillar bore the bud from side and ate away the ovary. This was regarded to be one of the major causes of flower drop. The caterpillar was not found in any other flush of the year. The pest is under indentification.

3. *The inflorescence, flower and fruit :* The main stalk of a panicle in the variety 'sour' is greenish, while its branches are light pinkish. In 'sweet' the main stalk is dark purple and its branches are purplish. Details of floral morphology along with several abnormalities observed in floral parts have been reported earlier (Nand, 3). The fruit is normally ovoid in shape with five prominent longitudinal lobes and looks like a star in cross-section. However, lobes of fruits ranging from three to eight in number were also observed (Nand, 5). The flesh of the fruit is translucent, soft, juicy and attractive, having 2-4 small-sized, thin, flat seeds. The sepals and styles are persistent in developing fruits. The edges of lobes are purplish in 'sweet' and green in 'sour'. On maturity the fruit of 'sour' becomes light golden yellow in colour and its maximum breadth is towards the basal end.

The edges of lobes are thick, smooth and roundish throughout the length and comparatively more thickened at the basal end of the fruit. The fruit stalk is light greenish, and some time having pinkish tinge. The mature fruit was 8.9 x 6.4 cm in size and 80.0 g. in weight.

The fruit of the 'sweet' was comparatively smaller in size (6.8 x 4.3 cm) and lighter in weight (67.5 g.). On mautrity, it acquires a slightly darker colour than that of the 'sour'. The fruit has a uniform shape having maximum breadth in its mid-portion. The edges of lobes are thin and sharp. The fruit stalk is purple in colour with reddish tinge.

4. *Floral count and duration of opening of flowers in panicles :* Data collected in this connection are presented in Table 1, which shows that the mean number of flowers opening in a panicle of 'sour' is less than half to that of the 'sweet'. The duration of opening of flowers is lesser in 'sour' than that of the 'sweet'.

Table 1

Floral count and duration of opening of flowers in panicles of the carambola (Var. 'sour' and 'sweet')

Variety	*Date of opening of first flower*	*Date of opening of last flower*	*Duration of opening of flower in all the panicles in days*	*Duration of opening of flower in a panicles*			*Number of flowers opening in a panicle*
				Days	Hrs.	Mins.	
Sour	25.9.63	17.10.63	23	14	4	48	16.5
Sweet	25.9.63	24.10.63	30	21	4	48	37.6

5. *Panicle development :* The size of panicle at the bud-burst stage was approximately 2 mm. each, in length and spread ('sour' and 'sweet'). The development of panicle was slow upto the fourteenth day from the bud-burst and this increased suddenly between the fourteenth and twently first day, of the growing period. The panicle of 'sweet' was slightly longer than that of the 'sour'. During the development of panicle, the flower buds go on increasing and after attaining full size at the end of the twenty first day, the buds start opening. The bud at the top of the panicle blooms first.

6. *Flower bud development :* There was practically no difference in varieties 'sour' and 'sweet' with regard to the phases of bud development. All the nine stages are described as under:

Stage 1—In the first stage the bud which had just appeared on the panicle looked like a very small, roundish, light pinkish protuberance. This was approximately a milimetre in diameter. The sepals fully enclosed the petals.

Stage 2—On futher growth (3.0 x 2.5 mm.) the apex of the bud becomes prominently pointed. The sepals, though enclosed the petals, start losening.

Stage 3—The carolla becomes slightly visible after rupture of the sepals at the top of the bud. The visible portion of carolla lobe is pointed and approximately a milimetre in length. The whole bud was 4.0 x 3.0 mm. in size.

Stage 4—The carolla lobe elongates (length 2.3 mm.) and the margins along the union of petals become distinct. Size of the whole bud is 6.3 x 3.0 mm.

Stage 5—The carolla lobe elongates to a length of 3.5 mm. The size of the whole bud becomes 7.5 x 3.5 mm. (maximum thickness at the calyx tube). A small opening appears at its top from where the petals begin to separate. Anthesis started at this stage.

Stage 6—Broadening of the carolla opening continued and this reached a diameter of 2.0 mm. Size of flower and carolla tube remained the same as in stage 5.

Stage 7—The opening of carolla tube widened to a diameter of 3.0 mm. and equal to the thickness of the calyx tube. This gave the flower a tubular appearance. Size of flower remained as in stage 5.

Stage 8—The carolla tube further widened to a diameter of 4.5 mm. and the petals reflexed outwards. The thickness of calyx tube remained as in stage 7.

Stage 9—The broadening of carolla tube continued and the flower attained a fully open position. The calyx tube in this stage swelled to a thickness of 4.0 mm.

Time taken by the bud to complete various stages of its development is presented in Table 2.

Table 2

Chronology of bud development in the carambola (Var. 'sour')

Time required for completion from one stage to next in days, hours and minutes

Bud-burst to 1st stage	*1st to 2nd*	*2nd to 3rd*	*3rd to 4th*	*4th to 5th*	*5th to 6th*	*6th to 7th*	*7th to 8th*	*8th to 9th*	*1st to full bloom (9th stage)*
7-0-0	11-4-0	0-21-0	0-22-0	0-3-35	0-0-10	0-0-10	0-0-15	0-0-15	13-3-25

It may be seen in Table 2 that the time required from appearance of bud on the panicle (stage-1) to full bloom stage of the flower (stage-9) was 13 days, 3 hours and 25 minutes.

7. *Anthesis :* As mentioned earlier, anthesis in a fully developed flower bud starts from the top and this stage of flower bud development comes under the 5th stage. After passing through various stages, the flower, is fully open at the 9th stage of bud development. Total period required for anthesis, as evident in Table 2 was 50 minutes. The 5th stage reaches at 7.30 A.M., while the 9th stage reaches at 8.30 A.M.

Data on time of anthesis are presented in Table 3. It may be seen that the maximum anthesis in both varieties took place between 8 A. M. and 10 A. M.

After completion of anthesis, the petals bent inwards, met at the tips and the flower closed. This gave a pointed tip to the carolla lobe of the closed flower.

The length of the closed carolla lobe was 8.5 mm. The closing of flower took place at 7 P. M. on the very day of opening. Time taken from full bloom to closing stage of flower was 10 hours and 35 minutes.

Table 3

Time of anthesis in carambola (Var. 'sour' and 'sweet')

Date of observation	*Sour*			*Sweet*			*Temperature °C*		*Relative humidity per cent*	
	'P'			'P'						
	8-10 AM	10-12 AM	Total No. of flower recorded	8-10 AM	10-12 AM	Total No. of flower recorded	Maximum	Minimum	7 AM	2 PM
3-10-63	100	-	10	100	-	8	33.3	20.0	90	55
4-10-63	100	-	16	88.2	11.8	17	31.6	20.0	88	60
5-10-63	100	-	24	100	-	16	32.7	18.6	90	41
6-10-63	100	-	18	94.7	5.3	19	32.7	18.6	81	42
7-10-63	100	-	10	96	4.0	25	33.3	18.6	81	42
8-10-63	100	-	17	100	-	19	33.3	18.9	85	42
9-10-63	100	-	15	95.1	4.9	41	33.3	17.7	92	41
10-10-63	94.1	5.9	17	82.0	18.0	39	33.3	17.8	90	38
11-10-63	100	-	19	58.8	41.2	17	33	16.9	84	34
12-10-63	-	100	23	-	100	41	33.6	15.6	86	26
Mean	89.41	10.59	16.9	81.48	18.52	24.2	-	-	-	-

'P' = percentage of flowers opened.

Note - The percentage of flowers opened in both varieties during the periods (i) before 6 A.M. (ii) 6 A.M. to 8 A.M. (iii) 12 A.M. to 2 P.M. and (iv) 2 P.M. to 4 P.M. was nil.

Discussion

Bearing habit of carambola on naked shoots or small branches, as observed in these studies, agrees with the observations of Bailey (1). However, in the present studies flowering and fruiting were also observed in axils of leaves ('sour' and 'sweet'). The variety 'sweet' was found flowering also at the apical end of growing shoot. Some time flowering and bearing took place on large and thick branches, which was in agreement with the results reported by Chittenden (2). Appearance of cluster panicles in both varieties of carambola was in agreement with the findings of Randhawa and Damodaran (6) in mango.

Watts (7) reported that carambola blossoms in rainy season and fruit ripens in December-January. Hayes (3) mentioned that flowers are borne profusely in rainy season and spring. Bailey (1) reported that carambola tree produces three crops a year. In this experiment flowering ('sour' and 'sweet') was observed in three flushes i.e., (i) April-May, (ii) July-August and (iii) September-October and fruits were ready for harvest from these flushes during July-September, November-December and January-February in the same order. The maximum yield, however, was obtained from the 2nd and 3rd flushes.

Summary

Blossoms in carambola generally appear on naked shoots and sometimes in the axils of leaves and on large thick branches in short panicles. Panicles were also seen at the apical ends of shoots in the variety 'sweet'. Flowers appeared in three flushes in April-May, July-August and September-October. The maximum yield was obtained during November-February from the 2nd and 3rd flushes. There were 16.5 flowers per panicle in sour, while 37.6 in 'sweet'. The duration of opening of flowers in a panicle of the 'sour' and 'sweet' was 14 and 21 days respectively. The flower took nearly 14 days for completion of various stages of bud development. Anthesis started between 7-30 A.M. and 8-30 A.M. Peak of anthesis was between 8 A.M. and 10 A.M. The fruit weighs nearly 80 g. in variety sweet and about 67 g. in variety sour.

Acknowledgement

Sincere thanks are due to Dr. Ambika Prasad, Director, Horticultural Research Institute, Saharanpur, for encouragement during the course of these investigations.

Pollination, Fruits Set and Fruit Development in Carambola *(Averrhoa Carambola Linn)*

In an earlier article results were presented on investigations in flowering, fruiting, floral count, panicle development and anthesis of carambola (Nand, 3). The floral morphology and abnormalities in floral parts and fruits have already been reported (Nand 1, 2). Pollination, fruit set, fruit drop and fruit development studies made at the Horticultural Research Institute, Saharanpur are detailed in this paper.

Materials and Methods

The present studies were carried out in 1963-66 and the materials utilised were the same as already reported (Nand, 3).

The viability of pollen was examined in acetocarmine (Randhawa and

Damodaran, 5). Observations were taken in ten different microscopic fields. The number of pollen grains studied in 'sour' and 'sweet' were 476 and 456 respectively.

The following methods were followed to find out the mode of pollination.

(i) Natural self-pollination - Normal panicles having well developed flower buds were bagged before blooming.

(ii) Hand self-pollination - Flower buds were emasculated, pollinated by hand with pollen of the same plant and bagged.

(iii) Natural open-pollination - Completely open flowers were marked in various panicles and left open for pollination through natural agencies.

(iv) Hand cross-pollination - Flower buds were emasculated, pollinated by hand with the pollen of other plant and bagged.

(v) Natural cross-pollination - Flower buds were emasculated and left open to see the extent of pollination through natural agencies.

(vi) Parthenocarpy - Flower buds were emasculated and bagged without pollination.

The extent of fruit set in each case was determined in the varieties 'sour' and the 'sweet'. The total number of flowers marked and fruits set, as evidenced by swelling and elongation of the ovary and change of its colour (observed on the fourth day from the date of opening of the flower), was recorded.

Fruit drop and fruit retention studies were carried out in the variety 'sour'. A week old fruits, which were approximately 10 x 4 mm. in size, formed the basis of these studies. One hundred such fruits were tagged at random on the trees on 20th August 1963 in 50 panicles. Thereafter, weekly counting-each of mature, immature and total fruits present on the trees, was done separately and noted till: the fruits attained maturity. The mature fruits, when once recorded for their presence on the trees (fruit retention), were excluded for counting in future irrespective of their retention on the trees till then. Data collected in this connection were recorded from 27th August, 1963 to 26th November, 1963. The number of fruits actually dropped during a week was found out by subtracting (i) the number of total fruits present during the previous week from (ii) the number of immature fruits which were present during the previous weak.

For finding out initial fruit set and fruit retention is a panicle, twenty-five panicles each of the 'sour' and 'sweet' varieties, which were ready to bloom, were tagged. The fruits initially set (judged by the elongation of ovary, already described under 'mode of pollination') under natural condition, were marked in each panicle. Similarly, retention of fruits in a panicle was marked by regularly observing the panicles during the period of ripening. The data thus collected were averaged and recorded. With the help of these data and number of flowers opening in a panicles (3) the percentages of fruit set and fruit retention per panicle was found out.

The one hundred fruits selected and tagged on 20th August, 1963 for determining the extent of fruit drop and fruit retention were utilized for developmental studies of fruits. Immediately after tagging, the length and maximum breadth of these fruits were measured with a vernier callipers and recorded. Weekly measurements of the growing fruits were then taken and recorded till maturity. From the data relating to those fruits, which could actually be obtained in mature condition, at the end of the fifteenth week mean of the percentage growth of mature fruits at the end of each week was found out.

Observations and Results

1. Dehi scence of anther and receptivity of stigma-anthers dehisc with the opening of flower. The whole dehi scence of an anther was complete on the day of anthesis. The optimum time for collecting pollen was between 8 A.M. and 10 A.M. With the increase of atmospheric temperature and humidity, the time and rate of dehi scence appeared to have hastened and delayed respectively. The stigmatic surface was considered to be most receptive when it looked bright, moist and creamy in appearance under a hand lens at the time of anthesis. When the stigmatic surface lost its freshness and attained a dull appearance, the receptivity was regarded to be lost.

2. Pollen and pollination studies: The pollen grains of the carambola are very sticky (l) and look yellowish after dehi scence. An individual grain is barrel-shaped in dry condition under the microscope. When stained in acetocarmine, the grain immediately became roundish and its exine could be clearly seen. The outline of the exine had fine appendages. All the grains got fully stained and looked normal in size.

Therefore, the fertility of the pollen was taken to be 100 per cent. Honey bag bees, flies and other insects were seen visiting the flowers during the time of anthesis. The insects were found most busy and buzzing actively round about 8 A.M. to 10 A.M. These insects, therefore, were regarded to be responsible for transfer of pollen from flower to flower, as reported earlier(3), the flower after the full bloom stage, closes at 7 P.M. the same day. Thereafter, carolla lobe is loosened from the base by the next morning. This ultimately appears in a dry black colour on the tip of the young fruit and sheds off the same day or few days after set. At set the fruits of the 'sour' is greenish and 6.0 x 2.8 m.m. in size and that of the sweet is whitish or yellowish and 4.0 x 1.9 mm. in size.

The extent of fruit set under each mode of pollination, as specified earlier has been represented in table 1.

From table 1 it is quite evident that the extent of fruit set under 'natural open-pollination' was highest both in 'sour' (52.65 per cent) and 'sweet' (66.9 per cent). The results under 'hand self-pollination' and 'hand cross-pollination' were more or less similar but not encouraging in both the varieties. Under 'natural cross-pollination' fruit set was quite negligible ('sour'-8.33 per cent, 'sweet'- 7.20 per cent). There was no fruit set under natural self-pollination' and 'parthenocarpy' in any of the two varieties.

3. Fruit drop and fruit retention - The extents of fruit drop and fruit retention have been presented in figure 1. It may be seen that 84 per cent of the developing fruits drop off from the tree and 16 per cent reach final maturity. The maximum drop (17 per cent) took place between the first two weeks followed by the period between seventh and eighth weeks (14 per cent) of fruit development. Thereafter, there was a gradual decline in the rate of drop. The dropping continued throughout the growth period of the fruit. About half of the total drop was complete by the end of seventh week (recorded on 1. 10.63) and the rest occured between seventh and fifteenth weeks. Count of the matured the fourteenth week (recorded on 19.11.63) and 10 per cent at the end of the fifteenth week (recorded on 26.11.63) of the fruit development. After maturity the fruits remain on the tree hardly for a week and then drop off. Such drops were actually not included in recording the observations on fruit drop.

4. Initial fruit set and fruit retention per panicle. The data collected on on fruit set and fruit retention per panicle are presented in Table II. It is obvious from table-2 that the Tnitial set in a panicle was lesser in 'sour' than that of the 'sweet'. Though, the mean number of ripe fruits obtained from a cluster (panicle) in the 'sweet' was approximately double to that of the 'sour', the percentage of flowers or fruits which reached final maturity was lesser in 'sweet' than that of the 'sour'.

5. Fruit Development— The mean percentage growth of the fruit ('sour'), has been indicated graphically in figure 2. It may be seen that the rate of growth in the fruit was slightly rapid in the first three weeks when about 25-27 per cent growth was complete. From the 3rd week onwards, the size of the fruit increased almost at a uniform rate except slight declines during 11th-12th and 13th-14th weeks. By the end of 11th week the extent of growth was about 75 per cent. This is worth noting that the growth of fruit continued till maturity. It has already been reported that the mature fruits remained on the tree for about a week (text on fruit drop and fruit retention). During this period there was absolutely no growth in fruits. The rate of fruit growth in length was almost uniform with that in the breadth. From the date of opening of flowers, it took

three days to set (text on mode of pollination) and since then the fruits ripended at the ends of 14th-15th weeks. It is, therefore, deduced that the total period required from flowering to ripening of the fruit ranged from 100-108 days. The growth of fruit, which was uniform in length with that of the breadth, continued till maturity, this is in conformity with the investigations of Teaotia and Chauhan (7) in bar (Ziziphua mauritiana Lamak).

Summary and Conclusion

Anthers burst with the opening of the flowers. The optimum time for collection of pollen was between 8 A.M. and 10 A.M. The stigma was considered to be most receptive when the stigmatic surface looked bright, moist and creamy in colour.

Pollen grains are sticky and look yellowish after dehi scene. An individual pollen is barrel-shaped under dry condition and becomes roundish under the microscope. The fertility of pollen was 100 per cent in both varieties.

The carambola is a cross-pollinated fruit. Honey bees, flies and other insects were regarded to be the chief pollinating agents.

The fruit set takes place on the fourth day of opening of flower ('sour' and 'sweet'). The fruit set under natural open-pollination was maximua (52.65 and 66.90 per cent in 'sour' and 'sweet' respectively) against 0 per cent set under natural self-pollination and parthenocarpy'. Fruit set under 'hand self pollination' in 'sour' and 'sweet' was 32.85 per cent and 30.26 per cent respectively, while under 'hand cross-pollination', the set was 35.60 per cent and 38 per cent in the same order. The set under natural cross-pollination was negligible 8.33 per cent in 'sour' and 7.20 per cent in 'sweet'.

Discussion

Singh (6) did not observe any set under natural self, pollination in mango and, therefore, found cross- pollination to be the rule. Since in carambola there was more than 50 per cent set under 'natural open-pollination' and no set under 'natural self-pollination' , it was confirmed that the carambola is a cross-pollinated fruit.

Occurrence of this phenomenon is further supported by the author is observations that the stigmatic lobe in the carambola flower remains above the staminal column (heterostyly). The phenomenon of heterostyly was already observed in pomegranate (4). However, about 46 per cent set was caused under 'natural self-pollination' because the distance of stigmatic head over the staminal column was reduced due to bending of the style (4). Such exceptions, however, were not observed in carambola. Since honey bees, flies, and other insects were found extremely busy during the peak of anthesis, these were regarded to be the chief pollinating agents.

Though the maximum drop (17 per cent) in fruit took place during the first two weeks of growth size of a fruit 1.45 x 1.15 cm.), fruits being smaller in size and lighter in weight, the quantitative loss of drop was negligible. Next to this, 14 per cent drop was noted during the 7th and 8th week (size of a fruit 5.25 x 3.71 cm). During this period, therefore, the quantitative loss is likely to happen more, inspite of the faest that the numerical loss was lesser than that which took place during the first two weeks. Further, since about 50 per cent of the total drop took place during later half of the growth period i.e. between 7th and 15th weeks of fruit development, it is presumed that a serious loss of crop would have occured by weight. This quantitative loss is the actual loss and of an economic significance.

Initial fruit set under natural condition per panicle was 58.9 per cent in 'sour' and 74.5 per cent in 'sweet'. The number of mature fruit obtained per panicle was approximately two in sour and four in sweet.

Out of the growing fruits, 84 per cent drop off from the tree and remaining 16 per cent reach final maturity. About half of the total drop occur during the later half period of fruit growth. Fruits mature at the end of 14th or 15th week after set and the total period required from opening of flower till maturity was 101 to 108 days. The growth of fruit continued till maturity after which it remained hardly for a week on the tree. During this period growth of the fruit remained completely ceased.

Acknowledgement

The author expresses his deep sense of gratitude to Dr. Ambika Prasad, Director, Horticultureal Research Institute, Saharanpur for taking interest during these investigations.

Literature cited

1. Nand, Darsana (1966). Floral morp Fcology and abnormalities in Averrhoa carambola L. Sc and Cul. 32(7) 369-70
2. (1967). Some interesting abnormalities in the carambola fruit (Averrhoa carambola), Sc and Cul. 33(5): 240.
3. (1967). Flowering and bearing behaviour of carambola (Averrhoa carambola, Linn) Indian J. Hort (submitted.)
4. Nath Nirmalendu and Randhawa, G.S. (1959). Studies on floral biology in the pomegranate (Punica granatum L)-III-pollination, fruit set and seed formation. Indian J. Hort 16(3), 136-40.
5. Randhawa, G.S. and Damodaran, (1961). Studies on floral biology and sex ratio in mango (Mangifera indica L) var. Chausa, Dasehari and

Krishnabhog III-Anthesis, dehiscence, recaptiveity of stigma, pollination, fruit set and fruit development. Indian J. Hort 18(1), 51-64.

6. Singh, R.N. (1954). Studies on Floral biology and subsequent development of fruits in the mango (Mangifera indica L.) varieties Daeehari and langra, Indian J.Hort 1 (3) : 69—88.

7. Teaotia, S.S. and Chauhan, R.S. Flowering, pollination, fruit set and fruit drop studies in bér (Ziziphua mauritiana Lamak) Indian J.Hort 21 (1) 40-45.

Mode of pollination and fruit set in the carambola

Variety	*Natural self pollination*			*Hand self pollination*			*Natural open-pollination*			*Hand cross-pollination*			*Natural cross-*			*Parthernocarpy*		
	1	2	3	1	2	3	1	2	3	1	2	3	1	2	3	1	2	3
Sour	433	0	0	207	68	32.85	659	347	52.65	205	73	35.60	300	25	8.33	387	0	0
Sweet	504	0	0	195	59	30.26	175	117	66.90	178	68	38.20	250	18	7.20	219	0	0

1. Number of flowers pollinated/marked for pollination/emaseulated.
2. Number of fruit set.
3. Percentage of fruit set.

Table II

Initial fruit set and fruit retention per panicle in carambola (var. sour and sweet) under natural condition

Variety	*Number of initfial fruit set*	*Percentage of initial fruit set*	*Number of fruits which reached final maturity*	*Percentage of flowers which reached final maturity (fruit retention)*	*Percentage of fruits carried to final maturity*
1	2	3	4	5	6
Sour	9.6	58.9	1.9	11.6	19.79
Sweet	28.0	74.5	3.5	9.4	12.5

References

1. Bailey, L.H. (1950). The standard cyclopedia of Horticulture. The Mac Millan Co. New York, I: 435-36.
2. Chittenden, F. J. (1956). The Royal Hort. Soc. Dictionary of Gardening, Clarendon Press, Oxford, I : 227.
3. Hayes, W. B. (1957). Fruit growing in India, Kitabistan, Allahabad.
4. Nand, Darshana. (1966). Floral morphology and abnormalities in Averrhoa carambola, L. Sc. and Cul., 32: 369-70.
5. Nand, Darshana. (1967). Some interesting abnormalities in the carambola fruit. (Averrhoa carambola, L. Sc. and Cul., 33 : 240.
6. Randhawa, G. S. and V. K. Damodaran, (1961). Studies on floral biology and sex-ratio in mango (Mangifera indica L.) Var. Chausa, Dasehari and Krishanbhog-II-Flowering habit, flowering season, panicle development and sex ratio. Indian J. Hort., 18 : 36-45.
7. Watts, W. (1889). *Dictionary of Economic products of India, Caucutta* 1: 359-60.

9

Grapes in India

Some Selections of Grapes in Uttar Pradesh

In northern India, work on improvement of grape cultivation is in progress in Punjab (Singh and Bakhshi, 1963), Himachal Pradesh (Thapar and Panwar, 1961), Indian Agricultural Research Institute, New Delhi (Randhawa and Singh, 1958) and Uttar Pradesh (Singh, 1961 & 1962). In Uttar Pradesh, climate is the limiting factor for growing grapes. The main problem which has caused a great setback to the grape industry in U.P. is that the period of ripening of berries synchronizes with the advent of rains. The rains cause cracking and fungus growth on berries and the whole crop is damaged. Therefore, for growing grapes on a commercial scale in this State, it is very essential to select early-maturing varieties of superior quality which may also be of prolific bearing habit. With this idea, the performance of a large number of grape varieties collected at the Horticultural Research Institute, Saharanpur, and planted by the trellis system, are under study. So far, *Chandigarh* (Singh, 1961), *Himrod* and *Delight* (Singh, 1962) varieties of grape had shown promise for U.P. The *Pusa Seedless* variety was found equally good. A pilot trial of these varieties was, therefore, laid out on selected cultivator's fields of this zone in the winter of 1963-64. The performance of these varieties with regard to their adaptability, quality and yield will be tested after the vines come to bearing.

Besides the above varieties, five varieties of grapes, namely, *Perlette, Beauty Seedless, Romulus, Motia and Schuyler White* have further been selected now at the Horticultural Research Institute, Saharanpur. These varieties have shown great promise from the commercial point of view. Their performance has been studied and their important features are described in this paper. The size and weight of a bunch and the number of berries in a bunch where mentioned are the average of at least five specimens. The size and weight of a berry have been given after averaging the data of 20 and 50 berries, respectively. The varieties which start ripening in the month of May and complete by the end of

May or first week of June have been classified as 'early' under U.P. conditions, those which ripen from the second to last week of June or first week of July as 'mid-season', and the varieties ripening from the second week of July onward as 'late'.

Description of Varieties

Perlette

An early-ripening variety of medium vigour. Clusters ripen from third to last week of May or first week of June. Peduncle light green to dull purplish, medium long, medium thick, 3.0 x 0.3 cm. Bunch large sized, 17.7 (L) x 10.7 (B) cm. long, cylindrical or tapering, slightly curved towards apical end, single, medium compact, 287.2 gm. in weight, having 312 berries in number. Pedicel pale green, medium long, thin, 0.5 x 0.1 cm., warty. Berries greenish white or light yellowish, medium sized, 1.27 x 1.27 cm., spherical, 1.49 gm. in weight; skin thin, cracking; pulp whitish, transparent, juicy, sweet, melting; flavour very good; total soluble solids 17 per cent. Seeds very soft, eatable, one to three per berry, greenish with yellowish tinge, small, 0.54 x 0.24 cm., long, thin, very slightly notched or almost rounded, beak long, pointed, very narrow, 50 seeds weigh 0.63 gm.; almost a seedless variety; while eating berries no feeling of presence of any seed. A very heavy cropper; yield of as much as 12.34 kg. can be had from a vine. Ripening uniform and quality very good.

Beauty Seedless

An early-ripening variety of medium vigour. Clusters ripen from third to last week of May or first week of June. Peduncle purplish green, medium long, medium thick, 3.5 x 0.3 cm. Bunch medium sized, 12.66 x 7.50 cm. long, irregular, tapering, single, medium compact, 187.40 gm. in weight, having 113 berries in number. Pedicel green, medium long, medium thick, 0.5 x 0.15 cm., warty. Berries dark purple or blackish with whitish bloom, medium sized, 1.29 x 1.30 cm., spherical, 1.18 gm. in weight; skin medium thick, cracking or a little tough; pulp greenish, translucent, juicy, sweet, soft; flavour good; T.S.S. 22 per cent. Seeds very soft, eatable, one per berry, greenish with yellowish tinge, small, 0.51x0.24 cm., long, notched ; beak long, pointed and narrow, 50 seeds weigh 0.71 gm.; more or less a seedless variety; berry gives the feeling of seedlessness while eating. A medium to heavy cropper; yield of as much as 8.05 kg. can be had from a vine. Ripening uniform and quality very good.

Romulus

An early-ripening variety of medium vigour. Clusters ripen from second to fourth week of May or first week of June. Peduncle green, short, thick, 2.1 x 0.4 cm. Bunch medium sized, 12.5 x 7.4 cm. long, conical, single, very compact, 248.7 gm. in weight, having 245 berries in number. Pedicel light green, medium long, thick, 0.52x0.18 cm., warty. Berries yellowish green with a little whitish bloom, medium sized, 1.49x1.29 cm., short, oval, 1.42 gm. in weight; skin medium thick, cracking or a little tough; pulp whitish, translucent, juicy, very sweet, soft to melting; flavour very good ; T.S.S. 21 per cent. Seeds soft, hollow, eatable, one to three per berry, straw to brown coloured, shiny, small, 0.46x0.25 cm., long, slightly notched; beak long, pointed, narrow; chalaza sunken, not very prominent; raphe slightly raised; 50 seeds weigh 0.78 gm. A medium to heavy bearer; yield of as much as 8.45 kg. can be had from a vine. Ripening uniform and quality very good.

Motia

A mid-season variety of medium vigour. Clusters ripen from last week of May to second or third week of June. Peduncle light green, short, medium thick, 1.75 x 0.32 cm. Bunch medium sized, 13.36 x 9.09 cm., long, conical, apex slightly curved in most cases, single, compact, 255.8 gm. in weight, having 171 berries in number. Pedicel light green, medium long, thin, 0.6 x 0.1 cm., warty. Berries greenish yellow with whitish bloom, medium sized, 1.40 x 1.36 cm., spherical, 1.36 gm. in weight; skin medium thick, cracking. Pulp greenish white, transparent, juicy, very sweet, soft; flavour good; T.S.S. 20 per cent. Seeds hard, two to four per berry, but sometimes only one, dark brown, medium sized, 0.63 x 0.41 cm., long to broad, very slightly notched or almost rounded; beak long, blunt, tip of the beak broad; chalaza above centre; raphe raised; 50 seeds weigh 2.15 gm.; seeds easily separated from the pulp. A medium to heavy bearer; yield of as much as 9.46 kg. can be had from a vine. Ripening uniform and quality good.

Schuyler White

An early-ripening variety of medium vigour. Clusters ripen from third week of May to first week of June. Peduncle purplish green, short, thin, 1.8 x 0.25 cm. Bunch medium sized, 11.8 x 6.2 cm. long, tapering, loose, 190 gm. in weight, having 113 berries in number. Pedicel green, long, thin, 0.6 x 0.1 cm., warty. Berries dark purple or blackish with whitish or bluish bloom, medium sized, 1.41 x 1.33 cm., spherical, 1.71 gm. in weight: skin medium thick, cracking or a little tough. Pulp green, translucent, juicy, sweet, soft; flavour good; T. S. S. 20 to 21 per cent. Seeds hard, one to four in a berry, straw coloured, medium -sized, 0.56 x 0.45 cm., broad, notched; beak short, blunt, broad and slightly bent towards ventral portion; chalaza above centre, slightly sunken or at level of back of the seed; raphe raised; 50 seeds weigh 2.03 gm., seeds easily separated from the pulp or sometimes with a little difficulty. A medium to heavy bearer; yield of as much as 9.50 kg. can be had from a vine. Ripening uniform and quality good.

The authors' studies at this Institute have shown that several other varieties of grapes appeared to be quite good in several respects. These still require confirmation after which some of these may also come out as promising. Studies in this direction are under way.

Effect of Severity of Pruning in Grape Varieties Perlette, Convent Large White and Schuyler White

The influence of pruning on fruit production in grape seems much more important than manuring and irrigation. Usually cane pruning (6 to 12 nodes) is recommended for vigorous varieties, while spur pruning (limited to 3 to 4 nodes) is said to respond well in non-vigorous varieties (4). However, severity of pruning may vary from variety to variety, which primarily depends upon vigour and bearing behaviour of the vine under local conditions of soil and climate. Studies on the proper number of nodes to be retained per cane after pruning, therefore, may provide a very useful guide line to growers. It was, thus, deemed of considerable importance to study the effect of pruning on some important varieties of this region at the Government Fruit Research Station, Basti.

Materials and Methods

The present work, based on preliminary studies made during 1968-69, was undertaken during 1970 on local varieties of Perlette, Convent Large White, (C. L. White) and Schuyler White (S. White). The vines were about 6-year old, trained on 4-arm Kniffen system and received similar cultural treatments. Vines of Perlette and C. L. White are of medium to heavy vigour, while the vigour of S. White is medium. In all six vines at 2 per variety, were selected for the experiment. Thirtyfive healthy canes of uniform growth each in Perlette and C. L. White and twenty five in S. White were marked at random on these vines. The number of canes marked per vine was approximately uniform (18 canes on 1st and 17 on 2nd vine in the case of Perlette as well as C. L. White and 13 canes on 1st and 12 on 2nd vine in S. White). There were seven pruning treatments each in Perlette and C. L. White and five in S.White (total: 19 treatments; 95 canes at 5 per treatment). Canes were pruned to 2, 3, 4, 5, 6, 7, and 8 nodes each in Perlette and C. L. White, whereas the intensity of pruning was 2, 3, 4, 5, and 6 nodes in S. White. The experiment was replicated 5 times, treating one cane as one replication in a randomised block design. Pruning was done in the middle of January.

Results

1. *Time of Bud-break, Flowering, Fruit-set and Maturity:* The bud-break started on an average within 51 to 51.8 days in Perlette, 51.2 to 51.8 days in C. L. White and 47.4 to 48.8 days in S. White after pruning in all the treatments (Table 1). It is, therefore, evident that the bud-break in S. White took place

Table 1. **Showing effect of pruning on bud-burst, emergence of panicle, blooming, fruit set, maturity, bunch size, bunch weight and position of bunch on the shoot in three varieties of grape**

	Number of days taken from						Bunch size	
1	2	3	4	5	6	7	8	9	10
Perlette									
2-node	51.6	3.0	24.2	3.4	47.8	285.50	17.31	10.08	3rd to 5th
3-node	51.0	3.8	25.4	3.2	48.2	287.00	17.55	10.52	3rd to 5th
4-node	52.4	2.8	24.0	3.0	48.2	286.50	17.50	10.30	3rd to 5th
5-node	52.8	2.6	23.6	3.6	48.8	288.70	18.00	10.63	3rd to 5th
6-node	52.6	3.0	24.2	3.4	48.2	287.50	17.98	10.61	3rd to 5th
7-node	51.8	3.4	24.0	3.4	48.8	284.70	17.48	10.64	3rd to 5th
8-node	51.8	2.6	24.2	3.4	48.2	281.60	17.38	9.95	3rd to 5th
CD. at 5%						2.21			
Convent Large White :									
2-node	51.6	3.4	19.8	3.6	73.6	215.70	11.70	7.77	3rd to 5th
3-node	51.2	3.6	19.0	3.4	72.2	214.75	11.58	7.79	3rd to 6th
4-node	51.4	3.8	18.6	3.8	72.2	216.95	12.33	7.56	4th to 6th
5-node	51.4	3.4	19.2	4.0	72.4	217.60	12.22	8.03	3rd to 6th
6-node	51.8	3.4	18.8	3.8	72.0	214.75	12.38	7.69	3rd to 6th
7-node	51.6	3.2	19.0	3.8	72.4	216.50	12.80	8.04	3rd to 6th
8-node	51.2	3.4	19.4	3.6	72.4	215.80	12.39	7.97	3rd to 6th
C.D. at 5%						N. S.			
Schuyler White :									
2-node	47.4	3.0	23.0	3.6	43.6	185.00	11.23	5.96	2nd to 4th
3-node	47.6	3.8	22.2	3.6	43.4	186.50	11.12	6.02	2nd to 4th
4-node	47.4	3.6	22.8	3.6	43.2	192.85	12.20	6.26	2nd to 4th
5-node	48.0	3.6	22.6	3.4	43.0	191.00	12.12	6.79	2nd to 4lh
6-node	47.6	3.6	22.4	4.0	43.2	188.70	11.69	6.06	2nd to 4th
CD. at 5%						4.79			

N.S.=Non significant

about three days earlier than each in Perlette and C.L. White. Again, Table 1 shows that the effect of pruning on time of emerence of panicle, blooming, fruit set and maturity was almost similar in all the treatments in one variety. This, however, differed in certain cases within the varieties. The period required from emergence of panicle to blooming averaged 23.6 to 25.4 days in Perlette, 18.6 to 19.8 days in C. L. White and 22.2 to 23.0 days in S. White under different pruning treatments. Besides these, from fruit-set to maturity it took 47.8 to 48.8 days in Perlette, 72.0 to 73.6 days in C. L. White and 43.0 to 43.6 days in S. White.

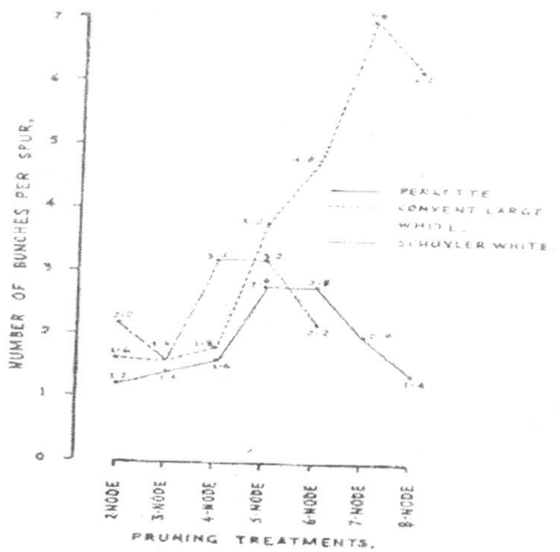

Fig. No- 4. Effect of pruning on yield of three grape varieties

2. *Yield:* Varying severity of pruning in canes gave interesting results as regards production of bunches also reveals that in Perlette the maximum number of bunches/spur (2.8) was obtained from 5 and 6-node pruning treatments, which are statistically significant followed by 7-. 4-, 3- , 8-, and 2-node pruning treatments.

In C. L. White the results from 8-, 7- and 6-node pruning treatments are statistically significant over other treatments at 5 per cent level of significance. The maximum number of bunches were obtained from 7-node treatment (7 bunches/spur) followed by 8-node (6.2 bunches/spur) and 6-node (4.8 bunches/ spur) treatments. The minimum yield (1.6 bunches/ spur) was obtained both from 2- and 3-node treatments.

Results in S. White, though statistically insignificant, were very promising under 4- and 5-node treatments, as each of these produced the maximum number of bunches (3.2/spur). Influence of these treatments, was superior over 3-node (1.8 bunches/spur) treatment. (Fig. 1)

3. *Bunch Weight:* The effect of different treatments of pruning of canes on bunch weight is shown in Table 1. It is clear from the table that in Perlette the treatment effects are highly significant at 5 per cent level of significance. The 5-node treatment gave the maximum bunch weight (288.7 gm) followed by 6-, 3-, and 4-node treatments. The minimum bunch weight (281.6 gm) was obtained from 8-node pruning.

The above table further reveals that in C. L. White, the 5-node treatment indicated a slight increase in bunch weight over other treatments, but statistically the results are not significant.

The effect of pruning treatments on bunch weight in S. White, on the other hand, was significant under 4-, 5- and 6-node treatments at 5 per cent level of significance.

4. *Length of the bunch:* Results of various pruning treatments on the bunch length are represented in Table 1. It is evident that bunch length in Perlette under 5-node (18.0 cm) and 6-node (17.98 cm) treatments increased slightly over the normal size (13) as well as over other treatments. Similar results were obtained in bunch length of C. L. White under 7-node treatment (12.80 cm) and of S. White under 4-node (12.20 cm) and 5-node (12.12 cm) treatments (5, 13). Likewise, the effect of various pruning treatments on width of the bunch, as well, was negligible.

5. *Position of bunch of the shoot:* In each treatment bunches were borne on 3rd to 5th node of the shoot in Perlette, 3rd to 6th node in C.L. White and 2nd to 4th node in S. White (Table 1).

6. *Activation of buds:* Irrespective of various pruning treatments, buds on the last few nodes (cut end) of a spur were activated and sprouted into productive or unproductive shoots, depending upon their potential. Buds on first few (basal) nodes of the spur were also stimulated.

In Perlette the buds, which gave rise to productive shoots on a spur, were on an average from 1.2 nodes (minimum) to 2.8 nodes (maximum) in number, maximum being on 6-node and minimum on 2-node treatments. Vegetative shoots were obtained from buds on 0.2 node (4-node treatment) to 1.6 node (8-node treatment) in number. Buds on 0.2 node (minimum) to 5.0 nodes (maximum) per spur remained barren, maximum being on 8-node treatment and minimum on 2-node treatment (Fig. 2A).

In C.L. White productive shoots were obtained from buds on 1.2 nodes (minimum : 2-node treatment) to 3.8 nodes (maximum : 8-node treatment) on a

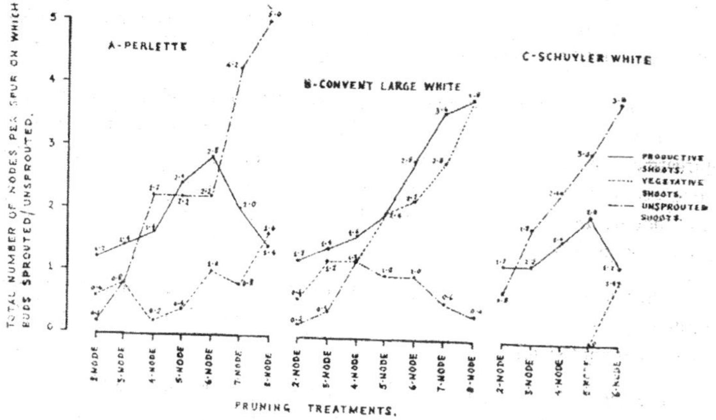

Fig. 2 Effect of pruning on activation of buds in three grape varieties.

spur. Vegetative shoots appeared from 0.2 node (2-node treatment) to 1.2 node (4-node treatment), while buds on 0.6 (minimum : 2-node treatment) to 3.8 nodes (maximum : 8-node treatment) remained barren (Fig. 2 B).

As regards Schuyler White, it may be seen further in (Fig. 2 C) that buds from 1.2 nodes (minimum : 2, 3, 6-node treatments) to 2.0 nodes (maximum: 5-node treatment) on a spur produced fruiting shoots. Further, it is interesting to note that buds from none of the nodes sprouted to vegetative shoots except from 1.0 node in 6-node treatment. Buds on 0.8 node (minimum : 2 node treatment) to 3.8 nodes (maximum : 6-node treatment) on a spur remained barren.

Figure 2 further reveals that the total number of nodes on which buds gave rise to productive shoots increased with the length of spur up to 6-nodes in Perlette and 5-nodes in S. White, i.e., upto the last bud of maximum yielding nodal treatment and later on showed a decreasing tendency. In C.L. White, however, the number of nodes (buds) sprouting into fruiting shoots increased up to the last (8-node) treatment, though the yield was maximum on 7-node treatment.

The number of nodes on which buds remained barren, increased with the length of cane up to the last treatment in all the varieties (Fig. 2).

Discussion

Since several varieties of grapes have now been selected for commercial adaptation both in western as well as eastern parts of Uttar Pradesh (5, 6, 7, 11 13, 16, 17), the present trial is of considerable economic importance, as the production of bunches greatly depend upon pruning techniques in vines.

Varying severity of pruning did not influence the time of bud-break, emergence of panicles, blooming, fruit set and maturity in all the grape varieties under study. This is in accordance with the observations of Tomkins and Shaulis (19) and Chadha *et al* (3) in Perlette.

Olmo (12) recommended spur pruning for Perlette. Chadha *et al* (3) reported 6-bud pruning producing highest number of bunches per vine and simultaneously insignificant difference between 6-bud and 5-bud pruning in Perlette. This supports the results obtained in the present trial on 5 and 6-node treatments in Perlette. However, in C.L. White and S. White, maximum bunches were obtained under 7-node and 4 to 5-node treatments (respectively). It is, therefore, evident that varying number of nodes on a cane have a dominating effect on bunch production in grape and the results vary from variety to variety. These observations are again supported by Mukherjee (10) who reported higher yield under 9-bud treatment in Pusa Seedless and 6-bud treatment in Bhokri grapes.

Chadha *et al* (3) observed longer bunches in 6-bud pruning over 3 and 5-bud treatment in Perlette. Tripathi (20) reported greater length and width of bunch in spur pruning over cane pruning in Perlette. These conform with the observations of the present trial under 5 and 6-node treatments, in Perlette, 7-node treatment in C.L. White and 4- and 5-node treatments in S. White.

The effect of various pruning treatments on bunch weight was very' encouraging in S.White, in which heavier bunches were obtained under 4- and 5-node treatments, which were significantly superior over other treatments. This is in accordance with the observations made by Tripathi (20), who found spur pruning resulting in higher bunch weight over cane pruning in Scarlet Grape.

Pruning treatments did not influence the position of bunch on the shoot (regardless of varieties). This agrees with the observations of Balakrishnan and Rao (1). Similarly, these did not differ as compared to the position of bunch on the shoot in normal course (6, 8).

Mostly the top buds and sometimes basal buds of the pruned canes (spurs) got activated to productive shoots (regardless of varieties and pruning treatments). This agrees with the views of Balakrishnan and Rao (1) who reported that first two nodes as well as the last node of spurs were found to be most fruitful and median portions, the least fruitful. These findings are further supported by Karuppuswamy *et al* (9), Rao (14) and Ritter (15). The number of fruiting shoots increased with the length of canes up to 6-node treatment in Perlette and 5-node treatment in S.White, after which these decreased. In C.L. White however, the number of fruiting shoots increased upto the last (8-node) treatment. These findings are supported by those of Spirov (18) in grape.

Bessis (2) reported lower percentage of bud-break as a result of long pruning in Carignan grape. Again Spirov (18) observed that an increase in length of canes resulted in reduction of the number of buds which opened. These findings provide full support to the observations made in the present trial.

Summary

1. Studies on pruning of grape varieties Perlette, Convent Large White (C.L. White) and Schuyler White (S. White) were carried out at the Government Fruit Research Station, Basti.
2. Vines were pruned in the middle of January to 2, 3, 4, 5, 6, 7, and 8 nodes in Perlette and C. L. White and 2, 3, 4, 5 and 6 nodes in S. White.
3. Time of bud-break, emergence of panicle, blooming, fruit set and maturity were not affected by various pruning treatments (regardless of varieties).
4. Pruning of vines to 5 to 6 nodes in Perlette, 7 nodes in C. L. White, and 4 to 5 nodes in S. White proved best in respect of yield.
5. The influence of bunch weight in Perlette and S. White was significant, while it was insignificant in C. L. White. The effect on size, on the other hand,was negligible.
6. There was no effect on position of bunch on the shoot in all treatments and all varieties.
7. Generally top buds of the spur were found most productive.
8. The number of nodes on which buds sprouted to fruiting shoots increased with the length of spur up to 6 and 5 nodes in Perlette and S. White. In C. L. White the increasing tendency was upto the last treatment (8-node).
9. The number of unsprouted buds (nodes) increased with the length of cane up to the last treatment in all varieties.

Acknowledgements

Thanks are due to Sri S. R. Kairati, Senior Statistical Assistant for statistical analysis and to Sri Udai Prakash, Photo Artist of this Research Station for preparing the illustrations.

Convent Large White - A Promising Grape Introduction

Selection of grape varieties for commercial growing in Uttar Pradesh is in progress for the last few years. Several varieties have been selected (2, 3, 4, 5) and are under extensive field trials. This note deals with another introduction, viz., Convent Large White, which is found to be a prolific bearer. This has been selected as a promising variety at Fruit Research Station, Basti in 1969.

Convent Large White (Fig. 1) is a pure vinifera grape introduced from National Hortorium, Meerut. The vines were trained on Kniffen system and pruned to 4-6 nodes in the last week of December, 1968. After pruning, 40 kg of farm yard manure, 1,355 gm. neem cake, 485 gm. ammonium sulphate, 1385 gm. potassium sulphate were applied per vine. Out of these, the total quantity of farm yard manure and neem cake, half of the ammonium sulphate and one third of potassium sulphate were applied immediately after pruning. The remaining half of ammonium sulphate and the other one-third portion of potassium sulphate were applied in the third week of March. The last one third part of potassium sulphate was applied in the middle of May. The different characteristics of the variety were studied in detail mainly following earlier recorded procedures (1, 2, 3, 6, 7, 8), modifying them wherever necessary.

Fig. 1 A bunch of Convent Large white grape variety.

Vigour, Flowering and Fruiting : The vine is of medium to heavy vigour and attains complete dormancy by the first week of January. Bud-break starts in the second week of March and panicles appear 3-4 days after bud-break. Flowers appear in the last week of March and set fruits 3-4 days after blooming. The vine is in full broom in the first week of April. Newly appeared inflorescence is whitish green, while rachis and other branches of growing inflorescence are light green. Seventy per cent of the productive shoots bear two panicles per shoot on 4th to 7th node, 20 per cent bear one on 5th to 6th node and 10 per cent bear three on 3rd, 4th and 6th node.

Bunch and Berry : The bunch is medium-sized (1.2 cm x 7.9 cm), short, conical, and loose to medium compact, 215 gm in weight having 127 berries in number (on an average). The berry is blackish red with a whitish bloom, large-sized (1.9 cm x 1.85 cm), and 3.52 gm in mean weight. The skin is medium thick, and the pulp green, translucent, very juicy, very sweet and melting with a good flavour. This is a seeded variety with 1-3 seeds per berry. Convent Large White is a mid-season variety and ripens from 2nd to last week of June. The ripening is uniform and quality is very good. This is a heavy yielder and an yield of about 16 kg can be had from a vine. At full ripeness the fruits have registered a T. S. S. of 20 per cent.

Earliness in ripening i.e., ripening of berries before the rains is an important factor in grape growing in this tract. This has been achieved by selection of sweet and prolific-bearing seedless and seeded varieties of grape like Himord, Delight (5), Perlette, Beauty Seedless, Romulus, Schuyler White and Motia (3), Kishmish Surkh and Gulabi (2) and Chandigarh (4). Convent Large White is one more addition to this list of early ripening varieties and should prove popular.

Literature Cited

1. Mustaffa, A. M. and M. A. Ginai, 1941 Grape growing in Baluchisten. *Imp. Council Agr. Res. Misc. Bull.* 40.
2. Nand, Darshana, 1965 Kishmish Surkh and Gulabi-two promising varieties of grapes-*The Punjab Hort. J.*5 : 177-80.
3. Prasad, Ambika and Darshana Nand, 1964. Some selection of grapes in Uttar Pradesh. *The Punjab Hort. J.* 4 : 145-47.
4. Singh, L. B.1961. An outstanding selection of grape for cultivation in northern India. *Ann. Rep. Hort. Res. Inst.* (Saharanpur) 68-71.
5. Singh, L.B.1962. Himrod and Delight, two outstanding grape introductions. *Ann. Rep. Hort. Res. Inst.* (Saharanpur) 124.
6. Singh, L. and S. Singh 1940. Distinguishing characters and behaviour of some grapevine varieties introduced at Lyalpur in the Punjab. *Indian J. Agric. Sc.* 10: 552-93.
7. Waugh, F. A. 1914. Describing grapes. Ch. 9 in *Systematic Pomology.* Orange Judd. Company, New York, 88-97.
8. Zeilenski, Q. B.1955. Grapes. Ch. 24 in *Modern Systematic Pomology.* W.M.C. Brown Company, Dubuque, Iowa, U.S.A., 224-32.

Kishmish Surkh and Gulabi—Two Promising Varieties of Grapes

Work on selection of suitable varieties of grape has been in progress at the Horticultural Research Institute, Saharanpur, U.P., for the last several years. As a result of this, several varieties have been selected by Singh (1961, 1962) and Prasad and Nand (1964). The present paper deals with the detailed flowering, fruiting, bunch and berry characters of two outstanding varieties of grape, namely, *Kishmish Surkh* and *Gulabi* selected in 1965.

Material and Methods

A large number of grape varieties collected at the Horticultural Research Institute, Saharanpur, U.P., from various parts of India and abroad were utilized for studying their performances. The vines have been planted 3.65 × 2.00 metres apart and trained by Kniffen System. The present investigations were carried out during the years 1963-65. The methods and terminologies employed for describing the various characters in a variety were on the lines of the work done by Mustafa and Giani (1941), Prasad and Nand (1964), Singh and Singh (1940), Waugh (1914) and Zielenski (1955), except those specified below :

Time of dormancy in vines was observed and noted from November to January. Observations on characters of inflorescences and flowers and times of bud-break, flowering, blooming and fruit set were taken from February to April. For finding out the number of inflorescences or bunches on individual shoots, ten bearing shoots, marked at random for each variety, were utilized from April to June. The actual nodes on which the inflorescences or bunches were borne, were counted from the bases of these shoots.

The bunch and berry characters, time of ripening and yield were studied from May to July. A bunch is 'medium compact' when the compactness of berries in a bunch is in between the conditions 'loose' and 'compact'.

The stalk of a bunch is called 'peduncle' and that of a berry 'pedicel'. Thickness of these parts was measured in their mid-portions.

For studies on seed characters, seeds were extracted from berries, thoroughly washed, sponged, weighed and used for further studies. The size of a seed, where given, is the average of five seeds. A seed is small, medium or large-sized, when the average of its length plus breadth is below 0.50 cm., from 0.50 to 0.55 cm. and above 0.55 cm., respectively.

Observations and Results

The observations taken and results obtained for each variety are reproduced below :

Kishmish Surkh

This is a variety of medium vigour possessing the characters of *vinifera* grapes and introduced from Mashobra, Himachal Pradesh, in the year 1957.

Flowering and Fruiting Characters

The vine is completely dormant by the last week of December. The bud-break starts in the last week of February or the first week of March. Flowers appear 2-3 days after bub-break, bloom in the first week of April, and set fruit 3-4 days after blooming. In the second week of April, the vine is in full bloom. The branches of growing inflorescences are light green or pale green in colour. Out of the bearing shoots, 90 per cent bear one inflorescence a shoot on the 5th node and 10 per cent bear two inflorescences a shoot on the 5th and 6th nodes. Flowers are hermaphrodite.

Bunch and Berry Characters

Peduncle light green, sometimes with purplish tinge, long, thick, 4.26 x 0.42 cm. Bunch medium-sized, 15.00 (L) x 14.60 (B) cm., short, more or less roundish or slightly conical, shouldered, single, medium compact, 473.60 gm. in weight, having 95 berries in number. Pedicel light green, medium long, thick, 0.54 x 0.18 cm., warty. Berries yellowish, sometimes having slightly pinkish tinge with thin whitish bloom, large-sized, 1.94 x 2.02 cm., spherical but slightly flattened, 4.48 gm. in weight; skin thin and cracking; pulp whitish, transparent, juicy, very sweet, melting; flavour very good; total soluble solids 22 per cent. Seeds hard, 3-4 per berry, sometimes only 1-2, mostly straw coloured, also darkish brown, large-sized 0.72 x 0.45 cm., broad, cordate, notched, beak long, blunt, broad; chalaza above centre, sunken, in some cases at surface level of the back; raphe raised; 50 seeds weigh 1.72 gm., seeds separate from the pulp very easily and automatically while eating. A mid-season variety; ripens from the last week of May to the second or third week of June; ripening uniform; excellent in quality and relished very much. A very heavy yielder; a yield of as much as 16 kg. can be had from a vine.

Gulabi

A medium vigorous variety of *vinifera* group, introduced from Poona, Maharashtra, in the year 1957.

Flowering and Fruiting Characters

The vine sheds its leaves completely in the first week of January. The bud-break starts in the last week of February or the first week of March, or sometimes even a bit later. Flowers emerge 2-3 days after bud-break, bloom in the first week of April and set fruit 3-4 days after blooming. The vine is in full bloom in the second week of April. The floral stalks in the inflorescences are light green in colour. One to four inflorescences are borne on the 4th to 7th nodes of an individual shoot. Out of the bearing shoots, 50 per cent bear three, 30 per cent two and 10 per cent four inflorescences, and the remaining 10 per cent only one a shoot. The developing flower buds are light green in colour. Flowers are hermaphrodite.

Bunch and Berry Characters

Peduncle light green, short, medium thick, 1.27 × 0.35 cm. Bunch large-sized, 18.00 (L) × 11.58 (B) cm., long, tapering, divided, loose, 254.60 gm. in weight having 95 berries in number. Pedicel light green, long, medium thick, 0.73 × 0.13 cm., warty. Berries blackish red with bluish bloom, large-sized, 1.79 x 1.78 cm., spherical, 3.21 gm in weight; skin medium thick, cracking; pulp whitish green, translucent, juicy, very sweet, melting, with a good flavour; total soluble solids 19 per cent. Seeds hard, 1-3 per berry but mostly two, pinkish, medium-sized, 0.70 × 0.40 cm., long, cordate, notched; beak long, blunt, medium wide; chalaza above centre and at the top of the seed, large, raised, in some cases also sunken; raphe raised; 50 seeds weigh 1.87 gm., separate from the pulp easily. A mid-season variety; ripens from the first to the third or fourth week of June; ripening uniform; quality very good. A very heavy yielder; a yield of as much as 28 kg. can be had from a vine.

Discussion

The grape industry in Uttar Pradesh could not flourish so far, as the ripening time of berries synchronized with the onset of rains. This caused cracking and fungus growth in berries and ultimately destruction of the whole crop. Earliness in ripening is, therefore, very important. An early ripening variety, at the same time, if disagreeable in taste and flavour or a poor yielder, will be of no use. Therefore, at the time of selection of grape varieties, three most important points had to be kept on a par for consideration. These are : (i) earliness in ripening, (ii) superiority in quality, and (iii) high yielding capacity. Considering the above points, this problem has now been solved, as many early-ripening varieties with all desirable characters have been found out.

Summary and Conclusions

Kishmish Surkh and *Gulabi* varieties of grape have been selected at the Horticultural Research Institute, Saharanpur, for commerical growing in Uttar Pradesh. Their characters have been studied and described in detail.

Acknowledgement

Grateful thanks are due to Dr. Ambika Prasad, Director, Horticultural Research Institute, Saharanpur, for encouragement during the period of these investigations and for critically going through the manuscript.

Influence of Different Media of Storage on Sprouting in Stem-cuttings of Grape

Grape in northern India, though of recent introduction, is making rapid strides and many superior varieties have been selected. Plants are easily propagated by stem-cuttings, which may be procured after pruning of vines in mid-January. The planting materials thus collected need immediate plantation either in pots, nursery or situ. These stem-cuttings sprout some time in the beginning or March and, therefore, an extra expenditure has to be incurred for their proper look after during the dormant period. On the other hand, if cuttings are not planted immediately, these dry up and fail to sprout. Again, to maintain the sprouting capacity in curtings during long transit, is another problem. Gandhi (1956) reported that grape cuttings can be imported by post as they can easily stand a journey of 15 to 30 days if packed in moist moss and wrapped in water-proof paper. However, no authentic data are available through which a definite recommendation can be made for a variety in a particular media of storage. To over come the above problems it is necessary to find out some suitable media in which grape cuttings could be stored or packed and kept at a place or transported to another for plantation at the time of sprouting. Keeping in view this pressing need, the present trial was laid out at the Government Fruit Research Station, Basti during 1970.

Materials and Methods

Three popular grape varieties Perlette (Prasad and Nand 1964) Pearl of Csaba (Singh,1968) and Convent Large White (Jauhari and Nand, 1969) were selected for these studies. Fresh stem-cuttings (each having four nodes) of uniform size: 168 in number were collected from each variety after pruning the vines on 17th January, 1970. In this trial there were six treatments for storing the cuttings under different media- one control and two replications insplit plot design. Varieties were allocated in the main plot and the treatments in the sub-plots. For each treatment twelve cuttings were utilized in one replication. As such in all 504 (12 × 7 × 3 × 2) cuttings were used.

Immediately after pruning, the cuttings with their ends dipped/without dipping in paraffin were stored in different media after wrapping in alkathene paper and placed in a cool dry place. The combination of various treatments were as under :

T_1 = moss + alkathene

T_2 = wax + moss + alkathene

T_3 = wax + alkathene

T_4 = only alkathene

T_5 = wax + saw dust + alkathene

T_6 = saw dust+ alkathene

Control = cuttings planted immediately after pruning.

N.B.- words "moss" and "saw dust" where mentioned mean "moist moss" or "moist saw dust".

Forty days after storage, the packages were opened on 26th February, 1970 and the stem-cuttings planted the same day in beds and proper care was taken. Before planting, the paraffin wax or other foreign material sticking to the cuttings was carefully removed. Weekly observations on sprouting of cuttings under each treatment were taken from the date of sprouting (4th March,1970) till final survival was noted on 1st July 1970.

Results

The observations on sprouting and survival in stem-cuttings of grape under various treatments provided very useful information and is described below:

Effect on Sprouting : The varieties do not approach to the significance among themselves (Table 1 Col. 9). The treatment means, however, are differing significantly at 1 per cent level of significance (table 1 Col. 2 to 8 against "mean"). It is apparent that Tl, T4, and Control have given maximum sprouts (89.4 per cent each) followed by T3 (61-1 per cent). Minimum sprouts were obtained under T6 (15.3 per cent).

The interaction between variety and treatment is statistically significant at 1 per cent level of significance due to the treatments being highly significant (Table l-Col.2 to 8 against varieties).

Maximum sprouting in perlette was obtained under T2 (91.7 per cent) followed by T4 (83.3 per cent) while the minimum was under T5 (8.3 per cent). There was no sprouting under T6.

As regards Pearl of Csaba, Tl, T3 and control gave maximum sprouts (70.9, 70.9 and 70.8 per cent respectively), followed by T5 (66.7 per cent). The sprouting was minimum under T2 (12.50 per cent) and nil under T6. None of the results were superior than control.

The sprouts in Convent Large White were maximum (75 per cent) both under Tl and T4 and these were also superior over Control (62.6 per cent). The sprouts were minimum (41.7 per cent) under T2 and T3.

Effect on Survival. All the varieties differed significantly at 5 per cent level of significance in respect of survival of cuttings. The maximum survial was found In Convent Large White (89.4 per cent). Though the survivals in Perlette and Pearl of Csaba were 81.6 and 71.2 per cent respectively, these are statistically similar (Table 2-Col. 9).

The effect of various treatments are also significant at 1 per cent level of significance as compared with T6 (mean survival-30.5 per cent: Table 2- Col.7 against mean). Other treatment effects were statistically the same.

The interaction between variety with treatment is significant at 5 per cent level of significance. In Perlette, the difference was observed statistically significant between T8 (0 per cent survival: Table 2- Col. 7) and all other treatments, maximum survival being under T2 and T5 (100 per cent each), which were also superior over Control (95.0 per cent). In Pearl of Csaba, the significant difference was observed between T6 (0 per cent), T2 (50.0 per cent) and all other treatments. The maximum survival was under T5 (94.5 per cent), followed by Tl (93.7 per cent). However in Convent Large White, though statistically there was no difference between various treatments, the maximum survival was found under Tl (95 per cent) and the minimum under T4 (83.4 per cent). Further, results under all the treatments were superior over control (79.5 per cent: Table 2-Col. 2 to 8).

Discussion

The effect of various treatments on sprouting of grape cuttings differed from variety to variety. Cuttings of Perlette stored under .wax + moss + alkathene (2) gave maximum sproute (91.7 per cent), while in Convent Large White and Pearl of Csaba the sprouting of cuttings were 41.7 and 12.5 per cent respectively, which is practically of no value.

Sprouting of cuttings stored under saw dust + alkathene (T6) was nil in Perlette and Pearl of Csaba and only 49.9 per cent in Convent Large White. The sprouting under wax + saw dust + alkathene (T5), on the other hand, was 8.3 per cent in Perlette, 54.1 per cent in Convent Large White and 66.7 per cent in Pearl of Csaba. This shows that saw dust has rather a detrimental effect on sprouting of grape cuttings except that in Pearl of Csaba the result under T5 was better over Perlette and Convent Large White.

Again wrapping fresh grape cuttings in Perlette and Convent Large White only in alkathene (T4), which was next to best in sprouting, proved better over wrapping in alkathene with their out ends dipped in wax, i.e. T3 (Perlette:T4-88.8 per cent, T3-70.9 per cent; Convent Large White : T-75.0 per cent, T3-41.7 per cent). However, in the case of Pearl of Csaba, sprouting under wax + alkathene (T3:70.9 per cent) was found superior over 'only alkathene' (T4:50.0 per cent).

Again in Pearl of Csaba it may be seen that cuttings when stored both under moss + alkathene (Tl) as well as wax + alkathene (T3) gave maximum but equal sprouts (70.9 per cent each). However, the results obtained under T3 is superior and economical over T1, since in T3 no media are required except dipping the cut ends in wax and then wrapping in alkathene, while in Tl, though the cut ends are not dipped in wax, moss is surely needed.

Similarly, though sprouting of cuttings under Tl and T4 in Convent Large White are equal (75 per cent each), T4 is definitely superior and cheaper over Tl, since in T4 nothing is required except wrapping in alkathene, while in T1 (as mentioned earlier) the presence of moss is essential.

Results under various treatments on survival of sprouts in Perlette and Pearl of Csaba were significant over T6 (saw dust + alkathene), since the actual sprouts in both the varieties were 0 per cent. Survival in Convent Large White, however, was insignificant.

Summary and Conclusion

1. The present experiment was conducted at the Government Fruit Research Station, Basti in 1970.
2. Fresh stem-cuttings of grape varieties Perlette, Pearl of Csaba and Convent Large White were planted in beds (i) immediately after pruning of vines (Control) on 17th January 1970 and (ii) on 26.2.70 after storing for 40 days in moss + alkathene (Tl), wax + moss + alkathene (T2), wax + alkathene (T3), only alkathene (T4), wax + saw dust + alkathene (T5) and saw dust + alkathene (T6).
3. The effect of various treatments on sprouting of grape cuttings differed from variety to variety.
4. Best results with regards to sprouting in Perlette (T2) (91.7 per cent) was obtained under wax + moss + alkathene followed by only alkathene (T4: 83.3 per cent).
5. In Pearl of Csaba maximum sprouts (70.9 per cent) were obtained both under moss + alkathene(Tl) and wax + alkathene (T3).
6. Maximum spouts (75 per cent) in Convent Large White were obtained both under moss + alkathene (Tl) and only alkathene (T4) and therefore T4 is deemed to be a superior method.
7. In general, the effect of saw dust appeared to be detrimental on sprouting.
8. Effect of various madia on survival of sprouts was almost insignificant in different varieties except in Perlette and Pearl of Csaba due to the sprouts being 0 per cent under saw dust + alkathene (T6).
9. From the results obtained in this experiment, it is gathered that there is no binding for plantation of grape cuttings immediately after pruning of vines but even after storing the material in suitable media. The stored planting material may thus be sent from one place to the other with success.
10. The results guarantee long transport and storage of grape cuttings to speed up the grape plantation at further distances without much loss.

Acknowledgments

Thanks are due to Sri S.R.Kairati for statistical analysis of data.

Table 1

Showing Mean Percentage of Sprouts in Grape Cuttings Stored Under Different Media

Treatment Varieties	*T1*	*T2*	*T3*	*T4*	*T5*	*T6*	*Control*	*Mean*
1	2	3	4	5	6	7	8	9
Perlette	62.5	91.7	70.9	83.3	8.3	0	75.0	55.9
Pearl of Csaba	70.9	12.5	70.9	50.0	66.7	0	70.8	48.8
Convent Large White	75.0	41.7	41.7	75.0	54.1	45.9	62.5	56.5
Mean	69.4	48.6	61.1	69.4	43.0	15.3	69.4	53.8

S.E. difference between two varietal means = 4.33 %

S.E. difference between subplot treatment means + 4.75 %

C.D. at 5 % = 9.98 %

S.E. difference for the same variety =4.36 %

C.D. at 5 % = 9.16 %

T1 = moss + alkathene

T2 = wax + moss + alkathene

T3 = wax + alkathene

T4 = only alkathene

T5 = wax + saw dust + alkathene

T6 = saw dust +alkathene

Table 2

Showing Mean Percentage of Survival of Sprouts in Grape Cuttings Stored Under Different Media

Treatment Varieties	*T1*	*T2*	*T3*	*T4*	*T5*	*T6*	*Control*	*Mean*
1	2	3	4	5	6	7	8	9
Perlette	92.9	100	88.2	95.5	100	0	95	81.6

Pearl of Csaba	93.7	50	88.9	83.3	94.5	0	87.9	71.2
Convent Large White	95.0	91.7	91.7	83.3	92.9	91.7	79.5	89.4
Mean	93.9	80.5	89.6	87.4	95.8	30.5	87.4	80.7

S.E. difference between two varietal means = 4.01 %

C.D. at 5 % = 10.31 %

S.E. difference between subplot treatment means = 10.39 %

C.D. at 5 % = 21.83 %

S.E. difference for the same variety = 9.53%

CD at 5 % = 20.2

Tl = moss + alkathene

T2 = wax + moss + alkathene

T3 = wax + alkathene

T4 = only alkathene

T5 = wax + saw dust + alkathene

T6 = saw dust + alkathene

References

1. G.S. Randhawa, and Singh, J.P. 1958. Varietal diversity and improvement of grapes. *Indian J. Hort. 15* (3 and 4) : 220-27.
2. Singh, K. Kirpal and Bakhshi, J.C. 1963. Grape improvement work in the Punjab. *Punjab Hort. J. 3* (I) : 19-21.
3. Singh, L.B. 1961. An outstanding selection of grape for cultivation in northern India. *Ann. Rep. Hort. Res. Inst.* : 68-71 (Saharanpur).
4. Singh, L.B. 1962. Himrod and Delight, two outstanding grape introductions. *Ann. Rep. Hort. Res. Inst* : 124 (Saharanpur).
5. Thapar, A. R. and Panwar, J. P. 1961. Grape cultivation in Baramati area of Maharashtra State. *Himachal Hort.* 2 (3) : 75-78.
6. Balakrishnan, R. and V. N. Madhava Rao. 1963. Effect of severity of pruning on growth flowering, yield and quality in grape *(Vitis vinifera,* L.). *South Ind. Hort.* 11 (3 & 4): 1-27.
7. Bessis, R. 1965. Analysis of the effect of long pruning on yield of

Carignan vine variety in Tunisia. *Hort. Abstr.* 35 : 324. (Orig. ref: J. Agric. Trop. Bot. appl., 1964, 11:3-11).

8. Chadha K. L., J. P. Nauryial and Harish Kumar 1969, Studies on pruning of Perlette grape. *Indian J. Hort.* 26 (1 and 2) : 15-20.
9. Gopalkrishna, N. and D. N. Kerwala, 1961, Spur pruning versus cane pruning in grape *(Vitis vinifera,* L). *Indian J. Hort.* 18 (3): 198-201.
10. Jauhari, O.S. and Darshana Nand. 1969, Convent Large White - a promising grape introduction (unpublished).
11. Jauhari, O.S. and Darshana Nand. 1970. Pomological studies on grapes. I - Seedless varieties. Allahabad Farmer (in press).
12. Jauhari, O.S. and Darshana Nand. 1970. Pomological studies on grapes. II - Seeded varieties Allahabad Farmer (in press).
13. Jauhari, O.S. and Darshana Nand and G. P. Srivastava, 1969 Studies on flowering, pollination and fruit set in grape. *South Ind. Hort.* 17 (1 and 2): 1-8.
14. Karuppuswamy, M.S., S. Krishnamurthy and V. N. Madhava Rao, 1960, Studies on growth, yield and quality of Anab-e-shahi grape (*Vitis vinifera*) in relation to disposition of shoots on the arbour. *South Ind. Hort.* 8 (3 & 4) : 1-16.
15. Mukherjee, S. K. 1968. Research findings on grape in North India. Grape (Andhra Pradesh grape growers association, Hyderabad). Andhra Writers Cooperative Society Ltd., Press. Troop Bazar, Hyderabad.
16. Nand, Darshana, 1965. Kishmish Surkh and Gulabi-two promising varieties of grape. *Punjab Hort. J.* 5 (2 to 4) : 177-80.
17. Olmo, H. P. 1948. Perlette and Delight. *Calif. Agr. Exp. Sta. Bull.* 705.
18. Prasad, Ambika and Darshana Nand, 1964. Some selections of grapes in Uttar Pradesh. *Punjab Hort. J.* 4 (3 and 4) : 145-47.
19. Rao, K. Radhakrishna, 1955 Training and pruning of grape wine in South India. *Indian J. Hort.* 12 (4) : 157-64.
20. Ritter, F. 1965. Trials on the horizontal and cordon training (of vines) at different spacings. *Hort. Abstr.* Vol. 35: 323. (Orig. ref : Weinberg U. Keller, 1964, 11 : 535-46).
21. Singh, L. B. 1961 An outstanding selection of grape for cultivation in Northern India. *Ann. Rep. Hort. Res. Instt.* (Saharanpur) 68-71.
22. Singh, L. B. 1962. Himrod and Delight, two outstanding grape introductions. *Ann. Rep. Hort. Res. Instt.* (Saharanpur) 124.

23. Spirov, M. 1965. Pruning Studies on the vine variety Chasselas Dora. *Hort. Abstr.* 35 : 566. (Orig. ref: Grad. lozar. Nanka, 1964, 1 (8) : 87-97).

24. Tomkins, J. and N. Shaulis. 1956. The Catauba grape in New York. *Proc. Amer. Soc. Hort. Sci.* 66: 209-13.

25. Tripathi, S. N. 1969. Preliminary studies on the methods of pruning Perlette and Scarlet grapes. *Punjab Hort. J.* 9 (1 and 2) : 24-27.

26. Mustafa, A. M. and Giani, M. A. 1941. *Grape growing in Baluchistan.* Imp. Counc. Agr. Res. Misc. Bull. No. 40.

27. Prasad, A. and Nand, D. 1964. Some selections of grapes in Uttar Pradesh. *Pb. hort. J.* 4, (3 and 4) : 145-47.

28. Singh, L. B. 1961. An outstanding selection of grape for cultivation in northern India. *Ann. Rep. Hort. Res. Inst.* (Saharanpur): 68-71.

29. Singh, L. B. 1962. *Himrod and Delight,* two outstanding grape introductions.

30. *Ann. Rep. Hort. Res. Inst.* (Saharanpur) : 124.

31. Singh, L. and Singh, S. 1940. Distinguishing characters and behaviour of some grape-vine varieties introduced at Lyallpur in the Punjab. *Ind. Jour. agric. Sc.* 10 : 552-93.

32. Waugh, F.A. 1914. Describing grapes. *Systematic Pomology* Orange Judd Company, New York. Chap. IX, 88-97.

33. Zielinski, Q. B. 1955. Grapes. *Modern Systematic Pomology* W.M.C. Brown Company, Dubuque, Iowa, U.S.A. Chapt. 24, 224-32.

34. Gandhi, S.R. (1968). Grape Culture in India. Ind. Coun. Agr. Res. Farm Bill No.12.

35. Jauhari.O.S. and Darshana Nand (1969). Convent Large White-a promising grape introduction (unpublished).

36. Prasad Ambika and Darshana Nand (1964). Some selections of grapes in Uttar Pradesh. Punjab hort. J.4 (3 and 4). 145-47.

37. Singh. S.N. (1968). Performance of some grape varieties under Kanpur conditions. Punjab hort. J .8(3): 147-51.

10

Some Other Fruits

Successful Rooting in Neglected Aerial Layers of Litchi

In an orchard of Litchi at Kasiá (Village Sabya) District Deoria, U. P. one hundred and fifty aerial layers were tied in the middle of August, 1954 with a view to multiply them. All the trees in the orchard were growing well in a good healthy condition.

For tying goottee a healthy dormant bud was selected on a healthy, mature and disease free shoot. A ring of about one and half inches length was prepared by removing the bark clearly from all round the shoot under a selected bud. The ring was covered with goottee soil and a piece of chatti and tied.

After tying, regular waterings were done in all the layers for about a month to keep the soil moist. But later on due to certain reasons, they were neglected with the result that the soil of the goottee changed into a dry and hard material. After that no watering was ever done to the layers except when they got moistened sometimes by natural resources.

Till the end of October 1954 no roots sprouted up from any of the layers. The soil at that time was absolutely dry and hard but shoots were quite green and healthy. The dry and hard soil of some of the layers were broken open and it was found that callusing had taken place on the ringed shoots. All the remaining layers, therefore, were left as such on their mother plants and were kept under frequent observations.

Throughout the whole year the layers remained green but no roots appeared. After about a year when the rains started, the layers were found to be giving out roots in the month of July 1955.

The layers were then injured from the mother plants and planted in the nursery where they are flourishing well.

By the above results it is concluded that due to certain unavoidable conditions, if the air-layers could not be looked after properly on the tree, they should never be destroyed, provided the shoots are green. The layers should be left as such on the tree to allow them to give out roots next year when the favourable weather condition prevails. This is of a great importance from the economic and commercial point of view.

Why Not Grow Thornless Variety of Ber (*Ziziphus - Jujuba*)

Thorns on a ber tree, in the strict sense, are leaf spines formed by the modification of stipules. They are very sharp pointed and densely distributed on the branches, which hinder much in picking of fruits. Thorns also create difficulty in pruning, spraying, ploughing, manuring, irrigation and other cultural operations in the orchard. The significance of thornlessness, therefore, in such fruit trees can never be over-emphasized.

A thornless variety of ber does not appear to have been reported so far. The present paper, therefore, deals with a thornless variety of ber observed by the author in December, 1957, in the orchard of Thakur Adya Prasad Singh, Taluqdar, Madhupur Estate, district Pratapgarh. Only a tree of this variety was found in the orchard which was about fifteen years old. The tree was about 25 ft. tall and its branches were spreading for about 18 ft. in diameter. Most of the branches of the tree were tending to be growing upwards.

The branches were found absolutely free from spiny stipules, the so called thorns in the common language. On close observations it was found that the leaves were actually not ex-stipulate like other varieties of this species. But it was observed that two whitish stipules were present on the branches on each side of the base of the leaf stalk. They were fine and velvety in character and absolutely free from spiny nature. The fruit is longer in shape in comparison to other varieties of ber. The average size of a fruit is about 2.1" (length) × 1.0" (thickness). The apex of fruit is distinctly drawn into a long and narrow beak. The base of the fruit is more or less flat. The fruit has a remarkable air cavity at its basal end and a slight air cavity at its apical end. The fruit as a whole is slightly curved throughout its length.

The fruit is very sweet and starts ripening late in the season somewhere in the last week of March, when other varieties of ber practically disappear from the market. The harvesting period continues from the last week of March up to the third week of April, after which the tree goes to rest.

The fruit, having its skin of medium softness, has a good keeping quality and can stand transport very well. This variety is a heavy bearer as well.

The seed is about 1.4" × 0.3" in size. It has a characteristic apex which is prominently drawn into a long and needle like beak.

Such rare plant characters and plant materials, having thornlessness, qualities of late ripening and heavy bearing, good size and taste of the fruit, its good keeping quality and transportability, are of a great commercial importance for an orchardist. There is a wide scope of its propagation and multiplication by vegetative means for distribution amongst fruit growers.

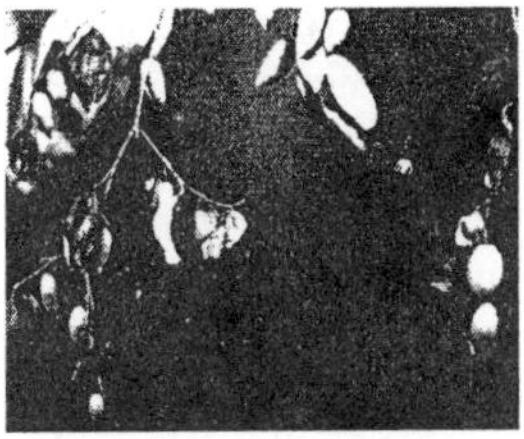

The variety may be named as "Madhupur Thornless", which may be recommended as a commercial variety of ber.

Acknowledgements

The tree of "Madhupur Thornless" variety of ber is standing in the orchard of Thakur Adya Prasad Singh, Taluqdar, Madhpur Estate, district Pratapgarh, U.P., to whom I wish to express my deep sense of gratitude for providing me necessary facilities throughout these investigations.

I am also thankful to Sri S.S. Singh, District Agricultural Officer, Pratapgarh, who encouraged me from time to time to carry out these investigations.

Maturity Assessment and Harvesting Techniques of Jamun

Jamun (Syzygium cuminii, skeels) of the family Myrtacease, is a delicious important fruit of Indian origin. Kala jam, phalani, phalinda, jambu, jambova, ra-jamun and jambul are other local names of jamun. Its English names, though, not very common, are Javaplum, black-plum jambolana, Indian black berry and jambul.

Jamun grows wild as well as along roads and occasionally in gardens all over the country. The small purple fruit of Jamun is extensively eaten. The better ones, which are bold in size, are less astringent and sourish which are very good in taste. These also have much pectin. This helps in successful setting of jelly from its juice.

Ripe jamun fruit is nutritious also. It has been reported that jamun fruit contains 50 to 65 per cent juice, 9 to 11.5 per cent total soluble solids, 2 to 2.3 per cent acidity and 2.3 to 3.7 per cent pectin. Again, per 100 gm of pulp, it contains 30 to 40 mg of vitamin C and 74 to 100 I.U. of vitamin A (Singh, I.S., 2001).

Its juice is used in preparing vinegar after fermentation, which has medicinal value and is very useful in stomach troubles. Jamun seed powder is also a medicine for diabetes. It is useful in urinary troubles. Doctors opine that jamun fruits are also useful for heart and liver patients. The fruit besides eating fresh and making vinegar and jellies is also used in preparing squashes and preserving juice.

Jamun seed is good nutritious cattle feed also. In Izatnagar experiments were carried out. There seeds were gradually added to concentrate mixture until these contributed 20 per cent of the concentrate. These were readily and tastefully eaten by the cattle. For this purpose fruits dropped under the trees may be collected by the villagers in their spare time, thoroughly smeared, washed and made available for use (Hayes, 1970).

Jamun is a very huge-sized evergreen, shady and ornamental fruit tree. It does not require much care. It is highly tolerant to usar salts and may survive also to some extent in water-logged conditions. On the other hand, it may also tolerate dry conditions. As such its plants may be planted at 9 × 9 meters apart along roads, highways, canals and in gardens, parks and on different types of waste lands. The trees may also be planted scattered or in groups near wells, grazing grounds, resting places, threashing floors and other such places. These are also planted as wind breaks along orchards of various fruits.

Maturity Assessment

Jamun fruit in a unripe stage is green in colour. Till the fruit is unripe it is of no use. The tree flowers in February-March and after that the growth of the fruit goes on. A fully grown up jamun fruit is equal to the size of a bold oval shaped 'ber' (Zyziphus mauritiana) fruit. As soon as the green colour of the fruit starts becoming pinkish, the grower must be alert to assess its maturity.

Gradually, the pinkish colour of the fruit darkens and ultimately on complete ripening, it becomes dark purple or slightly blackish in colour. The skin of the fruit is very thin and soft. The pulp is also very soft. As such, the fruit is high perishable. Even a slight slackness may injure and bruise the fruit.

The jamun fruit ripens in June - July. If there are rains during ripening, the ripening process is hastened. The proper stage of ripening and picking may also be assessed by touching the fruit. On touching, the skin a pulp should be tight and not loose. If such fruit is left on tree unpicked, the pulp and skin loosen and ultimately drop on the ground.

Harvesting Technique

Harvesting of Jamun fruit is a very important operation. Various techniques may be adopted for this, but in every case the picked up fruit must be saved from bruising. If picked properly the self life of the fruit continues from 2-3 days.

The branches of Jamun tree are very tender and therefore, the person who climbs on tree should be cautious on this aspect. Every fruit should be picked up individually and be kept in a wide-mouthed stiff cloth bag hanging on harvestor back. This may be done by using a ladder on the tree or by climbing direct on the tree. The contents of the bag should not exceed 3 to 4 kg at a time. The bag after picking should be sent down by means of a rope tied with the bag, which should be collected in wide mouthed airy basket, layered with newspaper sheets. The empty bag is then sent back to the harvestor.

Harvesting may also be done by giving jerks to branches of trees and collecting the fruits on wide cloth sheet stretched at all the corners by four persons under the tree.

The fruit after harvest should be disposed off as early as possible in the local or nearby markets to have proper income.

"Lecture delivered by the author in National Workshop, arranged in Hotel Shivalik View and organised by National Productivity Council, Chandigarh on 7th and 8th February, 2002."

Blossom Biology of Hog-Plum *(Spondais Pinnata, Kurz)*

The hog-plum (Spondias Pinnata, Kurz) syn. S. mangifera, wild; family Anacadiaceae; Common name - amra, is one of the various edible minor fruits of India. The fruit is astringent in taste with a little flavour. The portion near the skin is sour while that near the stone is sweet. Preserve, sweet and hot, pickles, curry, tart and chutney are some of the useful product made out of it. The fruit may also be dried and powdered for future use. It is of medicinal importance as well. The plant can easily be propagated by stem-cutting and seed. The hog-plum plant is also used as root-stock for Spondias Cytheria Sonn. (S. *dulcis* Forest). As such prospects of hog-plum appear to be bright. Knowledge of its blossom biology is essential for improvement through hybridization or other means. For this purpose well-established trees of hog-plum varieties 'oval' and 'round' growing within the premises of Govt. Gardens, Varanasi, (U.P.) were utilized. Results of these are presented as follows:

Flowering and Fruiting

Hog-plum was seen bearing terminally on last years growth. The tree commenced shedding leaves from the second week of December and acquired complete dormancy by the middle of January. The blossom bud, which consisted of a rudimentary panicle and enclosed with small brownish scales, started swelling in the second week of February. As a result of this, the brownish scales dropped off and a bright light green-coloured bud, known as rudimentary panicle (1.45 x 1.45 cm) appeared at the terminal end of each last year's shoot in the 3rd week of February. This stage was termed as bud-burst. The rudimentary panicle unfolded on the third day of bud-burst. This was the first day of emergence, when it attained the size of 1.54 × 1.58 cm (Table 1).

Table 1. Panicle Development in Hog-plum

Observations	Days after panicle emergence during February and March					
	0	4	8	12	16	20
	February		March			
	21	25	1	5	9	13
Length (cm)	1.54	2.89	5.87	11.38	16.93	21.27
Maximum Spread (cm)	1.58	2.97	6.18	12.33	20.11	25.90

The trees flowered during February-March. Fruits were found bearing in clusters, which were ready for harvest during July-August. The ripening of fruits took place by December-January. Off-season flowering and fruiting was never seen.

Inflorescence and its Structure

The inflorescence of hog-plum consisted of panicle which was composed of three types of shoots on the main stalk (rachis). These were primary, secondary and tertiary shoots. Each primary shoot possessed a fleshy bract at a base. The primary and secondary shoots were of racemose type, while the tertiary shoots were of cymose type. These floral shoots went on increasing in size towards the tip of the rachis, which ultimately gave a conical shape to the panicle.

Panicle Development

Ten freshly appeared panicles were marked at random and data on their length and maximum spread were recorded at 4 days interval in the pre-bloom stage (Table 1). During unfolding, the floral shoots of a panicle separated from each other. Soon after unfolding, the rachis and other floral shoots grew in size and the fleshly bracts dropped off. It is clear from table that about half of the growth of panicle was complete between 8th and 12th day of its emergence. The panicle in the pre-bloom stage attained the maximum size (21.27 x 25.90 cm) in 20 days. It was observed that the growth of the panicle was uniform. After passing the pre-bloom stage, the process of growth in the panicle continued till all the flowers below the tip, bloomed completely. At this stage, the panicle was 35.5 cm (length) × 43.8 cm (spread) in size having the girth of its main stalk as 4.47 cm at base.

Floral Count, Duration and Mode of Flower Opening

Five panicle were selected for these studies. The flowers which bloomed in each panicle, were counted and removed every day till these ceased blooming. The dates of opening of first and last flower were also noted (Table 2). Simultaneously, the mode of opening of flowers in panicle was closely observed and recorded. On an average, 1829.4 flowers bloomed per panicles. The duration of blooming in all panicles continued for 21 days, while it was 11 days in an individual panicle.

Table 2. Floral Count and Duration of Flower in Panicles

Date of opening of first flower	*Date of opening of last flower*	*Duration of opening of flower in all panicle days*	*Duration of opening of flower in a panicle days*	*Number of flowers opening in panicle*
March, 3	April, 2	21	11	1829.4

Generally, blooming started on first three or four primary shoots of a panicle towards the basal end of the rachis. The top most flowers in tertiary shoot opened first, followed by the flower situated at the base. Sometimes, the top basal flowers opened together.

Morphology of the Flower

The flower was observed as white, small (8.0 mm broad) and hermaphrodite. Sepals were 5 in number, united and greenish white in colour. Petals 5, united, white, thin, acute at apex 0.40 × 0.26 cm in size. Stamens 10, free inserted in a light cream-coloured disc; five of these were long (1.2 mm) alternating with petals and bending towards stigma; remaining 5 were short (1.0 mm), opposite and parallel to petals.

Pistil penta-carpellary, syncarpus; ovary superior, pentalocular and covered under the disc; style 5, short, free major portion of style was inserted within the disc and colour of top portion was seen mixed up with that of the disc; stigma 5, pointed opposite to stamens and all were alternating with petals.

Morphology of the Fruit

Ten fully developed fruits were utilized for each variety. The fruit was

3.8 × 2.7 cm in size and 10.78 g in weight (oval type) whereas round type was 3.6 × 3.6 cm in dimensions and 11.5 g in weight. The apical and distal ends of the fruit were roundish. The fruit possessed in itself a hard and large thick stone (seed), which resembled its own shape. The body of the fruit (oval) was dark green in colour having small dots thereon while the round was light green in colour.

Flower Bud Development

For this 25 flower buds (oval type) were kept under observation. The whole phase of flower bud development was divided into six distinct phases (Nand, 1970) which along with their chronology, are presented below:

Phases: The freshly appeared flower bud and bud on the panicle was tiny (1.0 mm), green and round. The calyx bound the remaining organs tightly in itself.

The flower bud swelled up in size (1.7 mm in diameter) till the calyx cracked and demarcated itself with the whitish carolla lobe.

On further swelling, the bud attained the diameter of 3.0 mm. the corolla lobe acquired a predominating creamy white appearance.

The creamy white carolla lobe further swelled up to 3.5 mm width and got loosened till it showed signs of separation of petals from each other through cracks in their margin. This was treated to be the initial stage of flower opening. The carolla lobe further opened and formed the shape of 'U' which was 4.5 mm in width.

The opening of the flower was taken as complete when this attained the shape of a saucer and the reproductive organs were clearly visible. At this stage the flower was 8.00 mm in width.

Table 3. Chronology of Flower Bud Development

Time required for passing from one phase to the other (Days, hours, minutes)						*Total period (Days, hours, minutes)*		
Bud-Burst	1st to 2nd	2nd to 3rd	3rd to 4th	4th to 5th	5th to 6th	From bud-burst to full bloom (6th phase)	From 1st phase to full bloom (6th phase)	For complete opening flower (4th to 6th phase)
6-0-0	9-0-0	7-0-0	0-18-48	0-2-57	0-1-15	22-23-0	16-23-0	0-4-12

Table 4. Anthesis, Fruit-set and Fruit Retention in Hog-plum (under natural-open-pollination, var. oval)

Anthesis			*Initial fruit-set per panicle*		*Fruit carried to final maturity (fruit retention per panicle)*		
Flowers opened (%)		*Total no. of flowers*	*Number*	*Percentage*	*Number*	*% of flowers*	*% of fruits*
2 to 4	4 to 6	16 to 22 March					
4.51	95.49	1405	1304.2	71.29	35	1.97	2.68

Chronology

From appearance of the tiny bud (phase 1) to full bloom (phase 6), it took 16 days and 23 hours (Table 3), while a period of 22 days and 23 hours was needed from bud-burst to full bloom (Table 3). The period required for complete opening of a flower (4th to 6th phase) was 4 hours and 12 minutes (Table 3). The times required from bud-burst to first phase and thereafter from one phase to the other have been indicated in (Table 3.)

Anthesis: Observations on anthesis were made on five panicles at an interval of two hours daily for a week. Flowers which opened in each panicle (judged by the sixth phase of flower bud development) were counted, recorded and removed.

Anthesis started at 1.48 hours in the 4 phase of flower bud development, which was completed at 6.0 hours in the 6th phase. Further anthesis was at its peak (95.49 per cent) between 4 to 6 hours (Table 4). This was therefore, regarded to be the actual time of anthesis.

After opening of flower, the petals refluxed backwards at about 18 hours and by 10.0 hours anthers of the five longer-sized stamens were seen lying over the stigmas. The remaining shorted-sized stamens, however, remained parallel to the petals as usual. Next morning the flower lost its freshness and showed signs of shivering.

Dehiscence of Anthers and Pollination

Anthers were found bursting with the opening of flower and the dehiscence was complete the same day. Pollen grain was yellow and dusty. Honey-bees, flies and various other insects were found buzzing actively around the flowers between 4.0 to 6.0 hours, which was the optimum time for collecting pollen. It was, therefore, believed that these insects were among few of the agencies responsible for transfer of pollen from flower to flower.

Receptivity of Stigma and Fruit-set

Five panicles, which were to bloom, were selected. The initial fruit-set under natural-open-pollination (indicated by a small, light pinkish protuberance over the disc) was recorded on the fourth day of flower opening. As such the number of fruits obtained finally on each panicle (fruit retention), was also counted and recorded. The percentage initial set and fruit retention were determined based on number of flowers per panicle.

The stigma was considered most receptive when its appearance was bright and fresh. Three days after opening of flowers, the style elongated, which along with the stigma became clearly visible. The ovary covered under the disc developed in size and came out of the disc in the form of a small light pinkish fruit. On further growth, this turned dark pink and later on to reddish-purple colour. It was observed that initial set under natural-open-pollination was quite good (71.29 per cent) in a panicle (Table 2).

During the course of development of fruit the disc was found suppressed, which later on became flat. The fruit turned green in colour and grew in size till it matured in about 14 weeks. On an average 35 fruits per panicle (1.973 per cent of bloomed flowers and 2.68 per cent of fruits) were carried to final maturity (Table 4).

Bearing behaviour of hog-plum at the terminal end of last years growth agrees with that of mango, which too belongs to the family Anacardiaceae. The tree of hog-plum bore pure panicle, which agreed with that of mango (Mallik, Indian J. Hort.; 14(1): 1-23, 1957; Randhawa and Damodran, Indian J. Hort., 18(l):36-45, 1961). Flowering took place on naked shoots with the advent of spring season, which is also the main flowering flush in mango as reported by Mallik in 1957. Flowers opened during odd hours and another dehisced with the opening of flowers.

The structure and shape of inflorescence in hog-plum were found similar to those of mango as found by Singh in 1954. Flowers were observed as heramaphrodite, which counted 1829.4 in number per panicle. This was in contrary to a total number of 1213 flowers in Dashehari and 1061 in Langra mango.

Pollen grains were dusty. The initial percentage set of flowers under natural-open-pollination was quite good, as compared to very nominal set in mango. Thirty-five fruits per panicle reached final maturity in hog-plum against only 0.34 fruits in Dashehari and 0.29 fruits in Langra mango as reported by Singh., R. N., India J. Hort., 11(3):69-88,1954.

BAEL- A Sacred Indian Fruit

Bael is one of the most nutritious, sacred and medicinal fruit of Indian origin. Bael fruit is very important in the case of dysentery and diarrhoea. For this doctors have advised to consume raw fruits. In the case of swelling of liver and problem of tuberculosis also bael fruit is of a great utility. It is also of utility in the case of disease of brain and in heart troubles. Raw fruit of bael is astringent and encourages constipation but useful in stomach-ache and digestion. The pulp of bael fruit is laxative and clears bowels.

The medicinal properties in bael fruit is mainly due to presence of a colourless crystalline substance 'Marmelosin'. This material is available in the fruit to the extent of 0.03 to 0.37%. Green fresh leaves and tender shoots of bael, flowers and fruits all are aromatic. These yield essential oil. Raw fruits are mostly used for preparing preserves, which are very useful for proper upkeep of stomach. Ripe fruits are eaten fresh and turned into ready to serve drinks (sharbat) which is good for stomach and has cooling affect. Pulps of ripe bael fruits are also transformed into jams, squashes, nectar, toffees, shreds and Baelpapar (Belawat). Pieces of dried ripe bael fruit are turned in Bael-powder. Presence of a scented compound named as 'Coumarene' has also been found out in central portion of the fruit. Leaves also yield a chemical 'aegelin'.

Bael fruit has a hard shell and its pulp is full of mucilaginous material and many white coloured flattish seeds. The fruit pulp contains 61.5% moisture, 1.8-5.12% protene, 0.39% fat, 1.7% mineral matter, 31.8% carbohydrate, 1.4-7% fibre, 22 to 44% total soluble solids and 0.36 to 0.75% acidity. Again per 100 gm of pulp makes available carotene (vitamin-A) 55 mg, vitamin-B1 (Thiamine) 0.13 mg, vitamin-B2 (Riboflavin) 1.19 mg, Niacin (Nicotinic acid) 1.1 mg and vitamin-C 18-21 mg. The whole fruit has the edible pulp as 57 to 74%. The fruit also contains tannic acid. Its seeds are also aromatic seeds also yield about 32% scented oil. Seeds have 3% carbohydrate, 3% ash and 62% protein.

Bael has been known to India from pre-historic times and Vedic period. It has been mentioned in various religious books.

Its tree, being sacred is also worshiped. At the religious occasion and festival of Maha Shivaratri, Lord Shiva is offered specially bael leaves (bael patra) and bael fruits. Bael is found growing scattered near temples and various other places, in groups, in forests and as orchards in whole of the country. It also grows in Shri Lanka, Mynmar, Bangladesh, Thailand, Pakistan and Southern Asia as well as at places at a height of 1219 metre above the sea level. It grows in Uttar Pradesh, Bihar, Orissa, Madhya Pradesh, West Bengal, Panchvati and hills of Chitrakoot.

Bael is an evergreen tree of the family 'Rutaceae'. However the tree sheds its leaves for sometime between ripening and picking. The tree grows to a height of 7-8 metre and sharp thorns in its branches. Its leaves are trifoliate, two side ones are smaller and the middle one wider and longer with a long tip like a 'trishool'. In English it is known as bael and also, as Bengal quince. In

Hindi it is known as Bael, Sripal or Bilva. Its botanical name is Aegle marmelos or Cratavia marmelos.

Climate and Soil

The tree of bael is very hardy and can tolerate several climatic hardy conditions like forst, too, dry atmosphere etc. It can grow in worst and unfertile soil, banjar, ravines and even in marshy lands. It can grow in acidic as well as alkaline soil having pH range between 5 and 10.

Varieties

Several varieties have been selected, which have be given local names like 'Kaghzi Etawa', 'Kaghzi Gonda', 'Kaghzi Faizabadi', 'Rampuri', 'Deoria Large', Mirzapuri', 'zmati', 'Ojha-ka-Purwa' and 'Narendra Bael'.

Propagation

Besides seeds bael is now propagated by shield or patch budding. For this seedling root stock should be of 1½ to 2 years age and scion stick should be one month old. Budding is done in May-June. Root-suckers coming out of bael tree roots, may also be taken out and utilized for growing as vegetatively propagated plants.

Top working of trees growing in forests or of undesirable varieties may be done with improved varieties. For this the trunk of the tree is beheaded at a height of 120 cm from ground in February-March and budding is done on shoots coming out from top of the cut portion of truck.

Plantation

Before plantation, pits of the size of $1\times1\times1$ metre should be dug up in April-May at a distance of 9×9 metres (30×30 feet). These should be left for about a month in hot sun and then filled up tightly with 2/3 of surfac soil and 1/3 of cow dung manure 15 cm above soil surface. Plants should be planted during rains in centre of the filled up pits. In this way 120 plants can be planted per hectare of land (48 plants per acre.) If there are no rains, irrigate and plants immediately after plantation.

Flowering and Fruiting

Bael trees flower and fruit in 4-5 years in the case of vegetatively propagated plants and in 7-8 years in the case of seedlings. The tree flowers and fruits in February-March. From flowering to ripening Bael fruits remain hanging on the tree for about a year.

Picking of Fruits

Generally fruits ripen in April-May. At this stage the colour of hard shell acquires yellowish tinge. After this the fruits are collected by cutting its stalk from the tree with about 4 cm stalk attached with are placed together and when these ripe fully the stalks are automatically released from the fruits. On ripening the fruits has a pleasant flavour and the shell becomes more brittle.

Yield

One tree of bael yield 200 fruits of average to large size. If the fruits are small number may exceed to 300. These fruits weigh from 1 ½ to 2 quintals. After harvesting marketing should be arranged. Fruits may be transported in gunny bags, but should be properly handled so that hard shell of fruits may not break. So grow and consume bael fruit, as it is restorative and a very good tonic.

Refreshing Phalsa

Phalsa is a cooling and refreshing summer season Indian fruit. It is available in May and June. Phalsa is nutritious also. It contains juice 60-70%, Total Soluble Solids (TSS) 18-20%, Sugar 11%, Acidity 2-3%, Minerals including Iron and Phosphorus 0.4 to 0.6 %, Vitamin-C 35-40 mg and Vitamin-A 700-750 IU per 100 gm pulp.

Besides eating, fresh fruits are turned in ready to serve syrup and squash. It is a digestive tonic and stomachic. It is more or less a medicine for constipation, fever, inflamation, heart and blood disorders.

Phalsa belongs to be family 'Tiliacea' and grows in the form of a shrub or a small tree. It sheds its leaves during December - January and sprouts again in February - March with tender shoots bearing there on first small yellow flowers and the small round green fruit in axils of leaves. Fruits when ripe become purplish and then blackish, which are slightly sourish or sweet according to ripeness. Green fruits are used for making chutney and pickles. Leaves are used as dining plates after stitching.

Its wood is used or making golf shafts and the stems for baskets, since these are pliable. Botanically phalsa is known as Grewia subinaequalis as well as Grewia asiatica. In English and Hindi both it is named as phalsa.

Varieties

Phalsa varieties have not been established so far except that one is a shrubby variety and the other a small tree, which is rarely seen. However, there is no difference in fruits.

Climate and Soil

Phalsa requires a hot dry climate. However, if rains fall during ripening, these enhance ripening. Plants are cold and frost resistant. The plants are leaf-less during winters. Well drained loam soil suits best. However, it can very well carry on in any unfertile soil, banjar, alkaline, clayee, sandy loam or on other waste land.

Propagation

Plants are propagated by seeds. Propagation is also done in the month of December - January, by stem cuttings of 25 - 30 cm length. Sprouting of cuttings (shoots and roots) take place easily if the cuttings are dipped in the solution of Indol butyric acid - a harmone.

Plantation

First of all the proposed land for plantation of phalsa is plough and planked during November - December twice and thrice. Then lay out is done at 180 cm apart each side. Pits of the size 50 x 50 cm are dug at each mark. Pits are then sterilized by burning leaves and other dry matter in them. Each pit is then filled up with a mixture of equal quantity of surface soil, cow dung manure and pond soil and well pressed 15 cm above the soil surface. Before planting the whole plot should be irrigated so that the soil of each filled up pit may come down at the surface level.

The best time for plantation is December - January. After the filled up pit is ready to receive plants, uproot the planting material from the nursery after slightly loosening the under soil. Bring these to the planting place without earthen ball after covering the roots. Dig small pits in the centre of the filled up pits to accommodate the plants in such a way that the roots of plants may spread up properly. After planting, cover the small pit with soil and then tighten each plant from sides. Plant phalsas also in kitchen gardens. Children will enjoy much.

Irrigation

Irrigate the plot soon after plantation. After that irrigation should be done at 15 days interval. No irrigation should be given after rainy season and during winters unless required after any special operation. Irrigation may be given during the growth of fruits and after manuring. Hoeing and weeding should also be done from time to time.

Inter Cropping

Winter, summer, rainy season vegetables may be taken in between the vacant spaces as inter crop, keeping in view that phalsa roots do not get water during winters.

Pruning

Pruning of phalsa shoots should be done in the end of December to mid of January. Pruning should be done every year in each plant at a height of one metre from the soil surface (light pruning). The prunes are utilized for propagation and basket making purposes. At this stage the plants are dormant.

Manuring

After pruning dig a 45 cm wide and 22 cm deep furrow all round each plant. After about a week furrow of each plant should be filled up with a mixture of surface soil, pond soil and 15 kg compost or farm yard manure with 200 gm neem cake or castor cake and 100 gm single super phosphate to cover the roots. Then irrigate the plants immediately.

Flowering, Fruiting, Picking and Yield

The plant of phalsa flowers and fruits in the second year. A reference of flowering and fruiting has been made earlier. In March - April plants are filled up with flowers and fruits. In May - June plants are loaded with ripe fruits. All fruits don't ripe at a time, hence the operation of picking and marketing should be done daily.

If a spray of 0.4% ferrus sulphate (4 gm $FeSO_4$ and 1 liter water) and then 0.4 % zinc sulphate after a week is done before flowering and after flowering, one may have fruits of better size and more juicy as well. Picking, handling of fruits should be done carefully. About 5 kg of fruits may be expected from one phalsa plant.

Grow Mulberry

Mulberry is a summer season refreshing fruit of the family Moraceae. It is a deciduous tree of medium size of the genus Morus. In English it is known as 'Mulberry', while in Hindi it is called 'Shahtoot' or 'Toot'. It may be grown in plains as well as on slopes of hills. In India it is grown in Uttar Pradesh, Punjab, TamilNadu, Karnataka and other parts of South India. The highest area under mulberry is in Mysore.

The fruit is sweet and sourish sweet in taste. Its T.S.S. is 9-11%, acidity 1.0%. It has minerals 0.5 to 0.7% and edible part 100%. It makes available vitamin-C 20 mg, vitamin-A 16 I.U., vitamin-B1 0.6 mg, vitamin-B2 0.9 mg, Niacin 0.2 mg, Calcium 60 mg, Phosphorus 20 mg, Iron 2.6 mg and Calorific value 55 calories per 100 gm pulp. Fruits also provide carbohydrate 12.2%, Protein 0.7%, Fat 0.7%.

Varieties. Mulberry has two varieties on the basis of colour, species etc., i.e. Morus alba and Morus nigra. The fruit of Morus alba are whitish green, which is often called white mulberry. Generally silk worms are reared on leaves of Morus alba to develop silk industry (Sericulture). Actually this species is a native of China/Japan. Its fruits are 2 cm long tasteful and very sweet leaves of this variety/species are green, broad, shining roundish and ornamental. Its leaves are good fodder for animals. Its fruits are dried and turned into powder which are used as feed in poultry and piggery. The wood of Morus alba is useful for manufacture of hockey and other games and sports articles.

The fruits of Morus nigra are black in colour, very sweet and juicy. It is a native of Western Asia. It was introduced in India from Iran. Black mulberry is also called Krishna Toot.

There is another species of mulberry - Morus rubra. Its tree is of large size with thick trunk. Its leaves are green and deeply lobed. In unripe condition fruits are reddish and sourish in taste. On ripening these become sweetish. Its wood is used as building material. For planting, first of all dig pits of the size l x l x l metre at 16 metres (50 feet) apart each way in the month of April - May. After about a month or so, fill in the pits will 2/3 parts of surface soil and 1/3 part of farm yard manure (cow dung manure). This organic manure should be well-rotten and old. Pits must be filled before the start of rains. These should be filled also tightly about 15 cm above the soil surface. After the rains start, soil comes down equal to the surface of soil. Then the plant should be planted in the center of the filled up pit in the month of July - August. The plant should be lifted from the nursery with the earthen ball around the roots and planted as such and then the soil around the earthen ball should carefully be tightened with the help of the wooden handle of a khurpee. As such 42 plants cover a hectare of land (17 plants per acre). After these are planted in soil, if there are no chances of rains, these should immediately be irrigated. Till the plants are small irrigation should be continued at an interval of 7 to 15 days according to requirements. In between two irrigations, hoeing and weeding should also be done for proper sun light and aeration in soil or better growth of the plants. When roots of plants reach quite enough deep under the soil, then gradually the number of irrigation may be reduced. However, full and proper care with regards to irrigation should be atleast for two years. Generally, a khirni plant / tree does not need manuring, but for a better crop about 50 kg. of F.Y.M. may be applied to a bearing tree in September - October and be irrigated thereafter.

Flowering and fruiting start after eleven or twelve years of plantation. The tree flowers in February - March, after which these bear small green fruits which go on developing and maturing. These get fully ripe for eating purposes in May - June. Picking of fruits should be done by climbing on the tree and collecting the fruits in bag tied or hanging on shoulders. About 700 to 800 kg. of fruits may be expected from a milk tree.

Khirni - A Summer Season Tasty Fruit

Khirni is a beautiful tasteful fruit of summer season. Its fruit on ripening is just like the shape and size of a 'neemauli' (ripe neem fruit), except that its colour is shining golden yellow and very attractive. The fruit is very sweet and milky. The fruits of Khrini are available in May - June, when fruits of ripe phalsa are also available. Generally the fruit sellers keep khirni fruits here and there in lots of phalsa fruits and decorate the whole lot to attract the customers. As such customers purchase both fruits the tasteful khirni and refreshing phalsa fruits. Khirni fruit is eaten fresh as well as after drying. It has a cooling effect and is thirst quenching also. It provides, strength to the body. It is useful for the patients of tuberculosis. It removes acidity and for get fullness and provides strength to heart also. Khirni fruit is also said to be useful in senselessness.

Khirni (Manilkara hexandra, syn. Mimusops hexandra), belongs to the family 'Sapotaceae' to which Sapodilla (Sapota) and Mahua (Madhuca indica syns. M. latifolia and Bassia latifolia) belong. Ordinarily in Hindi khirni has been name as 'Khirni' and 'Khinni' as well. In English it is called 'Milk Tree'. The khirni tree is a huge shade providing evergreen fruit-tree. It is grown in Uttar Pradesh, M.P., Delhi, Gujarat, Maharashtra, Andhra Pradesh and other plane areas of tropical and subtropical climate. Milk-tree may be planted in groups in the form of groves or scattered at various places and along highways. Its trees are also found growing wild. Plants of milk-tree may also be planted in mixed orchards, on grazing land near tube wells and threshing floors for shade as well as for fruits. It's leaves are shining and ornamental. These may be planted in wasteland, ravines, and in 'banjar' in groups or as orchards, as khirni may be planted in any type of soil.

No special varieties of milk-tree have been established so far. However, if some good varieties are observed by chance, these may be selected and multiplied through grafting or budding. The root stock of milk-tree is utilized for grafting sapodilla varieties to get original characters of the variety. For the time being its plants are propagated by seed. One fruit has generally one long black (also some portion black and some white) shining conical seed. Seeds may be taken out from the fruit and sown in well prepared beds immediately. Fruits are available in May - June as mentioned earlier. After germination plants should be regularly watered after every 7-10 days interval. After the seedings are of one year age, these are fit for shifting and planting at the proper place. During growth if there are chances of damage of young plants by hot sun or hot wind, each plant should be thatched separately. Thatches should be on upper and western portion of plants.

Besides eating fresh, fruits are utilized as ready to serve 'sharbat', jams, jellies, squashes and others. The fruit juice is useful in removing fever and in clearing throat. The extract of bark of black mulberry is laxative and kills worms. Various medicines are made from its roots. Extract of its roots create constipation and simultaneously kills worms of intestines.

Since Morus alba trees are of industrial use in sericulture the planting distance is minimised from normal distance to have more of vegetative growth and greater leaf area for rearing silk worm. Silk worms (caterpillars) eat the leaves and are reared on leaves. Later on these pupate and are transformed into cocoons which are utilized in collecting silk fibres for weaving silk cloth.

Climate and Soil

Mulberry grows in plains as well as on heights as stated earlier. Its tree shed its leaves in winters and has no adverse effect of frost or cold wind and hot wind. The tree also tolerates dry and other adverse conditions. Mulberry can flourish in any type of soil but clayey loam soil is best suited.

Propagation

Propagation of Mulberry is easily done by stem cutting. For this cutting of 25-30 cm length is prepared from last years shoots. One cutting should have 4-5 buds. The upper cut should be slanting above a plump bud which should lie on the back side of upper slope. The lower cut should be a horizontal one below a plump bud. Cuttings are prepared from pruning the tree in January (Details of pruning will follow). Insert 2/3 part of the cutting in soil in January in a slanting way, so as the top cut end may be visible protecting thereby the plump bud under the upper slope. The nursery bed should be well prepared with leaf mould and sand. Cutting may also be inserted in filled up polythene bags or in wooden boxes. After planting the cuttings, these should be lightly irrigated and care should be taken that soil may remain wet. Cuttings sprout in the last week of February or first week of March. These are nurtured in nursery and are fit for plantation as orchards next year. Ring budding may also be adopted in the month of April. Shield pudding and Inarching (attached grafting) are also possible. For these root stocks are also prepared by cuttings.

Lay Out and Preparation of Soil

For plantation of mulberry, lay out the orchard at a distance of 7.5 × 7.5 m (25 × 25 feet) in the month of October-November and spot out the planting point. After this pits of the size 60 × 60 × 60 cm (2 × 2 × 2 ft.) should be dug. Leave these as such for a month and burn leaves and other dry shoots in the pit to make soil worm-free. Fill in the pits with surface soil mixed with four baskets of farm yard manure, cow dung manure or compost, press it well and give it a finishing touch when the mixture of soil and manure in the pit is tightly filled 15 cm above the soil surface.

Plantation

Run water in the laid out orchard through prepared irrigation channels, so that filled up pits may come down parallel to surface soil. When the soil becomes friable, plant the mulberry plants in the centre of the filled up pits in January. For lifting plants from nursery, loosen the soil from all round the plant and uproot these from the soil with roots but without earthen ball. At this time plants are leafless and in dormant condition. At the time of planting prepare holes so that roots of plants may spread all round. After planting tighten the soil from all round the plants. A light irrigation should be given after plantation. Have a watch that soil may remain wet till rains start.

Grow Mulberry also

For this weekly irrigation, hoeing and weeding should be continued. Sprouting of plants start by the end of February or 1st week of March.

In this way at the above mentioned distance one hectare will accommodate 172 plants, while one acre will accommodate 69 plants. For sericulture plants planted at the distance of 2 to 2.5 metre each side (8 x 8 feet) a hectare of land will accommodate 1780 plants. On the other hand, one acre land will accommodate 680 plants. These plantations will specially be utilized for rearing silk worms on leaves of plant for production of silk (sericulture).

Pruning

After plantation let the plant grow and prune from time to time, so that the plant may have a strong framework. The height of the stem of the plant should be 74 cm (1.5 feet). Cut the plant growing above at this height and from the top of the plant 4-5 branches should be allowed to grow and spread all round.

In fruiting trees, leaves shed off by December-January. Annual pruning should be done in such trees in the middle of January. For this all the branches spreading above 75 cm of the trunk should be pruned to healthy and thick portions and the top portion be removed. Any weak and dry or diseased shoot appearing on the tree should be removed from the base. Any branch growing downwards or crossing each other should by set right by pruning. Sprouts appearing on trunk should be rubbed off.

Manuring

After pruning, soil all round the tree should be dug up and left for a fortnight. After that spread in dug up soil 4 basket of FYM per trees, leaving one metre all round from the trunk. Mix the manure in soil.

Irrigation

After manuring irrigate the tree immediately. Again, after sprouting of pruned shoots continue watering at 8-10 days interval. After sprouting when fruits are borne on new growing shoots, then irrigate weekly for development of fruits.

Flowering and Fruiting

Mulberry trees start bearing in 4-5 years. After pruning and manuring when sprouting is started in February flowers and fruits start developing. Trees bear unisexual as well as bi-sexual flowers. As a matter of fact each fruit is formed in combination with small fruitlets (Catakins). According to variety fruits are first green or slightly pinkish and then turn to their characteristic whitish or black colour on ripening. Fruits are available from April-May to June. The durability of mulberry fruits is hardly for two days. As such disposal of these should be done as early as possible.

Diseases and Pests

Mulberry canker is a disease caused by fungus Fusarium lateritium, which produce protuberated spots on leaves and twigs. In Dieback disease shoots start drying from the top and move towards base. Ultimately the whole shoot or branch dries up. Under such circumstances the shoot or branch upto healthy green portion in both cases of canker and dieback should be pruned off. The prunes thus released should be burnt. Mulberry blight is another disease caused by bacteria (Bacterium mori) and affect the leaves and young shoots. Black spots appear on these parts. Spray of Bordeux mixture prevents the attack of disease.

Yield

About 10-15 kg of mulberry fruits may be had from a well established fruiting tree. As regards trees grown for sericulture, 500 to 800 kg leaves may be plucked per hectare of plantation. Leaves should bee plucked from March to May.

Maturity Standard and Post Harvest Management of Roselle (*Hibiscus Sabdariffa, L*)

India has been making rapid strides in vegetable production during the past several years. As a result, India has been declared second largest producer of vegetables in the whole world next only to China.

Earlier, the area under vegetables was estimated as 5.5 million hectares, producing thereby 53.8 million tonnes of vegetables annually, which contributed roughly 12 per cent of the world production. Now the production of vegetables has reached nearly 81 million tonnes from an area of 6.2 million hectares of land.

Of these, roselle is also an important useful crop. It is also, known as 'Jamaican sorrel' and 'Red sorrel' in English and "Lal ambri", 'Patwa' or 'Vilayati Patwa' in common language. Roselle is a biennial small shrubby plant of the family Malvaceae.

It is a native of West Indies and is grown in hotter parts of India and Sri Lanka. In damp climate of lower India it grows better in damp climate. West Bengal, Assam, Punjab, Andhra Pradesh, Tamil Nadu, Bihar, Uttar Pradesh and some other are the chief growing areas of roselle.

Roselle is grown for its fleshy persistent calyces, which are rich in protein and acid. Vitamin-C is also available in roselle to the extent of 20 mg per hundred gm of fresh calyces. These are sour in taste and utilized in preparing drinks, tarts, chutneys, jellies and other confections.

Fleshy calyces are also dried for further use. Fresh fleshy calyces yield their $1/11^{th}$ part dry material. These are powdered and applied in curries, pulses and other preparations. Fresh tender leaves and shoots are eaten as salad and also as sour flavoured vegetables or condiments.

Its fruits when immature are green and used in preparing curries and pickles. Mature ripe seeds of roselle are eaten after roasting in hot sand. It is medicinal like others. An infusion of roselle calyces is refreshing and cooling and helps in digestion. It is a mild laxative and intestinal antiseptic as well. Stem fibre of the plant may be used as a substitute for jute. It may be used for making ropes and cordage.

Roselle seeds are sown in well-prepared beds open to sun light in June - July at 1 x 1 metre apart and 1.0 cm deep in soil. Seeds start germinating on the 4th day of sowing. The germination is complete on the 7th day. The plant grows up to a height of 1.0 to 1.5 metres. Flowering and fruiting start in the last week of September and continue up to the end of December. Flowers, on opening, have yellow colour petals like those of lady's finger flowers.

Maturity and Picking Standard

Calyces or roselle in an immature stage are thin, pliable and slimy in nature. At full maturity, the calyces attain bright dark pink colour, which may be judged better by experience. These calyces look very beautiful and shining in the rays of sun. Maturity assessments by observations and experience have been made in other horticultural produce also.

An average fully grown calycate fruit of roselle is 4.45 cm in length and 1.95 cm in thickness (maximum). The maximum thickness of the fruit is at its basal end, which goes on narrowing towards the apex and acquires a conical shape at the apical end.

Further, at full maturity, main green fruits covered under the calyces show dryness and signs of longitudinal crack from apical towards basal end, confirming thereby symptoms of ripening. In certain cases, the cracks are seen widened as if these fruits are prepared just to burst and release their seeds.

In the initial stage, picking of fruits may be started in the first week of November, for day to day use. However, fruits get fully mature for picking by the last week of December. At this stage peduncles of the fruit cannot easily be plucked by hand. These should, therefore, only be harvested by cutting the peduncles with the help of a secateur or a sharp knife without giving any jerk to the plant. It may be noted that on an average one plant of roselle yields 32 nos. Calycate fruits, which are 148 gm in weight and these yield 74 gm of fleshy calyces.

Post Harvest Management

A huge amount of loss takes place between harvesting and consumption of vegetables, due to their being quite perishable in nature. As such, an amount of Rs. 10,000 million worth of vegetables, and fruits has been estimated as annual loss in India, of which more than 50% loss has been shared by vegetables. On the other hand, in India annual post harvest losses in vegetables have been referred, on an average, as 25% worth Rs. 8000 crores.

Besides various techniques of post harvest management, processing of vegetables into durable products have been found very useful in reducing post harvest losses.

As regards roselle, turning the fleshy calyces in the form of jelly has appeared as the most successful technique. The shelf life of these calyces is hardly for 3-4 days. Therefore, soon after harvesting, these should be utilised in jelly making as soon as possible.

For this, the calyces should be taken out of the calycate fruits of roselle quite neatly and thoroughly with a sharp stainless steel knife. These are collected in a stainless steel container. In general, the method adopted for preparation of roselle jelly is almost the same as reported for guava and other jellies (Brochure CFTRI, 1951, 18, My Survey). However, some details appear necessary to be mentioned.

The fleshy calyces thus collected should be well washed to remove dust and other particles sticking to these. These are then placed in a wide mouthed stainless steel container. Fresh and clean water should then be added to the container just to cover the surface of calyces. The whole material is then boiled for only ten minutes to extract pectin and acid in the juice. After this the cooked material is strained through a muslin cloth or a jelly bag and the juice is collected in another wide mouthed stainless steel container.

Now sugar is added to the strained juice according to richness of pectin in the juice. No citric acid and colour is required to be added. After adding sugar the container is again put on fire and the juice is continuously stirred to avoid charring of sugar in the bottom of the utensil and allow the sugar to dissolve soon in the juice. This juice is again strained to remove dirt of sugar and have neat and clean juice.

The material thus obtained is finally boiled and cooked to a temperature of 222°F without stirring the pulp. This is the end point for jelly making. Judging the end point of jelly is very important. The end point of roselle jelly may also be confirmed by flake sheet test; for this while cooking the pulp, a little pulp is taken in the ladle, cooled in air and made to drop. If the cooked pulp drops in flakes or thin sheets, it means the end point has reached. The cooked material should then be removed from the fire and placed away from fire and allowed to cool for 4 - 5 minutes. During this period the scum formed on the surface of the finally cooked material, should gently be removed with a ladle without stirring or disturbing the cooked material.

Now the clear bright cooked material is poured into the wide mouthed sterilized glass bottle. One kg of roselle calyces is obtained from 2 kg of calycate fruits of roselle, which are 400 in number. Juice obtained from these calyces, yield 6.5 bottles of roselle jelly of one pound capacity. (Sugar added half the quantity of the obtained juice, pectin being medium in the juice).

Preparation of roselle jelly is easier and less time taking than that of guava jelly. The roselle jelly thus obtained is very palatable and has a very transparent and beautiful colourful appearance. Setting of the roselle jelly was also very appealing. This could be judged by the quivering nature of a piece of jelly cut with sharp stainless steel knife, placed in a plate, which also attained sharp edge.

"Lecture delivered by the author during International Conference on Vegetables, organized by P.N. Agri. Sc. Foundation and Indian Soc. of Vegetable Science, New Delhi from 11th-14th Nov. 2002 in ITC Hotel Windsor Shereton and Towers, Bangalore".

11

Rare and Newly Introduced Wonderful Vegetables

Among a large number of vegetables grown in India, there are still several vegetables, which are either less known to people or remain under-utilized for lack of proper awareness. Some are newly introduced, though most of the common vegetables are already of foreign origin, which have been acclimatized in India, some are not known to all, because these are grown and utilized only in a certain area and many portion of the vegetables are thrown away thinking that these have no value. Keeping all these points in view, efforts have been made to make awareness among the public about such rare, nutritious and wonderful vegetables.

Broccoli or Sprouting Broccoli

(Harigobhi, light purple gobhi - Brassica oleracea var. italika plenk; Crucifereae)- Broccoli is actually a word of Italian language. Its original place is also Italy. Broccoli plant forms a cauliflower like head except that these are either green or light violet or purplish in colour. Broccolis are of two types. One is that which bears the green head over the top of its stem. These green heads are formed by groups of small solid protuberated green flower buds and their small delicate branches. Broccoli is used for preparing curries just like cauliflower. While planted in beds, these buds should never be allowed to open and must be harvested before opening. This Broccoli is also called sprouting Broccoli. After cutting the broccoli from the stem, these again sprout and small broccoli are formed in axils of leaves with thin long stems. All of these should be plucked off and curries may be prepared in the same way along with tender and soft stems also.

Green broccoli is very nutritious. It contains water 87.5%, carbohydrate 5.5%, protein 3.3% and fat 0.2%. Further, each 100 gm of green broccoli provides 900 I.U. Vitamin-A, 33 mg Vitamin B-l (Thiamine), 137 mg Vitamin-C, 205 mg Iron, 1.29 mg Calcium, 24 mg Copper, 1.26 mg Sulphur, 1.97 mg Iodine, 3.52 mg Potassium, 93.5 mg Phosphorus, 26.2 mg Sodium with its calorific value as 37 calories. It is rich in Riboflavin (Vitamin B-2) also. 'Calabrese' or 'Italian Green sprouting' and 'Pusa broccoli- K.T.C.-l' are improved good varieties of Green broccoli.

Broccoli is a vegetable of winter season. Its seedlings are planted in September-October in well prepared beds at 45 × 45 cm apart from both sides. Heads are read for harvest within 2 ½ to 3 months.

Another type of broccoli is that, heads of which are either whitish like cauliflower or purplish in colour. These are also called 'Heading Broccoli'. This broccoli is also nutritious. It contains protein 3.3%. It is rich in Vitamin -A, B-l, B-2 and Vitamin -C also. 'Bronzino' is one of the best varieties of Purple broccoli.

Selection of such soil for Broccoli cultivation should be done, which is loam and rich in humus. Seed rate of broccoli is 300 - 400 gm seeds per hectare of land. In one hectare of space 48400 plants may be planted. Accordingly in the month of February - March about the same number of heads are yielded. Other cultural operations are just like cauliflower.

Red Cauliflower

In Canada a variety of such cauliflower (Brassica oleracia L. var botrytis, L., Crucifereae) has been reported, the plant of which bears orange coloured heads. Due to presence of orange colour it is very rich in carotene, ultimately very rich in Vitamin-A. In this connection scientists from Himachal Pradesh of Agricultural University Palampur are said to have gone to Institute of Horticultural Research, Walesbourn, England to make further studies and introduce it in Palampur (Science Times - News and Views, April - June, 1993).

Pollution Removing Cauliflower

Scientists like Andrew Smith and Ute Kemar of Oxford University could be able to find out the presence of such metals in cabbage, cauliflower and Brussels sprouts, with the help of which soil pollution may be removed to a large extent. This could be found out through Genetic Engineering. Actually many poisonous metals like lead, zinc, copper, nickel have already reached sufficient deep into the soil in a large area of land. Probably this might have been due to heavy industrialization earlier in that area. These scientists made available the information that the plant of Allium lasbiacum has capacity to absorb the poisonous metal Nickel in itself and keep them stored in their green tissues: These are then made poison-free inside the plants, so that plants may not be harmed. Again, there are also some such plants, which absorb zinc, copper, manganese and chromium, etc. As such it is expected that these vegetables in future may be planted even in polluted soils (United Bharat, Alld., Indradhanush 20th February 2002). Further, it was also investigated that the plant of Allium lasbiacum contains an acid - histideen, which is useful for cleaning and shining Nickel articles.

Bud-bearing Cabbage/Brussels Sprouts (Button gobhi: Brassica oleraceae-var. gemmifera, D.C. crucifereae). Brussels sprouts or button gobhi or bud-bearing cabbage is a modern vegetable, which was earlier grown in Brussels town of Belgium or in other places near Brussels. This is the reason that this vegetable was named as Brussels sprouts. Now it is grown in many parts of the country but still unknown to the common people.

The plant of Brussels sprouts grows upto a height of 30 to 45 cm on thick fleshy stem. In Northern India these are planted at a distance of 45 x 45 cm in October-November. About 2½ months after planting small round or oval sprouts of the shape of cabbage start appearing in axils of leaves and also on its main stems all round and from top to bottom. Since these sprouts are small and also of the shape of cabbage, these have been called by different names like 'button gobhi' or "Choti Band gobhi" in Hindi and miniature cabbage besides Brussels sprouts. In vegetable mandies these are sold in the name of small band gobhi i.e. small cabbage and people on seeing get surprised and purchase them with interest.

After picking, these are turned into curry, salad, soup and pickles. An improved variety of Brussels Sprouts is 'Hilds Ideal' one plant gives out 40 - 50 sprouts, weighing 300-400 gm. This small cabbage makes available water 84.0%, carbohydrate 4.1%, protein 4.5% and fat 1.4%. Further, 100 gm of its pulp makes available Vitamin-A215 micrograms, vitamin B-2 (Riboflavin) 0.11 mg, Vitamin-C 115 mg, Niacin (Nicotinic acid) 0.2 mg, Iron 0.7 mg, Calcium 26 mg, Phosphorus 7.7 mg, potassium 4.5 mg and Sodium 6.0 mg. For producing Brussels sprouts all the cultural operations should be done as in cabbage.

KALE or BORE COLE (Brassica oleracea, L var. acephaea D.C., Crucifereae) Kale is a rabi vegetable which has become very popular in Kashmir Valley, Maharashtra, Baroda, Assam and other parts of India. This plant has cabbage like broad thick fleshy spreading leaves. These leaves are very rich in Vitamin-A and Vitamin -C. One or two leaves as and when required are picked and utilized for preparing curry, salad, soup and others. Leaves and soft stems all are utilized. The Kale plant is planted in pots and as an ornamental plant. A variety with crinkled dense leaves is very ornamental.

This plant grows well in every hardy situation. This may be planted at 60 × 60 cm a part. Its crop may be taken for the whole year.

CHINESE CABBAGE (Brassica pekinensis Ruhr; Brassica chinensis var. pekinensis sims. B. petssai Bailey; crucifereae. Chinese cabbage is also named as Shantung cabbage. In common language it is called Cheeni Paatgobhi. Chinese cabbage is a native of China. Its cultivation and production is done in China, Southern Eastern Asia and in India also just like cultivation methods of cabbage. The plants form generally loose heads and sometimes only broad spreading fleshy leaves with white leaf stalks. The head forming species-petssai has two varieties - Chihili and 'Wong Bok'. The head of 'Chihili' is long, thin and ovoid and that of 'Wong Bok' is small and thick. Some varieties of Chinese cabbage like 'Pakchoi' - do not form heads and leaves of plants remain open. These are deep green fleshy with while leaf stalks and midribs. All these portions are utilized in preparing curry, soup and salad.

The head or leaves of Chinese cabbage possess in themselves water 95%, carbohydrate 3.0%, protein 1.2% and fat 0.1%. Again each 100 mg of these portions contains Vitamin - 150 I.U., Vitamin B = 0.04 mg, Vitamin -C 25 mg, Nicotinic acid (Niacin) 0.6 mg, Calcium 4.3 mg, phosphorus 40 mg, Potassium 2.5 3 mg and 14 calories energy.

BUCK-WHEAT LEAVES (Fagopyrum esculantums Moench - Polyganoceae- Kutu). Buckwheat is a herbacous annual plant native of central Asia. Its plants are mostly grown on hills, valleys and also in plains. Kutu seed flour is utilized during fast in the form of poories and halwa. Seeds are brownish and three cornered. Its light green triangular leaves and tender shoots are chopped, fried and relished as curry. It is slightly sourish like Portulaca due to which the preparation further becomes tasteful. Its leaves are rich in Calcium, Iron, Phosphorus and Vitamin-A, D and 'Rutin' a drug.

Its seeds may be sown direct in soil in well-prepared beds. Sowing should be done in October - November in rows 45 cm apart and 1 - 2 cm deep in soil. After germination plants in each row should be thinned, so as to bring the plants at 30 cm apart in each row.

RAT TAIL RADISH (Raphanus caudatus L, r. sativus var. Caudatus, R. sativus var. mongri; Crucifereae) - Rat tail radish commonly known as 'Sengri". "Sengra" or 'Mongra' is another species of radish. In radish its roots are relished in many ways but in Rat tail radish, roots are of no worth and its long hanging fruits on plants only are utilized as curry and pickles. Fruits are long, thin like cowpeas except that its fruits are tapering and go on becoming thinner from basal end to apex, where it becomes very acutely conical. It's a Rabi crop. Though it is grown in many parts of the country but not known every where. Even it is not known in Eastern U.P. but in Western U.P. and Delhi this is well known. These fruits are very succulent and are chopped and used. These are available in the months of December-January.

SPINE GOURD (Momordica cochinchinensis spreng; M.mixta Rox., Cucurbitaceaes)-Spine gourd is an annual twining plant vegetable available in rainy season. The plant bears green, round or slightly elongated fruits. It is broader at basal end and conical at apical end with green soft spiny protuberation on the whole body. It may be grown in plains and valleys as well, where these are called;. 'Van-Karela', 'Kheksa' 'Kakrol' and 'bhat karela'.

CELERY (Apium graveolens L., native of Europe, umbelifereac) - Celery is an annual herbaceous plant, which is utilized like lettuce. Its plant grows straight upwards with long large light green soft leaves. Its leaves are utilized as salad or soup. Its soft fleshy white stems, thick leafstalks and mid-ribs of leaves are used for curry. Celery is of two types. One is that stems of which are white, while that of the other is purplish-reddish.

Leaves of Celery are very nutritious. These possess moisture 93.%, carbohydrate 3.55, protein 0.8%, fat 0.1%, fibre 1.2% and minerals 0.9%. Again every 100 gm of its pulp contains vitamin-A 867 I.U., vit. B-l (thiamine) 0.12 mg, Vitamin B-2 (Riboflavin) 0.05 mg, Vitamin C 6 mg, Nicotinic acid (Niacin) 0.3 mg, Iron 4.8 mg, calcium 30 mg, phosphorus 38 gm and heat energy 189 calories.

Celery is a Rabi crop. Its seedlings are planted at 45 x 15 cm in September-October. Its seed rate is 250 gm per hectare. Seeds are very fine. These are also used as spice. Its plants are shallow rooted and, therefore, irrigation and organic manuring should be done accordingly. 'Standard bearer' and 'Wright Glove Grant' are two important varieties of celery. Yield per hectare of land is 200 quintals of leaves.

PARSLEY - (Petroselinum crispum Nym -, P.hortense Hoffm., Apium crispum Mill. Umbelifereac, native to Europe) - Parsley is a leafy annual herbaceous vegetable of winter season. Its leaves resemble more or less those of Coriander and are also scented. Leaves are used for flavoring food material, preparing soup, dishes of salad and curry also.

Its leaves are rich in Vitamin-C. Its seeds are sown direct in the field in rows 45 cm apart and later thinned at 15 cm apart in each row. Seedlings of these may also be prepared by sowing in well prepared beds and then transplanted as above, 'moss curled' (dwarf with fine leaves) and "Hamburg" are two important varieties of Parsley. Other cultural practices are followed as in Coriander.

KASERU (Scirpus grossus L. S. Kysoor Roxb. ; Cyperaceac:0 - kaserus is an Indian tuberous nutritious vegetable. Its tubers are small black hairy and flaltish. These are borne on herbaceous perennial plants deep in marshy land or in ponds or at places where water remains collected. Its tubers are sometimes seen in market sold by village persons in rainy seasons. Its hairs are a bit hard. Fresh Kaseru tubers after peeling are white milky and may be taken as such like waternut. These may also be taken after frying. Only boiled and peeled tubers are also relished with salt. These may also be turned into curry and pickles as well. It is very rich in carbohydrate and, therefore, may also be utilized like potato, water-nut and others. It is cooling and dieuretic and removes constipation. It is highly rich in Iodine and, therefore, acts like a medicine in the disease 'g'goitre, Kaseru is said to be a tonic.

Leek (Allium ampeloprasum L. var. porrum (L Gay; Allium porrum L.; Alliaceac, Amarylidaceae; Native of Switzerland and Mediterranean Ocean areas). Leek is a perennial herbaceous plant vegetable like garlic and onion. In Hindi it is known as 'vilayati lahsun', 'vilayati pyaz', 'gandina', 'kirs' and 'kirath'. This is grown in India also but people rarely know about it. Though the plant of leek does not form bulbs like garlic and onion, even then its green long leaves and soft fleshy stems are used for pickles, curry, salad and soup. Its plant grows to a height more than that of onion. Its leaves are less pungent than garlie and onion. Leaves contain moisture 78.9%, carbohydrate 5.0%, protein 1.8%, fat 0.1%, minerals 0.7% and fibre 1.3%. A hundred gram of its pulp makes available Vitamin-A 30 I.U., Thiamine (Vitamin B-l) 0.23 mg, Vitamin C 11 mg, Iron 2.3 mg, phosphorus 70 mg and heat energy 77 calories. It is rich in Vitamin 1 E. also.

Seedlings of leek are produced like onion. These are planted in October-November at a distance of 45 × 15 cm in pre-prepared trenches of 25 cm depth and width. After about 1½ months or so, when plants become stout the trenches should be gradually filled up to the level of surface of soil. Before doing so the solid should be well prepared with 120 kg, N 75 kg P and 150 kg K. The soil should be fertilized with above in the form of organic manures. A hectare of land will yield about 300 quintals of leaves and soft stems of leek.

Meetha Kerela (Cyclantheras pedata L; Cucurbitaceae, native of Central America - Meetha Karela is an annual creeping vegetables. Its vines bear fruits 5 - 6 cm long and 2- 3 cm thick in the middle and tapering at both the ends forming conical shapes. The fruit is also filled with fine spiny protuberances. Its curry is prepared after slicing with peels and relished. It is not bitter in taste. Generally meetha karela has been found growing on hills and valleys of North India. Ripe fruits after slicing (outer portion yellowish and inner porton bright red) and removing seeds have been seen in winter season in Garhwal (now in Uttarakhand) drying in sun and watched by women for use in the period of off-season. Its propagation is done by seeds.

Other cultural operations in meetha karela are like those in bitter gourd. Its cultivation may be extended in plains of India.

Parsnip (Pastinaca Sativa L., peucedanum sativum L., Umbellifereae; native of Europe and also some parts of England and Siberia) - Parsnip is a herbaceous vegetable grown for use of roots as curry. There are two varieties of Parsnip. One is 'long rooted' and the other is 'short rooted' like turnip. The long-rooted one is supposed to be better, but it has not become very popular in India, so far.

Indian Spinach or Malabar Nightshade (Basella alba, B. rubra; Basellaceae)- Indian Spinach, commonly known as 'poi' is a summer season climbing leafy vegetable. Its leaves are broad heart shaped thick and green. These along with tender green succulent steams are utilized for preparing curry. This green leaved with green twigs type of 'poi' is actually basella alba. Another specieis of 'poi' is basella rubra. Leaves and twigs of this species are dark pink or purplish and are equally useful. These are rich in Vitamin A and are grown in some parts of plains in India and rarely seen in West and East U.P. Its propagation may be done by sowing seeds 3 - 4 cm deep in soil in February — March or by inserting hard-stem cuttings in soil during rains at 150 × 150 cm apart. Vines are spread on wooden or bamboo trees. About one kg of seed of 4500 cuttings will be required for one hectare of land.

Water Spinach (Ipoemea reptanes (L) Poir, Convulvulno reptans L, Ipoemea aquatica; Convubulaceac) - Water spinach also called water leafe is a trailing herbaceous vegetable plant, leaves and vines of which are chopped into pieces and fried to make a tasteful curry. These plants are available during rainy season, which grow in ponds, marshy places and along nullas. Its vines are hollow and leaves are small long thin or somewhat wide and conical. Vines root at nodes and as such these may be propagated by cittings and may also be grown under shade of trees. This vegetable has more importance during a festival 'Harchatthai' celebrated in Hindu families. In common language this aquastic or semi-aquatic vegetable plant is known by the names of 'Karemuka saag' 'naali ka saag', 'kalmi saag' or 'surnali'.

BROAD BEAN (Vicia faba L., Faba vulgaris Moench; Leguminoceae - Papilionaceae) -Broad bean commonly known as 'bakla' is a winter season proteinous and nutritious vegetable. The plants grow to a height of about one metre and give out upright shoots. These bear dark green slightly hairy soft fleshy pods. Bakla pods are 3 - 4 cm long, roundish in thickness and 1/2 to 1.0 cm thick. Pods appear on plants in bunches in axils of leave. Shape of its seeds is like peas with slight elongation. Green and soft bakla pods are chopped with peels for making curry. When peels of pods become stiff, green seeds are taken out from these and fried and relished with tea or as break fast. Fresh seeds may also be ground and cooked as pulse or curry. Dry seeds are used as pulse. Two varieties of broad bean have been seen. One is white seeded and the other one is black seeded. It is grown in many parts of India but not every where, though it may be grown very well in plains every where, but it is less known and has not become popular. However, there are many vegetables, which are quite nutritious but either these have not been introduced in India or have not become popular and require attention.

These are 'shallot' (Allium ascalonicum L; Alliaceae-common name "gandana" or 'gandhan'); 'Swiss chard' (Beta vulgaries var. cicla; Chinopodiaceae); 'Rhubarb' (Rheum rhaponticum L., Polygonacea); 'Horse radish' Armoracia rusticana Gaertn., A. lapathifolia Gilib., Cochlearia ormoracia L; Crucifereae): 'Rutabaga' (brassica napobrassica; Crucifereae); 'chocory' (chicorium intybus L., 'kasni,); 'Endive' (Chicorium endivia L; 'Vilayati kasni) and many others.

Leaf Mustard (Brossica juncea (L) Czern and Coss. Subsp. Integrifolia (West) Thell; Crucifereae; Hindi- 'Raaiee') - Leaf mustard or Raaiee is a leafy vegetable of India commonly grown in tarai areas of Nainital, West Bengal and Assam. Its young leaves and tender shoots are utilized for preparing curry after frying. A variety of Raaiee is grown on hills, valleys and plains also, leaves of which are long and broad. Its leaves, midribs and shoots are soft, chopped and fried and relished. This is known as 'Pahari Raaiee'. Two types of this are available. One is green coloured and the other one is purple coloured. The purple one is ornamental.

12

Food Problems

How to Solve Food Problem

High food prices, poverty, malnutrition, starvation, famine, drought, scarcity of rains, fire, floods and various natural calamities are some of the main dominating problems of many countries of the world, including India. All these events hinder food security and ultimately lead to serious hunger crisis. An estimate of United Nations Agency has shown that one in six people remain hungry every day in the world. Presently about 1.02 billion people remain hungry in the world (F.A.O. report, Times of India, New Delhi, 2nd June, 2009). The day to day fast increase in population and illegal migration in India have further produced food crisis. Between 1947 and 1991, Indian population was more than doubled. In July 2004 this population was more than 106 crore and in July 2007 it shot up to more than 112 crore. As regards migrants, illegal migration from Bangladesh to India are going on speedily specially in Delhi, Bihar, Mumbai, Uttar Pradesh and other parts of the country. These practices have created further great economic burden on the country, besides polluting the environment, creating further food and hunger crises. A Government panel has reported that 50% Indians are living below poverty line and recommended that 50% Indian population may be issued below poverty line cards (*Times of India* 1st July, 2009, page 1). The result of these is that India has to import wheat, rice and even sugar from foreign countries.

This position is very alarming. Earlier a Washington news agency opined that with the soaring food prices sparking protest in many countries, Americans have the highest per capita daily consumption in the world, eating 3,770 calories a day, more than a Canadian at 3,590 calories or an Indian at 2,440, as per data from U.N. Food and Agricultural Organisation (Washington, News 2008 - U.S. overeats as world fights hunger: *Times of India*, New Delhi, 30th July 2008).

Calorific requirements of an ordinary working man and woman per day are 3,000 and 2,500 calories in the same order. The requirements of calories may be fulfilled or supplanted by eating, besides cereals, many staple vegetables and fruits like potato, sweet potato, banana, mango, jackfruit, Mahua, Waternut and others. These provide carbohydrate, fat, fibre and nutrition. Carbohydrate and fat provide body heat energy and fibres bulk for fulfilling hunger. These may fulfill calorific requirements. Again in these hard days of food crisis one must change his food habit and should not depend on cereals only and eat fruits and vegetables also as a supplement or supplant to cereals. There is a glaring example of an 82 year old resident of Madhya Pradesh of Shahdol Sri Satya Narain Aggarwal - Atal. He was eating potato for the last forty years during the year 1991. He ate 2 kg of boiled peeled potato every day and took 500 gm milk over that and lead a healthy and cheerful life. Besides these, many yams, e.g., Dioscoreas are also staple food. Dioscorea is a flowering vine of the family 'Dioscoreacea' of tropical subtropical and temperate climate as Dioscorea grows well in the planes and vallies of India. It is a perennial herbaceous tuberous plant which grows to a height of 2 to 10 metres. The leaves are broad betel-leaf shaped and arranged spirally on the stem.

Dioscorea bulbifera L. is commonly known as 'air-potato' and 'potato yam' in English and 'daal ka aloo', 'gaithi' and 'arua' in Hindi. It is native to Africa and Asia but now grown well all over India, specially in South India and Northern Indian planes and vallies as well. The vine bears succulent bulbils in leaf axils of twining stems and more larger tubers under the ground. These tubers are of the shape of oblong potatoes. Both aerial bulbils (aerial potato) and underground tubers are edibe and used as vegetable. These must be eaten after boiling. The bulbils on the vines, if not plucked, sprout at a later stage to form new plants. These twist around each other to form mat. When the whole plant is cutout from the ground level afterwards, the tubers or portions of tubers left under the soil, will again sprout and give out new shoots and produce a new plant. Airnotato is medicinal also and is said to be remedy for ailments like dysentery, diarrhea and conjunctivities as well.

Another one is **Dioscorea alata L.** This is native to East Asia and is grown in Philippines, Hawaii and Tahiti, where it is highly esteemed and the tubers, which are formed beneath the soil of the vine are cooked with sugar to prepare 'halwa'. In India it is grown in almost all parts of the country, specially in Assam, Bengal, Tamil Nadu, Baroda, Madhya Pradesh and U.P. as well. A synonym of D. alata is aloo D. purpurea Roxb. In English this is known as 'purple yam', 'white yam', 'greater-yam', and Asiatic yam. In Hindi, it is called 'Khamalu', 'Chaprialu' and 'ratalu'. The tubers of this climbing vine are large in size and irregular in shape and may easily be utilized as staple food like potato, banana and sweet potato.

Dioscorea esculenta Lour. Burkill syn. D. spinosa Roxb. ex. Wall is further a useful yam grown in Assam, Bengal, Orissa, Uttar Pradesh, Madhya Pradesh, Andamans, East Himalayas, Khasi hills and Nagaland. Its vines are prickly and bear softer semi-soft spines or hairs on nodes of tubers under the ground.

These tubers are like long and thick colocacia or even somewhat bigger than that. In English this is known as 'lesser yam' and 'Karen potato'. In Hindi it has been named as 'susnialu' and this may be called by a common name 'suthni' as well. The tubers are edible and eaten after boiling like potato and sweet potato, etc. Two varieties of this Dioscorea have been found. One 'white' and the other 'black'.

Dioscorea pentaphylla L. syn. D. digitata. This is native to tropical Asia and grown throughout whole India. Its Hindi name is 'Kanta alu' and this also may be named as 'Suthni'. Tubers like other Dioscoreas are edible after boiling.

Dioscorea elephantipes syn. **Testudinaria elephantipes** is further a tuberous flowering vine native to South West/ South Africa. Its tubers are of the shape of elephant's foot in appearance and quite big in size about 3 metre in circumference and with a height of also one metre above the ground. It contains high amount of starch and carbohydrate. In English it is known as 'Elephant's foot' and 'Hotten lot bread'. In Hindi, this may be called as 'haathi-chak'. Several decades back, these Dioscoreas were being grown very well in collection block of National Hortorium Circuit House, Meerut, but unfortunately with the end of this temporary scheme, the collected plants also vanished. As regards cultivation of Dioscorea, same practices and cultural methods of deep digging and ploughing the land, high manuring and earthing etc. may be followed in deep loamy soil as in the case of potato, sweet potato, elephant yam (*Amorphophalus campanulatus, H. Zaminkand, Suran: Araceae*), taro or arum (*Colocasia esculenta. C. antiquorum, H. Arvi, Banda, Ghuiya: Araceae*:) and other underground vegetables.

However, besides growing and consuming these food vegetables and fruits, their production per cultivated area also requires to be increased. All out efforts were made from time to time in this direction, but there is limitation to this practice also, as area remains the same and consumers have increased a lot in number. Presently the area of cultivated land is getting reduced for Industrialisation. The burning example of grabbing forcibly farmers' lands by West Bengal Government and handing over to the Industrialist Ratan Tata for manufacture of Nano cars in connection of which a large number of agitators for their lands had to loose their lives-cannot be forgotten. However, hunger strike by the president Trinamul Congress and Chief Minister of West Bengal, Mamta Banerjee, well wisher of farmers, got the Nano project shifted from West Bengal. The farmers got their lands back but lives, which have gone in this agitation, cannot come back.

Similarly a project for running a train Ganga Express Highway on a very long route from one end of Uttar Pradesh to the border end of U.P. and Delhi (Noida) is in offing. In this project innumerable farmers had/have to loose their several hectares of cultivated lands, creating thereby a serious food shortage. Presently the Allahabad High Court has banned this project and what happens in future - God knows.

The following steps if taken will be a relief to a certain extent to meet the food crisis.

1. Increase in population must be got controlled by administration without considering cast and creed. This will be in public interest.
2. Illegal migrations must be stopped immediately and those who have already migrated must be sent back to their countries.
3. A change in food habit of all the citizens must be brought into practice and one should not depend only on cereals but supplement or supplant the cereals with banana, mangoes, jack fruit (Ripe) Mahua preparations, boiled potato, sweet potato, water nuts, various Dioscoreas and others.
4. If some where there is any scheme 'Food for Work', where cereals are given to workers instead of cash, 'Food' must be replaced with 'Potato'.
5. World Food Day is celebrated on 16th October every year. We all should try to bring this in practice.

Potato Has Potential to Fight Hunger

Hunger, poverty, malnutrition, starvation, famine, drought, untimely rains, over rains, flood, disasters like fire, landslides, earth quakes, breach in dams, catastrophe are some of the dominating problems of many countries of the world including India, hindering thereby food security. This is all due to not only scarcity of habitual cereal food, but also it may be better to say - mainly because of population explosion throughout the whole world, along with further addition in it through migrants from Bangladesh (*Times of India*, New Delhi, 13th Aug. 2008, *T.O.I*, N.D. 26th Aug. 2008). Food crisis also develops as most of us are habituated of consuming chapattis, rice or other cereal preparations ignoring, thereby fruits and vegetables. This is when many of these like banana, potato, sweet potato and Dioscoreas contribute much in solving food problem.

Potato is the world's 4th staple food after wheat, rice and maize. Further, India is the 3rd largest producer of potato (2,63,00,000 tonne) after China (7,20,00,000 tonne). Russia (3,57,18,000 tonne). India produces above potatoes from an area of 14 lakh hectare of land whereas the world produces about 32 crore tonne from an area of 1,92,00,000 hectare land (Vigyan, July, 2008). Potato has the potential to face the food problems of the whole world. This is potato, which was utilized earlier in saving lives of those starting in different countries and army persons in past world wars. Potato is a nutritious wholesome food, which is specially due to presence of rich carbohydrate and total solids in it. Carbohydrate provides energy (calories) and solids and fiber provides bulk to the body, which satisfies hunger.

The requirement of calories per day for an ordinary working man and woman is 3,000 and 2,500 calories respectively. The requirement of calories may be fulfilled by eating only potato, instead of chapattis etc. for this one will have to change his/her food habit psychologically. If only potato is taken as food a male will have to consume 3 kg potato per day, while a female will have to consume 2.6 kg of potato per day. If about 300 g of milk is also taken, along with it far so good.

As regard changing food habit, there was a glaring example of an 82 year old resident of Madhya Pradesh India of Shahdol (Village and P.O. Chandi). Mr. Satya Narain Aggarwal - 'Atal'. He was eating potato for the last forty years during the year 1991. He ate 2 kg of boiled peeled potato every day and hand 500 gm of milk over that and was living a happy life. He was known as "Aaloo Samraat" {Potato King} for this contribution. Similarly others may also do likewise (Aaloo ki Kheti, Gram Vikas Prakashan, Allahabad 1992).

How to eat Potato: The best way to eat potato is eating after boiling and peeling. Frying must be avoided. It is said that after boiling, if potatoes are dipped immediately in cold water, this helps in better digestion. In this connection the author has gone through a literature, which says that starch is the predominant form of carbohydrate found in potatoes. A small but significant portion of the starch in potatoes is resistant to enzymatic digestion in the stomach. This resistant starch is considered to have similar psychological effect and health benefits of fibre, which provides bulk, improved glucose tolerance and insulin sensitivity, lower cholesterol and possibly reduce fat storage also. The amount of resistant starch of potato is very much dependent on methods of preparation. The starch of cooked potato stuff contains about 7% resistant starch which increases about 13% on cooling after cooking.

Potatoes may also be eaten after roasting in hot ash, sand or salt to have change in taste. The skin of roasted potato may provide more fibre i.e., bulk also.

Nutrition

Nutrient contents available in potatoes are as follows:

Nutritive content available in per 100 gm fresh potato:

Content	*Amount*	*Content*	*Amount*
Moisture	74.7 gm	Sodium	11.9 mg
Total Solid	25.3 gm	Copper	0.20 ml
Carbohydrate	22.6 gm	Sulphur	37 ml
Protein	1.6 gm	Chlorine	16 ml

Fat	0.1 gm	Iron	0.7 ml
Fibre	0.4 gm	Vitamin (Thiamin)	0.1 mg
Minerals	0.6 gm	Vitamin B2 (Riboflavin)	0.01 mg
Calcium	10 mg	Vitamin C	17 mg
Magnesium	20 ml	Nicotinic Acid (Niacin)	1.2mg
Oxalic Acid	20 mg	Vitamin A	401 mg
Phosphorus	40 mg	Heat Energy	99 calories
Potassium	247 ml		

Besides providing bulk and fibre to satisfy hunger, potato is also nutritious as clear from the above. It contains necessary vitamins and minerals to keep the body healthy.

The year 2008 was declared as International year of potato by the United Nations (Global Potato Conference, 2008, 2, 3). This was just to apprise the citizens of all countries regarding importance of potato, which being a staple food may solve food crisis, hunger and poverty.

However, Washington News says that with the soaring food prices sparking protest in many countries and more than 800 million people going hungry every day, U.S. food portions are under scrutiny. Portion sizes in the U.S. not only exceed those in less developed countries, but also in developed world. In fact Americans have the highest per capital daily consumption in the world, eating 3,770 calories a day more than a Canadian at 3590 calories or an India at 2,440 as per data from U.N. Food and Agricultural Organisation (*Washington News*, T.O.I., N.D. 30th July 2008, 38).

As regards poverty, it has been reported that 4 out of 10 Indians live in poverty. Inflation is running at over 12% and high prices have historically caused larger scale deprivation. High prices benefit farmers but hit consumers. The net outcome will surprisingly be declined in poverty ratio by 0.8 percentage point (*Time of India,* ND, 27th Aug., 2008, 18).

No poverty brings happiness - Where there is no poverty people remain happy and prosperous. For this, one will have to do hard labour and earn money for livelihood. As a result of this, there are 10 happiest nations in the world, according to survey made by the British University of Leicester (*Mail Today*, N.D., 10th Aug., 2008, 22). Denmark has been ranked first, where poverty is negligible; 2nd Switzerland, where public money is utilized for health care; 3rd is Austria where public money is utilized in health care; 4th is Iceland - very little poverty; 5th is Bahamas - poverty rate high but all citizens life style keep them smiling; 6th is Finland - poverty rare; 7th is Bhutan - poverty rare; 8th is Swedenall citizens remain happy; 9th is Canada which is one of the most happiest country; 10th is Brunei - non existent poverty.

Potato a cash crop - An easy way of removing poverty among farmers is to take up potato farming. This will remove food crisis as well as enable one to earn money in a very short period. Kufri Chandramukhi (A-2708) is such a variety of potato, which maybe harvested from the field within 80 - 90 days. It is a white flattish oval variety, tubers of which are smooth and beautiful. It yields 25 - 30 tonne of tubers per ha. Its tubers may even be harvested even within 60 days in raw stage to earn immediate cash. Curries of such potatoes are very tasteful. Kufri Kuber (O.N. 22360 and K. Alankar 93649) are also short term varieties. Kufri Bahar (E-3797), K.L. hima (B.S. 1753)., K. Sheetman, K. Kundan and K. Jyoti are some of the mid-term varieties. Among late ripening varieties. Kufri Sinduri (C-140), K. Badshah, K. Deva, K. Gulal and K. Kumar are the chief varieties.

Main precautions to be taken in Potato growing:

1. Earthing should properly be done and tubers should in no way come out of soil in light, otherwise, these become green. Green potatoes contain glycoalkaloids toxic compounds, most common of which is Solanine. Such potatoes, if consumed, cause vertigo, headache, vomiting and food poisoning. One should, therefore, be cautious in this direction.
2. **Irrigation:** While irrigating potato-crop, care should be taken that water reaches in the whole length of furrow. Simultaneously irrigation water should not reach more than half the height of the ridge.
3. **Digging:** While digging and handling tubers, one should see that potatoes may not be damaged by cuts and bruises.

Let us start eating boiled peeled potatoes from now atleast once or twice a week to make the heavy burden on cereals lighter.

Bananas Can Solve India's Food Problem - 1

The World Food Day was celebrated on October 16. The author, former Deputy Director of Horticulture, Allahabad Division projects banana as a healthy item that can solve India's food problem. All that one has to do is to make changes in our food-eating habits.

Banana is one of the most sumptuous, tasteful and favourite wholesome fruits. It has the capacity to supplement and even to supplant various cereals like wheat, rice, maize sorghun (jowar) and pearl millet (bajra) etc. It is consumed daily in bulk as food in Indian families. To solve our day to day food problem, we have to change our food habit by supplementing these with many fruits and vegetables like banana, mango, potato, sweet-potato and others. Of all these, table bananas besides others are specially liked by children and old persons very much due to their sweat, pleasant taste and of flavour. Ripe table banana fruit is easily digestible. This is due to its being rich in sugar and less in starch. In green unripe banana pulp, the presence of sugar is very nominal (1 to 2 per cent), whereas the starch in it is quite in plenty (20 per cent). This is the reason why unripe bananas are digested with some difficulty. During the period of ripening, most of the starch of the pulp convert itself into sugar. Ultimataly, the pulp keeps in itself hardly 1-2 per cent of starch and simultaneously increases its sugar content as 20 per cent. However, in plantains (vegetable varieties) even after ripening, the starch still remains in the pulp to the extent of approximately 6 per cent.

In ripe banana pulp, the quantity of reducing sugar, i.e. glucose (grape sugar) and fructose (fruit sugar) is more than non-reducing sugar (sucrose or cane-sugar), which is more useful and refreshing. Banana is served as nutrient to the patients of intestines. For children, when it becomes difficult to consume carbohydrates in coeliac diseases, banana is easily digested.

The fresh pulp of ripe banana, contains in itself moisture of about 70 to 75 per cent, reducing sugar by 4 to 11 per cent, non-reducing sugar by 6 to 16 per cent, starch by 2.93 to 6.56 per cent and total carbohydrate by 27 to 36.4 per cent, acidity by 0.08 to 0.3 per cent, protein by 0.48 to 1.49 per cent, fat by 0.2 to 0.5 per cent, ash 0.70 to 0.84 per cent, pectin 0.7 per cent, calcium 0.01 per cent, phosphorus 0.05 per cent and total soluble solids (T.S.S.) 18.6 per cent.

Besides these, per l00 gm of fresh ripe banana pulp, the availability of Iron is 0.4 mg, Vitamin- A 1.5 to 2.0 mg, Vitamin B-1 (thiamin) 0.34 to 0.6 mg., Vitamin B-2 Riboflavin) 0.23 to 0.87 mg. Vitamin B-63.2 mg and Vitamin - C 20 to 340 mg. in dry pulp of banana the percentage availability of calcium is 0.03 to 0.05, phosphorus 0.18 to 0. 30, potash 1.2 to 3.0, nitrogen 0.5 to 1.2, silica 0.03 to 0.02, magnesium 0.2, sodium 0.2 to 0.9 and that of sulphur trioxide is 0.05 to 0.06 again traces of copper, iodine, manganese, zinc and cobalt are also said to be available in pulp of banana.

As regards calorific value of banana, every 100 gm of ripe banana pulp produces 153 calories of body heat. Besides, this sufficient quantity of solid material is also available in ripe banana pulp (38.6 per cent). Therefore, banana is good enough to be consumed as food to remove one's hunger. To achieve the required calories of energy for the whole day a working man and a working woman will need respectively 1.96 and 1.63 kg of bananas to eat per day. Further, taking some milk also along with these bananas will prove as complete food.

In India, next to mango, the maximum coverage of area and production is of banana. India produes 42,73,500 tonnes of banana from an area of 2,74,400 hectares of land. As such the averages production of banana per hectare of land comes to 15.03 tonnes which is, though more than average production of banana in the world (12.69 tonnes per hectare), far less than that in Argentina (34.02 tonnes), Costarica (33.17 tonnes), Paraguay (32.35 tonnes) and Senegal (32.22 tonnes).

Chief banana growing areas from commercial point of view in our country, are Maharashtra (Jalgaon), Mysore, Andhra Pradesh, Tamil Nadu, West Bengal Bihar (Hassipur, Bhagalpur, Munger), Orissa, Karnataka, Kerala, Assam, Gujarat and Tripura. Besides these states bananas are also grown in Himachal Pradesh Nagaland, Mizoram, Manipur, Meghalaya, Andaman and Nicobar Islands and Uttar Pradesh as well. Out of the above states, the maximum area covered under bananas is in Kerala (45,600 hectares). Next in the sequence are Tamil Nadu (37,800 Ha), Maharashtra (32,600 Ha), Karnataka (18,400 Ha), Assam (20,200), Andhra Pradesh (16,600 Ha), Bihar (97,200 Ha), Gujarat (11,700 Ha), Madhya Pradesh (1,700 Ha), Orissa (13,500 Ha), Tripura (3,400 Ha), Meghalaya (3,000 Ha), Manipur (1,400 Ha), Mizoram (900 Ha), Uttar Pradesh (700 Ha-now further increasing). Andaman and Nicobar Islands (300 Ha) and Himachal Pradesh (100 Ha).

Indian bananas are also exported to foreign countries. In 1971, it was planned to export 9,000 tonnes of banana to Kuwait. This plan was chalked out according to the understandings made between two partners of Kuwait and Gujarat Cooperative Fruit and Vegetable Marketing Federation Ltd and Jalgaon Distric Cooperative Fruit Marketing Society, Maharashtra. According to this plan, Gujarat was to export 3,600 tonnes, while Maharashtra was to export 5,400 tonnes of banana. An exportable banana variety named as 'Bhaskara Banana' was evolved by an Andhra Pradesh Horticulturist-Bhaskara Raju after 10 years of extensive research. The fruit is about 14 inches long and two and a half inches in diameter. On ripening the skin acquires an attractive golden yellow colour. In 1970 Bhaskara bananas were being exported to six Europeen countries, including Britain to create a market for Indian bananas abroad. Bhaskara Raju told newsmen in Delhi on 20th, September 1970 that every week he was selling 25,000 bananas to Delhi's posh hotels at Rs. 12 a dozen and the export price was Rs. 24 a dozen. Bhaskara bananas are very sweet and are not easily perishable. (Pioneer 21st Septs 1970). The most favourable point in banana export is that their are not the least chances of wastage or damage during transport. This is because the bunch after full maturity is harvested in green and hard stage. The bananas later on start ripening in the way. This plus point further encourages one to increase the area under this tasty and important fruit. As such by increasing banana production in our country opportunity for earning foreign exchange becomes better. Now the production and area under banana in India has different. According to a reference from College of

Horticulture, Gujarat Agricultural University, Navasari, the total area under this crop in India is about 2,82,800 ha with an annual production of 46,26,200 tonnes, the average production being 16.36 ha (FAO 1987) (National symposium on optimization of productivity and utilization of banana, September 22 and 23, 1992, page 25., College of Agriculture, Pune). On the other hand, another report from Indian Institute of Horticultural Research (I.I.H.R) Bangalore shows the area under banana in India as 3.39 lakh ha with an annual production of 61.76 lakh tonnes and productivity as 18.21 Ha (Souvenir, Golden Jubilee Symposium, Bangalore, May 24 to 28,1993, page 4).

Bananas Can Solve India's Food Problem - II

Banana requires warm and humid climate with plenty of rains. Dry wind, dust storms and hurricanes in summers and severe cold and frosty weather in winters are harmful for banana crop. This is the reason that in Uttar Pradesh the cultivation of banana had been limited except Tarai areas like those of Basti, Gorakhpur, Padrauna, Deoria, Gonda, Bahraich etc, which are immensely suitable for banana growing. Few places like Campierganj and Peepiganj of Gorakhpur district, Sitapur, Lakhimpur, Pilibheet, Faizabad, Mangalore of Saharanpur Distt (Near Roorkee), Maghar, Mehdaval, Khalilabad, Baansi, Siddharthnagar and others are well known for intensive banana cultivation. However, the varieties grown in these areas are not amply suitable for table use. When ripened, though not highly esteemed, these are consumed locally. As such with a view to finding out some suitable table varieties of banana for commercial growing in Uttar Pradesh, about ten decades back a large number of banana varieties were collected at the Fruit Research Station (Now Horticultural Experiment and Training Centre) Basti from various sources by the then Founder Horticulturist of this Research Station—Dr. S.S. Teaotia (Former Director Horticulture, U.P.) As a result of studying their performance many such varieties were selected, some of which are detailed herewith.

Basrai dwarf : This variety is also known as Bhusawal, Kabuli and Vaman Kabuli and Vamankali. Basrai Dwarf banana is commonly known as "Bhusawali kela," which is the leading choice variety of Maharashtra. The plant is dwarf and grows to a height of two metres with a thick and stout pseudostem and comparatively smaller and broader horizontal growing leaves. Due to its being dwarf, this variety is highly adoptable to windy situations. Again, it is better suited to drier areas than the taller varieties. It is also economical to grow them as a large number of suckers are accommodated per hectare of area (3025 suckers at 2 metres apart). Its plant bears a big and heavy bunch containing 200 to 250 large and slightly curved fingers (fruits). On ripening the skin still remains more or less greenish of course with a slight yellowish tinge, which is the symbol of its ripening. That is why people often confuse Basrai Dwarf banana fingers with those of the variety Harichhal which is a different variety.

The pulp of Basrai Dwarf banana is creamy yellow, soft and sweet with adorable flavour. This is highly esteemed by the consumers. There is no difference between the Bhusawali bananas being produced in Uttar Pradesh and those transported in U.P. from Bhusawal, as regards taste, flavour and other good qualities.

Harichhal (Bombay green): This is also a leading choice variety of banana, next to Bhusawal in Maharashtra. This variety is actually a sport of Basrai banana. Its fingers, taste and flavour are more or less like Basrai dwarf, except that fingers are without curve and the skin on ripening continues to be green. Further the plant is also taller (2.5 to 3.5 metres) than Basrai Dwarf.

Poovan (champa): This is a leading taste ful variety of south India. It is known as Champ in West Bengal, Poovan in Tamil Nadu and Malabar, Lalvelchi in Maharashtra and Karpura Chakkarkeli in Andhra Pradesh. The plant is slender and 3 to 3.5 metres tall. The bunch is large and heavy with about 300 small to medium sized fingers having well-developed mamillary tips. The skin is thin and on ripening attains attractive golden yellow colour. The pulp is creamy and sweet with slight sourish tinge which further adds to its taste and flavour.

Chini champa: This is a famous variety of Haajipur (Bihar). The plant is 3 to 4 metres tall and the preudostem is thick. It bears a big bunch having 200 to 300 small beautiful fingers, closely arranged in the bunch. The skin of the fruit is thin, which changes into yellow colour on ripening. The pulp is light creamy in colour, firm, sweet with a sub-acid pleasant flavour.

Malbhog: This is a most popular variety of West Bengal, where this is grown under the name of 'Martman'. The plant is, though 3 to 4 metres tall, can very well resist hurricanes and strong winds, as it enjoys a very good root system. The term 'malbhog' is used in Bihar for this variety. In Maharashtra, it is known as 'Mutheli, and in Tamil Nadu as 'Rasthali'. Its bunch yields on an average 130 to 140 fruits. The size of the fruit is more or less just like that of 'Poovan' (Champa), except that it is thicker in girth and the tip is not developed. The skin of the finger is very thin and acquires a bright ivory yellow colour on ripening. Its pulp is white, firm and very delicious.

Mohanbhog: The plant of this variety is about 3 metres tall, which bears heavy bunch of 100-200 fingers. The fruit is long, thick, sweet and tasty. It is mostly grown in Bihar.

Alpan: This is also a variety of Bihar. The plant grows to a height of 3 metres, which bears a bunch having 200 to 250 medium sized frurts. The pulp is thick, tasteful and with a sub-acid pleasant flavour.

Besides the above table (dessert) varieties, some culinary (vegetable) varieties were also found suitable. These were specially fit for cooking purposes. Chief of these are 'Kothia', 'Hazara' and Campierganj. Kothia is a well-known variety of Bihar and grows to a height of about 3 metres. It is resistant to drought and many diseases. The bunch contains about 120 large and thick fingers. "Hazara" is a commercial cooking variety of Gorakhpur division which is also known as 'Ballia'. The plant is tall and bears heavy bunch having upto 450 thick and long fingers. 'Campierganj' is a local culinary variety of the town Campierganj of Gorakhpur district, where it is grown on a very large scale even in 17 to 20 hectares of blocks. The plant is tall and bears 200 to 300 medium sized thick fingers in a bunch. Though not of agreeable taste and flavour, people eat these locally on ripening to remove their hunger. Most of the growers earn their livelihood thereby producing Campierganj bananas in plenty.

However, of all the collected varieties of banana the performances of which were studied at the fruit research station Basti, 'Basrai Dwarft' (Bhusawal) variety was found the best in quality and yield for commercial growing in Uttar Pradesh. Efforts were, therefore, made to cultivate this selected and exportable important variety and make its extension first in the districts of Gorakhpur division and then to other Tarai areas and later to other districts and areas of UP. Gradually the area under Basrai dwarf banana covered various parts of Basti district, chief of which are Mahsa, Hailaur, Ahra, Buxar.

Bananas Can Solve India's Food Problem - III

Bananas provide all the required nourishment and can be substituted for food. We have spoken of several varieties. Let me now talk of the extension of Basrai Dwarf banana done in various places and towns of Gorakhpur district which are Jagdishpur, Ramganj, Dumraila, Khorabar, Campierganj, Peepiganj, Kauriram, Ramchaura, Gularahia, Jungle Kauria, Charganwan, Sardarnagar, Barhalganj, Pipraich, Pharenda, Bhathat, Doma, and Nichlaul.

The areas covered in district Deoria are Premwalia, Delipnagar, Kasia, Sargatia, Jauran, Fazilnagar, Shahpur, Rampur Karkhana, Dhampur, Parsauli, Mahrani, Padrauna, Kanhauli, Nagwa, Rudrapur, Mauni Patti, Mahadia, Tamkuhi, Kunrhwa, Barhhara, Dhondha, Hata, Nawapar, Sukrauli, Teekar, Bhenrhihaari and Khadda. Similarly, the areas covered under Bhusawal or Basrai Dwarf Banana in Azamgarh districts are Azamgarh, Nizamabad, Phariha, Semraha, Kotwa, Charhai, Rani-ki-Sarai, Sardaha, Lakhanpur, Tahbarpur. Saadarpur, Barauli and Phulpur.

This variety extends to various towns and places of Faizabad, Gonda, Bahraich, Sitapur and other districts also. In Fatehpur district now Bhusawal or Basrai Dwari bananas are grown successfully on a large scale in places like Deomal, Bhitaura, Hanswa, and Telyani. In Deomal Vikaas Khand of Fatehpur district Sri Sarjoo Singh grows Basraif Dwarf banana in his village Poore-Meetau (Meetau has not to worry for marketing of his bananas. All his plants remain healthy, disease free and good-yielding as observed by the author earlier. By seeing the crop of Sri Sarjoo Singh of the village Poore Meetan, orchardists of village Jamrawan, Husainganj, Lalepur Nauganwan, Asni, Gopalpur, Jaitpur Onaha, Talikpur, Saraila, Chandipur, Jagatpur-Aadil, Maheshpur and others started growing these bananas. Similarly orchards of Basrai Dwarf bananas may be seen in villages of Khajua block on Bindki road in Fatehpur distt. Now it has almost become a custom of growing Basrai Dwarf bananas in Fatehpur proper, Allipur, Bilanda, Aamapur, Dhayamau, Bindki, Khajua, Faridpur, Paharwapur, Aaboonagar, Radhanagar and other neighbouring villages of Hanswa and Telyani blocks ot Fatehpur distt. The area under this fruit crop is going on increasing day by day in these regions. Kanpur district is also not behind. Villages of Sarsaul, Prempur and Bara Gaon of Kanpur Nagar are the chief Basrai dwarf banana growing areas on large scales. Sulem Sarai area of Allahabad/Kaushambhi is also now growing Bhusawali bananas on a commercial basis. On a road journey from Lucknow towards-Fatehpur, orchards of Basrai dwarf bananas may easily be seen throughout on both sides of the road, where these bananas are being grown with much interest.

Banana is a herbaceous, ever green monocotyledious plant, having succulent psendostem and leaves. The plant has an underground original stem in the form of a solid heavy rhizome, having several raised comical eyes all round by its side. These eyes later on develop into suckers. The plant has of fibrous root system. Banana comes under the order — 'Scitamineae' and belongs to the family 'Musaceal'. Its generic name is 'Musa' but the specific name differs according to thc use of the fruit. Specific name of table/dessert varieties (those eaten fresh after ripening) has been termed as Sapienturn. As such its botanical name forms as 'Musa sapienture', which has been named 'Banana' in English. The specific name of cooking culinary varieties (vegetable varieties) has been termed as 'paradisiaca' and as such its botanical name forms as 'Musa paradisiaca,' which in English is called as 'Plantain.' However in Hindi both banana and plantain are called 'Kela' and in Sanskrit 'Kadali' Banana is a pious plant and is worshipped by Hindu families. Its psendostem and leaves are used at various religious and social functions. It is also said to be the "native" of India.

Well-drained fertile loam or clayee loam friable soil full of organic matter (humus), is the best suited for banana cultivation. Sandy soil must be avoided for banana plantation, specially due to its roots being shallow.

Propagation : Banana is propagated by division of suckers. Suckers sprout from the original underground stem, which grow by the side of the main growing plants. These suckers are separated from the plant and planted at the proper place to establish a banana orchard. Only 'sword suckers' should be selected for plantation. To identify a sword sucker, see that the leaves are narrow, conical and sword or spear-shaped. Further the basal portion of its psendostem should be thick and heavy and the top portion be thinner and lighter. The selected 'sword sucker' should also be 2 to 2-1/2 months old and 70 to 90 cm in height. 'Water suckers' should be rejected straight away. These have broad leaves and thin and weak pseudostem of equal thickness throughout from top to base.

Preparation of land and plantation : Before actual plantation first of all the soil of the land should be well-prepared. For this the whole land should be ploughed 2-3 times and smoothened by planking. After this laying out of the banana orchard may be done at a distance of 1.8x1.8 metres (6x6 ft) from both ways i.e. by a square system. After laying out, the actual point of plantation should be marked by fixing pegs. Then bits of the size 50x50x50cm should be dug up in the month of May. After the soil and pit is fried up in the seorching heat of the sun for about 20-30 days, each pit is tightly filled up with top soil and 20-25 kg of farm yard manure (cow-dung manure) 15 cm above the soil level.

In addition to this 90 gm of phosphate (562.5 gm single super phosphate) required for the whole life the plant should be applied at a time and mixed with the top portion of the filled up pit. After rains when the raised portion of the pit comes to the level of the land, plantation may be done. If there are no fank watering should be done to bring the pit to the soil level.

Bananas Can Solve India's Food Problem - IV

Before planting one third portion of the sucker should be chopped off from the top. After this the underground stern should be dipped in 0.25 per cent solution of Agallol-3 or Seresan with water (2.5 gm medicine and one litre water) for 1/2 to 1 minute. After this treatment, the sucker should be planted just in the middle of the filled up pit. After planting, the soil around the plant should be well tightened with the wooden handle of a 'khurpee'.

Though the plantation time of banana is the rainy season, yet the best time for planting Basrai Dwarf banana is from the middle of June to middle of July. As such one hectare of land will accommodate 3025 suckers of banana by square system. Besides this, 15% additional plants can be accommodated in the same area by using hexagonal (Equilateral triangular) system of layout.

Manuring: Each plant of banana needs 200 gm Nitrogen, 90 gm phosphate and 170 gm of potash in its whole life time. These are applied in several instalments and these too within six months of plantation for this the whole quantity of phosphate is applied at a time in the filled up pit, as indicated earlier. As regards nitrogen, it is divided into four equal parts, while the potash in two equal parts. The first 1/4 part of nitrogen and first half of Potash are applied to the plant just one month after plantation. The second and third 1/4 part of nitrogen are added three and five months after plantation in the same sequence. The fourth and last 1/4 part of nitrogen and second and last half of potash—both are applied in the sixth month of plantation in the last. The manures and fertilizers should be applied to a depth of about 5 to 10 cm deep in soil all round the plant under its dip, leaving about one ft all round from the prese pseudostem. Nitrogen may be applied in the form of urea (46 per cent 'N'), Ammonium sulphate (20% N) or Calcium Ammonium Nitrate (20 per cent 'N') Potash may be applied either in the form of Potassium chloride (Muriate of Potash: MoP:— 60 per cent Potash) or Potassium sulphate (50 per cent Potash).

Irrigation, hoeing, weeding, mulching: After manuring plants should be irrigated immediately. Though banana needs plenty of water for better growth, water-logging in banana field is in no way acceptable. Therefore, the field should be divided into several beds and connected with irrigation and drainage channels. Light irrigation many times is better than few heavy irrigations. However, during summers weekly irrigation is essential, but in winters irrigation after fifteen days interval is good enough. From the very beginning of plantation till harvest, thirty irrigations are required to the maximum (during about a year). In the initial stage light weeding after every one or two irrigations must be done to keep the land neat and clean and free from pests and diseases.

Mulching the soil with paddy straw or covering the soil with thick black polythene sheets, will save many number of irrigation, hoeing and weeding. Simultaneously mulching operations will enhance the growth of plants. It is supposed that as speedily, the banana plant grows, the flowering and fruiting will also follow with the same speed, when generally it takes about a year to harvest the banana crop.

Intercropping: The interspace between the banana plants in the banana orchard may be utilised well by growing seasonal vegetables and spices and earn additional income without any loss to the main crop. Okra, lobia, brinjal, tomato, chilli, turnip, radish, carrot, beet-root, cauliflower, knol-khol, cabbage, soya, fenugreek, fennel, black cumin (kalouji), onion, garlic, turmeric, coriander and bitter gourd crops may easily be taken in these vacant spaces. Cereal crops, which generally do not require regular hoeing and weeding and some which require flooding like paddy, berseems, wheat, jowar, bajra, maize etc. should be avoided to grow as intercrop. Since vegetables and spices need regular hoeing and weeding, these are quite suitable crops for growing as an intercrop, which will simultaneously benefit the banana crop also.

Desuckering: The banana plant during its growth throw out side-suckers from time to time. If these suckers are allowed to flourish, these share with the food material of the main plant. As such this practice will result in a poor crop yield. Therefore, as soon as such side suckers are seen sprouting above the ground, these should immediately be clipped off from near the ground level. Further the visible cut portion left in the ground should also be immediately crushed with some heavy material, so that this may not sprout again. Desuckering, therefore, becomes one of the most important operations to be done specially in cultivation of Basrai dwarf banana.

Thus one has to keep himself always vigilant. The removed suckers thus collected may best be utilised as fodder for milch cattle and other animals. These may also be turned into organic manure as compost. However, if side-suckers are actually required for further plantation or gap filling, these may be separated from the mother plant very gently, without giving any jerk to it. Further, one sucker may be allowed to grow only after the main plant comes into flowering for taking a ratoon crop.

Flowering and Fruiting: During the growth of banana plant, leaves come out one after the other on the aerial stem (Pseudostem). As such generally 30 functional leaves come out on a Basrai dwarf banana plant. After this a last leaf also appears standing upward on the top of the plant, which is very small but enough broad like the shape of a showel. This is the signal of appearance of flowering bunch in the initial stage.

At this stage the conical portion of the closed coppery beautiful flowering bunch (Spathe) being upwards is seen coming out of the heart of the plant and resting at the top. This stage reaches after five months of plantation the function of the small, showel-shaped broad leaf besides photosynthesis is to protect the bunch from scorching heat of sun and other undesirable elements.

After flowering, further appearance of any fresh leaf on the plant stops. Later on in about three months the flowering bunch appears in full, hanging at the top of the plant. It is, therefore, clear that from actual plantation till appearance of hanging flowering bunch at the top, it takes about eight months. Again about two weeks are further spent from appearance of flowering bunch to its opening and appearance of all hands of the bunch in full. After this the fingers of the bunch further take three months to reach their full maturity. As such from plantation the banana crop becomes harvestable in 11½ months to a year.

As the spathes of the flower bunch go on opening, hands of Banana also start appearing and developing banana fruits actually develop without fertilization. That is why the fruits are seedless generally nine to ten well developed healthy hands are said to be good in a Basrai dwarf banana plant.

Removal of hanging inflorescence: After all hands come out and fingers start developing to maturity, a little portion of male/sterile flowers covered in the cone of the closed spathes is left over at the end (actually at the apical portion) and remain hanging. This cone should be cut and removed from the bunch, else these will start utilizing the food material of the main crop for their existance. As such the fingers of the hand may remain underdeveloped. However, the flowers inside the removed cones may be utilised in preparing tasteful curry after removing the stigmatic/staminal portion. Again, this may be given to milch cattle to eat or be utilised in composting.

Bananas Can Solve India's Food Problem - V

Staking (Propping): As the banana fingers go on increasing in size and weight in the bunch, the bunch goes on becoming heavier. The plant, therefore, goes on bending towards the ground due to the heavy bunch weight. As such to save the plant form falling on the ground or uprooting, it should be given support of bamboo clutches or of thick, long and strong sticks. This practice is called 'staking' or 'propping'. Besides staking, each plant should be tightly earthed up all round the pseudostem up to height of about 30 cm or so. Further, instead of earthing up of individual plant, the whole row of plants may be strongly earthed up. These practices will also save the plant from strokes of strong wind and hurricanes.

Protection of Plantation and Bunch, Green Manuring : As the new leaves come out of the plant on the upper portion, the older ones on the lower portion go on becoming yellowish, which later on become halfdry and remain hanging around the pseudostem. These should be allowed to hang as such, because these protect the pseudostem from the scorching heat of sun.

However, if there are completely dry leaves on the plant, these should only be removed by gently cutting these with the help of a sharp knife leaving the green sheath enclosing the stem. These should never be stripped off by hand. Banana fingers of the bunch on the plant should be protected from sun scald by covering (The bunch with paddy straw, newspapers, gunny bags or even banana dry leaves also. Further some quick growing plants like 'jait' (Sesbania acgyptiaca) and gliricidia septum should be densely planted as wind break on the Norther, Western and Southern side of the banana orchard. This will save the crop from strong hot and cold wind and hurricanes. From time to time green leaves and tender shoots of these leguminous plants may be pruned and spread in the banana orchard to be utilised as green manure.

Again, sowing of sun hemp seeds in vacant space just at the time of plantation of banana, will further be useful. When after germination, the plants. The stalk of the bunch should be protected from sun-scald by tying over it the top spathe leaf of the plant become six weeks old, these may be uprooted and left on the surface for rotting during rains. After rotting this should be tilled and mixed in the soil to act as a green manure. This will further encourage the plants in their healthy growth.

Besides above wind breaks plants of Morus sp. (shahtoot) and some tall plantation plants may also be planted to serve the purpose of windbreak. However, if the banana orchard is established amidst old orchards of mango, litchee, guava, ber, jackfruit and others, there is no need of planting these windbreaks, as these orchards of various fruits provide the best protection to the banana crop against hot and cold waves of wind. When there is fear of frost, soil should be kept moist and smudging should be done in the banana orchard in the night by burning leaves at various spots.

Harvesting and Marketing: The banana crop is ready for harvest when all the fingers of the bunch get fully matured. At maturity, the top leaves of the plant start drying. At this stage the fruits should still be hard and the dark green skin should change into lighter colour. However, in the case of Basrai dwarf banana, the skin should also have a yellowish tinge. At the same time, the fruits should be plump and their sharp corners must become roundish in every case. After full maturity the bunch should be severed from the plant by means of sharp knife or sickle, leaving about 30 cm of the stalk with the bunch.

Generally, the growers auction or sell their crop to the contractors, who further arrange for their marketing and disposal. Bunches should only be harvested just before transport for marketing. After harvest do not allow the naked bunches to expose in the rays of sun, else these will be scorched and become blackish, which will lower the market value. Precautions should also be taken that the skin of fruits are not bruised. If any how during handling these get bruised, again these will blacken. For sending to mandies or market, bananas are trans-rted on trucks or in railway wagons covered with dry banana leaves. According to the place of destination these are also transported on carts, trollies and others. In many cases during long journey bananas start ripening in the way before reaching the destination.

Removal of Pseudostem (Mattocking): One plant yields only one banana bunch. Therefore, after harvest its pseudostem must be removed to allow the ratoon sucker to flourish. If pseudostem of the mother plant is left as such, this will unnecessarily utilise the food material of the ratoon crop. However, the pseudostem should not be removed all of a sudden, otherwise the food material, which it had been consuming so far, will suddenly be transferred to the sucker of the ratoon crop, which will be far more than what is actually required for it. As such there will be overfeeding in the ratoon sucker. This will result in abnormal growth of the sucker, thus affecting the ratoon crop yield adversely. For removing the pseudostem first of all it should be kept alive for about 20 to 30 days. Then the top 1/3 portion of it should be chopped off with the help of a sharp implement or "mattock'— an implement formed by the combination of an axe and a hoe. Next cuttings and removals of remaining portions of the pseudostem should be done in three to four installments at an interval of fifteen days, the last cutting from the ground level should be done within 2½ to three months of harvesting. After finally removing the pseudostem, its rhizome should be dug up and chopped off into pieces. These pieces may be relished in the form of chaat. These may also be utilised as fodder for cattle and other animals. The cut portions of pseudostem may also be chopped off into pieces and used as fodder. The inner soft portion inside the middle of pseudostem is used in curry or pickle making.

Ripening: For ripening, the cut end of the stalk of the bunch should be painted with lime. To keep the bananas fresh and protected for a longer period, the cut end may be covered with wax or vaseline. The harvested banana bunches may also be collected and heaped in a closed chamber and covered with dry banana leaves or gunny bags or paddy straw. The fruits in this way will ripen within a week in summers and in two weeks in winters.

Another method of banana ripening is that bunches are hanged on bamboo or iron bars above 1.5 to 2.0 metres from the ground in a chamber. Instead of hanging the bunches, these may also be arranged on the ground in rows. After arranging bunches, the chamber should be smoked for 20 to 24 hours by burning cow-dung cake in the chamber. Then these bunches should be transferred to another smokeless chamber and closed therein for 2-3 days, after which the bananas will become ripe. The bananas will also ripen if covered with green leaves of 'Adoosa' (Justicia odatoda) and closed in a chamber placed in a big and broad earthernware on a small scale and covered with another holed, small earthern pot.

Pests and Diseases

Banana Beetle: The young and adult banana both-harm the banana crop. These are green in colour and are found moving inside the newly coming out folded leaf at the top of the plant. These eat away the chloraphyl and soft portion of the leaf. If their attack continues these eat away the soft portion of inflorescence and skin of young banana fingers of the bunch developing inside the heart of the plant. As such, these beetles create scratches on leaves and fruits as well. The scratches later on turn brown and then black in colour. Such scratches on banana fruits give an ugly appearance and brings the market value down. The banana grower, therefore, is put to a great financial loss. The scratches on leaves on the other hand, hinder in manufacturing food material for the plant through photosynthesis. The beetles remain active throughout the rainy season. As such to get rid of the menace spray 200 ml of Nuvan 100 E.C. mixed with 100 litres of water (0.2 per cent) from the top of the plant all round the inner portion of the growing and opening folded leaf. The prepared solution may also be sprayed on the soil all round the plant. It will further be better if spraying of Nuvan is done in July-August. Banana stem and Rhizome under-ground) Weevil–grubs of the banana weevil burrow the underground stem (rhizome) of banana and multiply therein by laying eggs. The grubs eat away the rhizome and check growth of the plant. Further, these also move above inside the pseudostem and eat away the central tender portion, which later on blacken and rot inside. The plant as such fell down from near the ground and thus the crop is destroyed. Sometimes weevils bore inside from the aerial stem also and destroy the plant and crop as above. To have a check on this pest, the rhizome should be dipped in lime water before planting. Spraying the stem with 0.02 to 0.04 per cent Dimecrow or Rogor 40 twice at an interval of 15-20 days may prevent the weevil to attack the plant. Besides this the land all round should be maintained quite neat and clean and the soil be tilled from time to time. The affected and fallen banana plants by the attack of weevil should be lifted and burnt.

Thrips: Theses are small insects which suck up the sap from tender parts of the plants. Spraying the plant with 0.2 per cent of Malathion will be useful.

Bunchy top disease and aphids: This is a virus diseases of banana, which may occur in the very young stage or even after flowering. The leaves get shrunk up and the top growing portions of the plant get bunched up with each other and form a rosette-like appearance. The plants remain stunted and margins of leaves get rolled up. The inflorescence does not develop fruits. The disease is spread, when the plant is infected through and aphid (Pentalomia nigro-nervosa). On seeing the attack of bunchy top disease, the whole plant should be uprooted immediately and burnt, otherwise the aphids will transmit the disease to other healthy plants. The soil from where it has been uprooted should also be drenched with some disinfectant.

Bunch Stalk Rot—Drying Up of Dorsal Surface of Peduncle

The dorsal surface of the stalk (peduncle) of the hanging banana bunch on the plant generally starts browning/ blackening and then shrivelling and drying at the bending point. The disease later on spreads below and as such fingers of few hands are also affected, which ultimately remain under-sized. The disease may start at the young stage of the bunch also. Generally the bunch-stalk disease occurs, when the bunch grows in hot season or when the bunch hangs towards sun. Thus the stalk and fruits get damaged due to sun scold. In severe cases even the tips of banana fruits get damaged. It has also been opined by some that there is some species of the fungus gloeosporium, which is responsible for spreading the disease and for its remedy fortnightly spraying of burgundy mixture has been recommended for spraying in young stage of bunches.

However, the main cause has been the scorching sun. As such to save the bending bunchistalk, it should be covered with the small broad showel-shaped spatheleaf standing like a flag on the top of the plant, which should also be tied with a soft string. Again the fruits should be protected by covering, rather thatching with dry banana leaves. Bunches hanging in directions other than those of the sun, have been found free from bunch stalk disease.

Anthracnose: This disease, caused by a fungus, spreads on leaves and fruits in which black round spots are produced on leaves and skin of fruits. This results in drying of leaves and dropping of fruits from the bunch. Spraying with 0.3 per cent of any copper fungicide twice or thrice at an interval of fifteen days may prevent the crop from this disease.

Non Emergence of Inflorescence

Sometimes in some plants due to some physiological disorders and unbalanced water supply, the inflorescence does not emerge out. Under such conditions incision should be made in the pseudostem from the blocking point downwards (vertically) for about 1–1½ ft through a sharp knife with the precaution that the inside bunch stack does not get any scratch from the knife. The incision should be made towards that side on which the inflorescence shows the trend of bending. In this way the banana bunch will come out like a normal bunch to hang and mature.

Panama disease or wilt—Panama disease or wilt in banana is caused by a soil-borne fungus fusarium oxysporum. Sudden yellowing of lower leaves of the plant, starting with the margin is the chief symptom of this disease. Later on the whole leaf becomes yellow, hangs and dries up. By and by all leaves dry up and hang along the pseudostem. The inner central middle and soft portions of the pseudostem blackens and dry up. There is no immediate affect on the rhizome but afterwards it becomes brown from outside and black streaks are formed inside it. If bunch has already been formed in the plant, it remains undeveloped and then dries up. Roots of the plant also rot and stop functioning. This results into drying up of the whole plant including the top flag leaf. The dry plant remains standing for some time and ultimately falls down on the ground. Such plants should immediately be dug up along with the underground stem and already sprouted suckers and removed. The whole dug up portions of the plant should be burnt up. The soil all round the plant should be stirred and disinfected with lime and sulphur. After treating the soil some other crop may be taken up in such soil and no banana crop should be taken for three years. No suckers from such plants should be utilised for multiplication of banana orchards. Flooding of the land during the start of the disease is supposed to kill the fungus. Lands covered with banana crop continuously for several years, unfertility of soil and poor drainage system are said to be more prone for incidence and spread of this disease.

Yield: Since 3025 plants of Basrai dwarf banana plants are accommodated per hectare of land, about the same number of healthy and sound banana bunches are expected from a hectare subject to scientific cultivation done as above.

Besides taking fresh, ripe banana pulp may be transformed into jams and other tasty products. Unripe green banana and plantain pulp may be sliced into chips and fried. Grinding of dry pulp may also be done to turn it into flour. Banana/plantain flour may be utilised for preparing 'chapaties' after mixing it with wheat flour. Banana is also of great medicinal importance.

Sixteenth October is observed as the 'world food day'. The theme of 'world food day-2000' is 'A millennium free from hunger', as announced by the United Nations Food and Agricultural Organisation (FAO, NIP Alld. 20th July 2000).

After banana, potato is another horticultural food crop to reduce the day to day increasing load on cereals due to population explosion in our country. An average working man requires 3,000 calories of heat energy in his food per day to remove his hunger. Similarly a woman's requirement is 2,500 calories per day. Potato is rich in carbohydrate (22.9 per cent) over which depends the actual quantity of the material to be used to fulfil the calorific requirement. About 26.6 per cent total solids is also available in potato which provides bulk to the food. As such 100 gm of potato provides 99 calories of body heat. Accordingly a man requires 3 kg and a woman 2.63 kg of potato to eat per day to fulfil his/her calorific requirements. For this boiled potato is better to take. Further, taking 300 gm of milk in addition makes the potato food complete and balanced. Regarding others, the availability of carbohydrate in sweet potato is 31.0 per cent, while the total solids is 31.5 per cent, with its calorific value as 132 calories per 100 gm of material. To fulfil one calorific requirement/hunger, therefore, a man per day will need 2.32 kg and a woman 1.59 kg of sweet potato. Again in dry water chestnut pulp or its flour, the availability of carbohydrate and total solids are 68.9 and 86.2 per cent, with its calorific value as 336 calories per 100 gm material. A male and female adult as above will need 0.89 kg and 0.72 kg material to fulfil their requirements of calories/hunger per day. One may live on dates also (man 1.34 and woman 0.88 kg per day) along with some milk, as these are rich in carbohydrate (67.3 per cent), total solids (73.9 per cent) and fibre (2.1 per cent) also. Its calorific value is 283 calories per hundred gm dates. Dates are also rich in iron (10 mg/ 100 gm), protein (3 per cent) and vitamin-A 600 i.u/100 gm) also.

Dry potatoes may also be transformed into potato flour which has 81.7 per cent carbohydrate and 93 per cent total solids and 8.4 per cent protein along with 349 calories/ 100 gm potato flour. Potato flour may also be utilised in preparing chapaties by mixing it with wheat flour. As regards potato growing it may be grown in well-drained loam, light loam or sandy loam fertile soil during winters. The actual time of sowing potato is from 10th October to 15th November. The seed rate is 25-30 quintals tuber seeds per hectare of land. Only disease-free seeds obtained from certified agencies should be sown.

Among the short term varieties of potato (80-90 days duration), the chief of these are Kufri Chandramukhi (A-2708), Kufri Kuber (O.N. 2236), Kufri Alankar (3649). The mid-duration varieties (91-110 days of potato are Kufri Bahar (E-3797), Kufri Lalima (B.S. 1753), Kufri Kundan, Kufri Sheetman (3745) and Kufri Jyoti. The chief late duration varieties (111 to 120 days) and kufri sinduri (c-140), Kufri Badshah (J.F. 4870), Kufri Deva, Kufri Kumar and Kufri Gulal. Some new varieties namely Kufri Ashok (90- 100 days, Kufri Sutlaj (90-100 days) and Kufri Jawa (100-110 days) have also been evolved these yield about 200 to 250 quintals of tubers per hectare of land.

Now true potato seeds (TPS) are also being produced at various research stations like Central Potato Research Institute (CPRI), Shimla and Bangalore-based centres for technology development' through tissue culture. These seeds are very small like tomato or brinjal seeds. Only 100 gm of such seeds, i.e. true potato seeds (TPS) is sufficient for sowing a hectare land TPS—grown plants are disease-free and produce disease-free uniform-sized tubers. Further, potato is of a great medicinal value also. Crushed fresh potato tubers heal burn injuries of body and provide a soothing effect. Again boiled potato peels have proved very useful on bum injuries, when used as bandage. This technique of potato peel bandage (PPB) evolved by the burn injury unit of Vadia Hospital Mumbai. Potato peel bandage heals the burn injuries of the body soon and can be removed from the wound easily and comfortably without any trouble.

So let us grow bananas, potatoes, sweet-potatoes, dates, water chestnuts carrot, turnip, onion and others and improve and increase their production and productivity and change our food habit by supplementing/ supplanting cereals with these fruits and vegetables and observe "World Food Day" successfully and with a sportsman spirit.

13

Environment Sustainability

Smoking, Tobacco Chewing - Very Risky

Medical officers, doctors and health experts have already declared that tobacco, whether through smoking or chewing, has a definite link with several cancers including those of lungs, mouth, throat, larynx, urinary bladder, kidney, pancreas and possibly cervix and liver. Tobacco can also cause coronary heart diseases, chronic obstructive lung diseases, tuberculosis and paralysis as well.

Further, Indian Cancer Society has warned that contrary to popular presumption, beedi smoking is twice as dangerous as cigarette smoking. The practice of putting the lighted portion of beedi or cigarette in mouth in some parts of Andhra Pradesh leads to oral cancer and so does betel leaves.

Again tobacco smoking also gives birth to unwanted deposits on teeth and gums and diseases like bronchitis, cough and asthma. A study in California has revealed that people who smoke increase their risks for leukemia as well as cancer of bone marrow known as multiple myeloma. The word leukemia refers to one of a number of frequently fatal cancers of the white blood cells and blood forming organs of the body. Tobacco chewing is also very popular in India. It is said to be a causative agent for cancer of mouth and throat.

Dr. Rajani Bhisey of Cancer Research Institute, Bombay found that alarming evidences of chromosomal damages were detected among women and children beedi rollers of Kamatipura in Central Bombay. According to information received during a campaign against tobacco in Bombay and also as reported by Dr. S.D. Chibate a cancer specialist, "In the whole world maximum number of throat cancer patients is in Bombay". Again, of all cancer patients of Bombay, 40 per cent are those of throat cancer.

Dr. K.S. Reddy of All India Institute of Medical Sciences pointed out that lady-smokers are more likely to have menstrual problems including missed and irregular periods. An average woman smoker reaches menopause two years earlier than non-smokers and chances of miscarriage, premature birth and cervix cancer are more among smokers. Also a large number of non-smoker women fall prey to tobacco related diseases through passive smoking. If a woman is a smoker or is subjected to passive smoking during pregnancy, the chances for still birth and low birth weight will increase. The newly born babies are also prone to infectious diseases and respiratory problem. Experts say that smoking or passive smoking by pregnant lady results in either abortion or 10 per cent under-weight of the baby. All such babies have their heads comparatively smaller in size, who also become physically and mentally retarded. Also a smoker pregnant woman has more chances of falling victim of ovary cancer.

Another information further reveals that in India still-birth rate for tobacco chewing women was 50 per 1000 live births, compared to only 17 per 1,000 non-tobaeeo chewing women. A child may be a victim of tobacco from birth and even earlier if the mother smokes during pregnancy. The resulting damage to the foetus has the risk of respiratory infections in the newly born child or children living in smoking atmosphere.

Children of regular smokers passively smoke 30 to 80 cigarettes worth of nicotine a year, or a quarter of cigarette every day. As a result of this chronic cough, phlegm and wheezing were found more common in children of smoker parents, specially the mother. Finding themselves in such an atmosphere, they also become permanent smokers.

Passive smoking is several times more fatal than normal active smoking. Dr. Ronald M. Davis of USA reports that tobacco smoke in the home and working place could be killing 46,000 non-smokers each year in the United States. Out of these 3,000 die due to lung cancer, 11,000 from other cancers and 32,000 from heart diseases.

It has been further opined that the risk to a non-smoker in a typical office is about the same as the risk for a non-smoker whose spouse smokes. The smoke released by a smoker, possesses in itself 3-times more of nicotine, 4 times more of tar and many times more of other dangerous chemicals, than those present in the smoke, which a smoker inhales through his own cigarette, beedi or cigar. As such a smoker in a family keeps the lives of his family members, specially of his wife and children in danger.

The most fatal chemical in the tobacco is nicotine. Experts say that nicotine leads to last palpitation of heart and high blood pressure. On account of this, blood of the body gets coagulated, which increases the possibilities of heart failure.

Nicotine takes only seven seconds to reach from lungs to brain. If nicotine equal to the quantity of that present in a cigarette, is injected to a person, he may die then and there. Similarly, if a person does not release smoke of a full cigarette from his mouth, he may die immediately.

The carbon monoxide gas of the tobacco smoke absorbs the oxygen present in the blood and, therefore, the supply of oxygen to brain is reduced. This results in fast breathing and other troubles. Carbon monoxide gas also makes the fat of inner layers of blood vessels coagulate. This results in blockage of blood vessels, increasing thereby the dangers of heart failure.

The next fatal chemical after nicotine in tobacco smoke is tar or charcoal. Tar contains cancerous chemicals like benzopyrine, nitrosamine and others. Various gases like acrolene. acetaldehyde, formaldehyde, hydrogen cyanide are also present in tobacco smoke. These gases block the passage of nose and thus create breathing troubles.

Out of many vitamins required in human body through daily diet, the maximum quantity required is that of vitamin-C. Smoking of one cigarette reduces 25 mg. of vitamin-C from serum of the body, which gives birth to several diseases.

Doctors have also pointed out that smoking of only one cigarette reduces 5 minutes life of the smoker. As such if a person has to live for 60 years, he will live only for 55 years. It has been estimated that 30 lacs people die every year in the world due to tobacco consumption. Out of this 20 lacs die in developed countries and 10 lacs in developing countries. Out of these, 3,90,000 people die only in USA. In our country 7.2 crores females and 14.2 crores of males above the above of 15 years are victims of tobacco.

Indian Council of Medical Research has estimated that in India 8,03,000 people die every year and more that 2200 die every day due to tobacco related diseases. World Health Organisation has indicated that tobacco related deaths have now gone up manifold in developing countries due to a surprising increase in number of tobacco consumers. This is because western cigarette manufacturers of multinational companies are facing strict legal and social prohibitions in their countries and, therefore, they are going on unloading their products in developing countries.

The World Health Organization has, therefore, warned - 'if this practice will continue, 70 lacs (7-fold) people will die every year in developing countries by the year 2020 due to excess tobacco consumption, as compared to the existing figure of 10 lacs'. As such the number of smokers in developed countries is decreasing and that in developing countries like India is increasing, where there is no legal binding.

However, if there is any such legal prohibition, that is not being followed strictly. This is because nobody wants to take pains to watch the progress of prohibition act or legislation at site and punish the defaulters then and there, as they themselves are victims of smoking and tobacco chewing. This is unfortunate. Wooden or card board sheets written there on as 'Smoking prohibited' remain hanging on walls of hospitals and patients/visitors sitting there on benches go on smoking and polluting the air. Doctors themselves do not hesitate in smoking or tobacco chewing.

As regards social prohibition, it has not the least value in India, specially in social and public gatherings, where smokers become slaves of fashion, keep themselves in grips of complexes, go on polluting the environment and forcing non-smokers to inhale dirty and poisonous life-killing gases blown by them from their mouths and noses, for which they have no right at all.

Commerce ministry has reported that in India 60 billion cigarettes were sold in 1986, which rose to 85 billion in 1991. Similarly sale of beedies was 10 to 12 times more than that of cigarettes.

Indian Council of Medical Research has further pointed out that tobacco is a major source of revenue in India. This may be the main reason for not imposing a total ban on smoking and consuming tobacco or tobacco products and also on tobacco cultivation in our country. It has been presumed that by imposing ban, there will'be a total loss of revenue gained by Tobacco. This is something ridiculous and misleading, as ICMR has further revealed that against a receipt of revenue from Tobacco, heavy amount would be spent in treatment of tobacco related diseases. It means our country, instead of gaining something, would be losing considerable amount for nothing.

The Director General of World Health Organization in his visit to India told that there are 11000 deaths daily in the world only due to tobacco use and as such 2200 deaths per day in India (N.I.P. Alld 01-06-2001). Regarding revenue received from tobacco in another reference it has been mentioned that in India there is a receipt of Rs.6,000 crores, while the expenditure in treatment of tobacco related diseases is Rs.27,000 crores (*Amar Ujala*, Alld. dt. 31st May, 2,000). It may thus be seen how tobacco growing in India and tobacco chewing and smoking is justifiable.

To save people from hazards of smoking, 87 countries in the world have totally banned advertisements of cigarette. Out of these any type of advertisement concerning tobacco is prohibited. Twelve European countries including Greece, Belgium, France, Italy, Portugal and others have started a campaign against smoking by strictly discouraging advertisements and representations of cigarette on radio, television, magazines and newspapers, etc.

In France even showing cigarette packets on the screen is prohibited in cinema houses. Even those scenes, in which actors or actresses are smoking, are also prohibited for showing in the cinema. Contrary to this in India no picture, telefilm or serial is complete unless the actors/actresses are shown smoking. In Singapore, cigarette or beedi smoking or tobacco chewing have been legally banned. They are implementing this practice in their flights also.

Several measures have been taken from time to time and acts and legislations passed in India also to fight with hazards of smoking and tobacco chewing. Also every year World Health Day is celebrated on 7th April, World-No-Tobacco-Day on 31st May and World Environment Day on 5th June, but to our great disappointment, the laws passed or instructions issued against smoking or tobacco consuming menace are not being strictly followed.

Recently smoking has been banned in Manipur jails and Tihar jail of Delhi. Government had also announced in parliament that they would introduce a legislation to ban tobacco advertisements in the country. Further, it was also announced that smoking at public-places will be banned and that cigarette and tobacco shops existing near Government offices and schools etc. will be removed. On the other hand smokers, tobacco chewers, tobacco growers and their supporters are claiming that smoking and tobacco chewing are original human rights (*Dainik Jagran*, Varanasi, 28th October, 1990 page 9; Our Leader. 15th March, 1994 page 8), which is ridiculous.

Even then, smoking of beedi, cigarette, cigar, hukka and chewing of tobacco, pan masala, khaini and use of other tobacco products like 'gutkha', 'chutki', etc. are continued in full swing in trains, buses, taxies, rickshaws, cinema houses, hospitals, dispensaries, nursing homes, offices, banks, treasuries, courts, railway stations, bus stations and educational institutions. Similar is the case in hotels, restaurants, canteens, dhabaas, shops, markets, hair cutting saloons, conferences, symposia, religious and social gatherings, gardens, parks and other public places. Even morning and evening walks on roads have become difficult, for instead of fresh air one has to inhale dirty and poisonous smokes of beedies and cigarettes released by uncultured persons passing on roads from all sides.

Drivers in school buses and school rickshaw trollies go on smoking and enjoying, but playing with the health of young school-going children, sitting in these vehicles. Drivers and conductors in trains and buses themselves smoke and pollute the atmosphere. Therefore, the question of stopping smoking in trains or buses does not arise even after raising objections by non-smoker passengers. Writing there 'Dhumrapaan varjit hai' has no meaning. However, if non-smoker passengers are bent upon fighting with smoker passengers for the whole night and day during their journey without sleeping or taking rest, that is another point.

Sale of cigarette, beedi, tobacco and all other tobacco products, advertisements through newspapers, magazines, big-sized sign boards, are still in practice. Tobacco cultivation and cigarette and beedi-making have not been stopped and are going on as usual.

If tobacco cultivation provides employment and means of livelihood to a large number of people, tobacco growers may choose other crops for growing, which exist in a large number in our country. There is no justification for them to have employment and earn their bread at the cost of inconvenience, health and life of others.

It is true that warnings like - "Smoking is injurious to health" and Danger Sign are displayed on cigarette packets, so that by reading this, people may not smoke. This is not a solid step to stop smoking. However, if this display is actually a correct step, why this has not been adopted on a beedi packet specially when it is more harmful than cigarette. Further when it is very well known that these things are harmful to health, why are these being manufactured and why are these being imported. Is it not playing with one's life? Who is responsible for all these? It is a matter of great concern.

The only solution to get rid of hazards of tobacco chewing, smoking, therefore, is to legally ban all the above mentioned tobacco-related activities immediately. Further, only passing an act or legislation will not suffice. The administration will be required always to be vigilant and make surprise checking in trains, buses, cinema houses, offices, hospitals and all other places pointed out earlier and handle the defaulters strictly under the laws and acts framed by the Government.

The author is campaigning to stop the Hazards of Tobacco Chewing and Smoking through various articles in Magazines and Newspapers etc. from time to time.

Dumping of Garbage

Environment, pollution and maintenance of ecological balance have become burning topics of the day, not only in India but in the whole world. Debates, meetings, workshops, seminars, symposia and conferences are arranged from time to time for discussion among students, teachers, scientists, environmentalists, administrative officers, political leaders, general public and others. These are also being held on National and International levels. The International Earth Summit held in June 1992 in Rio deganeiro (Brazil), is a clear example of such conferences.

Coverages are also done on such important issues in newspapers, magazines, periodicals, radio and television etc. through various articles, interviews, advertisements and other means. Efforts are also being made from time to time to have a neat and clean environment and create public awareness through dramas, telefilms, cultural programmes etc.

To achieve this goal several schemes, campaigns, drives and other programmes like plantation, afforestation, lessening of poisonous gases coming out of running vehicles, factories etc. and general sanitation have been started from time to time. For proper implementation of these, various acts and legislations have also been passed on certain aspects.

Inspite of all these, the environment of our country is going on polluting day by day, disturbing thereby the ecological balance. Deforestation is going on. Cutting of trees and orchards are continuing. Spreading in air, of black smoke with poisonous gases comming out of running vehicles, factories and other sources are going on as usual. Increasing number of smokers and tobacco chewers are also going on releasing poisonous gases and dirty smell in the atmosphere. People have to inhale all these with the result that they are becoming victims of various diseases and troubles.

Similar is the case with dumping of garbages. It has become a general practice that sweepings, wastes and various types of garbages are dumped at various spots on public places, making thereby the entire atmosphere polluted with harmful, unhealthful, foul and poisonous gases. There are many sources of such garbages.

1. Garbage from Houses : These include dust particles, pieces of papers, clothes leaves and stems etc. collected after brooming houses. The broomings also consist of polythene bags, peels of fruits and vegetables, tea leaves, other kitchen wastes, pieces of coal, wood and many other types of house wastes.

All these wastes are daily collected from each house and thrown outside either in front of one's own house or in front of his neighbour's house. In many cases these are also thrown on roads, in drains, in garbage containers or at any place where one likes, depending upon his/her own sweet will. In the case upper floor houses or in special circumstances, these garbages are thrown even on heads of persons passing through that area.

"These garbages remain dumped for a long period at the same places", where these were thrown. During that period these go on rotting and polluting the atmosphere. Stray animals like pigs, dogs, asses etc. further spread these in search of food material. These are also spread by young boys and girls roaming for collection of polythene bags and other material useful for them. Dust particles of these also blow through wind, which deposit on plants, trees and other articles.

These garbages are lifted only when it is convenient for the sanitary employees, without having any consideration of inconveniences caused to public. It is not a must for them that the garbages are removed immediately.

2. **Garbage from Roads, Footpaths, Lanes, Railway and Bus Stations, Railway Lines, Railway Platforms**: These garbages consist of sweepings and collections from roads, lanes and foot paths of towns, cities, colonies, mohallas etc. by municipal or town area sanitary employees. These also include

collections from railway and bus stations, railway lines and railway platforms. All these include many types of rubbish with leather and rubber pieces, cow dung, horse dung, excreta of pigs, asses, dogs and other stray animals, night soils, packing material, fruit-vegetable waste, paddy straw, factory wastes plus house garbages dumped at various places.

All these, whether lying here and there or collected at a place, create dirty atmosphere. Often it becomes difficult even to pass through these areas. During this period if there are rains, the whole garbage becomes wet and start further rotting and emitting foul smell.

Portions of garbages which are dry, are also burnt at various places to lessen their volumes. Their dense smoke and foul smell of rotting material, besides spreading in the atmosphere, also reach inside houses where family members are forced to inhale directly poisonous gases like carbon monoxide, carbon dioxide, sulphur dioxide, methane, lead and others. The passers already have to inhale these from the polluted atmosphere.

Roaming of pigs have already been declared as one of the important spreaders of the most dangerous disease encephalitis (brain fever) in human beings. Even then they are seen wandering here and there, as if they are the permanent original residents of the area.

3. **Filth Collected in Drains and Nullahs** : Generally it has been observed that drains and nullahs remain blocked at several places due to solid and muddy garbages. These start rotting in drains and nullahs alongwith night soils etc., which go on giving out foul smelling dirty poisonous gases in the air.

These continue rotting for a long period. Even whenever drains are cleaned, the garbages are collected along drains on road sides. These garbages are also removed after months or so and are not lifted immediately in the pretext that these garbages are wet, when these can very easily be lifted. Till then the environmental pollution continues. Stagnant dirty muddy water in drains and nullahs also favour mosquito breeding, spreading, thereby, malaria and many other diseases.

4. **Over-flowing Sewers and Underground Drainage** : Sewer lines and underground drainage pipes are often found blocked with garbages. These, therefore, overflow and the sewage and other dirt start spreading over the ground. These start emitting bad-smelling gases and thus polluting the whole environment. Even if sewers are cleaned, the sewage and rotting garbages are again stocked at various points, where these also remain for long like other garbages.

At certain places drainage systems are extremely defective and poor. Therefore, during rainy season or whenever there are heavy rains, people have to pass through knee-deep dirty, unhygenic rotting filthy polluted muddy water. These are also mixed with garbages, which are also seen floating there. People passing on foot, cycles and rickshaws through such places are the greatest sufferers. Such places are also sources of spreading epidemics.

Besides these, people have also to keep their lives in danger, while passing through these places. Some people also become victims of felling in these muddy, watery mini-graves. The sufferings caused to these people due to such nuisance, may very well be imagined. The space between Niranjan talkies and Surajkund police outpost towards K.P. Training College crossing in Allahabad, specially under the Surajkund bridge, is the best example of such occurrences. These are being observed for the last several decades.

Even in normal cases also both sides of road and footpath remain in wretched condition and full of such heaped garbages and filth under this bridge that it becomes difficult even to pass through this area. A large amount of money has been and is being spent from time to time in repair and making improvements in this area but the chronic troubles and inconveniences are still prevailing as ever.

5. **Pollution of Environment Through Garbage in Uncovered Manholes**: Manhole covers of sewers are often removed and stolen away by thieves and mischief-mongers. These manholes remain open for long here and there on or along roads, until some mishappenings do not take place. Open manholes not only give way for spreading foul smell of sewage in the environment, but also become dangerous points for young boys and girls and also animals. They fell in the manhole, due to inattentive and irresponsible attitude of the concerned authorities, lose their lives and further pollute the environment.

6. **Garbage of Dead Bodies of Animals**: Often dead bodies of animals are thrown along roads. These rot and spread foul gases in air, which are unhygenic and sources of various epidemics.

7. **Garbage of Dust** : Even metalled roads, besides others, are covered with thick layers of dust and dust heaps at several places. This is because roads are lightly broomed and dust garbages are not lifted. Thus the dust further spreads through wind and running vehicles. In this way the whole atmosphere is filled up with dust, which also deposit on walls, articles of houses, shops, food material and leaves ofstanding trees.

8. **Pollution Through Shifting of Garbage on Uncovered Garbage Carriers** : If and when dumped up garbages of city and town are lifted and shifted through garbage carriers (municipal trucks) for unloading on main proper dumping place, these go on polluting the atmosphere throughout the way with their foul smell. Besides this, pieces of garbage and other filthy material go on flying, dropping and collecting on roads, fresh fruits-vegetables

and eatables of the market, shops and also on persons passing through. This practice, therefore, creates an unhealthy and unhygenic condition. This is all for the simple reason that firstly the garbage carriers are over-heaped and secondly these are kept uncovered during shifting.

Conclusion : The observations made above reveal that besides so many sources of environmental pollution, various types of city and town garbages heaped on road-sides, road crossings, railway platforms, railway and bus stations and other public places, also play vital roll in polluting the environment. Thus by emission, in air, of smoke and various deadly and poisonous gases like methane, carbon dioxide, carbon monoxide, sulphur dioxide etc. and spreading of dust and other filthy material from heaped and burnt garbages and forcing everybody to inhale the same, people, become victims of many dangerous diseases.

Layers of these dust smoke, besides depositing on several articles, also get deposited on leaves of plants and trees, which are the main sources of supply of oxygen. Deposits of such layers on surfaces of leaves, cover their green pigment-Chlorophyll. Thus the manufacture of food i.e. photosynthetic (carbon assimilation) activities in plants and trees are lessened or stopped.

The cycle of absorption of carbon dioxide and other harmful gases and release of oxygen from and in the atmosphere, therefore, get disturbed. These harmful gases, as such, go on polluting the environment and simultaneously the condition of plants and trees also go on deteriorating day by day, which also become shabby and unhealthy. Such observations have also been reported earlier. Attention of concerned authorities have also been drawn from time to time for improvement on certain aspects, but to no affect. The whole ecological balance, therefore, is adversely affected.

Remedies

1. Brooming and cleaning of roads, drains and other public places should be done in early morning, when number of persons there, are the minimum. Further, as the dust particles during night become wettish on, account of dew formation, chances of spreading dust particles in air in early hours, specially during brooming, are lessened.
2. Suitable places should be allotted and Marked or garbage containers placed along roads in cities, towns, colonies and mohallas in the vicinity of houses for throwing house garbage.
3. Strict acts/legislations/laws should be framed, so that it may be a 'must' for throwing house-garbage at the allotted places or in garbage containers only.
4. For implementations of these laws and acts, regular timely and surprise

checkings should be done by the administration openly and confidently and catch hold of defaulting house-garbage throwers. They should also be liable for punishment under these acts. Such a checking should also be a 'must', as mere making and passing of laws and acts will never be useful, unless their implementations are thoroughly monitored.

5. Simultaneously, such acts and laws should be widely publicised among all citizens through road to road and lane to lane announcements, newspapers, magazines, radio, T.V., cinema and other means, before taking any such action.
6. Sweeping and cleaning of roads, lanes, footpaths, drains, nullahs and sewers in every part of the area, must be done every day by municipal sanitary employees. Drains should also be washed daily. Roads, footpaths and lanes should always be dust-free.
7. None of these garbages should in any case be heaped here and there or in front of houses or along roads, whether these be from roads or drains. These should be lifted immediately and dumped at the allotted marked places or in garbage containers, as the case may be.
8. Cleaning and removal of all such garbages should also be done under supervision of some responsible employees and they should see themselves that all the cleanings have been done according to norms.

   Timely, regular and surprise checkings by the administration should be done in this case also and the defaulting employees should be dealt with seriously then and there.
9. Garbages from allotted marked places and garbage containers, before these are over-filled, should be collected in garbage carriers (municipal trucks) at regular specified intervals and shifted and dumped to pre-allotted main garbage dumping place.
10. Shifting of garbage to main garbage dumping place should always be done in covered garbage carriers only and never in open carriers.
11. Roaming of pigs, dogs, asses, horses and other stray animals in cities, colonies, towns, roads, lanes and other public places should be stopped by law. This will prevent pollution of environment through them and the chances of spreading dangerous diseases like encephalitis will also be reduced in the area.
12. Underground and all drainage must be well improved, so that the passers may remain free from filth and may not have to face the inconveniences as they have always facing under the Surajkund bridge in Allahabad.

13. Encroachers and outsiders living in unauthorized ways in cities, colonies, mohallas etc. must be ousted. The administration should also keep a thorough check and watch that their families and children may not wander and further spread dumped up garbages, ease from their natural calls, here and there or in drains. This has also to be checked they may not act as thieves and mischief mongers. The area should remain free from such hazards.
14. Practice of burning of garbages near residences, shops, markets and public places must be stopped.
15. Throwing of dead bodies of animals on road-sides, residential and public places should not be allowed and a thorough watch should be kept for stopping this practice.
16. Some portions of garbage shifted and dumped at main garbage dumping places, may be utilized for composting and manuafacture of biogas and paper.
17. Foliar feeding of trees and plants on road-sides, parks, gardens, residences, institutions and other public places should be done from time to time with forceful water showers. This may be done through sprayers, tubes, syringes etc. This practice will wash the leaves and make them atleast dust-free, facilitating thereby photosynthetic activities in plants and trees.

Maintain the Environment Neat and Clean

Environment has become one of the most burning topics of the day. It is going on polluting day by day due to one's own selfish action. Under such critical circumstances of ecological imbalances, people are forced to pass unhealthy and unhygienic lives. As such it has become a world-wide issue and for this very reason the whole world celebrates 'WORLD ENVIRONMENT DAY' on FIFTH JUNE every year. This is done just to remind public for maintaining a neat and clean environment.

Now the environment has become so much polluted that it has become almost impossible to lead a peaceful life. The whole atmosphere is filled up with various poisonous gases and chemicals like carbon monoxide, carbon dioxide, sulphur dioxide, lead oxide, tar, nicotine, etc.

Among various polluting sources, population explosion is the most important one. Efforts made for check on growing population in the past appear as failures. Population must be controlled by forcing family planning without consideration of religion, cast and creed. No Prizes should be awarded to those who follow family planning and facilities given by Government should be withdrawn from those who do not follow. Bangladeshi intruders stepping in the country must be stopped and those who have stepped in must be ousted, as these people further add to the population of the country.

Use of polythene bags is still in use with a greater speed than earlier, in spite of ban imposed in Allahabad, Delhi and other places. Burning of heaps of garbage having polythene bags, dirty clothes etc. on road-side and in moving garbage trollies and trucks and in garbage containers placed at different places has become a common practice. These emit black foul smelling smoke/ poisonous gases as mentioned above, which are inhaled by people and become victims of dangerous diseases.

The black fumes deposit also on leaves of fruit and other trees which are already covered with dust of roads. Deposit of such layers on leaves stop photosynthetic activities in plants/ trees. As such these become unhealthy and weak, stop manufacture of food material (carbohydrate), create dearth of life-saving gas oxygen and further give rise to environmental pollution as well as to economic loss.

Due to irregular electric supply people are compelled to operate generators. Kids and others have lost their lives from generator fumes in the past in Delhi. As such use of generators must be strictly banned and strictly followed up by the administration. Simultaneously, the administration should strictly ensure regular supply of electricity, so that people may not have inconvenience.

Polluting vehicles must be strictly checked up and removed. Again, number of three/four wheelers, rickshaws, rickshaw-trollies, hand driven trollies, thelas etc. must be limited for a particular city to reduce pollution.

Use of tobacco could not be stopped as yet in spite of several Government, orders. This can only be stopped after very seriously interfering by the administration and Heads of various departments.

All the polluting fatal gases and chemicals mentioned above, when emitted and inhaled, cause many fatal diseases like cancer, heart trouble, breathing problems, T.B., Asthma, etc.

Soil erosion should be controlled by planting suitable plants like Guavas along river banks as already done from Nawabganj to Bithoor in Kanpur. Similarly, Mangroves should be planted on ocean/sea-shores, as a safeguard from Tsunami hazards, occurred recently on 26th Dec. 2004, (Black Sunday) in Chennai, Andaman Nicobar, Indonesia, Thailand and others.

A large area of waste lands is lying in our country. These should be turned in greenery by planting fruit and other plants/trees. Aonla, Bael, Jamun, Ber, Mahua, Phalsa, Guava, Karonda, Jatropha curcas and others may be included in these plantations. These green patches will make a great improvement in the deteriorated environment. Cutting of orchards should never be allowed unless the Department of Horticulture UP and Uttaranchal permit only on genuine grounds. Similarly, forest department should not permit to cut jungles and trees. They should also not interfere in the activities of Horticulture Department and keep themselves busy in increasing forest area for better environment (avoiding urban areas).

Deteriorating Environment

Environment has become one of the most burning topics of modern era. Environmental degradation is going on increasing day by day due to inhabitants own faulty selfish actions. Under such critical circumstances of ecological imbalances, human beings are forced to pass unhealthy and unhygienic lives and become victims of several dangerous diseases.

Now, the problem of polluted environment has become a world-wide issue. That is why on 5th June the whole world celebrates 'World Environment Day' every year, just to remind the citizens for maintaining a neat and clean environment. The environment consists of such a large number of pollutants that it becomes very difficult to deal with all of them at a time.

These pollutants have made 'pollution and environment' - a very wide and exhaustive subject.

As such, only a few most important issues of pollution are being highlighted.

Destruction of Orchards and Forests: Green growing orchards, trees and forests are valuable wealth of Nature. These are symbols of a prosperous country. Unfortunately besides other countries, the practice of continuous destruction and cutting of trees is going on in India in full swing.

This results in dearth of life-saving gas-oxygen and excess of poisonous gases in atmosphere. These include carbon dioxide, carbon monoxide, sulphur dioxide, tar) nicotine, formaldehyde, methane, chlorofluorocarbons (C.F.C.), lead oxide and others. Therefore, in such polluted environment, it becomes very difficult to remain alive for human beings and all other living creatures as well.

Further, trees spread their roots in the soil in such a way that their root hairs continue binding of soil particles within themselves and save soil-erosion and land-slides. Besides planes, this issues is specially of great significance on hills and mountains.

In this connection, it will not be improper to mention here that on 23rd September, 2004, the hill/mountain in Uttar Kashi got sunkup due to sudden land-slides. This resulted in damage of about 1/4 part of the city (United Bharat Alld. 29th Sept. 2003). From that very day, sliding of rocks and huge-sized heavy stones remained continued alongwith soil-erosion for several days, killing thereby many families and innocents. Later on l/4th portion of the city further got damaged. These caused a huge loss of about Rs. 1.0 crore, affecting, thereby, 1000 families (Star T.V. 3rd Sept. 2003, 10 A.M.; T.V. Sahara Samaya U.P.; 1st Oct. 2003, 3.45 p.m.).

Again, from the night of 2nd October 2003, sliding and falling of large stones of Varuna Vata Mountain alarmed the residents from the fearful noise created by the rocks. The electricity arrangements also got very much disturbed. Thus the whole city was plunged into darkness (Times of India, N.D., 3rd Sept. 2003; T.V. Aaj Tak, 3rd Oct., 2003, 7.30 A.M.).

Several buildings situated on Gangotri highway near the areas adjoining hotel Bhandari and colony of Horticulture department started reaching the stage of demolition. The road running from Gangotri for entrance in Uttarkashi also got closed up. Buildings of eollectorate and treasury also reached the same stage and the population of Uttarkashi city was reduced to only 1/3 of the total population.

According to information, about 357 families and 2833 persons were put to serious troubles and complications due to this severe dangerous landslide. The Government of India has decided to help such families. In addition to cutting and damaging trees and forests from mountains and making them tree less, there may be some other reasons also for such disasters. Swami Chinmayananda and other agencies have arranged for geological survey in this direction.

In recent past a Gangotri-related workshop was arranged in Lucknow. There, it was predicted that in the near future 'Gangotri Himnadi rik ho jaaegi' (Gangotri Himnadi will be empty). Pollution problems caused by landslides and soil-erosion in the adjoining areas were also predicted (Vigyan, June, 2003).

As such a critical vigil on protection and proper maintenance of orchards, trees and forests should be a must. In no case these should be cut or destroyed. Further, public awareness should be there for planting and protecting as many fruit trees, flowering, other ornamental, shady and fodder trees as possible every year on suitable available places. Plantations may be done in groups, in the form of orchards, forests or even in scattered forms and also along roads, railway lines and in waste lands.

Population Explosion

For the last about five decades family planning campaign is in vogue in India, but all the efforts made so far are utter failures. The growing population of our country has become one of the very major sources of pollution. For reducing the birth rate and adopting family planning, and birth control, every year 11th July is celebrated as 'World Population Day'.

Due to population explosion the poisonous gases like carbon dioxide and others as stated earlier, are going on mixing up in air. Urban people are facing many complications caused by growing population and resulting in increasing environmental pollution. Scarcity of trees and turning green-growing leaves of existing trees into unhealthy conditions, further create pollution problems. This is because such leaves hardly absorb poisonous gases from air. The population of India has already exceeded 100 crores.

Besides citizens of our country, infiltrators getting protection contribute much in increasing population of the country. They are illegally migrating in India and living with their families in unauthorized sheds (Jhuggies and Jhoparies) in many residential colonies and vacant places of various cities. They are going on producing children and adding fuel to the fir by making additions in the present huge population.

Bangladeshi intruders have become serious problems for the country. Over 50,000 Bangladeshis are staying only in Allahabad (U.P.) for the last several years. (NIP Alld. 3rd. October, 2002) Not a single day, apparently passes without some 25,000 Bangladeshis migrating illegally into India (NIP 6th March 2004).

In a two crore population of North Bengal, about half of the people are Bangladeshis and all of them are having more than one wives. Again, in India 24,443 Bangladeshis are residing continuously for a long period (NIP 20th Feb. 2003). In this connection Delhi High Court has instructed Delhi Government to submit a programme for ousting 13 lakh Bangladeshis staying in the capital (United Bh., 16th Oct. 2003).

Of course, there is no food shortage in our country, but in view of the increasing population, importance is being paid on improving the production and productivity of cereals and horticultural crops like potato, sweet potato, onion, turnip, dioscoreas and banana, etc. These vegetables and fruits will further supplant or supplement the cereals and will also solve food problem of the country, if any. For all these also 'World Food Day' is celebrated every year on 16th October.

Though population control is a world-wide campaign, but just against the international campaign, there is a bizarre. President Omar has an Al-Basheer of Sudan had instructed the residents of his country during 2003 to keep as many wives as they could, so that there may be a rapid increase in population of his country (Delhi Times, 28th August, 2003) astonishing is it?

Thus to have a proper control over such a huge population of India, first of all public awareness towards family planning is very necessary. Then in the next step to bring the family planning programme into practice, people should be seriously dealt with. Adopting family planning should be made a 'must' and not left on option. Hardest action should be taken against the defaulters. They should rather be discouraged by withdrawing all necessary facilities provided to them by Government. Any financial offer for adopting family planning will be of no use. This will only be wastage of Government money.

Further, inflow of Bangladeshis and other infiltrators in India should immediately be stopped. Again, those who have already intruded in the country should be ousted at any cost. Such actions may prove more useful in carrying out the campaign successfully, as it is hoped.

Generators

In absence of electric supply, people are forced to operate generators to bring the electricity - run appliances into use, though these also emit same poisonous fatal gases as emitted by factories and running vehicles etc. as already indicated above. Generators besides producing air pollution also produce noise-pollution and invite deafness as well.

Generators have already found places in houses, institutions, hospitals, offices and shops, etc. However, if generators are brought into use at most of the above places at a time, what will happen? The whole atmosphere will be full of black smokes, having all the above fatal poisonous gases, thereby, making people victims of vertigo, asthma, bronchitis, cancer, heart diseases and others.

Anyway, if generators are operated under some special circumstances, one should remain very cautious, as a slight slip in this direction may be fatal. In West Patel Nagar, New Delhi, due to failure of electricity, a generator placed in the night of 8th July 1996, the generator was sufficiently near the bed-room of the house, when a 16-year girl 'Ekta' and a 17-year boy 'Kunal' were sleeping with their 45-year old maid-servant.

Next morning on 9th July none of them were found in senses due to the choking black smokes of the generator. After hospitalizing them, the boy and maid servant lost their lives the same day (H.T. N.D., l0th July 1996; T.O. India, N.D., 10th July 1996). The girl on the other hand remained fighting with her life and death. The dangers caused by generators are going on increasing. As such the use of generators has become a very serious considerable issue.

Under such dangerous and alarming circumstances, should one expect freedom for use of generators and producing pollution in the environment? Certainly not. One will have to stop its use and the time has come for that also. Delhi High Court has enquired from the Ministry of Environment regarding the possibilities of banning the use of generators. Most probably these have been banned for Commercial Institutions. In spite of knowing various important utilities of generators, but simultaneously considering its fatal affects also, the Allahabad Administration had for the time being banned the use of generators (w.e.f. 13th March 2003) for commercial and Industrial use (NIP, 13th March, 2003).

Electricity Supply

The actual reason of operating generators is irregular and insufficient supply of electricity. Had these been regular electric supply, why one could has to be forced to inhale fatal poisonous gases. Due to mismanagement, the prevailing problem of electric supply is going on increasing day by day. Sometimes informed or uninformed roistering, trippings and sut downs for repair of faults take place, sometimes transformers get burnt up and sometimes there are grid failures also.

On account of grid-failures in the year 1996 the whole Northern India was plunged into darkness from the very morning of 20th December (Rashtriya Sahara, Lucknow, 21st Dec. 1996). This resulted into sudden stoppages of running trains in Uttar Pradesh, Punjab, Jammu-Kashmir, Haryana, Himachal Pradesh and Rajasthan. The routine activities of inhabitants, therefore, were badly affected. There was already a grief failure just about two weeks earlier than this failure (NIP 21st Dec., 1996). Again same conditions prevailed in the year 1998 on 18th March and then in the year 1999 on 22nd Sept. (NIP 23rd Sept. 1999).

Grid failures also occurred on 5th November 2003 in West Maharashtra and the electric supply was held for about 2 $^1/_2$ hours (NIP, 6th Nov. 2003). Then again a very severe grid-failure took place on 6th December 2003 in Maharashtra and some parts of Gujarat. Now electricity problems are often found in Delhi also - the Capital of India.

On one side the stoppages of all routine activities due to insufficient electric supply and on the other hand several utilities of generators and further forced imposition of ban on use of generators due to black fatal smokes and gases-all these have become very important and burning issues.

Such disastrous electric problems have prevailed not only in India, but in foreign countries also, (On 14th and 15th August 2003 many cities of USA and Canada remained in total darkness for 12 - 13 hours due to grid failure (Hindustan, N.D., 16th Aug. 2003).

Later on Rome and many other cities of Italy plunged into darkness on 28th Sept. 2003 due to mismanagement of electricity (NIP, 29th Sept. 2003). Therefore, considering the ill-affect of generators, use of these will have to be essentially stopped. Simultaneously regular electric supply must be ascertained under all circumstances and for that hardest steps will have to be taken. This is the only remedial measure for saving people from inhaling these poisons.

Light Pollution

A fresh issue of light pollution has recently crept in before Indian scientists, though it is already prevailing in foreign countries like USA, Europe, Japan, etc., where some rules in this direction have also been formed. According to Mukherjee (United Bharat 17th Oct. 2003) scorching artificial light sources like flood-light, halogen, tube light, street light and bulbs etc. produce light pollution.

The light produced through these artificial sources mingle with the molecules of moisture vapor and dust particles of the atmosphere and come back towards earth. This results in formation of an undesirable layer of light spreading between earth and sky. giving rise to light pollution. Light pollution makes the starts of the sky invisible except few very bright starts. Twinkling stars are not the least visible. About 27 years back, the sky was very clearly seen, but now it is not so. The visibility of sky at present is 27% less than earlier.

Agarwal and Mukherjee (United Bh. 17th Oct. 2003) further opined that in foreign countries, now scientists are getting success in developing artificial light sources like micro-chips and others through advanced technology. These chips are called 'Light Emitting Diode' (L.E.D.), such chips and energy sources will supply light and economise consumption of electricity as well. Further, these chips solve light-pollution problems also.

Out of these improved developed sources of light, there are some such types of bulbs which never break and consume about 80% less electricity than the present traffic light. Researches on improved light sources are also going on in Australia (Sahara Samaya, 25th Oct. 2003).

As such to avoid unwanted light pollution, only highly improved sources of artificial light as chips should be brought into use.

Note: Translation of lecture delivered by the author in Hindi on 20th February 2004 during the occasion of All India Vigyan Sammelan - 2004 in the auditorium of National Physical Laboratory in IARI, Pusa Campus, New Delhi.

Utilization of Horticultural Waste

Fruits, vegetables and ornamental plants are the main components of Horticulture. Spices, potato and other tuber crops, medicinal, aromatic, plantation crops and bamboo are also included in Horticulture. For keeping the body system fit, use of fruits and vegetables have become a must in our daily diet, especially in the present era of environmental pollution. The production of fruits in India is 469.71 lakh tonnes from an area of 45.40 lakh ha of land (Verma, 25). As regards vegetables, the production is 715.94 lakh tonnes from an area of 53.35 lakh ha of land (Shukla, 18). Earlier India ranked first in the world fruit production (Chadha, 2) and second in vegetable production after China (PTI,14). However, presently India is ranking as second largest producer of fruits and vegetables and largest producer and consumer of cashew nut, tea and spices in the world (Preamble,15). In spite of all these productions, India has to bear a great wastage loss of Horticultural produce. In 1992 this loss was worth Rs. 3000 cr (PTI,14) each year. Now the Ministry of Food Processing of India has estimated the wastage of agricultural produce worth Rs. 58000 cr every year (Martin,5).This loss occurs for want of post harvest facilities like storage, refrigerated transport, processing, linkage between growers and processors and fruit-vegetable markets (PTI 14, UNI, 22; Pari News, 10, Bhandarker,1).This loss has been estimated as 30 per cent of the total annual production of fruits and vegetables (UNI, 22; Bhandarker, 1).

As regards processing, only 10 per cent of total production of fruits and vegetables is processed in our country, against 70 per cent in some developed countries (UNI, 22). On contrary, in 1992 out of India's total fruit and vegetable production, it processed barely 1.5 per cent and exported less than 1.0 per cent of it, whereas Brazil and Philippines process over 70 per cent (Bhandarker, 1). Further, only a meager quantity of 40,000 to 50,000 tonnes of fresh and processed fruits are exported to foreign countries (Jagtiani, 4). In terms of money, it has been mentioned elsewhere that India exports a meager Rs. 317 cr worth of fresh fruits, vegetables and onions and about Rs. 120 cr worth of processed items (Bhandarker, 1). Out of the exported quantity too, more than part consists only of mangoes. As regards fresh fruits of mango, it has been estimated that 1,200 tonnes of only Alphonso and Dasehri mangoes are exported from India (Srivastava,19). Besides above, only 60-70 per cent portions of these fruits and vegetables are actually consumed and rest are treated as wastes. These wastes consist of peels, seeds, stalks, cores, leaves, flowers and remains of various products and byproducts.

Generally in many fruits and vegetables, portions just under the skin and near seeds are comparatively richer in nutrition. If these are removed and wasted, most of the nutrition and useful bulk are lost. Similarly, many seeds, leaves and flowers are valuable. As such losses occurred on account of these wastes and those wasted for want or post-harvest facilities, may be made up to a great extent, by further utilizing these wastes in original form or by turning them into various products/byproducts. These may be for human, industrial or therapeutic use or useful as cattle feed. For actually bringing these wastes into use, the bulk may be collected from canning and processing factories/ institutions, hotels, canteens, restaurants, messes, residential places, *mandies,* markets, orchards, cold storages, sorting and grading centres.

Mango Waste

Mango peels left after eating/sucking fresh fruits, canning, preparation of squash, and mango leather have sufficient pulp within themselves. These peels along with damaged ripe fruits may be utilized in manufacture of alcohol after fermentation. Peels of unripe mangoes may be used in pickling and also as cattle feed. The mango seed kernels make excellent confectionery fat, which is exported by West African countries to Europe and US (Jagtiani, 4). The quantity of fat present in the kernel is to the tune of 8-10 per cent (Srivastava, 20). After extraction of fat, the residue serves as a good cattle feed. The kernel may also be ground into flour, which may be utilized for preparing chapattis after mixing with wheat flour. This is nutritious also as the seed kernel contains in itself 69.21 per cent carbohydrate and 5.56 per cent protein. The outer hard portion of the stone, however, serves as a good fuel. Fresh mango stones are useful for raising root-stocks. Dry mango leaves play an important role during raising mango root-stocks. For this when mango stones are spread in nursery beds, these may be covered with only dry mango leaves and watered. These wet leaves keep the stones moist for a longer period and (i) provide the least resistance to sprouting seeds, (ii) help in early sprouting and (iii) protect plants from attack of termites due to presence of resin in leaves (Nand, 8).

Guava *(Psidium qua Java* L: Myrtaceae) Waste: Peels and cored portions had from guava halves during canning / bottling, must be utilized in jelly making. The pulp remains thus obtained should further be used in preparing guava cheese/toffee after separating seeds. These guava seeds again will be relished by cattle as feed. Further, unripe guava fruits which drop on ground or plucked from the tree during rains for having good quality winter (main) crop may be pickled after scraping them into shreds.

Aonla *(Emblica officinalis Gaerth.:* Euphorbiacease) **Waste**: Injured aonla fruits and those destroyed by birds, may be utilized in preparing *chutney,* candy, sucking pills, toffee, pickles, *chyavanprash* and aonla hair oil etc. Such fruits may also be dried and powdered for cleaning dirt of body and hair, Remains of aonla stones after collecting seeds serve the purpose of fuel. Seeds are useful for raising root stocks. Leaves and flowers which shed under aonla trees, should be ploughed, which will provide organic manure to trees. All parts of aonla tree are medicinally important.

Jamun *(Syzigium cumin ii Skeels:* Myrtacease) **Waste**: Jamun fruits dropped on the ground and other injured ones may be collected, fermented and turned into vinegar. *Jamun* vinegar is said to be of a great therapeutic value, especially in stomach troubles. Again, *jamun* seed powder is said to be a boon for controlling diabetes and urinary troubles. Seeds may also the sown for raising root stocks for budding. *Jamun* seeds are also rich in protein, calcium and carbohydrates and, therefore, can compensate 15-20 per cent of concentrates given to cattle as feed (Thapar, 21).

Citrus Fruits Waste: The outer portions of rinds of oranges and lemons are useful for extracting orange and lemon oil, which are good for flavouring beverages (Gandhi, 3). Seeds of citrus fruits also yield oil. The inner white portions of citrus fruits are rich in pectin and, therefore, are valuable for making jellies and marmalades. Further, the rag and inner white peels of oranges, if taken with juice and pulp, are said to create laxative effect. Peels of malta and santra are good for preparing shreds for marmalades. Powder of dried santra peels are useful as tooth powder, while paste of dried santra peels soaked in milk serve as a good face cleaner. Kagzi lime peels after extracting juice may be utilized in pickling simply with salt. Inner parts of these peels, which remain wet with juice, are good for cleaning and brightening utensils, as well as for cleaning dirt from face and other parts of the body. *Khatta* lemon may be used for pickling and seeds should be sown for raising root-stocks after extracting juice. Decorate drawing room with small beautiful *'Hazara Oranges'* (Kumquat) and then put them in wide mouthed bottles with sufficient salt and have tasteful pickles.

Jack Fruit *(Artocarpus integrifolia* auct: A. *heterophyllus* Lamk: Moraceae) **Waste:** Peels of ripe or unripe jackfruit and its leaves are good cattle feed. Fleshy portions of peels of unripe fruits make tasteful curry, after scraping green conical portions. Jackfruit seeds may tastefully be taken as curry. These may also be relished with salt after boiling or roasting in hot sand/ash. Jackfruit seed is rich in iron, phosphorus, carbohydrate (38.4 per cent), protein and calcium. Its flour can be utilized in making chapattis after mixing with wheat flour. The latex of the tree is useful in plugging holes of earthen wares or buckets etc.

Grape (*Vitis vinifera* L.: Vitaceae) **Waste**: Soviet scientists have developed a new vitamin - "Ammivit" in group-B from wastes of wine prepared from grapes. It's flavour is like that of lemon and is brown in colour. A Soviet scientist Dr. E.O dintsova developed the technology for extracting "Ammivit" from these wastes by microbiological methods. "Ammivit" can be added to tea and fruit juice. An amount of 5 gm of Ammivit contains that amount of vitamin B, which is present in whole available blood of a human being. It has a special value for athletes, as they require larger amount of vitamins of 'B' group (USSR Inf. Ser, 24). Prunings of grape vines should be utilized for multiplying plants by cuttings.

Plantain- Banana (*Musa sapientum* L. : *M. paradisiaca* L. : Musaceae) **Waste :** Unripe plantain peels may be utilized in preparing curry and pakoras after scraping outer green portion. Unutilized remains of these peels may be given to cattle. Pulpy portion from ripe banana peels may be scraped and utilized in preparing banana toffee and rest are good for cattle use. Ripe banana peels after drying may be burnt for cleaning atmosphere. Sterile flower buds enclosed in reddish spathes and hanging at the end of inflorescence, after formation of fruits, should be cut and utilized in preparing curry. Underground stem is useful for preparing *chaat* and curry and also for propagation of plants by bits. Inner tender portion of pseudostem is also used in curry making.

Banana-plantain leaves are good dining plates. All these are also good as cattle feed. Banana fibre is useful for tying buddings. All remains of pseudostem, under ground stem, inflorescence, leaves and banana-plantain bunches, should be cut into pieces and given to animals/dumped in compost pits to have organic manure.

Pineapple (*Ananas cosmosus* Merr.: A. *sativus* Schult, f.: Bromeliaceae) **Waste**: Juice extracted from cores and peels of pineapple are useful for manufacture of citric acid or alcohol. The refuse thus obtained is good as cattle feed. The remains of pulp after extracting pineapple juice may be turned into *chutney*. Pineapple leaves are source of strong white silky fibre, which may be used for making pine cloth, strong cords, fishing nets. Leaves of pine apple are considered as anthelmintic (medicine for intestinal diseases). Pineapple waste is a good source of oxalic acid (Singh et. al, 17).

Monkey Jack (*Artocarpus lakoocha* Roxb.: Moraceae) **Waste**: Male flowers of monkey jack drop on the ground. These should be picked up and utilized in curry making or pickling. Latex of the tree contains resin. Roots are useful for extracting a dye. Refuse obtained after eating ripe fruits are good as cattle feed.

Apple Waste: Remains of apple pulp after juice extraction are good for preparing chutney. Unutilized portion in centre of pulp of the fruit should be given to cattle.

Bael (*Aegle marmelos* L. : Rutaceae) **Waste**: Rind of the fruit yields tannin. The mucilaginous material embedding seeds, are good adhesives. This is also used in varnishes and may also be utilized in plugging cracks of wooden domestic appliances, furnitures and windows etc.

Wood-Apple *(Feronia limonia* Swingle; *Kaitha* L.: Rutaceae) **Waste**: Hard rind of the fruit is useful for preparing snuff boxes. Leaves and seeds yield useful oil. Branches of the tree excrete gum.

Ber *(Ziziphus mauritiana* Lamk.: Rhamnaceae) **Waste**: Prunings of ber tree are good for fencing. Remains of prunings may be used as fuel. Leaves are good as fodder. Seeds are used for raising root stocks for budding.

Phalsa *(Grewia subinaequalis* DC., Tiliaceae) **Waste**: Phalsa prunings are suitable for making baskets. Leaves may be stitched as dining plates. Seeds if not eaten with *phalsa* fruits may be sown for raising plants. The bark of *phalsa* tree/plant is fibrious and may be turned into rough ropes. Its wood may be used in making golf shafts.

Carambola (*Averrhoa carambola* L.: Oxalidaceae; Averrhoaceae) **Waste**: Fruits cut or injured by birds or otherwise may be utilized for making *chutney*, squash or pickles.

Lasora *(Cordia, myxa : Ehretiacea)* **Waste**: Seed kernel is said to be useful in curing ring worm. Bark of the tree is useful for making rope and is also rich in tannin. Leaves, bark and seeds-all are of therapeutic value. Utilize green fruits in pickling and rest be given to cattle.

Mahuwa *(Madhuca indica* J.F. Gmel.; Sapotaceae) **Waste**: Flowers which drop on the ground may be picked up and utilized for manufacturing alcohol. Juice of flowers is sweet and can very well be used in preparing *halwa* or sweet *poories.* Flowers may also be dried for eating in future. These are also good as cattle feed. *Mahuwa* is also medicinal. Seeds yield edible oil, which is also an important ingredient in soap making. Its leaves may be used as fodder. Unripe tender green fruits may be used as vegetable. *Mahuwa* flowers relieve from cough and decoction of bark of its tree cures bleeding gums and ulcers. *Mahuwa* cake is a good manure and its decoction may be applied on plants as organic pesticide.

Papaya Waste: Fruits thinned from papaya plants should not be destroyed but utilized in making curry or pickles. Peels may be utilized as cattle feed. Unripe peeled fresh green papaya pieces may be used as *'petha'* and pickles. All other remaining unused parts may be chopped into pieces for preparing organic manure.

Custard-Apple, Pear Pomegranate and Litchi Waste: Peels of these fruits may be utilized as cattle feed. Prunings of Pear, Pomegranate and remains of litchi fruit bunches may be used for propagation/fuel. Green tender fruits of FIG, *(Ficus carica* L.), CLUSTER FIG, *goolar- Ficus glomerata* Roxb.), HOG-PLUM *(Amra-Spondias pinnata),* ROSELLE *(Hibiscus sabdariffa* L.), ELEPHANT APPLE *(Chalta Dillenia indica* L) may be utilized in making curries and pickles. Calyces of *Roselle* and Elephant Apple may be used into beautiful tasteful jelly. Other wastes of these may be used as cattle feed/ manure.

Coconut *(Cocos nucifera* L.: Palmae **Waste**: Coconut water of unripe fruit is very sweet, nutritious and refreshing and is good for taking as beverage. When in plenty, these may be turned into alcohol after fermentation. The coir covering the hard endocarp (shell) is useful for filling in mattresses and for manufacturing mats, carpets, foot-mats, thermal insulation boards and ropes etc. The hard shell is good for preparing toys, combs, buttons etc. Whole shells are good for preparing containers for hukkas and halves are useful as lids, bowls, cups, small flower pots etc. Small pieces of shells and fibres may be used as fuel. The dust of fibre coir is useful for mulching and composting. The residue left after extracting coconut oil from copra (mature and dried kernel) is a useful cattle and poultry feed.

Tamarind *(Tamarindus indica* L: Caesalpiniaceae) **Waste**: Tamarind kernel powder, prepared after decorticating seeds, is a source of jellose (a polysaccharide), which acts as a substitute for pectin (Singh et al,19). Tamarind kernel powder is used as creaming agent for concentration of rubber latex and as conditioner and stabilizer of soil for brick-making and also as sizing material in textile industry (Singh et al,17). Unripe fruits are rich source of tartaric acid and bi-products like citric acid, lactic acid and ethanol (Singh et al,17). Tamarind leaves are used as poultice for removing pain. Leaves are also useful in swellings and boils. Wood is useful as fuel and timber. Flowers and tender leaves are edible. Flowers are also useful for preparing pakoras.

Drumstick *(Morninga oleifera* Lamk: Moringaceae) **Waste**: Drumstick seed oil is said to be having curative effect in gout and rheumatism. Mature dry seed powder has been found very effective for cleaning drinking water and removing turbidity from river waters (PTI,12; Vigyan varta, 26; U.B. News, 21) Prunings of branches are good materials for propagation and also as fuel. Drumstick *(Sahijan)* leaves are good fodder. Very tender green leaves and flower buds may be relished as curry. Fruits, besides curry, are useful medicine in pain of back and hips.

Okra *(Abelmoschus esculentus* Moench : Malvaceae) **Waste**: Okra *(Bhindi)* seeds yield edible oil, which is present up to 20 per cent in the seed. Roasted powder of the seed is said to be a substitute for coffee powder in Africa (Singh and Bhagchandani, 16). Mucilaginous material in stems and roots of okra are useful for cleaning sugar cane juice during gur making. Stems also yield fibre. During threshing of ripe dry okra pods, the refuse after separating seeds prove good for manufacture of paper, compost or for burning. Ripe seeds of *bhindi* contain 20 per cent protein as well. Its flour mixed with 10 percent of wheat flour makes agreeable breads, which are nutritious (PTI.11).

Potato Waste: Peels of mature potatoes may be cut into small pieces and taken after frying. Boiled potato peels may also be fried and taken with salt. Cut and bruised potatoes are useful in manufacturing alcohol and starch and as cattle feed also. Boiled potato peels may also be utilized as bandage known as 'boiled potato peel bandage'. This is said to be very soothing and useful in healing burn wounds, dressing very bad pressure sore, long standing nonhealing wounds and crush injuries, as experimented and established in Burns Unit of Wadia Hospital, Bombay by Dr. M.K. Keswani (PTI Feature, 13).

Water Chestnut *(Trapa natans* L. var *bispinosa,* T. *bispinosa* Roxb. : Trapaceae) WASTE : Water chestnut peels are rich in iron and iodine and make tasteful pickles. These are also good cattle feed.

Colocasia *(Colocasia esculenta* Schott: Araceae) **Waste**: Leaf stalks of colocasia should be scraped and utilized as curry or cooked with pulse.

Leguminous Vegetables Waste: Peels of **Cowpeas, Beans** (if green seeds already utilized) and GREEN PEAS should be utilized as cattle feed.

Root Vegetables Waste: Turnip, Radish, Carrot and Beet Root leaves are generally thrown away as waste. These green leaves are very nutritious and may be taken fresh as salad or may also be taken after frying. Turnip leaves possess 15669 IU of vitamin-A per 100 gm of leaves. In a reference regarding carrot, radish and turnip, Nayer (9) has reported like this- "The portion of green leaves discarded as waste material is in fact the most nutritious the darker the leaves the greater their nutritious content". Besides leaves, turnip peels should also be utilized after chopping and frying. These may also be consumed as soup.

Cole Crops Waste: Peels of Knol-kohl should be utilized like those of turnip. Cauliflower and knol-kohl leaves may be eaten after frying. Cauliflower and CABBAGE stalks may be made into curries, while thick midribs of their leaves may be pickled. Rest may be utilized as cattle feed.

Cucurbits Waste: Peels of Pointed Gourd, Round Gourd, Bottle Gourd, Ridge Gourd, Smooth Gourd and ripe Pumpkin are very precious. These should be chopped into small pieces, fried and tastefully eaten with meals. Peels of Cucumber and Ash Gourd (with pithy portion) should be utilized as cattle feed. Peels of bitter gourd may also be eaten after frying. Juice of peels of Bitter Gourd is also medicinal. After consuming reddish sweet pulp from Watermelon, the whitish thick pulp should be separated from the peel and utilized in *petha* making. Then its peel and that of the Musk-Melon serve as cattle feed. Seeds of watermelon and musk- melon are nutritious and are good for utilizing in preparation of sweets and refreshing drinks etc. after decorticating or grinding.

Khejari *(Prosopis) cineraria* Druce: Mimosaceae): Khejari plants/trees are extensively grown in arid/semi arid areas of Rajasthan specially in Bikaner, as seen in already pruned and sprouting condition in first week of March 2008. Its young pods are used as vegetable. The plant also yields gum. The wood after pruning may be utilized as fuel and other work. Its leaves are good fodder for cattle.

Bamboo *(Bambusa arandinaceae* Wild, Bambusaceac): Bamboo- *baans* cultivation is very remunerative for poors, who earn their livelihood by preparing baskets, huts and other articles of domestic and industrial use. Bamboo is also used for making paper. However, all the refuse and remains coming out of these preparations may be utilized as fuel or manure. Again very tender growing vegetative buds found in bamboo plants may be relished as curry or pickle.

Tea Leaves: Tea leaves after use should be washed and dried. These may be spread in flower or vegetable beds and ornamental pots for mulching, specially in summers. Rest may be turned into organic manure.

Flower Waste: Flowers offered to different gods in temples and used at many religious occasions, are later on immersed in Ganges. As a result of this, living fish were found dead in Varanasi by decreasing oxygen (Srivastava, Piyush, 20). The aromatic components in flowers react with chromium and other heavy metals (Due to presence of industrial waste in river water) to form certain non-degradable poisonous components. These deplete the oxygen level in river water. This phenomenon may prove fatal to living beings, specially in stagnant water (Mishra, P.K., 6). All such flowers at river banks and those thrown or lying here and there after functions, may be collected along with dry flowers from plants and also dropped flowers under trees, should be turned into organic manure. Scented Flowers like those of Maulsari *(Mimusops elengi,* L), HARSINGAR *(Nyctanthus arbortristis*) and many species of *Plumeria,* which bloom in night and shed from midnight to next early morning, may gently be had in plates and placed in drawing room. These will spread their fragrance and make the environment pleasant. After use these may also be composted.

Petals of Scented Indian Roses like *'Chaiti'* or *'Fasli gulab'* (Damask rose: *Rosa damascena* Mill) and *'Cheenia'* gulab (Edward rose: *Rosa indica* L, *R.chinensis* Jacq.) should be collected from flowers of plants after their full bloom. These may be placed in drawing room for fragrance or may be utilized in preparing *'gulkand'* with sugar, which is very nutritious and a very good laxative. These petals may also be dried *(pankhuri* and used in future for flavouring beverages. Those rose petals which shed from plants in beds, may be mixed in soil to make it fertile. Flower Buds like those of *Cordia myxa* (Sebestan), *Bauhinia purpuria (Kachnar)* and *Sesbania grandiflora* (Agati sesban- *Agast)* if in excess and liable to be wasted, may very well be utilized in preparing tasteful curry after frying with spices or *pakoras*. Even flower petals, of Rose, Marigold, Banana and Coriander flowers have been recommended for decorating salad dishes on dining tables and then relishing them with pleasure. (Mail Today,7).

Other Wastes: Rest of the wastes obtained from other fruits, vegetables, horticultural produce, leaves lying under the trees and other degradables must be utilized as cattle feed/manure/fuel according to suitability and requirements.

Ripening of Fruits - Now a Problem

Ripening of fruit was never a problem, but it has been made a problem now. One must keep patience to wait for maturity of fruit, when these should be picked up from trees for further safe treatments if needed. For example, mangoes hanging on trees, on maturity change there green colour into slight yellowish colour. Further on maturity the fruit will have a whitish blush over there and by thumping the fruit from fingers it will give a dull sound. Again a mature/ripe fruit of mango will drop from the tree. This gives a message that fruits are ready to be picked, of course all the fruits may not be mature at a time.

Then these may be put in baskets for transport, which will ripe themselves in the way. For home use these may be wrapped / covered with newspapers and within days these will ripen and safely eaten without fear of any poisonous material in them.

In the case of banana when the fingers of the whole bunch have come out, one sterile flowers bunch at the apex start hanging down. One should wait for proper growth and maturity of all the fingers. In the mean time the hanging sterile bunch of flowers should be cut down and be utilized for making curry or be given to animals specially to milch cattle. On reaching maturity the sharp corners of each finger will become roundish and the green colour will attain slightly yellowish colour. At this stage the bunch may gently be cut leaving about 15 cm of stem to make its handling easy. The cut end may be pasted with lime and stored in a dark-room in the corner wrapped with dry banana leaves or newspapers all round and the door closed. In summer all the fingers will ripen within a week and within two weeks in winters. In a kitchen garden the bunch remains hanging on the plant and members of the family go on picking fingers of ripe banana from the bunch and go on enjoying / eating. Such fruits are healthy and nutritious to eat.

Guavas should be picked by hand when yellowish tinge starts but still hard. So is the case with papaya. Guavas will ripen themselves at room temperature naturally and its shelf life is hardly for 3-4 days. Papaya should be wrapped in newspapers. Similarly other fruits may be picked up at maturity and get ripened by simple healthy process at room temperature. No need of applying any chemical.

Nowadays growers / contractors are in a hurry to pick up even unripe fruits, get them ripened by calcium carbide gas (CaC2) and extract as much money as they could at the earliest. They have no business to think if these fruits will be healthy to eat or make one ill. Such businessmen are playing with the lives of consumers. Carbide gas is a poisonous chemical and has become very common to ripen with this poisonous gas fruits specially Mango, Papaya and Banana. So many warnings have been given that those using carbide gas will be arrested and punished and many raids of godowns have been made in Allahabad and Delhi but these could not be implemented properly. Similar is the case with use of oxytocin for increasing the quantity of milk in milch cattle and increasing size of vegetables by injecting oxytocin, in spite of several warnings. (*Amar Ujala Agra*, 2nd July 2010, 08; Compact : *Amar Ujala Alld.* 19th Aug. 2010, 07, *TOI* 30th June, 2010, 15; Compact Alld. 23rd July 2010, 03; *United Bharat*, Alld. 28th July 2010, 04: NIP Alld. 18th Aug. 2010,04; U.B. Alld. 5th Aug 2010,01; Compact Amar Ujala, 15th Aug 2010, 07; Amar Ujala, Agra 2nd July 2010, 08; U.B. Alld. 8th August 2010,12; U.B.7th Aug. 2010, 11).

It is being noticed that oxytocin injection in vegetables create poisonous effect and on the other hand it is being publicized that it has no harmful effect. If it is so why these are being injected and why the Govt. is worrying for replacing carbide gas with Ethenyl. Carbide gas and Ethenyl or Ethelene- all are harmful and confusing and unnecessarily for ripening of fruits, use of Ethenyl is being recommended (NIP Alld. 18th Aug. 2010,11) when there is no problem at all. Why these fruits are not being allowed to ripen naturally and the vegetables being grown naturally. Of course organic farming must be adopted, but no chemical should be used for all these, as they pollute the environment also. All these Calcium Carbide, Ethenyl and oxytocin should be banned and strict vigilance should be there and the defaulters be strictly punished. It is also important to note that only framing of rules and laws will not suffice, unless these are thoroughly executed and timely checked.

Pollution Associated with Power Generation

Coal for Power Generation

The modem civilization is energy based. With increasing demand, there has been a continuous search for new sources of energy. While large dams are controversial, uncertain monsoon and dwindling rainfalls have made hydropower unreliable. Safety regulations and problems of waste disposal have given a back seat to nuclear power generation and high technology of harnessing "nonconventional" energy is yet to come to the forefront. Thus, fossil fuel, off which, coal being more abundant and easily available, is at present, the most preferred source for power generation. Presently, 65 to 70% of India's power requirements is met from coal only. Eighty and odd thermal power plants, belonging to various State Electricity Boards, NTPC, private organizations and captive power plants of industries have a combined installed capacity of 70,000 MW. This is expected to go upto 2,00,000 MW by next century.

India has a proved coal reserve of 180 billion tonnes with an annual production of 350 million tonnes, of which, 65% is used for power generation. Unlike European coal, Indian coal have high ash, to the extent of 30%, but fortunately of low sulphur (less than 0.3 %), the dreaded polluting element in fossil fuels. Large demand of coal in superthermal power plants can only be met by machine mining. Unlike manual mining, thin bands of shale (stones) in the coal seams can not be sorted out by machines during mining operation. Thus, the ash content of coal supplied to thermal plants, at times, goes as high as 50%, effecting the plant machinaries as well as efficiency of the power plants. In general, for every 100 tonnes of coal burnt in an Indian power plant, 30 to 40 tonnes of ash is generated. The total amount of ash generated in India today is about 60 million tonnes and this is expected to exceed 100 million tonnes by early next century. Disposal of ash is a mounting problem for the thermal plant authority. The Fly Ash Mission of Govt. of India is siezed with the problem of its utilization. It is said that, India's limit of power generation is dependant upon her limit in capability for fly ash utilization and disposal.

Environmental Impacts of Coal Combustion

Large scale combustion of coal, in the order of several million tonnes in thermal power plants results in various orders of environmental degradation. The first order degradations, easily observed are, air pollution, spillage and discharge of solid wastes around the plant, but are amenable to technological curative processes such as, installation of precipitators, scrubbers in the plant and safe storage of ash in ash ponds followed by ash pond management practices. The second order impacts are, land despoiling, acid rains, thermal pollution, folliage damage and impared health of people living around due to air pollution.The third order impacts, little understood, but more difficult to prevent are, emission of green-house and ozone depleting gases, "Oxygen Consumerism" and societal craze for electricity addiction including "Illumination-extravaganza". Every tonne of carbon (coal) burnt, consumes tonnes of oxygen of the atmosphere and we borrow it from the future generation. The present content of 21% oxygen in atmosphere, in which we breathe comfortably, was made possible by dissociation of the carbon-dioxide of the anoxic primitive atmosphere to carbon - dioxide of the anoxic primitive atmosphere to carbon and oxygen, followed by burial of the carbon as fossils fuels. The earth can not be returned back to the primitive anoxic atmosphere or fermentation ocean with man and other forms of life still existing on it.

The Flyt Ash Problem

The problem of fly ash disposal from therman plant does not lie, only on the magnitude of the amount generated but also on its environmental impact. Prevention of fly ash from a point source of stack emission by installation of efficient ESP (Electrostatic Precipitator) is obviously considered to be a technological achievement. However, its disposal (accumulation) in the ash pond after ESP collection enhances its dispersion four dimensions, i.e., length, breadth and depth of the pond and by leaching of pollutants in a span of time. As per today's technology of ash received from various points of collection in thermal plant is made into a slury and pumped into the ash pond. The supernatent pond liquid, rich in ash reachates, either pollute the surface water directly or percolates down to contaminate the subsurface water. The easily noticeable pollutant of the ash pond water is suspended solid (TSS), but significant increase of TDS (Total Dissolved Solids) is contributed by ash-water interactions.

Commonly, Indian ashes are alkaline and the leachates, therefore become alkaline due to the presence of alkalies and alkaline-earth elements such as Na, K and Ca. Addition of alkaline leachates to surface and subsurface waters increases the pH.Coal is known to contain significant amounts of toxic elements like Pb.Zn, Cd.Ge, Hg, As, Se, F etc., which get enriched in the ash after combustion. The mechanism of combustion, the texture and structure of ash particles as well as the mineralogy of the ash, combined, facilitate leaching of these heavy metals from the ash matrix. Thus, the ash pond becomes a strong source of toxic element contamination of the aquatic regime of the surrounding region.

Mitigation of Toxic Leachates

Leachability of ash is recognised and estimated by standard methods of leaching in laboratory experiments by way of Batch, TCLP and Cascade leaching or by percolation of water through ash column of standard specifications. If alarming level of leaching of heavy metals is detected, mitigational measures, such as treatment of effluent and sealing of ash pond with clay/or synthetic materials are recommended. Sealing or blanketting of ash pond is normally practised prior to dumping of ash in the pond, during selection of the pond site. However, the natural soil barrier around an ash pond plays important role to a limited extent, in adsorbing the toxic constituents emanating out of ash leaching.

Ash Utilization

Compositionally, ash is dominantly silicious and consists of quartz and alumnosillicates. The material is fine (size varies from 150 micron to less than a micron) with dominantly spherical particles, rarely solid but mostly hollow (Canosphere and Plirosphere). The develop large internal surface area known as specific surface. Large specific surface imparts strong reactivity in fly ash. Thus the ash has strong self-pozzalonic property, making it an ideal cement additive or a material for brick making. Utilization of ash for making brick is very much welcome as it will lead to save precious top soil, now being freely used for making of bricks. Beside brick manufacturing, a host of other uses have been proposed. A major promise on utilization aspect of ash is its application as a pesticide, pesticide carrier or as soil conditioner. When added to sticky, clayey and impervious soil, it increases the waterholding capacity and transmissibility of water. But for sandy and highly porous soil it helps to retain the water. Besides, alkaline ash added to acidic soil or acidic ash added to alkaline soil develop optimum soil pH as per requirement. Many trace metals in ash, such as Mn, Mo, Ni, Co etc. can be suitably mobilized as plant nutrient for increased biomass development, but elements like Hg, Cd, As, Se if present may result in phytotoxicity and when enter into edible parts of the plant push the toxic elements to human food chain. Like brick manufacturing, agricultural applications not only promise utilization of ash in large amounts and releive thermal plants from the large magnitude of ash generated, but also the biomass developed over ash dumps will generate extra oxygen by photosynthesis and compensate the oxygen consumed during combustion of coal. Thus, while brick manufacturing from ash is more desirable, biomass development on ash dumps may be most desirable in ash utilization.

In either cases of ash utilization, a note of caution is essential. Zeolite formation on surface of ash particles is an indication of subsequent mobilization of Na, Al, Ca and Si by interaction of slury or pond water and ash. It goes to prove that, long after the manufacture of brick, surface of ash grains, when get coated with zeolite, a soft mineral, will drastically decrease the cohesion between ash particles inside the brick, leading to decreased strength of the brick and failure. Similarly, ash is an azoic (abiotic) discordant material compared to the complex biotic soil. In other words, ash, when added to soil, can behave like an "antibody" with possibility of rejection. Therefore, long term filed experiments are needed to be performed before its recommendation as agriculture additive in large scale.

Alarming Population Explosion

The situation of increasing population day by day in India as well as in the whole world is very alarming. A report on situation of world population 2004 was released in a gathering organised by United Nations Population Cell and Health and Medical departments of Rajasthan Government at Jaipur. According to this report, in the year 1950 the world population was 2.5 billion and present world population of 6.4 billion may reach about 9.0 billion by the year 2050. Of these, population of 50 poorest countries will increase thrice reaching thereby near 1.7 billion (Jaipur, 15th Sept. 2004-United Bharat, Allahabad 16th Sept. 2004, page 11).

Various methods to control population have been applied in India from time to time for the last several decades, but all the efforts made so far were utter failures. In a seminar organised by an NGO 'Gram Kalp' at Shringverpur Dhaam, Allahabad, U.P. Integrated Village Development Minister -Vishambhar Prasad Nishad opined accordingly. He said despite the hectic efforts of Health Department, besides other major organizations, to curb the ever growing population menace, the same could not be controlled effectively. Policy adopted in China to control population, will have to be followed (NIP Alld. 18 January, 2005, a page 3). Due to population explosion the poisonous gases like Carbon dioxide and others are going on mixing up in atmosphere. Urban citizens are facing many complications caused by growing population and resulting in environmental pollution. Scarcity of vegetation and covering green leaves of growing trees with dust and black smoke further make the trees weak and pollute the environment. Though there is no food shortage in our country, but due to alarming increase in population, importance has to be paid on improving production and productivity of cereals, fruits and vegetables.

Regarding alarming population explosion, the Commissioner Allahabad division expressed his views that whatever the circumstances might have been there, the programme on population control was never taken up seriously. He further said after independence where production of food grains was registered by increase of three times, commendable achievements were registered in the fields of education, science and technology and others, population of our country increased from 32 crore to one billion mark, whereas China and Japan have well controlled their population (NIP Alld. 31st Dec. 2004. page 02 and United Bharat, Alld. 31 Dec. 2004, page 2).

The present population of India has exceeded one billion and has reached about 102 crore. The family planning programme is not in personal interest but in public and Nation's interest. Those who do not adopt family planning 'will be doing on their own risk. Only on these principles Haryana Govt. have cancelled the membership of a member of Nagar Palika Haryana due to not following the norms of two babies. Supreme Court has taken this step as correct and further said-hat curbing the increasing population is in Nations interest (United Bharat Alld. 13 Oct. 2004, Page 1).

Since the programme of family planning and curbing the increasing population are National programmes, there should be no question of religion, cast or creed. However, there are difference of opinions regarding norms of two babies in various groups and boards of Muslims. On release of census data during 2004 and reacting over statements of Maulana Kalbe Sadiq Vice President of All India Muslim Personal Law Board in New Delhi on 13 September 2004 favouring birth control and imposing the one or two baby norm, Maulana Rabey Hasan Naqvi president AIMPLB expressed his views against family planning. He said 'Family Planning among-Muslims is un-Islamic' and further said 'it is not proper to stop the birth of those whom God has destined to be born'. He also told family planning as unnecessary. Many other members expressed their views against the birth control and said those favouring this practice might be their personal views and there is nothing like birth control in the constitution. (NIP Alld. 15th and 16th Sept. 2004. pages 5 and 6). AIMPLB do notaccept the increasing population as a problem. They say that there is no place for faimily planning inslam (United Bharat Alld. 3rd Oct. page 14).

Again in a seminar held in Lucknow Maulana Kalbe Sadiq Vice President of AIMPLB said. It has been clarified in Islam that there should be control on population and also that this is the demand of time." On the other hand, the spokesman of the board Mr. Abdul Raheen Qureshi told media that there was no provision for birth control in Islam (United Bharat Alld.) 3rd January 2005 page 1). As mentioned earlier population control is a National work and as such birth control the - National campaign has to be forced upon each and every family. There'was no question of including this in the constitution of India.

Not only citizens of our country are responsible for increasing population, but the Bangladesh infiltrators getting protection contribute best in population explosion. They are illegally migrating in India and residing with their families in unauthorized constructed huts/temporary sheds in residential colonies of citizens and other vacant places in Allahabad, Delhi, Assam, West Bengal, Bihar, Jripura, Nagaland and other (United Bharat 12 Dec. 2004, Page 10). They are going on producing children and adding fuel to fire by making additions in the huge population of India.

Bangladeshi intruders have become serious problems for the country. Over 50,000 Bangladeshis are staying only in Allahabad (U.P.) for the last several years (NIP Alld. 3 Oct. 2002, page 3). Not a single day apparently passes without some 25,000 Bangladeshis migrating illegally in India (NIP Alld. 6 March 2004, Page 2).

In two croer population of North Bengal about half of the people are Bangladeshis and all of them are having many wives (Rashtriya Sahara New Delhi, 2 May, 1997). According to another information in India 24,443 Bangladeshis are residing continuously for a long period (NIP Alld. 20th February 2003, Page 5). In this connection Delhi High Court has instructed Delhi Govt. to submit a programme for ousting 13 lakh Bangladeshi staying in the capital (United Bharat Alld. 16" Oct. 2003, Page 10).

Supreme Court has further issued notices to Central Govt., West Bengal Govt. and Election Commission and asked them to explain their views on illegal migration of Bangladeshis on such a large scale in West Bengal and other parts of India (United Bharat Alld. 11th Dec. 2004, Page 1and 11). Defence Minister of India had admitted in Parliament on 11th Dec. 2004.that infiltration from Bangladesh had increased. For this Dhaka was requested to stop this but no cooperation was/is found from Bangladesh (NIP. Alld. 13th Dec. 2004, Page 06, Editorial). What steps are now being taken under such circumstances ?

As such to have a proper control over such a huge population of India first of all public awareness towards family planning is very important. Next step should be to bring the family planning programme into practice. People should be seriously dealt with. Adopting family planning should be a must and not left on option. It should be forced in each and every family. Religion or cast etc. should not be hindrances in the way. Hardest action should be taken against the defaulters. They should rather be discouraged by withdrawing all necessary facilities provided to them by Government, keeping in view that no inhuman treatment is done. Any financial offer for adopting family planning will be of no use except wastage of Govt. money. In a meet of information and Health Dept. and media regarding family planning awareness, Lok Ayukt Justice Sudhir Chandra Varma said it is not possible to control increasing population unless law for this framed. DM Allahabad stressed the importance of family planning (NIP Alld. 5th July 5 Page 3, United Bharat 5th July05, Page 5). Inflow of Bangladeshis and other infiltrators in India should immediately be stopped. Again, those who have already intruded in the country should be ousted under all circumstances. Such steps may prove more useful in carrying out this National Campaign successfully. Let us make a firm determination to carry out this National campaign with sportsman spirit on 11th July the World Population Day.

Television- Shwetabh Kumar

1. Ghar bathe picture daikhein television main.
   Cartoon bhee daikhen television main.
   Shakalaka boom-boom bhee daikhein television main.
   Sonpari bhee daikhein television main.
   Cricket bhee daikhein television main.
   Hockey, football, tennis bhee daikhein television main
   Badminton aur basketball bhee daikhein television main.
   Tabletennis aur snooker bhee daikhein television main.
   Golf daikhein, Polo ghorhadaurh bhee daikhein television main.
   Car race, boys - girls race bhee daikhein television main.
   High Jump long jump, kursi daurh bhee daikhein television main.
   Shotput, discus throw our sabhi sports daikhen television main.
   Jaadugar ke jaadu daikhein television main.
   Circus, haathi, ghorhe aur sher daikhein television main.
   Mukkebaazi aur pahalwaano kee kushti bhee daikhein television main.
2. Bagh bagheeche, pairh - paudhey daikhein television main.
   Rashtriya Vrikch - 'PEEPAL' daikhein television main.
   Aaam, amrood, anannas aur litchee daikhein television main.
   Cheeku, aonla, kaila aur papita bhee daikhein television main.
   Seb, loquat, anaar aur naashpaati daikhein television main.
   Angoor, Phalsa, Khirni aur jamun bhee daikhein television main.

Neeboo, Santre, mussammi daikhein television main.
Barhhal, kathal aur shareefa bhee daikhein television main.
Aaloo, gobhi aur pyaz daikhein television main.
Matar, tamatar, bhindi bhee daikhein television main.
Rang - birangi titliyan urhtee daikhein television main.
Sugandhit phool bhee daikhein television main.
Phoolon main mun bahlaate bacchon ko daikhein television main.
Rashtriya Pushp 'LOTUS' bhee daikhein television main.
Sabhi phal - vrikchon ko daikhen television main.
Anya upyogi vrikchon aur jungle daikhein television main.
Pradooshit Paryavaran shudh hotey bhee daikhein television main.

3. Daish - Vidaish ke samachar daikhein sunain television main.
Naach gaanon ke anand lein television main.
Drama - natak ke bhee anand television main.
Kisse-kahani aur paheli sunein television main.
Shiksha bhee praapt karein television main.
Samudra aur nadiyaan daikhein television main.
Aandhi - toofan daikhein television main.
Bhookamp, baarh aur Tsunami bhee daikhein television main.
Jwalamukhi aur baadal phatte daikhein television main,
Pashu-pakchi aur machlian bhee daikhein television main.
Tota, maina, kabootar aur Saaras daikhein television main.
Rashtriya Pakchi 'More' bhee daikhein television main.
Koo - koo karti koyal bhee daikhen television main.
Rashtriya Pashu 'BAAGH' daikhein television main.
Dilli, Mumbai, Chennai aur Kalcutta daikhein television main.
Jammu Kashmir, Srinagar aur Shimla daikhein television main.

4. Mandir, Masjid, Girjaghar daikhein television main.
Gurdwara bhee daikhein television main.
Badrinath, Kedarnath, Jerushalam daikhein television main.
Macca, Madeena, Meenakchi daikhein television main.
Tirupati Baala Ji, Saarnath daikhen television main.
Kushinagar, Dwarka, Ajmer Sharif daikhain television main.

Ayodhya, Sant Kabeernagar, Rameshwaram daikhein television main.
Kaashi - Mathura daikhein television main.
Ram, Krishna, Eesa, Moosa daikhein television main.
Guru Nanak aur Mohammad daikhein television main.
Gautam, Mahaveer, Kabeer bhee daikhein television main.
Christmas, Id, Prakashutsava manayen television main.
Holi, Deewali ka tyohar manaein television main.
Dushehra, Janma Ashthami bhee manain television main.
Shabe-barat ka bhee anand lein television main.
Sabhi tyoharon ka anand lein television main.

5. 15 August ko Swatantrata Diwas daikhein television main.
26 January ko Garthantra diwas daikhein television main.'
7 Sitamber ko deikhein 'VANDE MATARAM DIWAS' television main.
10 Maee ko daikhein 'Shaheed Diwas' television main.
5 June ko daikhein 'Vishwa Paryavaran Diwas' television main.
11 July ko daikein 'Vishwa Jansankhya Diwas' television main.
31 Maee ko daikhein 'Vishwa Tambaaku Vihin Diwas' television main.
16 Aktoober ko daikhein 'Vishwa Khadya Diwas' television main.
28 Faruary ko daikhein 'Rashtriya Vigyan Diwas' television main.
7 April ko daikhein 'Vishwa Swasthya Diwas' television main.
14 Sitamber ko daikhein 'Vishwa Hindi Diwas' television main.
22 April ko daikhein 'Vishwa Dharti Diwas' television main.
23 April ko daikhein 'Vishwa Pustak Diwas' television main.
5 Sitamber ko daikhein 'Rashtriya Shikchak Diwas' television main.
14 November ko daikhein 'Rashtriya Baal Diwas' television main.
26 Disamber ko daikhein 'Tsunami' television main.
15 Sitambar ko daikhein Engineers' Day television main.
17 Sitambar ko daikhein Vishwakarma Jayanti television main.

6. 23 March ko daikhein 'Shaheed Bhagat Singh ka Shaheed Diwas' television main.

27 Fabuary ko daikhein 'Shaheed Chandra Shekhar Azad ka shaheed diwas' television main.

2 Aktoober ko daikhein 'Gandhi aur Shastri Jayanti' television main.

14 November ko daikhein 'Jawahar Jayanti' television' main.

23 January ko daikhein 'Subhash Jayanti' television main.
14 Aprail ko daikhein 'Ambedkar Jayanti' television main.
Bhojya samagriyan bhee daikhein khayen television main.
Idly, dosa, chaomin daikhein khayen television main.
Maggy, Peeza, Burgar bhee daikhein khayen television main.
Poori, Kachori, chole, bathure, bhee daikhein khayen television main.
Kaile ke patton par bhaat-daal khate bhee daikhein television main.
Baati - chokha khate bhee daikhein television main.
Kaanta, Churi, Chammach se bhee khaate daikhein television main.
Yoga - kasrat, pooja paath bhee karte daikhein television main.
Gyan barhate rahein television main.
Lekin parhai ka nuksaan na hone paaye television main.

References

1. Bhandarker, Gayatri 1993. Processed Food. *Business Today*, Jan. 22 : 72-80.
2. Chadha, K.L. 1988. Introductory remarks given during inaugural session of National Seminar on New Horizons in production and Post Harvest Management of Tropical and Sub-tropical fruits held in New Delhi, 8th Dec. : 1-10.
3. Gandhi, S.R. 1956. Oranges, lemons and limes in India. ICAR Farm bulletin No.15.
4. Jagtiani, J. K. 1988. India poised for pink revolution. NIP (Alld.), 29th Sept., 4.
5. Martin, Max 2008. *Mail Today*. New Delhi, 17th May, 3.
6. Mishra, P.K. 2008. *Mail Today*. New Delhi, 5th May, Monday, 4.
7. M.T. 2008. Pretty and Edible. Mail Today, May 20, Tuesday, 31.
8. Nand, Darshana 1963. Secrets of mango grafting practices. Gardening, 4(11):43-51.
9. Nayer, G. Ravindran 1992. Health - Nutrition, myth and reality. NIP (Alld.) 28th Nov. : 6.
10. Parliament news 1992. Parliament Questions - Rajya Sabha - "Waste", NIP (Alld.), 1st Dec. : 9.
11. PTI 1975. Ripe bhindi seed a protein store. *HT*, 23rd February. : 3.
12. PTI 1990. Drumstick seeds can clear river waters. NIP (Alld.), 10th Sept.

13. PTI Feature 1991. Potato peel for burn heal. NIP (Alld.) 13th February.

14. PTI 1992. Rs. 3,000 cr, loss from fruits and vegetables. NIP (Alld.) 5th Dec. 6.

15. Preamble 2008. Third Indian Horticulture Congress, Bhubaneswar, 6-9 Nov., 2.

16. Singh, Harbhajan and Bhagchandani P.M. 1967. Bhindi cultivation in India. ICAR Farm bulletin (New series).

17. Singh, Umrao, Wadhwani, A.M. and Johari, B.M. 1983. Dictionary of Economic plants. ICAR, New Delhi: 224,17.

18. Shukla, Praveen Kumar 1999. Shaak Bhaaji kee uplabdhiyan tatha bhavishya ka paridrishya. Smarika Rashtriya Sangosthi, Janata College Bakewar, Etawa, U.P., 13-15th Feb.: 68-71.

19. Srivastava, K.C. 1985. Aam Utpadan. Central Northern Plane Fruits Horticultural Institute (ICAR), Lko. Extn. bull. No.1.

20. Srivastava, Piyush 2008. A death bed of flowers for the fish in Varanasi. *Mail Today*, New Delhi, May 5, Monday, 4.

21. Thapar, A.R. 1958. Passion fruit and Jamun in India. *ICAR Farm bull.* No. 42.

22. UNI, 1992. Suvidha ke abhav men phalon va sabzion ki barbadi. *Rashtriya Sahara* (NOIDA), 11th Oct.

23. United Bharat News Alld. 2008 Multiprovider Munga Jal Shuddhi mein sahayak. *United Bharat daily*, April 2, 05.

24. USSR Inf. Ser. 1983. A new vitamin - 'B' NIP (Alld.) 18th Aug. 1983.

25. Varma, Sant Ram 1999. Bharat mein baghwani vikas; Smarika Rashtriya Sangoshthi, Janata College, Bakewar, Etawa, U.P. 13-15 Feb., 66-67.

26. Vigyan Varta 1991. Sahijan ke beejon se jal ka prodooshan nivaran. *Dainik Jagran.* Varanasi (Alld.), 20th July.

Index